DELAWARE BIBLE RECORDS

Volume 6

Lu Verne V. Hall

HERITAGE BOOKS
2009

HERITAGE BOOKS
AN IMPRINT OF HERITAGE BOOKS, INC.

Books, CDs, and more—Worldwide

For our listing of thousands of titles see our website
at
www.HeritageBooks.com

Published 2009 by
HERITAGE BOOKS, INC.
Publishing Division
100 Railroad Ave. #104
Westminster, Maryland 21157

Copyright © 1998 Lu Verne V. Hall

All rights reserved. No part of this book may be reproduced or transmitted in any form or by any means, electronic or mechanical, including photocopying, recording or by any information storage and retrieval system without written permission from the author, except for the inclusion of brief quotations in a review.

International Standard Book Numbers
Paperbound: 978-0-7884-0982-0
Clothbound: 978-0-7884-7584-9

This Book is Dedicated

to

DONALD ODELL VIRDIN

A gentleman, my mentor, my friend

PREFACE

This book, "DELAWARE BIBLE RECORDS, VOLUME 6" is the last of the series that will be written. Insofar as we can determine, there is very little if any other information in the 13 volume set of the Delaware Bible Records - prepared by the Delaware Chapters of the Daughters of the American Revolution over a period of 31 years (1943-1974) - which would justify printing. In fact the author, Lu Verne V. Hall, has prepared an index of all the chapters and titles that have been previously printed so that there is no duplication.

The authors of this six volume set of books have made every effort to correct any errors that appear to have been made in the original text. It must be remembered that 200-300 years ago words were different and writing was difficult to understand. But notwithstanding this difficulty, in all the volumes and the thousands of names published to date, insofar as the authors have heard from the readers, there has been only one error. We have honestly put the facts as they were printed in the original 13 volume set of Delaware Bible Records. I think it is worth mentioning that the only error that has been reported to us is one from a gentleman in California, who wrote to say that he thought one date should be 1842 and we had 1843. The gentleman came to Washington and checked the date at the DAR Library and found that he was correct. We apologize for this error. But I believe this tells the diligence that has gone into the making of this 6-volume Delaware Bible Records.

As we previously stated, the Delaware Chapters of the Daughters of the American Revolution compiled this information over a period of 31 years (1943-1974). They located the information, copied, typed and bound them into the 13 volumes of the most complete collection of Delaware Bible Records ever assembled. As a result of their devotion to this task, it has been possible to print these books and they have been dedicated to those DAR members.

When the first of the Delaware Bible Records was prepared for publication, I secured the approval of the head of the DAR of Delaware, Miss Elizabeth Hancock. She has been given a copy of each of the Bible Records published to date. She lives in Wilmington, Delaware but she has made special trips to Washington to get these books in the DAR Library in Washington. She was happy that some honor had been given to the ladies who did this work and was delighted to see the material published.

Insofar as the authors are aware, there are only three sets of the original DAR Bible Records available. One is in the DAR Library in Washington, D.C.; another is in the Delaware State Archives Library in Dover, Delaware; the third set is in the Historical Society of Delaware Library in Wilmington, Delaware.

These Bible Records include not only Bible Records that have been located by DAR members, but also some narrative family histories written by members of the family or other people. Since all the records in the original 13 volume set had been approved by a DAR Committee as being correct, we had to take their word and assume that the facts were true. Although many of the Bible Records were owned or acquired by Delawarians, there are many that cover other states. The previous volume, Volume 5, covers many states in the mid-Atlantic region. As this author previously stated, this is an invaluable compilation of information for any genealogist working the several states in the mid-Atlantic region - including Delaware, Pennsylvania, Virginia, West Virginia, Maryland, Ohio and other states.

When the first book was published, it was not taken in sequence from the first book. It was selected, as were all the books the authors had published, from what we considered to be the most interesting or the most valuable data. We did not know originally that we would be able to complete the 6 volume set. They were not selected in any chronological or alphabetical order, but because they were well written, precise, and understandable.

Some Bible records have charts with only names and no dates. This information generally has been omitted because there was no real data helpful to a genealogist.

I might mention that Lu Verne V. Hall is the sole author of this Volume 6 - the last volume of Delaware Bible Records - and what a remarkable lady she is. I doubt if any reader knows her reputation as a good administrative assistant and an honest researcher. When she was working in the mid-West a famous and well known Senator was responsible for her move to Washington, D.C. and securing a job with the Federal Government. Mrs. Hall has worked in the White House and worked on two special White House Conferences. She has letters of commendation from Presidents and other high level dignitaries. I know Mrs. Hall would rather not have this in the preface, but if high level dignitaries convinced her to come to Washington, I think the public deserves to know what great abilities she has - what she had then and what she still has. She is a remarkable lady and I am honored to be able to call her my friend. She is the most honest individual I have ever known in my 85 years. Her work is almost flawless. She is a brilliant researcher and a person with outstanding judgment. She and her husband, Archie, have been happily married 33 years. I only wish it were possible for those who buy this book to meet her someday. God Bless her.

This is the largest book of Delaware Bible Records that has been published - over 400 pages and an index. We honestly believe, because of the many unusual and different pieces of information that can be found in this large volume, that anyone interested in genealogy of the mid-Atlantic region should buy a copy. They will never regret it.

Donald O. Virdin
February 1998

TABLE OF CONTENTS

ADAMS - EDGELL - TWIFORD	1
ALDRED FAMILY	2
ALLERDICE BIBLE RECORD	3
ALLMOND - GRUBB DATA	5
ANDERSON-NEEDLES-GRIFFITH-EDWARDS	9
JOHN ANDERSON-REBECCA SMITH BIBLE	11
ARTERBRIDGE BIBLE	12
THE ASH FAMILY	14
ASHBRIDGE BIBLE	16
ATKINS BIBLE RECORD	16
AN ACCOUNT OF THE BABB FAMILY	19
JOHN W. AND PHEBE H. (PEARSON) BABB	19
BACON - SCALES	22
BAILEY BIBLE 1821	22
JOHN E. BARCUS BIBLE	25
PETER L. BARCUS-SARAH A. BELL BIBLE	26
BARLOW - WHITCRAFT	29
WILLIAM L. BARLOW AND LEVENIA H. L. HANBY	32
BARR BIBLE	33
BASSETT	35
BEESON BIBLE RECORD	35
BEESON BIBLE RECORD	37
ELIZA BEESON RECORD	38

BELL-GREENLEA BIBLE	39
BENSON - NORTH BIBLE	41
THE ALFRED DUPONT BIRD FAMILY	42
JOHN BIRD - JULIANNA GRUBB	43
BLACK	46
WILLIAM H. BLACKISTON BIBLE	48
JOSEPH BOUGHMAN & LYDIA ANN	51
BOWERS - STRADLING - ANDERSON	54
BOWLES FAMILY, VIRGINIA	55
BOYCE FAMILY RECORD	56
JOHN G. BRACKLIN'S BOOK	57
BRADEN FAMILY	58
WILLIAM BROWN & CHARLOTE CARTER CHARLOTTE BROWN & FRISBY TULL	59
JOHN BUCKLEY & HANNAH CLEMSON AMER GRUBB & ANN BUCKLEY	62
BURTON FAMILY	65
CALEB BYRNES BIBLE	68
CANTWELL FAMILY - NEW CASTLE CO.	73
BIBLE OF THOMAS CARTMELL - BRANDYWINE HUNDRED, DELAWARE	74
GEORGE CASEY & CATHERINE MILLER	76
CHASE RECORD	78
JOHN S. CLARK - SARAH E. CONWELL	78
LOT & REBECCA CLOUD BIBLE	80
CONNELLY RECORDS	81

JANE CORD RECORD	87
WILLIAM COULTER BIBLE	88
COVINGTON RECORD	89
ESAU COXE BIBLE RECORD	93
THE DAVID CRANE BIBLE	95
PETER C. & REBECCA DAILEY	96
DARBY - LOFLAND BIBLE	97
DAVIDSON RECORD	99
DAWSON FAMILY RECORD	100
DAY FAMILY - BRANDYWINE HUNDRED, DELAWARE	103
BENJAMIN DEACON'S BOOK	105
J. W. DENNISON BIBLE	106
DERICKSON FAMILY	108
ABSALOM DODD BIBLE	110
JOSEPH DODD BIBLE	112
WILLIAM A. DODD'S BOOK	114
DRAGOO BIBLE	116
DUFF BIBLE RECORD	118
JOHN EASTWICK RECORD	120
EDWARDS - LAWSON RECORD	123
ELDER - FOSTER RECORD	125
ELLIS FAMILY RECORD	127
ENTRIKIN FAMILY	130
ESTELL FAMILY BIBLE	132

JOHN AND ESTHER FARRA	135
FENEMORE - DONOHO BIBLE	137
GEORGE W. FIELDS BIBLE	139
FLICKWIR - WOOD	141
WILLIAM J. & MAGGIE T. FORD	141
GEORGE FAMILY	142
GIBBONS FAMILY	144
ARTHINGTON GILPIN BIBLE	147
WILLIAM S. GOODLEY	148
GORDON FAMILY RECORD	151
RALPH P. GORDON - SARAH BRERENTON BIBLE	154
GRING BIBLE	155
GRUBB FAMILY BURYING GROUND	156
HAMILTON BIBLE	157
HANBY FAMILY	159
HANNUM-WALTER BIBLE	160
JAMES HARRIS BIBLE	161
HAY - BACON RECORD	163
HAY - BARNITZ - SEEBACH	164
HEFLEBOWER - GRING	168
DAVID HILL'S BOOK	169
HARRY HINKSON & VILETTA P. HANBY	171
HITCH FAMILY BIBLE RECORD	172
HORNER FAMILY	173
SAMUEL C. HUGHES & AMY E. LONGFELLOW	174

HUSSEY FAMILY OF DELAWARE	175
HUTSON BIBLE RECORD	177
MARY JANE HYATT BIBLE	178
JAMISON - VANDERGRIFT - MCWHORTER	180
WILLIAM JARDEN & MARY YOEST	182
JOHNS FAMILY BIBLE RECORD	183
ANDREW M. JOHNSON BIBLE	184
JOHNSTON FAMILY	185
JOYCE BIBLE	186
KELSO & FRIEDEL BIBLE	187
KENDALL BIBLE - 1831	189
KINSEY - WHITEMAN	191
KINSEY - WHITEMAN	193
KIRBY FAMILY RECORD	196
KIRBY RECORD	204
LACEY FAMILY RECORD	207
LANE - GALBRAITH	211
LAWSON BIBLE RECORD	212
CAPTAIN JOHN LOCKTON BIBLE	212
SAMUEL LODGE & TALITHA SOMERS	213
COL. ARMWELL LONG BIBLE	214
LUNT FAMILY OF MAINE & DELAWARE	215
LUNT FAMILY JOSHUA LUNT, JR. & JERUSHA M. WINSLOW	218
MACKENZIE - HAY RECORD	221

THOMAS E. MALIN & ELLA WEBSTER 221

MESSICK BIBLE 222

MESSICK-PUSEY RECORD 224

MARTIN MILLER AND ANN JUSTISON 226

MAURICE - VAN BUSKIRK 231

MILLIGAN RECORD 233

MARY LEVY MILLIGAN'S JOURNAL 235

MONTGOMERY RECORD 238

ROBERT I. MORROW & LYDIA ANN BARLOW 240

MURPHY, SIMPKINS, FRENCH,
DAVID, MORGAN 241

THE MCCRONE FAMILY, FARNHURST, DELAWARE 242

JOHN & ELEANOR (BYERLY) McCULLOUGH 243

McDADE - BLACK RECORD 244

McNEAL FAMILY 245

LOGAN - McNEAl 249

FRANCIS L. McSORLEY AND
ANNA MARIA LODGE 249

McWHORTER, JAMISON, FERRIS, ETC. 251

NORMAN BIBLE RECORD 252

THOMAS NORMAN BIBLE 254

NORMAN RECORD 255

JACOB Z. ORR AND SARAH A. MAXWELL 257

ROBERT ORR AND MARGARET LATIMER 259

WILLIAM S. ORR AND SARAH E. ZEBLEY 260

JOSEPH F. OUTTEN - MARY A. BRYAN	263
PAINTER FAMILY RECORD	264
PASSMORE BIBLE RECORDS	266
PATTISON RECORD	267
PATTON BIBLE RECORD	268
PENNINGTON BIBLE RECORDS	270
THOMAS PEPPER-RACHEL LAWLES BIBLE	275
FRANKLIN PETERS - CHARLOTTE EDWARDS	276
THE PETERSON FAMILY	277
WARREN J. & ELNOR ANN (JOHNSON) PHILLIPS	278
URIEL PIERCE & BRANDLING G. GRUBB OF BRANDYWINE HUNDRED, DELAWARE	280
JAMES PONSELL - MAMIE C. RASH	282
CLARENCE E. POTER & LAURA L. SIMON	284
WILLIAM NELSON POTTER & CLARA DAVIS HANBY	286
PRINGLE - CLARK	287
JOHN F. RASH & MARIAM TRUAX	288
JOHN H. RASH & MARTHA	290
REDISH BIBLE RECORD	292
REES - McNEAL	292
RICKARDS RECORD	295
JAMES ROBERTS BIBLE - SMYRNA, DELAWARE	300
ROBESON BIBLE	304
ROBESON BIBLE	305

MARTIN & CHRISTINE ROSINBERGER	307
SCALES - NICHOLS	308
SHADINGER RECORD	309
SHAKESPEAR FAMILY RECORD	311
SHAKESPEAR RECORD	312
JOHN A. SHELDON & REBECCA E. ERB	313
SHIPLEY BIBLE RECORD	314
ELIAS & SARAH A. WARREN SHOCKLEY BIBLE	315
WILSON & NANCY SHOCKLEY BIBLE	316
SHORT - COOPER BIBLE	318
THOMAS SILVER	320
JAMES SIMMONS - SARAH ANN DUBREE	330
CHARLES SIMON JUNIOR - LAURA A. PIERCE OF BRANDYWINE HUNDRED, DELAWARE	334
SIMPERS RECORD	335
JOHN & ELIZABETH (HENTON) SITES	337
SMITH - HITCHENS RECORD	338
SAMUEL SMYTH AND JANE	338
JEREMIAH SPRINGER	339
JOSEPH SPRINGER BIBLE RECORD	341
STEVENSON - BAILEY	343
STEWART FAMILY RECORD	346
ISAAC STIDHAM BIBLE	348
JOHN STONE & GRACE MILLER	349
THE LEMUEL STURGES BIBLE	349

TALLEY - MILLER	353
CHARLES TALLEY AND MARY ZEBLEY	358
TAYLOR BIBLE	361
THE TAYLOR BIBLE, KENT COUNTY, DELAWARE	361
WILLIAM TOWNSEND'S RECORD OF GOVEY TOWNSEND	365
ELIZAH TYSON & ARABELLA ROSS	366
VANDEVER FAMILY	367
VANDEVER RECORD	370
VANSANT FAMILY	371
CORNELIUS VANZANT FAMILY	373
VANZANT BIBLE RECORD	374
SAMUEL WALKER	375
WALTER FAMILY RECORD	376
AN ACCOUNT OF REBECCA WARDELL'S FAMILY	378
WATERS - KILLINGSWORTH RECORD	379
CLARK WEBSTER & ELIZABETH ABBITT	379
ISAAC WEBSTER AND SARAH E. WILSON	383
ISAAC WILDIN'S BIBLE	385
EXACT COPY OF WILL OF REBECCA WESTON - 1812	388
GEORGE W. & MARY E. WILSON	390
CHARLES I. WILLIAMS & ELIZA EDWARDS	392
WINSOR-BULLOCK BIBLE	393
WOLFE FAMILY RECORD	397

THOMAS WOLVERTON - REBECCA CRAWFORD 398
CHRISTOPHER & HANNAH YOEST 401
INDEX 402

ADAMS - EDGELL - TWIFORD

(Bible in possession of J. Herbert Edgell,
Greenwood, Del. Copied by Rev. Albert Bell,
1947.)

Peter Adams
    1. Henry Adams
        b. 7-29-1797
Mary   d. 8-10-1828
        m.
        Charlotty
        d. 12-27-1840

        1. Cornelay (ius) Adams
           b. 10-30-1822
        2. Francis Ray
           b. 4-16-1824; d. age 24
        3. Hester Ann
           b. 4-22-1825; d. age 2
        4. John Henry
           b. 5-16-1828; d. 17 da.

    2. Stansberry Adams; b. 3-31-1799
    3. James Adams; b. 12-24-1801
    4. Elizabeth; b. 6-14-1803

Charles Twiford
        Alan Twiford; m. Margaret D. Cranor,
        b. 4-16-1800   daughter of Joshua
Charlot   and Elizabeth
                              b. 1-1818;
                              m. 11-1-1832
        Charlottea

Jesse Edgin
        Wm. Edgen
Mary   b. 2-16-1818
        d. 6-30-1896
        Age 80

        Cornelay
        d. 3-5-1852

        2-10-1859
        m. Mary Ann
           Pratt

1. Mary E.; b. 9-27-1843
2. Charlotty A. Edgen
   b. 11-4-1844
       Thomas F. Obier
       b. 9-30-1862
   m. 12-19-1861
   Henson Obier
3. William H. Edgen
   m. Mary E. Hollis
   b. 9-12-1846
   m. 8-3-1876
4. John A.; b. 2-7-1849
5. James Edgen
   b. 4-4-1850
6. Martha Frances
   b. 1-11-1852

7. Sallie Edgell
8. George R.
   b. 11-15-1859
   d. 5-3-1904, age 44
   m. Belle Raughley
   11-22-1885.
   Belle d. 12-19-1893
9. Jessey G.; b. 5-30-1861
   d. 1-24-1862
10. Ida E.; b. 10-31-1862;
    m. Samuel F. Collison
    6-26-1881; d. 4-3-1944,
    age 81
11. Horace G.; b. 8-19-1864;
    d. 5-29-1946
12. Mary Effie; b. 12-19-1866; m. Clifton
    Coates 10-26-184;
    d. 11-6-1903, age 36
13. Carnelia; b. 12-16-1869;
    d. 1869
14. Erma; b. 4-29-1870;
    d. 1873
15. Sallie; b. 9-14-1872
16. Roland C.; b. 10-31-1874; d. 3-7-1878.

ALDRED FAMILY

(Bible is owned by John W. Day, Talleyville, Del. 1893, now owned by Thomas R. Day, Pittsburgh, Pa., son of John W. Revord. Copied by Mrs. Clara W. Bird, Wilmington, Del.)

William and Sarah Aldred's Book, 1737.

Hannah his daughter was born March 2, 1737.
John his son was born December 29, 1738.
Alice his daughter was born April 11, 1741.
Mary his daughter was born October 27, 1742.
Betty his daughter was born June 25, 1745.
Ellen his daughter was born June 25, 1747.
William his son was born September 22, 1749.
Margaret his daughter was born November 2, 1751.
John his son was born July 11, 1753.
Sarah his daughter was born September 7, 1755.

A daughter was dead born July 28, 1758.
William his son was born May 16, 1760.

> John Aldred, Scriptist
> December 22, 1766

William Aldred and Catherine Robinson were married July 5, 1783.
    Richard, their son, was born May 22, 1784; died October 23, 178?.
    Sarah, their daughter, was born June 18, 1785; died October 23, 178?.
    John, their son, was born August 11, 1786.
    Lydia, their daughter, was born March 8, 1788; died June 12, 17--.
    Mary, their daughter, was born Sept. 24, 1790.
    Ellen, their daughter, was born April 18, 1792.
    William A., their son, was born at Wilmington, Del., January 11, 1797.
    Sarah, their daughter, was born Sept. 17, 1801.
    Thomas Jefferson, their son, was born Oct. 3, 1803.

Members of the Aldred and Day families intermarried after settling in Brandywine Hundred.

> Clara W. Bird
> (Mrs. Charles)

ALLERDICE BIBLE RECORD

(Bible is now owned by the Delaware Historical Society, Wilmington. Record given by Mrs. Glenn S. Skinner, Newark, Del.)

Marriages

Abraham Allerdice and Eliza Shuff were married June 7, 1821 at Isabella Furnace, Virginia.

The following records were taken from the files in the Delaware Historical Society, Wilmington:

Abraham Allerdice Baptism, December 7, 1866; Presbyterian Church records. Born 9-20-1854; parents Joseph and Anna T. Allerdice.

Taylor-Allerdice 1862 May on the 8th at Calvary Church by the Rev. John Jenkins, D.D.
John Allerdice and Mary Taylor, daughter of the late Levy Taylor of Philadelphia.
James Henry Allerdice, parents Joseph and Anna T. Allerdice, Baptised December 7, 1866 at Presbyterian Church.
Sloan-Allerdice married May 22, 1849. David R. Sloan to Miss Jane E. Allerdice.
(Delaware Gazette, May 25, 1849)
(Delaware State Journal, May 22, 1849)
(Blue Hen's Chicken, May 25, 1849)
John A. Allerdice, March 27, 1867, at New Castle on Wednesday morning 27th inst., John A. Allerdice in the 43rd year of his age died. (Smyrna Times, April 3, 1867).
Brown-Allerdice married in Philadelphia at the Washington House on March 21 by Rev. Dr. Gilbert Allerdice Esq. to Miss Isabella Brown, all of Wilmington. (Delaware Gazette, March 26, 1850).
Joseph Emmor Allerdice, parents Joseph and Anna T. Allerdice, born January 18, 1856; Baptised December 7, 1866 (Presbyterian Church Record).

Births

Abram Allerdice was born December 27, 1795, his parents were Abram and Ruth Allerdice from Ireland.
Eliza Shuff was born May 26, 1803, her parents were John and Barbary Shuff.
Jane Eliza Allerdice, daughter of Abraham and Eliza Allerdice, was born April 4, 1822 at Isabella Furnace in Shenandoah County, Va.
John Alphonso Allerdice, son of Abraham and Eliza, was born February 12, 1824 at Isabella Furnace, Shenandoah County, Va.
James Allerdice, son of Abraham and Eliza, was born November 20, 1825 at Isabella Furnace, Shenandoah County, Va.
William Hilary Allerdice, son of Abraham and Eliza, was born April 24, 1828 at Wilmington, Del., New Castle County.
Joseph Allerdice, son of Abrahm and Eliza, was born February 16, 1831 at Wilmington, Del.
Mary Caroline Allerdice, daughter of Abraham and Eliza, was born February 26, 1833 at Wilmington, Del.

Deaths

Abraham Allerdice died March 21, 1864 at Wilmington, Del., age 69.
John Alphonso Allerdice died March 27, 1869 at New Castle, Del., age 43.
Sarah Isabella Allerdice, wife of John Alphonso Allerdice, died February 29, 1868 at New Castle, Del., age 44.
Joseph Allerdice died August 22, 1869 at Wilmington, Del., age 38.
James Allerdice died May 19, 1870 at Philadelphia, age 44.
Eliza Allerdice, wife of Abraham Allerdice, died August 8, 1876, age 73 years, 2 months and 16 days - buried in Wilmington Brandywine Cemetery.

Abram Allerdice
b. 1742
d. 2-1800
m. Ruth

1. Alphonso, b. 1802
2. Jane, b. 2-20-1786
3. Ruth, b. 8-7-1789
4. Abraham
   d. 3-21-1864

John Shuff
m.
Barbary

Eliza Shuff

1. Jane Eliza
   b. 4-4-1822
   m. 5-22-1849
   David E. Sloan
2. John A.
   b. 2-12-1824
3. James, b ?
4. William
   b. 2-24-1828
5. Joseph
   b. 2-16-1831
6. Mary C.
   b. 2-26-1833

ALLMOND - GRUBB DATA

(Sketch of the Allmond Family by Hon. Ignatius C. Grubb, January 1911. Addition by Charles M. Allmond, M.D., May 1, 1932. Record given by Mrs. Charles D. Bird, Wilmington, Delaware.)

By tradition the Allmond family is of French origin. They fled from the Province of Languedoc and the oppression of the religious and Civil Wars in France and sought refuge in England during

Elizabeth's reign. From England, two of the descendants (1) Joseph and (2) John Allemond or Allmond, emigrated to Delaware shortly after Penn's arrival.

Early records, 1685, Joseph Allmon, Planter and Margaretta, his wife, executed a conveyance of 200 acres of land on Blackbird Creek in New Castle County, Delaware and also in 1687 Ephraim Herman conveyed to Joseph Allman, Planter of New Castle Co., Del., 200 acres of land on North side of Duck Creek.

Thus it appears that Joseph Allmond or Allman had wife Margaretta - that they had a son Solomon and probably a son Benjamin and other children; that they were Episcopalians attached to Old Swedes Church of Christiana now Wilmington; that they owned lands in New Castle Co., near Appoquinimink settlement and that Joseph was a Planter and regarded as belonging to the gentlemen class in his day.

His brother (2) John Allmond, wife's name not known, left 3 children:
    (3) Thomas married Mary and had 2 sons, Thomas and John.

John, son of Thomas (3) and Mary joined the British forces in 1777 and his property was confiscated (Deed M2, 268). He died after his mother in 1794 and it is not known that he left any descendants.

John Allmond, son of (2) John Allmond, born about 1700; died in Brandywine Hundred, Del., Nov. 11, 1761. (See will H & I pages 548-9). On Nov. 13, 1761 Administration was granted (after his nuncupative will was proved) to his widow Barbara and to his brother William Allmond. (See Adms., Record 1 page 152.)

John Allmond married Barbara Macmillian, April 23, 1752 and after his death in 1761, his widow Barbara married Elias Reed, who died intestate in 1789. (Will Record N.I. 37). She died December 31, 1806 aged 75 years. Her will, devising her property to her son, John, and her three daughters

Elizabeth, Mary and Lydie, was proved 1807 (Record Z.I. 209).

In the year 1748, John Allmond was commissioned a Colonial Captain during the French and Indian Wars.

(10) Elizabeth Allmond was born Oct. 3, 1755; died 18--; married Feb. 27, 1781 to George Weldin (Old Swedes Records pp. 593-753).
(11) Mary Allmond, born Jan. 23, 1758; died 18--; married March 18, 1790 to Jacob Weldin (Old Swedes Records pp.593-764).
(12) John Allmond, born Feb. 2, 1761 in Brandywine Hd., near Edgemoor, died Feb. 18, 1832; married Beulah Grubb, who was born Jan. 18, 1775; died Feb. 19, 1832. She was the daughter of Amer Grubb and Anne Buckley. They are buried in Old Swedes Churchyard, Wilmington.

They had the following children:
John Grubb Allmond, born Dec. 29, 1796; died July 17, 1830; married Jane McClintock; born Dec. 12, 1803; died Nov. 16, 1882.
Children:
Beulah Ann, born 1-4-1824; died 4-18-1868.
John Bray Allmond, born March 1826.
Elizabeth Jane, born March 8, 1828.
John Grubb, Jr., born Aug. 20, 1830; died 1-12-1901.
Beulah Ann Allmond, married John Smith Beeson on 2-29-1844. Children:
Sarah, Joseph, William, Elizabeth, Ann, Emma, Harry, Addie L.
Elizabeth born Feb. 1, 1850; died 10-14-1876; married Henry Laban Jones on May 20, 1874 and had a son, Walter Beeson Jones, born 2-18-1875; married Georgianna N. Miller 11-25-1896 and had:
Ann Elizabeth Jones
Adeline Beeson Jones
Emma Beeson born 12-25-1852; died 11-18-1876; married Harry Husbands, no issue.
Harry Allmond Beeson born July 22, 1855; died 10-8-1919; married Isabella Snyder on 4-25-1887; died 1900. Children:

        Harry Snyder born 12-3-1888;
        married Alice C. Scholtz
        2-10-1910 and had:
            Harry 2d born 2-26-1911;
            married Mildred Myers 4-15-1931.
            Alice Isabella Beeson born
            11-17-1913; married Norman
            Daughady 2-21-1932.
            Gene Charles born 5-4-1920.
Addie Lucinda Beeson born 12-15-1867;
    married John Taggart 4-15-1891 and
    had:
        Beulah Jane Allmond Taggart
        born 3-3-1892; died 7-29-1892.
Anne Maria Allmond, born 12-12-1797;
    married Nov. 18, 1819 to George
    Griffin of Wilmington, Del. They
    had a son:
        John Allmond; married _____.
        He was born Dec. 16, 1821.
        Children: Helen, Anne,
            Frederick H.
Amer Bayard Allmond was born Dec. 22,
    1804; died Feb. 4, 1807.
Henrietta Matilda Allmond was born
    Jan. 20, 1810; died 2-15-1841;
    married March 14, 1833 Amer Grubb
    and later divorced him. No
    children. She left a legacy for
    the repair and renovation of Old
    Swedes Church, Wilmington, which is
    commemorated by the Vestry upon her
    tomb in said churchyard.
Beulah Carolin Allmond was born July 5,
    1814; died Sept. 10, 1852; married
    Nov. 7, 1832 Wellington Grubb of
    Stockdales, Grubb's Landing, Del.,
    who died Feb. 10, 1853 in Wilmington,
    Del., leaving a daughter, Louise O.
    Grubb and a son, Ignatius C. Grubb.
    He died June 20, 1927; was the
    writer of this sketch as heretofore
    stated. She is buried in the vault
    of her father and mother in Old
    Swedes Churchyard, Wilmington, Del.

This sketch was taken from a printed booklet owned by Mrs. Walter Jones (Georgia Miller) of Wilmington.

ANDERSON-NEEDLES-GRIFFITH-EDWARDS

(Bible was published by Mathew Carey, Philadelphia, T. Kirk, Printer.)

Cora Needles, daughter of Wilbur Needles and Anna his wife, was born May 19, 1882.
Samuel Needles, son of Wilbur Needles and Anna his wife, was born July 9, 1885.
Edith Needles, daughter of Wilbur Needles and Anna his wife, was born September 4, 1887.

James C. Anderson and Sarah Berry were married September 7, 1826.

Joseph W. Griffith and Sarah Anderson were married December 20, 1831.

James A Griffith, son of Joseph W. Griffith and Sarah his wife, was born October 5, 1832.
Rhody Ann Griffith, daughter of Joseph W. Griffith and Sarah his wife, was born December 6, 1834.
Mary Catherine Griffith, daughter of Joseph W. Griffith and Sarah his wife, was born March 31, 1838.

Andrew Edwards and Mary Ann Anderson were married December 22, 1829.
Rebecca Edwards, daughter of Andrew Edwards and Mary Ann his wife, was born November 7, 1830.
Lavania Edwards, daughter of Andrew Edwards and Mary Ann his wife, was born (torn).
Abner Edwards, son of Andrew Edwards and Mary Ann his wife, was born July 7, 1836.

James Anderson, son of John Anderson and his wife Cathron, was born January 21, 1791.

Lavania Saulsbury, daughter of John Saulsbury and Temperance his wife, was born March 1797.

Allie B. Needles, daughter of Samuel Needles and Catherine his wife, was born Nov. 11, 1853.
Wilbur Needles, son of Samuel Needles and Catherine his wife, was born June 26, 1856.
James Needles, son of Samuel Needles and Catherine his wife, was born Oct. 1, 1858.
Two entries follow but unable to read.

Mary Ann Anderson, daughter of James Anderson and
    Lavania his wife, was born Sept. 20, 1813.
Sally Ann Anderson, daughter of James Anderson and
    Lavania his wife, was born April 6, 1815.
John Saulsbury Anderson, son of James Anderson and
    Levenia his wife, was born Aug. 2, 1817.
Lizey Anderson, daughter of James Anderson and
    Levenia his wife, was born Dec. , 1820.
William Henry Anderson, son of James Anderson and
    Levenia his wife, was born April 1824.
George Warrington Anderson, son of James C. Anderson
    and Sarah his wife, was born Sept. 29, 1827.
Ann Elizabeth Anderson, daughter of James C.
    Anderson and Sarah his wife, was born June 24,
    1830.
Cathron Anderson, daughter of James C. Anderson
    and Sarah his wife, was born Nov. 27, 1832.

Levenia Anderson, wife of James Anderson, died
    June 12, 1825.
Sarah Melvin, wife of Brummel Melven, died
    March 13, 1831. She was the sister of James
    C. Anderson.
John Anderson, husband of Mary Ann Anderson, died
    March 21, 1831.
Ann Elizabeth Anderson, daughter of James and Sarah
    Anderson, died June 1, 1831.
Margarett Anderson, daughter of James C. Anderson
    and Sarah his wife, died Sept. 21, 1836.
Mary Ann Anderson, wife of John Anderson, died
    August 22, 1838.

Emily Anderson, daughter of James C. Anderson and
    Sarah his wife, was born July 24, 1837.
Joseph B. Anderson, son of James C. Anderson and
    Sarah his wife, was born November 15, 1839.
There are other entries but cannot read them.

Catherine Needles, daughter of James C. Anderson
    and Sally Berry, died March 11, 1917 in her
    85th year.
Samuel Needles, husband of Catherine Needles, died
    November 9, 1864. His funeral preached by
    Joseph Smith.

James C. Anderson died December 12, 1851.
Sarah Anderson, wife of James C. Anderson, died
    December 31, 1858.

On the back page of the Bible is:
Janes Bostick and Eliza Anderson were married January 15, 1839.

JOHN ANDERSON-REBECCA SMITH BIBLE

(Bible published by Mathew Carey, 192 Market St., 1812. Belonged to Wm. Anderson, born August 25, 1792; lived in Northern Delaware. Present owner, Mrs. Edna Talley Kallam, McDaniel Heights, Wilmington, Del. Copied by Clara Wallace Eyre, Caesar Rodney Chapter, D.A.R., June 20, 1962.)

John Anderson was married to Rebecca Smith on February 9, 1792.

Family Records

John Anderson was born October 28, 1742.
Rebecca, wife of John Anderson, was born June 18, 1768.

William Smith Anderson, son of John and Rebecca Anderson, was born August 25, 1792.
Mary Anderson, daughter of John and Rebecca Anderson, was born January 27, 1794.
Jacob Anderson, son of John and Rebecca Anderson, was born October 27, 1796.
Ann Anderson, daughter of John and Rebecca Anderson, was born September 22, 1798.
Elizabeth Anderson, daughter of John and Rebecca Anderson, was born March 20, 1800.
Rebecca Anderson, daughter of John and Rebecca Anderson, was born December 23, 1801.
Sarah Anderson, daughter of John and Rebecca Anderson, was born October 15, 1803.
Susannah Anderson, daughter of John and Rebecca Anderson, was born August 3, 1805.
John Anderson, son of John and Rebecca Anderson, was born December 8, 1807.
Catherine Anderson, daughter of John and Rebecca Anderson, was born November 6, 1810.

Elizabeth Anderson, daughter of Elizabeth, was born November 2, 1821.

Deaths

Rebecca Anderson, daughter of John and Rebecca
    Anderson, died September 28, 1846, age 45.
Rebecca Anderson, wife of John Anderson, died
    January 14, 1849, age 81.
Ann Anderson, daughter of John and Rebecca
    Anderson, died March 27, 1854, age 56.
Susannah A. Graves, daughter of John and Rebecca
    Anderson; born August 3, 1805; died
    January 24, 1887, age 82.
Isaac Graves died March 2, 1860; born May 23, 1797.
Mary Ann Graves, born Nov. 29, 1825; died
    Jan. 27, 1887.
John A. Graves, born Aug. 1, 1827; died Aug. 24,
    1890.
Sarah J. Graves (Talley), born March 16, 1836;
    died October 12, 1871.
James Graves was born February 2, 1838.
David Graves, born July 7, 1842; died Sept. 27,
    1843.
Marshall Graves, born November 29, 1843; died ?
Rebecca Graves (Kellam), born April 22, 1846;
    married John H. Kellam, son of Joseph Kellam.
Addie C. Graves was born July 14, 1850.

John Anderson
            Susanna Anderson
Rebecca Smith   Rebecca Graves
            Isaac Graves

            Joseph Kellam   John H. Kellam

ARTERBRIDGE BIBLE

(A small hand Bible, published by the American
Bible Society, D. Fanshaw, Printer. Owned by
Thomas Arterbridge, Lewes, Delaware. On front
Fly page: Bessie Johnson.)

Marriages

Abraham W. Johnson and Marthy J. Fisher were
    married October 8, 1851.

Births

Marthy J. Fisher, daughter of James and Sarah his
    wife, was born March 8, 1832.
Rasmus D. Johnson, son of Abraham W. Johnson and
    Marthy J. Johnson his wife, was born
    October 24 1852.
Benjamin Y. Johnson, son of Abraham W. Johnson and
    Marthy J. Johnson his wife, was born July 1,
    1854.
Nathaniel W. Johnson, son of Abraham W. Johnson
    and Marthy J. Johnson his wife, was born
    November 20, 1857.
Hannah E. Johnson, daughter of Abraham W. Johnson
    and Marthy his wife, was born Sept. 9, 1859.
James A. Johnson, son of Abraham W. Johnson and
    Marthy his wife, was born Nov. 11, 1861.
Conealy A. Johnson, daughter of Abraham Johnson
    and Martha his wife, was born April 10, 1864.

On a slip of paper in the Bible:
Charles E. Johnson, son of Abrum W. Johnson and
    Martha his wife, was born January 29, 1869.
Mary L. Johnson, daughter of Abrum W. Johnson and
    Martha his wife, was born November 10, 1875.
Georga P. Johnson, daughter of Abrum W. Johnson,
    was born October 27, 1877.

Nellie Pepper, daughter of Truitt Pepper and
    Bessie his wife, was born May 29, 1892.
Raymond Pepper was born March 23, 1896.
Ralston Pepper, son of Truitt Pepper and Bessie
    his wife, was born October 8, 1912.

Deaths
Rolley Johnson, son of Abraham W. Johnson and
    Martha J. Johnson, died December 21, 1872.
The daughter of Abraham W. Johnson and Marthy J.
    Johnson died November 18, 1852.
Rhoda Ann, daughter of Abraham W. Johnson and
    Martha J. Johnson, died January 18, 1857.
Rosa Johnson died July 12, 1884; born 1870-71.

Back Fly Leaf - Miss Prudie Johnson.
Bottom: Sarah J. Johnson, daughter of Abram W.
Johnson and Marthy his wife, was born Feb. 2,
1866.

James Fisher

Sarah

Abraham W. Johnson
m. 1851

Martha Fisher
b. 1832

Rasmus   b. 1852
Benjamin   b. 1854
Nathaniel   b. 1857
Hannah   b. 1859
James   b. 1861
Rhoda   d. 1857
Conealy   d. 1864
Charles   b. 1869
Mary   b. 1875
Georga   b. 1877
Rosa   d. 1884

Truitt Pepper

Bessie

Nellie Pepper
b. 5-29-1892
Raymond Pepper
b. 1896
Ralston Pepper
b. 1912

THE ASH FAMILY

The Emigrant to America was George Ash, a native of Germany who settled in Elkton, Maryland. He married twice. There were several children by his first marriage.

He married 2nd _____ Pusey. Their children:
1. John Ash
2. Matilda
3. Louise - Mrs. John Kinkard.

John Ash (2) was a merchant, later collector for the Chesapeake and Delaware Canal at Del. City. He died 1849. He married 2 times.

Married 1st Ruth Ann Smithers, Kent Co., Del.; bur. St. Georges. Children:
1. Amanda Ash; m. Wm. P. Caldwell, Phil.

Married 2nd Susan, daughter of Capt. Henry and Lackey Rowan, Wilmington. Her father was English and a Capt. of a vessel on the Del. R. His wife was Irish. She died at Mrs. McIntyre's 1883.

Children:
2. George C.
3. Cornelia (Mrs. Samuel Lambertson, Central, O.
4. Charles Granville, clerk and collector of Ches. & Del. Canal, 26 yrs.; Coal and Lumber bus.; stockholder and director of Del. City Nat. Bank, its 3rd President; Mason, democrat; married Mary Pennington Fields; d. 7-15-1889; bur. St. Anns; no children.
5. Child, died young
6. Laura C., wife of Francis McIntyre, cashier of Del City Nat. Bank.
7. Emma Louise; married Frank Belville, M.D.

Notes: Mary Rowan married Robert McCoy 2-23-1826. Henry Rowan married Mary Ann McCoy 10-26-1825.

John Belville
    Thomas Belville
Margaret
    Sarah Wood

    Rev. R. B. Bellville

    Mary
    George Ash

1. Thomas W.
2. Sarah, m. Isaac Clark
3. Margaret, m. Curtis B. Ellison
4. John P. Belville 1. *
   Mary Belville

John Ash
m. Ruth Ann Smithers
m. Susan Rowan

Rev. R.B. Bellville will 9-19-1845 Wife: Mary
Ch : Robert C.
    Ann K.
    Mary B.
    Ely
    Jacob
    Elizabeth W.
    Catherine
Son-in-law John P. Bellville

*1. Catherine Belville
2. Dr. Frank Belville
   m.
   1. Emma Louise Ash
   2. Geo. C. Ash
   3. Chas. G.
   4. Laura
   5. Amanda by 1st wife
   6. Cornelia
3. Mary Ann m. Henry Taylor
4. John P.
5. Allen L.
6. Robert B.
7. Thomas W.

- 15 -

ASHBRIDGE BIBLE

(Bible printed by T. Wright and W. Gill, printers to the University. Sold by S. Crowder in Pater noster Row, London and by W. Jackson in Oxford. MDCCLXXVII 1777.)

The names and time of birth of the children of George and Rebecca Ashbridge:

    Lydia, daughter, was born November 5, 1755.
    Mary, daughter, was born September 13, 1758.
    Susanna, daughter, was born September 30, 1761.
    Jane, daughter, was born November, 1764.
    Phoebe, daughter, was born September 8, 1767.
    George, son, was born August 17, 1770.
    William, son, was born August 2, 1773.

Rebecca (?) Ashbridge died September 24, 1777.
George Ashbridge died October 25, 1785.
Lydia Malin died January 7, 1796, age 40 years, 2 months and 31 days.
Phoebe Valentine died August 28, 1805, age 37 years, 11 months and 20 days.
George A. Downing, son of Samuel and Jane Downing, was born March 1, 1802.

Note: These records of George and Rebecca Ashbridge were very difficult to read as the proper names were in very large letters, and each name was one big blur. I believe that the above is fairly accurate as I spent a great deal of time and tried very hard to get the first names correct - C.W.E.

ATKINS BIBLE RECORD

(Bible was printed by William Young, Bookseller, No. 52-2nd Street, the corner of Chestnut Street. M DCC XCIV. The New Testament has the date of 1808 and they are sewed to the Old Testament. Owned by Miss Sara Atkins, Milton, Delaware. Record given by Mrs. D. A. Potter, Lewes, Delaware.)

(Marriage Certificate owned by Mrs. George Atkins of Milton: This Certifies that the Rite of Holy Matrimony was Celebrated between David T. Atkins of Milton, Del. and Annie F. Reed of Philadelphia, Pa., on January 17, 1867 at the house of the Pastor by William Hickman. Witnesses: Morris Duxfoot and Joseph P. Reed (or Reese - is not clear.)

Note: The oldest son of the above states that this marriage took place in Philadelphia.

George W. Atkins, son of Thomas C. Atkins and
    Arcada his wife, was born July 27, 1812.
Joseph C. Atkins, son of Thomas C. Atkins and
    Arcada his wife, was born July 20, 1813.
Lydia Atkins, daughter of Thomas C. Atkins and
    Arcada his wife, was born January 6, 1815.
Sarah and Leah R. Atkins, daughters of Thomas C.
    Atkins and Arcada his wife, were born
    June 10, 1816.
Thomas J. Atkins, son of Thomas C. Atkins and
    Arcada his wife, was born April 16, 1818.
John S. Atkins, son of Thomas C. Atkins (no
    dates shown).

On sheets placed in the center of the Bible:
    Thomas C. Atkins, son of Isaac Atkins and
    Sarah his wife, was born October 9, 1785.

Next item in different writing:
    and departed this life January 20th day one
    thousand eight hundred thirty and two on
    Friday 4 of the clock afternoon.

    Leah R. Rust, wife of James Rust, departed
    this life in perfect happiness and
    resignation to God in June 15th 1841.

Arcada Atkins, daughter of Thomas Simpler and Leah
    his wife, was born September 3, 1788.
Thomas C. Atkins and Arcadia Simpler were married
    March 28, 1811 by the Rev. Thomas Walker.
Arcada Atkins, wife of Thomas C. Atkins, died
    September 12, 1863.
George W. Atkins, son of Thomas C. Atkins and
    Arcada his wife, was born July 27, 1812.

Joseph C. Atkins, son of Thomas C. Atkins and
    Arcada his wife, was born July 20, 1813.
Lydia Atkins, daughter of Thomas C. Atkins and
    Arcada his wife, was born January 6, 1815.
Sarah Atkins, daughter of Thomas C. Atkins and
    Arcada his wife, was born June 10, 1816.
Leah Atkins, daughter of Thomas C. Atkins and
    Arcada his wife, was born June 10, 1816.
Thomas J. Atkins, son of Thomas C. Atkins and
    Arcada his wife, was born April 16, 1818.
John S. Atkins, son of Thomas C. Atkins and Arcada
    his wife, was born October 6, 1819.
Arcada E. L. Atkins, daughter of Thomas C. Atkins
    and Arcada his wife, was born Jan. 15, 1821.
Peter Edward Page Atkins, son of Thomas C. Atkins
    and Arcada his wife, was born July 12, 1822.
Henry W. Atkins, son of Thomas C. Atkins and
    Arcada his wife, was born May 18, 1827.

Henry W. Atkins, son of Thomas C. Atkins and
    Arcada his wife, died June 11, 1827,
    age 24 days.

Allen R. Atkins, son of Lydia Atkins, was born
    November 5, 1849.
Isaac I. Phillips was born in 1842.
Thomas Simpler, son of Phillip Simpler and
    Suzannah his wife, was born March 22, 1742.
Leah Simpler, daughter of William Rodney and Mary
    his wife, was born March 21, 1750.
Thomas Simpler died February 7, 1826, age 84.
Leah Simpler died February 10, 1826, age 76.

ATKINS CHART

1.	2.	3.
Phillip Simpler	Thomas Simpler	Arcada Simpler
b.	b. 3-22-1742	b. 9-3-1788
d.	d. 2-7-1826	d. 9-12-1863
m.	m.	m. 3-28-1811
Suzannah		
William Rodney		
b.	Leah Rodney	
m.	b. 3-21-1750	
Mary	d. 2-10-1826	

(Continued next page)

```
            Isaac Atkins           Thomas C. Atkins
            m.                     b. 10-9-1785
            Sarah                  d. 1-20-1830
```

4.
Children of Arcada and Thomas C. Atkins:
```
    1.  George W.      b. 7-27-1812
    2.  Joseph C.      b. 7-20-1813
    3.  Lydia          b. 1-6-1815
    4.  Sarah          b. 6-10-1816
    5.  Leah           b. 6-10-1816
    6.  Thomas J.      b. 5-16-1818
    7.  John S.        b. 10-6-1819
    8.  Arcada E.      b. 1-15-1821
    9.  Peter E.       b. 7-12-1822
   10.  Henry W.       b. & d. 1827
```

AN ACCOUNT OF THE BABB FAMILY

(This record was given by Miss Anna Sherrill of Philadelphia, some years ago. She gave the Bible to her nephew, by name of McGovern. Miss Anna died January 6, 1954. Record given by Mrs. Charles Bird.)

John Babb, born March 5, 1773, was a son of Samson, who was born in Calm, Chester Co., Pa. to Peter Babb. Peter Babb was born in Brandywine Hundred, New Castle Co., Del., a son of Thomas Babb, Sr. and his first wife, Bethsheba (Hussey), son of John of N.C.C., Del.

John Babb died in 1852 in his 79th year.
Lydia Babb died in 1854 in her 77th year.
B. Pearson Thockmorton, was born 7-23-1859,
    died 12-1-1932.

JOHN W. AND PHEBE H. (PEARSON) BABB

Marriages

John W, Babb and Phebe H. Pearson were married
    April 8, 1830.
John Babb and Lydia Clark were married March 24,
    1796.

James Clark and Hannah Hayes were married
    April 17, 1765.
D. Webster Chandler and Emma F. Babb were married
    January 21, 1852.
Jos. F. Thockmorton and Mary P. Babb were married
    March 6, 1854.
John L. Serrill and Rebecca S. Babb were married
    March 1, 1866.
Thomas C. Babb and Sarah E. Bradley were married
    July 28, 1863.
George Pearson and Mary Harper were married
    December 23, 1784.

Births

John Babb, son of Samson and Ann Babb, was born
    March 5, 1773.
Lydia Babb, daughter of Jas. and Hannah Clark,
    was born October 9, 1777.
Wm. H. Babb, son of John and Lydia Babb, was born
    January 18, 1800.
John W. Babb, son of John and Lydia Babb, was born
    December 7, 1801.
Thomas Babb, son of John and Lydia Babb, was born
    June 19, 1803.
Hannah Babb, daughter of John and Lydia Babb, was
    born October 6, 1804.
Samson Babb, son of John and Lydia Babb, was born
    February 18, 1806.

Emma Francis, daughter of John W. and Phebe
    Pierson, was born January 1, 1832.
Lydia Clark Babb (died 6-23-1836) was born
    April 26, 1836.
Rebecca Serrill Babb was born September 9, 1840.
Thomas Clark Babb was born September 13, 1842.

Deaths

Mary P. Thockmorton, daughter of John W. and Phebe
    H. Babb, died April 20, 1878. Interred at
    Mt. Vernon Cemetery, Philadelphia.
John W. Babb, husband of Phebe H.; son of John
    and Lydia, died March 26, 1879; interred Mt.
    Vernon Cemetery, Philadelphia.
Emma B. Chandler, daughter of John W. and Phebe H.
    Babb, died December, 1880; interred Mt.
    Vernon Cemetery.

Samson Babb, father of John Babb, died October 28, 1814; buried on his farm in Tioga Co., Pa. Second Fork in Pine Creek.
James Clark, father of Lydia Babb, died March 28, 1808, age 67 years, 10 months and 15 days.
Hannah Clark, mother of Lydia Babb, died Nov. 14, 1814, age 67 years, 9 months and 11 days.
Ann Babb, wife of Samson Babb; mother of John, Mary, Caleb, Jacob, William and Samson, died April 14, 1834, age 91 years, 10 months and 26 days.
John Babb died 1852 in his 79th year.
Lydia Babb died 1854 in her 77th year.
B. Pearson Thockmorton, born 7-23-1859, died 12-1-1932.

1.
Samson Babb
b.
d. 10-28-1814
m.
Ann
d. 4-14-1834
age 91

2.
John Babb
b. 3-5-1773
d. 1852
m. 3-24-1796

3.
1. William H.
   b. 1-18-1800
2. John Babb   4.**
   b. 12-7-1801
   d. 1879
   m. 4-8-1830
   Phebe Pearson

James Clark
b.
d. 3-28-1808
m. 4-17-1765
Hannah Hayes
d. 11-14-1814
age 67

Lydia Clark
b. 10-9-1777
d. 1854

3. Thomas
   b. 6-19-1803
4. Hannah
   b. 10-6-1804
5. Samson
   b. 2-18-1806

   4.**
1. Emma Babb, b. 1-1-1832; m. 1-21-1852, D. W. Chandler.
2. Lydia, b. 1836; d. 1836.
3. Mary, d. 4-20-1878; m. 3-06-1854, Jos. Thockmorton.
4. Rebecca, b. 9-9-1840; m. 3-1-1866, John Serrill.
5. Thomas, b. 9-13-1842; m. 7-28-1868, Sarah Bradley.

BACON - SCALES

George William Bacon, Journalist, married Amelia Scales. He died in 1901. Amelia was born October 1876 in Norwich, Norfolk, England.

Their children:
1. Millie Frances Bacon, born September 18, 1897.
2. Cecil Williams
3. Herbert

Millie Frances Bacon, daughter of George W. Bacon and Amelia (Scales) Bacon, was born September 18, 1897 in Norwich, England. She married July 8, 1922, James Hay, son of William S. Hay and Mary E. (MacKenzie) Hay.

Their daughter:
Edith MacKenzie Hay was born February 9, 1924 in Philadelphia. Pa. She was married April 3, 1948 in Ambler, Pa., to Daniel R. McNeal, Jr., son of Daniel R. McNeal and Clara Louise (Berlin) McNeal, and grandson of H. W. McNeal and his wife Myrie V. (Reese) McNeal.

Their Children:
1. Daniel R., III, born September 11, 1949; died April 15, 1951.
2. Debra Jeanne, born November 24, 1952.

(See McNeal, Berlin Record)

BAILEY BIBLE 1821

(Owned by the Delaware Historical Society, Wilmington, Del. Record was given by Mrs. Glenn S. Skinner, Newark, Del.)

Joseph T. Bailey and Priscilla Hatton were married February 7, 1822.
Edith Pritchett Bailey, daughter of Joseph T. and Priscilla Bailey, married George W. Concklin January 11, 1843.

Tatnall Baily and Jane Van Blarcom were married December 20, 1847.
Ann Elizabeth Baily, daughter of Joseph T. and Priscilla Baily, married Dr. Arthur H. Grimshaw on April 10, 1850.
Edith B. Concklin married Jesse R. Value on October 19, 1852.

- - - - - - - - - -

Joseph T. Baily, son of Joseph and Elizabeth Baily, was born January 5, 1799.
Priscilla Hatton, daughter of Joseph and Priscilla Hatton, was born April 18, 1803.
Tatnall Baily, son of Joseph T. and Priscilla Baily, was born January 19, 1823.
Edith Pritchett Baily, daughter of Joseph and Priscilla Baily, was born April 28, 1824.
William Pritchett Baily, son of Joseph T. and Priscilla Baily, was born December 5, 1825.
Ann Elizabeth Baily, daughter of Joseph T. and Priscilla Baily, was born March 31, 1827.
Sidney Ann Baily, daughter of Joseph T. and Priscilla, was born November 17, 1828.
Joseph Hatton Baily, son of Joseph T. and Priscilla, was born February 5, 1834.
James Edward Baily, son of Joseph T. and Priscilla Baily, was born January 22, 1837.
George William Concklin, son of George W. and Edith B. Concklin, was born April 4, 1844.
Joseph T. Baily, Jr., son of Tatnall and Jane Baily, was born September 20, 1848.
Brandt VanBlarcom Baily, son of Tatnall and Jane Baily, was born September 3, 1851.

Deaths

Priscilla Hatton, wife of Joseph Hatton, died May 20, 1837.
Joseph Hatton died May 4, 1842.
Elizabeth Baily, wife of Joseph Baily, died October 28, 1808.
Joseph Baily died January 31, 1843.
Edward T. Baily, son of Joseph and Elizabeth Baily, died May 18, 1843.
George W. Concklin died March 21, 1844.
Major James E. Baily, youngest son of Joseph and Priscilla H. Baily, died March 5, 1865 at Annapolis, Maryland, from wounds received at Hatcher's Run, Virginia, February 6, 1865.

1.
Joseph Baily
b.
d. 1-31-1843
m.
Elizabeth
d. 10-28-1808

    2.
1. Joseph T.
   b. 1-5-1799
   d.
   m. 2-7-1822

    3.
1. Tatnall   4.**
   b. 1-19-1823
   d.
   m.
    Jane Van
    Blarcom

Joseph Hatton
b.
d. 5-4-1842
m.
Priscilla
d. 5-20-1837

   Priscilla
    Hatton
   b. 4-18-1803

2. Edith
   b. 4-28-1824
   d.   1.**
   m. 1st
    1-11-1843
    Geo. Concklin
    b.
    d. 3-21-1844
   m. 2nd
    10-19-1852
    Jesse R. Value

2. Edward
   d. 5-13-1843

3. William P.
   b. 12-5-1825

4. Ann Elizabeth
   b. 3-31-1827
   d.
   m. 4-10-1850
   Dr. Arthur Grimshaw

5. Sidney
   b. 11-17-1828
6. Joseph
   b. 2-5-1834
7. James
   b. 1-22-1837
   d. 2-6-1865

4**:
    4.
1. Joseph T.
   b. 9-20-1848
2. Brandt
   b. 9-3-1851

1**:

1. George W.
   b. 4-4-1844

JOHN E. BARCUS BIBLE

(Bible - 1891 - New York International Bible Agency, 150 Fifth Ave., N.Y. Original owner, John E. Barcus and Edna R. Pigott. Present owner, Mrs. Donald F. Wright, 204 Saturn Drive, North Star, Newark, Del. Copied by Clara Wallace Eyre, Caesar Rodney Chapter, D.A.R. 1962.)

This cerifies that John E. Barcus and Edna R. Pigott were solomnly united by me in The Holy Bonds of Matrimony, at Chester, Pa., on the Twenty Second Day of April in the year of our Lord, One Thousand Nine Hundred and Three. Conformably to the Ordinance of God and the Laws of the State. In the Presence of Linda King Pigott.
    Signey by W.E.E. Barcus, Pittsburgh
    Conference, M.E. Church

Marriages

Wm. Herman Barcus and Viola Roberta Blittersdorf were married at Beaver Falls, Pa., on September 15, 1930 by Rev. W.E.E. Barcus, Pittsburg M.E. Conference.
Gilbert Laben Barcus and Frances Louise Jauss were married October 13, 1934 at St. James P.E. Church, West Philadelphia, Pa. by Rev. Wm. Roberts.
Rebecca L. Barcus and Edwin L. Jenks were married November 4, 1936 at Wilmington, Delaware by Rev. Frank Hicks.
Sarah A. Barcus and Donald F. Wright were married May 3, 1952 at Milford Avenue Methodist Church by Rev. Roy L. Tawes.
William Herman Barcus and Kate Claudia Ornsen were married November 24, 1960 at Whittier House, Swathmore, Pa., Friend's Meeting.

Births

William Herman Barcus was born April 14, 1904 in Dover, Delaware.
Rebecca Louise Barcus was born July 14, 1906 in Philadelphia, Pa.
Gilbert Laben Barcus was born March 11, 1912 in Darby, Pa.

Sarah Ann Barcus was born December 2, 1921 in
Darby, Pa.

Deaths

Edna P. Barcus, wife of John E. Barcus, died
December 3, 1933 in Milford, Delaware,
age 53 years. Buried in Arlington Cem.,
Drexel Hill, Pa., Lawnview Section, Lot 908,
Grave 1.
John Edgar Barcus died November 15, 1960 in
Milford, Del., age 59 years, 2 months and
25 days. Buried same, Grave 2.
Edwin L. Jenks, husband of Rebecca Barcus, died
September 1945 in Milford, Del. Buried
in Arlington Cem., Drexel Hills, Pa.
Viola L. Barcus, wife of Wm. Herman Barcus, died
December 20, 1958 in Media, Pa. Buried in
Arlington Cem., Drexel Hill, Pa., Lawnview
Section.

Memoranda

John Edgar Barcus, son of Sarah Anna Nell and
Peter Laban Barcus, was born August 20, 1871,
in Cheswold, Del. He enlisted in U.S. Army
on November 12, 1897 for a period of three
years. He served in Troop G, Third Cavalry,
during the Spanish American War. Engaged in
Santiago Campaign, Battle of San Juan Hill,
July 1 and 2, 1899. Discharged November 12,
1900.
Edna P. Barcus, daughter of Mary Louise Brogan and
William Pigott, was born July 8, 1880 in
Chester, Pa.

PETER L. BARCUS-SARAH A. BELL BIBLE

(Bible published by National Publishing Co.,
#724-726-728, Cherry Street. December 1881.
Presented to Sarah A. Barcus by Peter L. Barcus,
December 25, 1884. Present owner, Mrs. Donald F.
Wright, 204 Saturn Drive, North Star, Newark, Del.
Copied by Clara Wallace Eyre, Caesar Rodney
Chapter, D.A.R., April 23, 1962.)

Marriages

This cerifies that Peter L. Barcus and Sarah Ann Bell were united in the Holy Bonds of Matrimony, at Petersville, Delaware, the Thirteenth of October in the year of our Lord 1856. In the presence of: Sarah Meridith and Mary E. Bennett.
Signed by Rev. Peter Meredith

Martha Ellen Barcus and Edward Ford were married December 24, 1878.
Mary Elizabeth Barcus and William Joseph Phillips were married December 11, 1879.
Sarah Emily Barcus and James Ahab Pearson were married in 1885.
William Elmer Ellsworth Barcus and Anna Susan Aikens were married May 31, 1894 at Midway (Wash. Co.), Pa.
Peter L. Barcus, Jr., and Daisy May Shahan were married November 27, 1895.
Laura Etta Barcus and George W. MacNamee were married October 26, 1899 at Cheswold, Del. by Rev. W.E.E. Barcus.
John Edgar Barcus and Edna R. Pigott were married April 22, 1903 in Chester, Pa. by Rev. W.E.E. Barcus.

Births

Children of Peter L. Barcus and Sarah A. Bell:
Richia Ann, born July 30, 1857.
Mary Elizabeth, born September 22, 1859.
Martha Ellen, born October 16, 1864.
William Elmer Ellsworth, born April 18, 1864.
Sarah Emily, born March 14, 1867.
Peter Laban, born March 25, 1869.
John Edgar, born August 20, 1871.
Laura Etta, born January 12, 1874.
Anna Bell, born January 24, 1877.
James Herman, born May 29, 1881.

Deaths

Richia Ann, daugher of P.L. and S.A. Barcus, died February 7, 1859, age 1 year, 6 months and 8 days.
James Herman, son of P.L. and S.A. Barcus, died October 28, 1881, age 5 months.

Anna Bell, daughter of P.L. and S.A. Barcus, died August 3, 1882, age 5 years, 6 months and 21 days.

Sarah Ann Barcus, wife of Peter L. Barcus, Sr., died November 2, 1921, age 82 years, 6 days, married 65 years, 3 days.

Peter L. Barcus, Sr., died June 1922, age 90 years and 11 months.

Mary Elizabeth Phillips died June 1935, age 75 years, 8 months. Buried Bethel Methodist Cem. near Cheswold, Del.

Peter L. Barcus, Jr., died February 4, 1839, age 69 years, 10 months and 9 days. Buried in Bethel M.E. Cem. near Cheswold, Del.

William Elmer Ellsworth Barcus died December 3, 1940 in Crafton, Pa., age 76 years, 7 months and 15 days. Buried Robinson Run Cemetery, Noblestown, Pa. (South Fayette Twp., Alleghany Co.).

Laura Etta MacNamee died September 26, 1947 in Chester, Pa., age 73 years, 8 months and 14 days. Buried Bethel M.E. Cemetery near Cheswold, Del.

Sarah Emily Pearson died August 4, 1952 in Smyrna, Del., age 85 years, 4 months and 20 days. Buried Bethel M.E. Cemetery, Cheswold, Del.

Martha Ellen Ford died February 9, 1954 near Townsend, Del., age 92 years, 3 months and 23 days. Buried Bethel M.E. Cemetery, Cheswold, Del.

John Edgar Barcus died November 15, 1960 in Milford, Del., age 89 years, 2 months and 25 days. Lot 908, Grave 2, Lawnview Section.

Memorandum

Peter L. Barcus, son of Edward Barcus and Anna his wife, was born June 26, 1831. Served as a soldier in the War of the Rebellion 1861 (Civil War) and was twice wounded in said war.

Sarah Ann Bell, daughter of William P. Bell and Richa his wife, was born October 27, 1839.

This Bible was presented to Rev. W.E.E. Barcus by his father, Peter L. Barcus, Sr., November 6, 1921; W.E.E. Barcus gave this Bible to Sarah Ann Barcus November 17, 1939.

Rev. William Elmer Ellsworth Barcus was born April 18, 1864; died December 3, 1940. Born in Kent Co., Delaware. Graduate of Alleghany College, Meadville, Pa. and Drew Theological Seminary, New Jersey in 1891; joined Pittsburgh Conference 1892.

BARLOW - WHITCRAFT

(Bible published by William W. Harding, Phil. 1861. Owned by Harry M. Barlow, Grubb's Road, Wilmington, Del. 1957. Record given by Mrs. Charles D. Bird, Wilmington, Del.)

Marriages

Henry M. Barlow, son of Malachi and Eliza L. Barlow, and Eliza L. Whitcraft, daughter of Jacob and Mary Whitcraft, were married on January 1, 1857.

Parents
Henry M. Barlow was born August 10, 1834.
Eliza L. Barlow was born January 7, 1833.

Children
Mary Emma Barlow was born July 6, 1859.
Eliza Ella Barlow was born January 15, 1861.
Clara Belle C. Barlow was born August 9, 1863.
George Taylor Barlow was born May 25, 1865.
Willie Lewis Barlow was born March 18, 1867.
Margaretta Wilson Barlow was born October 7, 1869.

Deaths

Mary E. Barlow, wife of Wilmer Talley, died January 8, 1903, at her home near Harvey Station on B. & O. R. Road.
Maggie W. Barlow died March 3, 1886 on a farm in Brandywine Hundred.

MALACHI BARLOW AND ELIZA F. TAYLOR
Of Barndywine Hundred, Delaware

(Bible printed by Jesper Harding & Son, Philadelphia. 1857. Owned by Harry M. Barlow, Grubb's Road, Delaware. 1957. Record given by Mrs. Charles Bird, Wilmington.)

FAMILY RECORD

Marriages

Malachi Barlow and Eliza F. Taylor were married November 28, 1833.
Henry M. Barlow married January 1, 1857 in Philadelphia.
Mary Jane Barlow married Sepember 13, 1855.
Lydia Ann Barlow married November 8, 1856.
Susanna T. Barlow married January 27, 1863 at home.
Sarah E. Barlow married February 25, 1863 at home.
Emma L. Barlow married January 1, 1867, Phil.
Margaretta Barlow married March 14, 1868, Brandywine Hd.

Births

Malachi Barlow was born February 25, 1811.
Eliza F. Taylor was born August 5, 1814.

Henry M. Barlow was born August 10, 1834.
Mary Jane Barlow was born March 3, 1836.
Lydia Ann Barlow was born August 30, 1837.
Susanna T. Barlow was born March 25, 1840.
Sarah E. Barlow was born March 6, 1842.
Emmor L. Barlow was born January 25, 1844.
Margaretta Barlow was born November 16, 1845.
Anna Eliza Barlow was born February 14, 1849.
Hannah R. Barlow was born May 19, 1851.
Emma L. Barlow was born December 21, 1852.
Phebe Ella Barlow was born April 7, 1856.
Estella Barlow was born August 31, 1859.

Deaths

Malachi Barlow died June 21, 1888 in Wilmington.
Eliza F. Taylor died July 21, 1865, near Chester, Del., Co. Pa.

Lydia Ann Barlow died January 29, 1867, near
   Chester.
Hannah R. Barlow died January 26, 1879.
Emma L. Barlow died May 30, 1866, Marcus Hook.
Phebe Ella Barlow died September 21, 1856,
   Brandywine Hundred.

BARLOW CHART

1.
Malachi Barlow
b. 2-25-1811
d. 6-21-1888
m. 11-28-1833
Eliza F. Taylor
b. 8-5-1814
d. 7-21-1865

    2.
1. Henry M.
   b. 8-10-1834
   d.
   m. 1-1-1857
   Eliza
   Whitcraft

2. Mary J.
   b. 3-13-1836
   m. 9-13-1855

3. Lydia
   b. 8-30-1837
   m. 11-8-1856

4. Susanna
   b. 3-25-1840
   m. 1-27-1863

5. Sarah E.
   b. 3-6-1842
   m. 2-25-1863

6. Emmor L.
   b. 1-25-1844

7. Margaretta
   b. 11-16-1845
   m. 3-14-1868

8. Anna E.
   b. 2-14-1849

9. Hannah
   b. 5-19-1851
   d. 1-26-1879

10. Emma L.
    b. 12-21-1852

11. Phebe E.
    b. 4-7-1856
    d. 9-21-1856

12. Estella b. 8-31-1859

    3.
1. Mary E.
   b. 7-6-1859
   d. 1-8-1903
   m. Wilmer
      Talley

2. Eliza
   b. 1-15-1861

3. Clara
   b. 8-9-1863

4. George
   b. 5-25-1865

5. William L.
   b. 3-18-1867
   d. 11-29-1850
   m. 3-17-1891
   Levenia Hanby
   d. 1-20-1957

6. Margaret
   b. 10-7-1869
   d. 3-3-1886

- 31 -

Barlow Chart Cont'd.

                                                4.

1. Henry
   b. 3-28-1892
   m. 11-29-1917
   Rebecca Ford

2. Raymond
   b. 2-2-1894
   m. 4-4-1917
   Mary Ebright

3. Esther
   b. 9-5-1898
   m. 6-7-1920
   Ralph Ford

4. William G.
   b. 3-23-1903
   m. 12-17-1936
   Ella Moore

5. James W.
   b. 1-5-1912
   m. 10-7-1937
   Elizabeth Simon

WILLIAM L. BARLOW AND LEVENIA H. L. HANBY

(Bible owned by Mrs. Esther A. Ford, Landenburg, Pa. 1957. Record given by Mrs. Charles D. Bird.)

Marriage Certificate of Wm. L. Barlow of New Castle Co., Delaware and Levenia H. L. Hanby of New Castle Co., Delaware, were married at bride's home on March 17, 1891. In presence of Witnesses. Signed: A. P. Prettyman, Pastor of Bethel M. E. Church.

Births

Henry Myers Barlow was born March 28, 1892.
Raymond Hanby Barlow was born February 2, 1894.
Esther Anna Barlow was born September 5, 1898.

Wm. Gilbert Barlow was born March 23, 1903.
James Wilson Barlow was born January 5, 1912.

Marriages of children of Wm. L. Barlow and Levenia H. Barlow:
   Harry M. Barlow and Rebecca Ford were married
      November 29, 1917.
   Raymond H. Barlow and Mary E. Ebright were
      married April 4, 1917.
   Esther A. Barlow and J. Ralph Ford were
      married June 7, 1920.
   Wm. G. Barlow and Ella G. Moore were married
      December 17, 1936.
   James W. Barlow and D. Elizabeth Simon were
      married October 7, 1937.

Deaths

William L. Barlow, husband of Levenia H. Barlow,
   died November 29, 1950.
Levenia H. Barlow died January 20, 1957.

BARR BIBLE

(Printed and published by Mathew Carey, 1811. Owned by the Delaware Historical Society, Wilmington, Del. Record given by Mrs. Glenn S. Skinner, Newark, Del.)

Martin Barr was born October 17, 1793; married
   Jane Adams, November 3, 1815.

Births

John Adams Barr was born August 8, 1916.
Elizabeth Barr was born January 25, 1818.
Mary Chambers Barr was born September 13, 1819.
Elizabeth Barr was born October 8, 1821.
Joseph M. Barr was born March 25, 1823.
William H. Barr was born December 9, 1824.
Jane Barr was born April 5, 1827.
Franklin Barr was born February 17, 1829.
Eugene Barr was born January 10, 1831.
Virginia Barr was born February 26, 1833.
Marion Barr was born April 5, 1835.
Eugene W. Barr was born November 25, 1837.

Deaths

Elizabeth Barr died January 12, 1821.
Mary Chambers Barr died April 25, 1840.
Elizabeth Barr died August 10, 1848.
Eugene Barr died October 2, 1832.
Virginia Barr died July 12, 1835.
Marion Barr died May 20, 1836.
Eugene W. Barr died May 14, 1844.
Mary Adams died February 10, 1833, age 60 years;
   Mother of Jane.
Margaret Adams died April 11, 1834, age 24 years;
   sister of Jane.
Martha Adams died January 6, 1836; sister of Jane.
Jane Barr died February 22, 1841; age 46 years.
Elizabeth Barr died March 20, 1837, age 88 years;
   Mother of Martin.

Elizabeth
d. 3-20-1837   Martin Barr   1. John
m.   b. 10-27-1793   b. 8-8-1816
                  m. 11-2-1815   2. Elizabeth
Mary   b. 1-25-1818
d. 2-10-1833   3. Mary C.
m ----Adams   Jane Adams   4. Elizabeth
                  b. 1795   b. 10-8-1821
                  d. 2-22-1841   5. Joseph
                                         b. 3-25-1823
                                      6. William
                                         b. 12-9-1824
                                      7. Jane
                                         b. 4-5-1827
                                      8. Franklin
                                         b. 2-17-1829
                                      9. Eugene
                                         b. 7-10-1831
                                     10. Virginia
                                         b. 2-26-1833
                                     11. Marion
                                         b. 4-5-1835
                                     12. Eugene
                                         b. 11-25-1837

BASSETT

One of the old and honored colonial families of Salem County, New Jersey is the Bassett Family. They have been represented here for over two centuries. Following closely in the wake of the first few brave voyagers of the Mayflower fame, the good ship "Welcome" (?) plowed her way across the Atlantic Ocean in 1621 and, among the courageous souls who thus sought a home and "freedom to worship God" in the new land of promise, there were two young men by the names of Bassett - William and Joseph.

Many of their descendants continue to dwell in the vicinity of Lynn and Boston, Mass., where they landed, while others live in Rhode Island and Connecticut.

In 1691, William Bassett emigrated from Lynn to Salem, New Jersey and here he and his posterity found happy homes and an abundance of this world's goods in return for their labors.

BEESON BIBLE RECORD

(Bible was printed in Edinburgh, by Alexander Kincaid - His Majesty's Printer. 1762. Owned by Mrs. William Trianer, New Garden, Pa. Record given by Mrs. David R. Eastburn, Sr., Newark, Del.)

John Beeson, son of John and Alice Beeson, was born August 21, 1739; died November 23, 1793, age 54 years, 2 months and 2 days, after 11 days sickness with Palsy.
Hannah Beeson, daughter of John and Mary Simmons Beeson, was born April 21, 1765.
Elizabeth Beeson, daughter of John and Mary Simmons Beeson, was born December 24, 1768.
Esther Beeson, daughter of John and Mary Beeson, was born May 6, 1769.
Martha Beeson, daughter of John and Mary Beeson, was born December 29, 1770.

Mary Beeson, daughter of John and Mary Beeson, was
    born December 27, 1772.
John Beeson, son of John and Mary Beeson, was born
    May 12, 1774.
Sarah Beeson, daughter of John and Mary Beeson,
    was born March 7, 1776.
Ann Beeson, daughter of John and Mary, was born
    November 28, 1778.
William Beeson, son of John and Mary Beeson, was
    born September 4, 1780.
Lydia Beeson, daughter of John and Mary Beeson,
    was born October 9, 1783.

John Beeson, son of John and Mary Beeson, died
    June 18, 1775.
William Beeson, son of John and Mary Beeson, died
    August 30, 1836.

Children of William Beeson and Elizabeth Mansel
Beeson:
    John Beeson, son of William and Elizabeth
        Beeson, was born September 27, 1802.
    Mary Beeson, daughter of William and
        Elizabeth Beeson, was born December 16,
        1803.
    Hannah Beeson, daughter of William and
        Elizabeth Beeson, was born April 28,
        1805; died November 3, 1828.
    Susannah Beeson, daughter of William and
        Elizabeth Beeson, was born August 2,
        1806; died April 22, 1825.
    Esther Beeson, daughter of William and
        Elizabeth Beeson was born December 2,
        1807.
    Elizabeth Beeson, daughter of William and
        Elizabeth Beeson was born February 14,
        1810.
    Ann Beeson, daughter of William and Elizabeth
        Beeson, was born October 31, 1811; died
        March 16, 1813.
    Lydia C. Beeson, daughter of William and
        Elizabeth Beeson, was born May 6, 181?

Elizabeth Beeson, daughter of William and Susanna
    Mansel, wife of William Beeson, was born
    January 20, 1781; died May 12, 1862.

Amanda McCullough Beeson, wife of John M. Beeson,
    died September 14, 1862; age 55 years.

John Beeson, son of John and Amanda Beeson, was
    born March 22, 1832; died September 18, 1832.
Philena Beeson, daughter of John and Amanda Beeson,
    was born January 18, 1834.
John Franklin, son of John and Amanda Beeson, was
    born April 8, 1836.
Elizabeth Ann, daughter of John and Amanda Beeson,
    was born May 23, 183?
Sallie Ann, daughter of John and Amanda Beeson,
    was born March 8, 1841.
Amanda Beeson, daughter of John and Amanda Beeson,
    was born July 29, 1843.
George Beeson, son of John and Amanda Beeson, was
    born January 20, 1845.
Jethron Beeson, son of John and Amanda Beeson, was
    born January 28, 1848.

BEESON BIBLE RECORD

(Bible owned by Mrs. H. McVaugh, Hockessin, Del.
Record given by Mrs. David R. Eastburn, Sr.,
Newark, Del.)

Taken from Mary B. Beeson Dixon's Bible.

Deaths

William Beeson died August 31, 1836.
Elizabeth Beeson died May 12, 1862, age 83 years.
Hannah P. Beeson died November 3, 1828.
Sussan H. Beeson died April 22, 1825.
Sarah Ann Beeson died 1831.
John M. Beeson died December 25, 1849, age 67 years.
William Mansil died February 11, 1818.
Susannah Mansil died May 16, 1841; age 85 years.
William Mansel, Jr., died July 25, 182?,
    age 37 years.
Anna Reed died November 1, 1841, age 54 years.
Mary Davis died July 27, 1834, age 56 years.
George P. Mansil died January 29, 1849; age
    61 years.
James Mansel died September 6, 1845, age 63 years.
Susannah Mansel, Jr. died August 5, 1865.
Sarah Boyce died October 5, 1870.
Hannah Buckley died April 1877.

ELIZA BEESON RECORD

(Bible was published by John B. Perry, 198 Market Street, Philadelphia. 1856. Owned by Charles Robert Guest, Gordon Heights, Delaware. Record was given by Mrs. Charles Bird, Wilmington, Delaware. Presented to Eliza Beeson, by her mother, December 25, 1856.)

Marriages

Clara Mae Crossan and Charles Edgar Guest were
    married November 26, 1908 in Chester, Pa.
    at the First Baptist Church. J.M.T.
    Childry, Pastor, Chester, Pa.

Births

William Beeson was born July 18, 1824.
John Beeson was born November 26, 1825.
Henry Beeson was born August 10, 1827.
_____ was born October 16, 1829.
Eliza Beeson was born July 31, 1831.
Mary Jane Beeson was born May 25, 1834.
Edward Beeson was born July 31, 1836.
Lydia Ann Beeson was born March 29, 1839.
Anna Maria Beeson was born February 5, 1842.

Albert Reuben Guest was born May 5, 1912.
Charles Robert Guest was born October 11, 1914.

Charles Edgar Guest was born November 27, 1859
    at New Castle County, Delaware.
Clara Mae Guest was born October 19, 1874 at
    Wilmington, Delaware.

Deaths

William Beeson died October 6, 1826.
Henry Beeson died March 11, 1834.
John Beeson died June 7, 1834.
Edward Beeson died January 15, 1840.
Charles Edgar Guest died August 19, 1940.
Clara Mae Guest died April 4, 1954.
Edith Barton Guest died September 6, 1955.
Harry Beeson Guest died January 17, 1954.

From a hand written paper in Eliza Beeson's Bible:
Charles Edgar Guest was born in New Castle
County, Del., November 27, 1859.
Alice Rebecca Guest was born in Chester
County, Pa., September 8, 1859.
Edith Barton Guest was born in New Castle
County, Del., December 3, 1884.
Harry Beeson Guest was born in New Castle
County, Del., September 27, 1886.
Fred Harrison Guest was born in Los Angeles
County, Cal., October 5, 1888.

Children of Reuben and Lydia Crossan, all born in Wilmington.

George A. Crossan was born February 26, 1871; died March 10, 1897.
Clara M. Crossan was born October 19, 1874.
Anna E. Crossan was born November 3, 1876.

Reuben Crossan and Lydia E. Chandler were married November 18, 1862 at Kennett Square, Pa., by Rev. J. L. Heysinger, Presbytor of Epis. Church.

Reuben Crossan was born March 4, 1848; died May 15, 1914.
Lydia E., his wife, was born October 12, 1844 in New Garden Township, Pa.

Reubena Roderick was born September 30, 1899 in Chester Co., Pa.; died October 18, 1899 in Chester, Pa. She was the daughter of Anna Crossan and Theodore Roderick.

Charles E. Guest, of New Castle County, Delaware, and Alice R. Patterson, of New Castle County, Delaware, were married December 5, 1883.

BELL-GREENLEA BIBLE

(Bible published by Hogan & Thompson, 30 N. 4th Street, Philadelphia, Pa. Copied by Clara Wallace Eyre, Caesar Rodney Chapter, 1962. Original owner

Wm. P. Bell and Richie Greenlea, Kent Co., Del.
Present owner is Mrs. Donald F. Wright, 204 Saturn
Drive, North Star, Newark, Del.)

Marriages

William P. Bell and Richie Greenlea were married
    January 10, 1839.

Births

Sarah Ann Bell, daughter of William P. Bell and
    Richie Bell his wife, was born Oct. 27, 1839.
John G. Bell, son of William P. Bell and Richie
    Bell his wife, was born March 23, 1842.
William Bell, son of William P. Bell and Richie
    Bell his wife, was born May 18, 1844.
William H. Bell, son of Wm. P. Bell and Richie
    Bell his wife, was born October 16, 1846.
Mary Elizabeth Bell, daughter of Wm. P. Bell and
    Richie Bell his wife, was born April 22, 1850.
Edward Bell, son of Wm. P. Bell and Richie Bell
    his wife, was born September 5, 1852.

William P. Bell was born February 15, 1816.
Richie Bell was born September 15, 1814.

Deaths

William Bell, Jr., son of Wm. P. Bell and Richie
    his wife, died May 14, 1846, age 2 years
    lacking 4 days.
William H. Bell, son of Wm. P. Bell and Richie his
    wife, died June 24, 1848, age 1 year, 8
    months and 8 days.
John G. Bell, son of Wm. P. Bell and Richie Bell
    his wife, was killed by the kick of a horse
    May 18, 1849 at Bowers Beach, age 7 years,
    26 days.
Edward Bell, son of William P. Bell and Richie
    Bell his wife, died January 28, 1859, age
    6 years, 4 months and 23 days.

William P. Bell, son of William P. Bell and Ann
    his wife, died January 20, 1858.
Richia Bell Billings died November 16, 1900,
    age 86 years, 2 months and 1 day.

BENSON - NORTH BIBLE

(Now owned by Genealogical Society of Pa., Philadelphia.)

FAMILY RECORD

Alexander Benson was born in Baltimore, Md., on November 21, 1794.
Sarah North was born in Philadelphia, Pa., on April 9, 1798.

Alexander Benson and Sarah North were married April 27, 1824 by Rev. G. T. Bedell.

Births

Emily North Benson was born March 29, 1825.
Mary Louisa Benson was born January 24, 1827.
Harriel(t) Smith Benson was born December 19, 1828.
Alexander Benson, Jr., was born March 3, 1831.
Theodore Benson was born January 15, 1833.
Rosalie Benson was born November 21, 1835.
Washington Benson was born June 26, 1838.
Edwin North Benson was born January 16, 1840.

Deaths

Caleb North, a Colonel of the American Army in the War of the Revolution, and the father of Sarah Benson, died November 1840.
Lydia North, mother of Sarah Benson, died February 16, 1845.

Richard Benson, father of Alexr. Benson, died February 20, 1844.
Alexander Benson, Sr., died May 13, 1870.
Alexander Benson, Jr., died August 5, 1870.
Sarah, wife of Alexander Benson, died April 16, 1859.
Emily North Benson died December 1, 1830.
Mary Louise Benson died December 8, 1830.
Theodore Benson died December 17, 1833.
Washington Benson died August 28, 1838.
Alexander Benson, Jr., died August 5, 1870.
Rosalie Benson died June 11, 1879.
Harriet S. Benson died September 3, 1902.
Edwin North Benson died April 18, 1909.

Richard Benson
d. 2-20-1844   Alexander Benson
                  b. 11-21-1794
                  d. 5-13-1870
                  m. 4-27-1824
Caleb North
d. 11-1840   Sarah North
                  b. 4-9-1798
Lydia   d. 4-16-1859
d. 2-16-1845

THE ALFRED DUPONT BIRD FAMILY

(Bible was published by White & Yost, 309 Market St., Philadelphia, Pa. 1855. Bible is now owned by Charles D. Bird, Jr., 9 Rodman Road, Wilmington, Delaware. His wife is a member of Caesar Rodney Chapter N.S.D.A.R. Record copied by Mrs. Alban Shaw.)

Records of Alfred DuPont Bird of Claymont, Delaware.

A. D. Bird was born January 16, 1826.
E. E. Bird was born November 5, 1929.

This certifies that Alfred Dupont Bird of
   Philadelphia, Pa., and Ellen Elizabeth Lawson
   of the same, were united by me in the bonds
   of marriage on December 11, 1850, conforming
   to the ordinance of God and the laws of the
   State of Pennsylvania.
                          Joseph H. Kennard
                          Minister of the Gospel.
   New Castle County, Claymont, Del.

1. Emma Rebecca, daughter of Alfred D. and Ellen
      E. Bird, was born October 31, 1851.
2. John Lawson, son of Alfred D. and Ellen E.
      Bird, was born October 6, 1853.
3. Edward Mississippi, son of Alfred D. and
      Ellen E. Bird, was born October 26,
      1858.
4. William Suddards, son of Alfred D. and Ellen
      E. Bird, was born March 24, 1861.
5. Charles Deacon, son of Alfred D. and Ellen
      E. Bird, was born August 6, 1863.

6. Laura Craven, daughter of Alfred D. and Ellen E. Bird, was born December 9, 1866.
7. Julia Grubb, daughter of Alfred D. and Ellen E. Bird, was born April 18, 1871.
8. Ellen Wardell, daughter of Alfred D. and Ellen E. Bird, was born March 23, 1873.

Deaths

Horace Greeley, infant son of Alfred D. and Ellen E. Bird, died October 26, 1857 in Philadelphia, Pa., age 2 months and 14 days.
Emma Rebecca DeValinger, daughter of Alfred D. and Ellen E. Bird, died February 16, 1885 in Claymont, Delaware.
Laura Craven Wilson, daughter of Alfred D. and Ellen E. Bird, died January 23, 1897, age 30 years, 1 month and 14 days.
Alfred D. Bird died February 18, 1908, age 82 years, 1 month and 2 days.
Ellen Elizabeth Bird died April 8, 1921; age 91 years, 6 months and 3 days.
Charles D. Bird, Sr., died January 16, 1935, age 73 years, 5 months and 10 days.
Laura E. Bird, wife of Charles D. Bird, Sr., died September 24, 1939, age 77 years, 5 months and 8 days.
Alfred D. Bird, son of Charles D. Bird and Laura E. Bird, died April 13, 1937.
Nellie A. Bird, wife of A. D. Bird, died January 17, 1952, age 70 years, 4 months and 29 days.

JOHN BIRD - JULIANNA GRUBB

(Bible was published and sold by Kimber & Sharpless at their Book Store, No. 93 Market St., Phila., Pa. Stereotyped by E. White, New York. 1824. Now owned by Charles D. Bird, Wilmington, Delaware.)

Marriages

John Bird and Julianna Grubb were married March 21, 1816.

Alfred DuPont Bird and Ellen Elizabeth Lawson were
married December 11, 1850, by Rev. Kennard,
Philadelphia.

Births

John, son of Thomas and Mary Bird, was born
December 29, 1784.
Julia Ann Grubb, daughter of Amer and Ann Grubb,
was born February 12, 1791.

1. Edward Grubb, son of John and Julianna Bird,
was born September 27, 1816.
2. Charles Cheyney, son of John and Julianna
Bird, was born January 26, 1818.
3. Mary Ann, daughter of John and Julianna
Bird, was born October 20, 1820.
4. Anna Mary, daughter of John and Julianna
Bird, was born January 23, 1822.
5. Alfred, son of John and Julianna Bird, was
born February 18, 1824.
6. Alfred DuPont, son of John and Julianna Bird,
was born January 16, 1826.
7. Thomas Babb, son of John and Julianna Bird,
was born March 7, 1828.

- - - - - - - - - -

1. Emma Rebecca, daughter of Alfred D. and Ellen
E. Bird, was born October 31, 1851.
2. John Lawson, son of Alfred D. and Ellen E.
Bird, was born October 6, 1853.
3. Horace Greeley was born August 12, 1856.
4. Edward Mississippi, son of Alfred and Ellen
Bird, was born October 28, 1858.
5. William Suddards, son of Alfred and Ellen
Bird, was born March 24, 1861.
6. Charles Deacon, son of Alfred and Ellen
Bird, was born August 6, 1862.
7. Laura Craven, daughter of Alfred and Ellen
Bird, was born December 9, 1866.
8. Julia Grubb, daughter of Alfred and Ellen
Bird, was born April 18, 1871.
9. Ella Wardell, daughter of Alfred and Ellen
Bird, was born March 23, 1873.

Deaths

Julianna, wife of John Bird, died July 23, 1828,
age 37 years, 5 months and 16 days.
John Bird died August 28, 1858, age 72 years,
7 months and 30 days.

1. Mary Ann, daughter of John and Julianna Bird, died October 20, 1821, age 6 months and 28 days.
2. Alfred, son of John and Julianna Bird, died October 19, 1825, age 1 year, 8 months and 1 day.
3. Anna Mary, daughter of John and Julianna Bird, died July 16, 1828, age 6 years, 5 months and 23 days.
4. Charles Cheyney, son of John and Julianna Bird, died December 23, 1855 at New Orleans.
5. Thomas Babb, son of John and Julianna Bird, died January 20, 1856, age 27 years, 10 months and 3 days.
6. Edward Grubb Bird, son of John, died January 20, 1890. Died at Americus, Jackson County, Mississippi, age 73 years and 4 months.
7. Alfred DuPont, son of John and Julia Bird, died February 18, 1908, age 82 years.

A clipping pasted in this Bible, dated November 3, 1938: "A house built in Boston in 1635 by Thomas Bird is still occupied by his descendants and remains in good condition."

Deaths Continued:

Julia G. Patton, daughter of Alfred and Ellen E. Bird, died November 7, 1951, age 80 years.
Ellen Elizabeth Bird, died April 8, 1921, age 92 years.
Emma Rebecca DeValinger, daughter of Alfred D. and Ellen Bird, died February 16, 1885.
Laura Craven Wilson, daughter of Alfred D. and Ellen E. Bird, died January 23, 1897, age 31 years.
John Lawson Bird, son of Alfred D. and Ellen E. Bird, died May 9, 1928, age 75 years.
Edward Mississippi Bird, son of Alfred D. and Ellen E. Bird, died Feb. 8, 1932, age 74 years.

William Suddard Bird, son of Alfred D. and Ellen
E. Bird, died May 21, 1934, age 73 years.
Charles D. Bird, son of Alfred D. and Ellen E.
Bird, died January 16, 1935.
Laura E. Bird, wife of Charles D. Bird, died
September 26, 1939.
Charlotte McNeill, daughter of Harry and Emma
DeValinger, born March 4th, 1884; died
November 7, 1946 at St. Petersburg,
Florida. Granddaughter of Alfred and
Ellen Bird.

These records were given by Mrs. Charles D. Bird,
Penny Hill, Wilmington, Delaware.

BLACK

Robert Black, born in Ireland 1796, was the son of
John Black. He was one of the pioneer
settlers of Pittsburgh, Pa. He died July 21,
1872 in Pittsburgh. Is buried in Allegheny
Cemetery there. He married Margaret Black -
no relation - who was born in Ireland 1800;
died January 30, 1883 in Pittsburgh and is
also buried in Allegheny Cemetery.

It took Margaret and Robert Black twenty days to go
from Philadelphia to Pitsburgh. They made
the trip by covered wagon (Conestoga) which
was drawn by six horses.

Their Children:

1. Thomas Black, born May 21, 1832.
2. John
3. William R.
4. Margaret E.
5. Mary

Thomas J. Black, son of Margaret and Robert Black,
was born May 21, 1832 in Pittsburgh; died
July 6, 1894 in Pittsburgh; is buried in
Allegheny Cemetery, Pittsburgh.

He married March 13, 1855 in Pittsburgh, Mrs.
Sarah Jane (McDade) McCracken, who was born
December 22, 1829 in Pittsburgh; died

January 1, 1908 at Wilkinsburg, Pa., and is also buried in Allegheny Cemetery.

Sarah Jane McDade McCracken was the daughter of James McDade (born in Ireland) and Elizabeth _____(?) born in Belfast, Ireland. Their children:

1. Clara Amanda Black, was born December 6, 1855.
2. John Wesley, born February 23, 1858; m. Sarah Burke; died Feb. 7, 1898.
3. Ida Jane, born Sept. 4, 1860; m. H. W. Davis; died Feb. 5, 1924.
4. Thomas Howard, born Aug. 3, 1863; died March 7, 1883.
5. Kate Young, born April 6, 1869; m. Jacob Kuhns; died June 27, 1937.
6. Minnie, born November 18, 1871.

Clara Amanda Black, daughter of Thomas J. and Sarah Jane Black, was born in Pittsburgh on December 25, 1855; died June 2, 1936 in Pittsburgh; buried in Allegheny Cemetery. Married George W. Berlin, June 24, 1880 in Pittsburgh. He was the son of Joseph Berlin and Jane Braden Schall. Their daughter:

Clara Louise Berlin, was born June 5, 1892; m. Daniel R. McNeal, son of H. W. McNeal and Myrtie V. (Reese) McNeal.

(See McNeal, Berlin, Braden Records)

WILLIAM H. BLACKISTON BIBLE

(Published 1890 by A. J. Holman & Co. Owned by William H. Blackiston. Now in the possession of his oldest daughter, Elva R. B. Taylor (Mrs. Paul W. Taylor), 12 Silverside Rd., Wilmington, Del. Credit of Clara Wallace Eyre, Caesar Rodney Chapter.)

Marriages

William E. Blackiston of Wilmington, Delaware, and Mary E. Roberts of Smyrna, Delaware, were married December 4, 1877. In the presence of Thomas J. Johnson, Etta Middleton.
                Signed, Enech Stubbs, Pastor

Elva Roberts Blackiston and Paul Woolley Taylor, son of Samuel W. Taylor and Lauretta J. Miller Taylor, were married April 25, 1898, Union M. E. Church, Wilmington, Delaware.

James Voshell Roberts Blackiston and Elsie May Webster, daughter of Henry and Temperance Alston Webster, were married December 4, 1906 at Asbury M. E. Church, Wilmington, Del.

Helen Irene Blackiston and Arthur Green Webber were married (no dates).

Florence Voshell Blackiston and Leon Wilde Crawford were married November 7, 1911.

Anna Jones Blackiston and Charles M. Poplos were married April 15, 1922.

Births

Elva Roberts Blackiston, daughter of Wm. H. and Mary E. Blackiston, was born January 5, 1879, Wilmington, Del.

Bertha Watson Blackiston, daughter of William H. and Mary E. Blackiston, was born December 9, 1880, Wilmington, Del.

Florence Veshell Blackiston, daughter of Wm. H. and Mary E. Blackiston, was born November 7, 1882, Wilmington, Del.

William Edgar Blackiston, son of Wm. H. and Mary E. Blackiston, was born February 3, 1885, Wilmington, Del.

James Voshell Roberts Blackiston, son of William
    H. and Mary E. Blackiston, was born
    January 10, 1887, Wilmington, Del.
Helen Irene Blackiston, daughter of Wm. H. and
    Mary E. Blackiston, was born April 25, 1889,
    Wilmington, Del.
Albert Watson Blackiston, son of William H. and
    Mary E. Blackiston, was born June 4, 1890,
    Wilmington, Del.
Mary Elizabeth Blackiston, daughter of Wm. H. and
    Mary E. Blackiston, was born September 20,
    1891, Wilmington, Del.
Herbert Keyler - Triplet   Children of Wm. H.
O. Lee   - Triplet   and Mary E. Blackiston,
Anna Jones   - Triplet   were born December 8,
                                 1892, Wilmington, Del.
John Wesley Blackiston, son of Wm. H. and Mary E.
    Blackiston, was born July 23, 1894, Wilmington,
    Del.
Gwendolyn Pyle Blackiston, daughter of Wm. H. and
    Mary E. Blackiston, was born November 18,
    1902, Wilmington, Del.

Mary E. Blackiston attested these records all to
be correct and so signs her name - Mary E.
Blackiston.

Deaths

Bertha Watson Blackiston, daughter of Wm. H. and
    Mary E. Blackiston, died December 7, 1880;
    buried New Years Day, 1881, Smyrna, Del.
O. Lee Blackiston, triplet son of Wm. H. and Mary
    E. Blackiston, died December 12, 1892.
Mary Elizabeth Blackiston, daughter of Wm. H. and
    Mary E. Blackiston, died July 12, 1911.
Herbert Keyler Blackiston, triplet son of Wm. H.
    and Mary E. Blackiston, died July 5, 1893.
Gwendolyn Pyle Blackiston, daughter of Wm. H. and
    Mary E. Blackiston, died July 2, 1905.
Albert Watson Blackiston died December 27, 1890.

Note: William H. Blackiston was christened
    William Watson Blackiston, This is an
    error by the Church. His name should have
    been on their books William H. Blackiston.
    The H stands for Holding.
            Signed, Wm. H. Blackiston

Elva R.B. Taylor states: My father never signed his name any other way from the time he could write to the time of his death in his 97th year, and many times he mentioned this error to me as did also his mother, brothers and sister. He never used the Holding.

      Elva R.B. Taylor, June 25, 1962.

<u>Samuel Roberts</u>
b. 1788
d. 2-15-1827   <u>James Roberts</u>
m.   b. 4-10-1818   1. Anna Spruance
<u>Eliz. Price</u>   d.   b. 1846
        m. 5-8-1845   2. Irene b. 1848
<u>Humphry Green</u>   3. Charles C. b. 1850
       <u>Arianna Green</u>   **(1. See
<u>Hannah</u>   d. 12-27-1850   4. John   Below)
3   m. 1-25-1853   b. 1854
*Daniel   Mary A.   5. James V. b. 1856
<u>Voshel</u>   <u>Voshel</u>   6. <u>Mary Elizabeth</u>
       b. 11-12-1816   b. 1858
Eliz   d. 2-20-1892   d.
<u>Crockett</u>   m. 12-4-1877
                <u>Wm. H. Blackiston</u>

*   1   2
Obediah, Sr.   Obediah, Jr.

** 1.   <u>Elva Roberts Blackiston</u>
     b. 1-5-1879   Bayard B.
     m. 4-25-1898   m. Ellen Ford
      <u>Paul W. Taylor</u>   Joseph Pyle
     b. 12-21-1876   Daniel
  2. Bertha   David W.
  3. Florence   Paul W., Jr.
  4. Wm. E.   James V.
  5. James V.
  6. Helen
  7. Mary Eliz
  8. Herbert
  9. O. Lee
 10. Anna m. J. W. Jones
 11. John W. m. Anna Spruance
 12. Gwendolen
 13. Albert

JOSEPH BOUGHMAN & LYDIA ANN

(Bible was published by Judd, Loomis and Company. 1836. Owned by Mrs. Mary J. Longstaff, Wilmington, Del. 1957. Record given by Mrs. Charles Bird, Wilmington, Del.)

FAMILY REGISTER

Marriages

Lewis T. Boughman and Anna Fusselbach were married July 23, 1882.
Henry R. Boughman and Sarah A. Bracklin were married November 19, 1874.
Samel James Longstaff and Mary Jane Boughman were married March 29, 1898, at her father's home, Wooddale, Delaware.

Births

Children of Joseph and Lydia Ann Boughman:
Joseph Boughman was born November 16, 1807.
Lydia Ann Boughman was born August 18, 1811.

William B. Harrison Boughman was born April 26, 1832.
Hannah Boughman was born February 18, 1834.
Joseph Boughman, Jr. was born August 29, 1835.
Mary Ann Boughman was born January 18, 1838.
Jacob Boughman was born February 23, 1840.
John Boughman was born September 28, 1843.
Susan Boughman was born December 20, 1844.
Henry Boughman was born August 15, 1847.
Manuel G. Boughman was born July 19, 1851.
Lewis T. Boughman was born March 27, 1855.

Children of James S. and Mary A. Lindsey:
Harriett G. Lindsey was born June 21, 1863.
Joseph E. Lindsey was born June 11, 1865.

Children of Henry and Sarah A. Boughman:
S. Lukens Boughman was born September 3, 1875.
Mary Jane Boughman was born August 22, 1876.
William Hanson Boughman was born November 4, 1878.
Fanny G. Boughman was born November 9, 1882 at Foulkland, Del.

Florence I. Boughman was born October 4, 1885 at Faulkland.

Sarah Elizabeth Longland was born March 1, 1911.
Elizabeth Jane Waters was born August 25, 1936.
Edith D. Longstaff, daughter of Samuel James and Mary Jane Longstaff, was born Sept. 30, 1899.
James Howard Longstaff, son of Samuel J. and Mary Jane Longstaff, was born June 2, 1901; died July 12, 1928.
William Henry Longstaff, son of Samuel J. and Mary Jane Longstaff, was born July 13, 1904; died August 18, 1905.

Deaths

Children and Grandchildren:
William Harrison Boughman died July 26, 1833; age 1 year and 3 months.
Emanuel G. Boughman died 1854 in infancy.
Lydia A. Boughman died November 13, 1876.
Joseph Boughman died November 14, 1898.
Mary A. Lindsey died January 1, 1916.
Susan G. Woodward died January 30, 1918.
Fannie Boughman Springer died February 18, 1920.
Elizabeth R. Boughman, wife of William W. Boughman, died November 18, 1926.
Lewis T. Boughman died March 4, 1929.
John G. Boughman died 1928, age 85 years.
Sarah A. Boughman died February 27, 1930.
Henry R. Boughman died December 4, 1933.

First born of Henry and Sarah Boughman, I. Lukens Boughman, died September 4, 1875, age 1 day and 5 hours.

Funeral notice in Bible:
Mary Ann Woodward, buried from her late residence in Baker Stree below Eighth, this afternoon, Tuesday, July 31, 1838 at 10 o'clock.
 Crozier, Printer, 151 S. 6th St.

Near Ashland, Delaware, May 24, 1941, Ida B., wife of William H. Boughman. aged 63 years.

Note:
Mrs. Longstaff said that Joseph Boughman married Lydia Ann Grubb, daughter of Peter and Hannah (White) Grubb.

Boughman Chart

Joseph
Boughman
b.
d.
m.
Lydia Ann
Grubb
b. 8-18-1811
d. 11-13-1876
dau. of Peter
Grubb and
Hannah (White)

1. William, b. 4-26-1832
   d. 1833
2. Hannah, b. 2-18-1834
3. Joseph, Jr., b. 8-29-1835

4. Mary Boughman
   b. 1-18-1838
   d.
   m. 3-29-1898
   Samuel
   Longstaff
   1. Edith
      b. 9-30-1899
   2. James
      b. 1901
   3. William
      b. 1904

5. Jacob
   b. 2-23-1840
6. John
   b. 9-28-1843
7. Susan
   b. 12-20-1844
8. Henry
   b. 8-15-1847
   d.
   m.
   Sarah
   Brackin
   1. S. Lukens
      b. 1875
   2. Mary
      b. 1876
   3. William
      b. 1878
   4. Fanny
      b. 1882
   5. Florence
      b. 1885

9. Manuel
   b. 7-19-1851
   d. 1854
10. Lewis T.
    b. 3-27-1855
    d. 1928
    m. 7-23-1882
    Anna Fusselbach

BOWERS - STRADLING - ANDERSON

(Copied from an old Bible by James M. Holm, Upper Darby, Pa.)

Marriages

George S. Bowers and Melinda Anderson were married September 13, 1883 at Trenton, N.J.
Henrietta H. Bowers, of Bordertown, N.J., on November 16, 1913 by Rev. Elder A. R. Sandborn, Trenton.

Births

George S. Bowers was born July 31, 1839 at Trenton, N.J.
Melinda A. Bowers was born November 18, 1860.

John Draper was born July 7, 1884 at Bordertown, N. J.
Mary Ann Bowers was born July 21, 1886 at Bordertown, N.J.
Henrietta H. Bowers was born April 25, 1894 at Bordertown, N.J.
Walter Quigley Bowers was born June 10, 1897.

John Draper Bowers Stradling was born June 15, 1914 at Bordertown, N.J.
Mary Elizabeth Stradling was born July 30, 1915 at Borderown, N.J.
Charlotte Melinda Stradling was born January 7, 1924 at Philadelphia, Pa.

Deaths

George S. Bowers, father, died May 3, 1913 at Bordertown in his 74th year. Husband of Melinda A. Bowers.
John Draper B. Stradling died February 24, 1916.
Henrietta H. Stradling died February 18, 1926.

Delilah Missimer, her Book.

She was born in the year of our Lord one thousand eight hundred and sixteen, December the 10th.

Sarah Lovering Skean (or Hean), daughter of Theodor and Delilah Skean (?) his wife, was born on the 9th day of April in the year of our Lord one thousand eight hundred and thirty eight in the morning at 9 o'clock.

BOWLES FAMILY, VIRGINIA

Founder
John Bowles came to Virginia 1610, with the expedition of Sir George Somers and Sir Thomas Gates. He returned to England 1612 and came back to Virginia, 1621 with Sir Francis Wyatt, and settled on the East side of Warwick Co., Virginia. He died 1664. He left a son, John Bowels, 2.

John Bowles, 2, m. Sarah Knight. They had a son, Benjamin Bowles; b. after 1700; d. 1762; m. 1725, Nancy. They had: Patriot.

David Bowles, born 1725/30; died 1806; m. 1st Sarah. David served as a Private in Capt. Samuel Jordan Cabell's Co., 6th Va. Regt. commanded by Lt. Col. James Hendricks.

Ref. D.F.P.A. Lineage Book v 28 p 86.

David Bowles was born Hanover Co., Va. 3-1-1750; died Bourbon Co., Ky. His wife's name was Sarah, family name unknown. His 2nd wife was Winney Rice. He was an Elder in the Dover Baptist Ch. of King William Co., Va. 1785. He had two children by his 1st wife: (Will Book C, p. 195.)
    1. Elizabeth; m. John Payne
    2. Jesse; m. Hannah Perkins - 10 children.
Other children mentioned in will:
    3. Nelson
    4. Thomas

Jesse Bowles will - Will Book F, p. 353.
wife-Hannah.
Sons: Jesse, Davis   Daus: Elizabeth Thomas
      Stephen   Sarah A. Turpin
      also Hughes
      Robert   Mourning Sandusky-
      David   Sally
                                 Betsy
                                 Isaac
writen 3-29-1820; proved 6-1820
Exc. David, Stephen, Hughes.

Stephen Bowles had a daughter, Hannah, who m. Jacob Smalley.

Hannah Bowles and Joseph Smalley m. 1-25-1819 by R. Thomas - Ref. Marriage Register #2, Bourban Co., Ky. They had:
1. Jacob Smalley
2. Stephen
3. Elizabeth
4. Matilda
5. Nancy
6. Joshua   1. Wm. Smalley 1854-1908
7. **Oliver F. 1832-1865**; m. Ch:
                     2: Jacob F. 1856-1925,
                        Marion, Ind. father of
                        author F. M. Smalley
                     3. Elizabeth
                     4. Matilda
8. Frances
9. Richard T.D.
10. Marly L.
11. Hannah

<u>BOYCE FAMILY RECORD</u>

Gertha Martin Boyce, son of John S. Boyce and
   Minnie his wife, was born February 19, 1891.
Iou (?) May Boyce, daughter of John S. Boyce and
   Minnie his wife, was born October 6, 1892
Mina Ruth Boyce, daughter of J. S. Boyce and
   Minnie his wife, was born September 3, 1895.
William Minous Boyce, son of J. S. Boyce and
   Minnie his wife, was born September 3, 1895.
Dawson Noah Boyce, son of J.S. Boyce and Minnie
   his wife, was born July 2, 1906.

JOHN G. BRACKIN'S BOOK

(Printed by D. Fanshaw for the American Bible Society. 1844. Owned by Mrs. Mary J. Longstaff, Wilmington, Delaware. 1957. Record copied by Mrs. Charles Bird.)

John G. Brackin's Book, April 20, 1846.

Marriages

John G. Brackin and Jane Foot were married
   March 7, 1843.

Births

Watson Brackin was born April 21, 1844.
Mary Brackin was born February 23, 1846.
Sarah Ann Brackin was born June 12, 1848.
Elizabeth R. Brackin was born March 13, 1850.
John F. Brackin was born June 22, 1853.
William H. Bracken was born November 28, 1857.
John G. Brackin was born April 10, 1818
Jane Foot was born October 20, 1817.

Deaths

William H. Bracken died February 12, 1861, age
   2 years, 2 months and 15 days.
John F. Bracken died February 11, 1867, age
   49 years.
Elizabeth R. Bracken died December 29, 1877,
   age 27 years.
Jane Bracken died October 16, 1899, age 82 years.
Watson Bracken died December 21, 1926, age
   82 years.
Sarah A. Bracken died February 27, 1930, age
   82 years.
Mary Bracken Fisher died January 2, 1932,
   age 84 years.
John F. Bracken died January 29, 1932, age
   79 years.

BRADEN FAMILY

James Braden was a native of Ireland and immigrated to America, locating in Derry Township, Westmoreland Co., Pa. about the close of the 18th Century.

Bradenville, Pa., between Latrobe and Greensburg on the Pennsylvania Railroad, is named for this family whose ancestors settled here in 1770.

James Braden, born in Ireland, died 1832 in Westmoreland Co., Pa. He married Elizabeth Jane Kelly, who was born 1794. Their children:

1. William, born 1811.
2. **Jane**, born 1815; m. 1st Andrew Schall; m. 2nd Joseph Berlin
3. David, born March 17, 1821; m. Elizabeth Offner.
4. John L., born 1824; m. Anna M. Perishing.
5. George L., born 1827; m. Maria _____.
6. Margarett, m. Jacob Strickler.
7. Edward

Ref. Westmoreland Co., Pa. Administration Book A, page 249, 1832 A.D. states: "Be it remembered that on the 5th day of December A.D. 1832, Letters of Administration on the estate of James Braden, late of Derry Twp., deceased, was granted unto William Braden and Andrew Schal, they having given bond in $800.00 for the faithful performance thereof."

This establishes that Jane was married to Andrew Schall before this date.

Jane Braden married Andrew Schall before 1832 - had 3 sons by him: Absolom, Andrew, Andrew J. Schall. She then married Joseph Berlin, son of Jacob Berlin and Susannah (Brinker) Berlin. He was born April 9, 1821; died Sept. 28, 1904. Their son:

George Washington Berlin, married Clara Amanda Black, daughter of Thomas J. and Sarah J. McCracken. Clara was born December 25, 1855; died June 2, 1936. George W. Berlin was born Dec. 20, 1846; died June 22, 1928. Their daughter:

Clara Louise Berlin married Daniel Raymond McNeal, son of H. W. McNeal and Myrtie V. (Reese) McNeal. She was born June 5, 1892 in Pittsburgh, Pa.; married October 15, 1919, in Pittsburgh, to Raymond McNeal, born September 5, 1892. Their son:

Daniel R. McNeal, Jr., born August 20, 1920 in Philadelphia, Pa.; married Edith MacKenzie Hay, daughter of James Hay and Millie Frances (Bacon) Hay. She was born February 9, 1924 in Phila. Their children:

Daniel Raymond, III.
Debra Jeanne.

(See Berlin, Brinker, McNeal Records)

WILLIAM BROWN & CHARLOTTE CARTER
CHARLOTTE BROWN & FRISBY TULL

(Bible published by N. & J. White, 108 Peach St., New York. 1833. Owned by Mrs. Elwood A. Davis, Wilmington, Del. 1957. Record given by Mrs. Charles Bird, Wilmington, Del.)

Marriages

William Brown and Charlotte Carter were married
    April 12, 1832.
Frisby Tull and Charlotte Brown were married
    January 9, 1838.

Births

John Frisby Tull was born September 30, 1774.
Elizabeth Osbourn was born May 23, 1776.
Sarah Tull, daughter of John and Elizabeth Tull,
    was born January 28, 1798.
Thomas Peregrine Tull was born March 16, 1800.
Mary Ann Tull was born October 28, 1801.

Francina Tull was born February 8, 1804.
John Tull was born April 11, 1806.
Frisby Tull was born August 14, 1808.
Elizabeth Tull was born June 11, 1811.

William Brown, son of William and Elizabeth Brown, was born January 1, 1807.
Charlotte Brown, wife of William Brown, was born March 16, 1810.
Newton C. Brown, son of William and Charlotte Brown, was born March 2, 1833.

Elizabeth Osbourn Tull was born August 15, 1843.
Hariette Parker Tull was born April 26, 1846.
Robert Frisby Tull was born April 14, 1850.

Deaths

Sarah Tull, daughter of John F. and Elizabeth Tull, died August 23, 1801.
William Brown, consort of Charlotte Brown and son of William and Elizabeth Brown, died June 30, 1833, age 26 years and 6 months.
Hariette Parker Tull died June 19, 1853; age 7 years, 1 month and 23 days.
Charlotte Tull, wife of Frisby Tull, died August 29, 1879.
Dr. Robert Frisby Tull died April 6, 1885.
Lizzie O. Tull, daughter of Frisby and Charlotte Tull, died January 9, 1887; age 43 years, 4 months and 25 days.

TULL CHART

John F. Tull
b. 9-30-1774
d.
m.
Elizabeth
Osbourn
b. 5-23-1776

1. Sarah Tull
   b. 1-28-1798
   d. 8-23-1801
2. Thomas
   b. 3-16-1800
3. Mary
   b. 10-28-1801
4. Francina
   b. 2-8-1804
5. John
   b. 4-11-1806
6. Frisby Tull
   b. 8-14-1808
   d.

1. Lizzie O. Tull
   b. 8-15-1843
   d. 1-9-1887

Tull Chart Cont'd.

              m. 1-9-1838   2. Harriette
              Charlotte   b. 1846
              <u>Brown</u>   d. 1853
              b.   3. Robert F. Tull
              d. 8-29-1879   (Dr.)
                                b. 4-14-1850
                                d. 4-6-1885
        7. Elizabeth
           b. 6-11-1811

BUCKELLEW FAMILY
New London, Chester Co., Pa.

<u>John Buckallew</u>
b. 2-9-1756 1. Garett
d.   Buckelew, b. 2-20-1780
m.   2. <u>Abraham Buckelew</u>
<u>Catherine</u>   b. 3-19-1783 1. Jeremiah
b. 6-26-1763   d.   Buckelew
               m.   b. 11-21-1807
               _____   2. Garrett
            3. Frederick   Buckelew
               b. 4-7-1785   b. 12-28-1809
            4. Catherine   3. Samuel
               b. 5-28-1787   b. 2-1-1812
            5. Ann   4. Abraham
               b. 10-7-1791   b. 4-10-1815
            6. Sarah   5. Eliza
               b. 12-25-1795   b. 9-15-1817
            7. Jane   6. William
               b. 3-20-1798   b. 3-27-1820
            8. Samuel   7. Margaret
               b. 6-10-1800   b. 2-14-1822
            9. George   8. Thompson
               Washington   McCarrell
               Buckelew   Buckalew
               b. 5-31-1803 9. John
                                10. Jesse
                              11. Howard
                                   <u>Buckelew</u>
                                   b. 1-6-1829 1.**
                                   d. 12-29-1911

11. Howard Buckley Cont'd.
      m.
      Sarah Jane
      <u>Howard</u>

1**
1. John Alexander
   Buckelew
2. Ann Elizabeth
   b. 8-5-1855
3. Phobe Jane
   b. 7-11-1858
4. Margaret Ellen
5. Mary Emma
   b. 7-3-1862
   m. Charles H.
   Rigdon 7-12-1882
6. Lydia Belle
   b. 4-23-1865
7. Franklin Thompson-
   *Warren Thomas
8. Theodore Howard
   b. 3-6-1871
   m. Fannie
   dau. Mary Emma
   b. 4-20-1903
9. Rachel Eva
   b. 10-26-1874
   d. 4-1-1900

Note: Warren Thomas Buckelew, b. 9-22-1901.

JOHN BUCKLEY & HANNAH CLEMSON
<u>AMER GRUBB & ANN BUCKLEY</u>

(Bible of John Buckley, Brandywine Hundred, Claymont, Delaware. Printed in England. 1752. Owned by Mrs. Raymond Zebley (Mabel Vernon), Claymont. 1957. Record given by Mrs. Charles Bird.)

Note: The paper in this Bible is very brittle and the corners are torn, which has prevented Mrs. Bird from completing some of the entries. In several places the pages have been sewn together with a needle and white thread.

THEE FEAR GOD
AND THOU SHALT BE BLESST

Beulah Buckley was born September 5, 1750.
Hepzibah Buckley was born December 22, 1752.
Ann Buckley was born April 24, 1755.
_____ Buckley was born June 16, 1757.
Mary (?) Buckley was born February 4, 1759
_____ Buckley was born 15th (?).
John Buckley, father of the above Buckley's,
   died July 19, 1799, age 79 years and
   9 months.
(The lower part of the page is missing.)

John Pyle, son of Beulah Pyle, was born
   January 1, 177?
Buckley Pyle was born February 24, 1777.
Nicholas Pyle was born March 20, 1783.

Beulah Grubb was married December 16, 1795.
Matilda Grubb was married November 2, 179? (edge
   of page is gone).
Charlotte Grubb was married March 5, ? (edge
   of page is gone).
Joseph Grubb was married the 12th ? (edge of
   page is gone).
Hannah Grubb was married (edge of page is gone).

Julianne Grubb, daughter of Amer and Ann Grubb,
   died July 1828 in five days of typhus fever.
Hannah Perkins, daughter of Amer and Ann Grubb,
   died Aug. 17, 1828 of typhus fever.
Joseph Grubb died May 15, 1828 of consumption.
Beulah Allmond died February 20, 1833.
John Allmond died February 18 of same month,
   48 hours between their deaths.
Harriett Amelia Grubb, daughter of Amer and Ann
   Grubb, was born February 25, 1789.
Juli Ann Grubb, daughter of Amer and Ann Grubb,
   was born February 12, 1791.
Buckley Grubb, son of Amer and Ann Grubb, was
   born October 15, 1792; died October 30,
   1792, aged 15 days - died of head fall.

John Grubb was born November 5, 1684; died
   March 15, 1757.
Rachel Grubb was born April 4, 1690; died
   December 15, 1752.

John Clemson died January 17, 1794, age 92 years.

Beulah Pyle died October 18, 1794, age 44 years - by a tedious illness which held her two years and terminated in consumption.
John Pyle, son of Beulah and John Pyle died 1795, age 24 years - of consumption which held him one year and a half.
John Pyle, father of above, died October 18, 1787 in Baltimore.
My father, John Buckley, was 78 years old Oct. 27, 1797.
Ann Grubb, wife of Amer Grubb, died March 9, 1798, age 43 years - of consumption.
John Buckley died July 19, 1799, age 79 years and 9 months.
John Allmond died June 1831, of consumption.

At the top of the next page:
 Ann Grubb, her Bible, given her by John Buckley. Her beloved Father and its My Desire after my Death that my Daughter Matilda Grubb shall have this Bible.
May 15, 1785.

Charlotte -----, May 15, 1785.

This Bible is a present from Matilda Babb to Amer Grubb Forwood, her nephew, as a mark of respect for his good behavior.
August 27, 1841.

Amer Grubb died September 26, 1817, age 67 years; born October 14, 1749.
Charlotte Harker died August 4, 1837.
Matilda, wife of Thomas Babb, and daughter of Amer and Ann Grubb, died May 22, 1844, age 68 years.
Robert Forwood died May 30, 1844, age 77 years, 12 days.
Amer Grubb Forwood was born July 23, 1831; died November 18, 1897.

Children of Amer and Ann Grubb:
 Beulah Grubb was born January 18, 1775.
 Matilda Grubb was born October 21, 1776.
 Charlotte Grubb was born January 12, 1779.
 Joseph Grubb was born March 16, 1781.
 Heneretta Grubb was born December 8, 1783.

Heneretta Grubb died February 28, 1784, age
   11 weeks and 2 days.
Buckley Grubb was born March 13, 1785.
Hannah Grubb was born April 9, 1787.

Mary E. Forwood was born December 10, 1836 (1834)?;
   died October 13, 1887.
Harry Garland Forwood, son of Amer Grubb and Mary
   E. Forwood, was born December 17, 1852.

BURTON FAMILY

(Bible was published by William W. Harding, No.
326 Chestnut Street, Philadelphia. 1865. Owned
by Mrs. Helen Burton Marsh, Angola, Del. Record
given by Mrs. D. Anthony Potter, Lewes, Del.)

Marriages

Cornelius T. Burton (written in a different hand)
was born July 24, 1820; died July 15, 1886.
Hannah W. Clifton (written in a different hand),
born January 9, 1835; died June 6, 1922, were
married December 10, 1851.

William S. Edwards and Clara W. Burton were
   married February 21, 18--?
Lewes E. Clarkson and Virginia Burton were
   married (no dates shown).
Martin E. Holloway and Annie E. Burton were
   married January 1, 1885.
John C. Burton and Annie B. Quillen were
   married January 13, 1884.
Enols B. Kerbin and Jennie E. Clarkson (Virginia
   E. Burton) were married March 16, 1887.
Fred Burton and Mary M. Murray were married
   January 30, 1888.
Elizabeth Burton and Edward Quillen were married
   December 25, 1893.

Children of John C. Burton and Annie B. Burton:
   1. Clara W. Burton, born Aug. 30, 1885.
   2. Lidie E. Burton, born Feb. 12, 1888.
   3. Helen M. Burton, born March 27, 1890.
   4. Wm. H. V. Burton, born July 6, 1896.
   (In a different hand) died June 14, 1942.

5. Hannah Mae Burton, born Feb. 14, 1899; died July 12, 1936.

Annie B. Quillen, wife of John C. Burton, was born Sept. 15, 1865.

Marriages of above children:
1. Clara Wilmina married Oct. 7, 1914 to Campbell Williams; born Dec. 1, 1890 - no issue.
2. Lida Emerson married Aug. 31, 1908 to Harry Messick Maull; born Nov. 8, 1885. Children:
   1. Lewes Delaware, b. Feb. 23, 1910.
   2. John Burton, b. Sept. 14, 1911.
   3. Harry Edward, b. Jan. 8, 1914.
3. Helen Mae married Oct. 17, 1909 to Edward Walker Sturdivant; born Oct. 4, 1876; died Jan. 18, 1918 - Issue:
   1. Ethel May, b. Aug. 21, 1910.
4. William Virden married Dec. 25, 1917 to Helena Ennis Morrik, born Sept. 20, 1895. Issue:
   1. Jane Ennis, b. 11-23-1918.
   2. John Clifton, b. 3-13-1920.
   3. William V. Burton, Jr., b. 4-1-1935.

Helen Sturdivant married June 16, 1927 to Roland S. Marsh. Issue:
Donald Shankland, born June 5, 1929.

Deaths

Clifton Burton died November 24, 1858.
William E. Burton died June 16, 1874.
Clara W. Burton died July 27, 1881.
Cornelius T. Burton died July 15, 1885.
Virginia Kerbin died November 21, 1893.
John C. Burton died December 5, 1926.
Lewes Delaware Maull died March 10, 1910.
J. Burton Maull died May 22, 1935.
H. May Burton died July 2, 1936.
Emma Quillen died April 6, 1944.

Libbie Quillen died April 29, 1946.

Births

These are the children of Cornelius and Hannah W. (Clifton) Burton:
> Clara W. Burton, born Nov. 8, 1852; died July 27, 1881.
> Mary H. Burton, born Nov. 16, 1854; died April 25, 1907.
> Virginia Burton, born Jan. 30, 1856; died Nov. 20, 1893.
> Clifton Burton, born Oct. 2, 1858; died Nov. 24, 1858.
> John C. Burton, born Feb. 28, 1860; died Dec. 5, 1926.
> Fred Burton, born Feb. 27, 1863.
> Annie E. Burton, born Aug. 16, 1865.
> Cecilia K. Burton, born Sept. 7, 1868; died Sept. 11, 1921.
> Kate R. Burton, born Mar. 19, 1871; died Sept. 11, 1921.
> Elizabeth Burton, born June 4, 1872.
> Willie E. Burton, born May 2, 1874; died June 16, 1974.

Married:
> E. Edward Maull, April 18, 1938 to Irene Jeanette Turner. Issue:
> > Henry Edward, Oct. 31, 1939.
>
> Leo G. Lenhoff, Sept. 30, 1933 to Ethel May Sturdivant. Issue:
> > Jeame (?) C. Lenhoss, Aug., 7, 1936.
>
> Donald Shankland March, June 8, 1953 to Jean Stambaugh.

CALEB BYRNES BIBLE

(Bible was published in Trenton and sold by Isaac Collins, 1791. Now owned by Delaware Historical Society, Wilmington. Record was given by Mrs. Glenn S. Skinner, Newark, Del.)

Susanna Byrnes was born November 22, 1760.
Tacy Byrnes was born March 27, 1763.
Martha Byrnes was born April 18, 1765.
Jonathan Byrnes was born April 18, 1768.
Rachel Byrnes was born March 4, 1771.
Daniel Byrnes was born March 17, 1773.

Charles Byrnes died May 12, 1794, age 74 years.
Mary Byrnes died January 5, 1794, age 60 years.
Caleb Byrnes died January 11, 1794, age 62 years.
Daniel Byrnes died March 28, 1804, age 33 years.
Rachel Byrnes - confined to her bed for 2 years.

Martha Stroud died April 5, 1833, age 63 years.
Joshua Stroud died April 4, 1834, age 80 years.
Cousin Rachel Byrnes died March 30, 1833,
    age 80 years.
Sister-in-law, Elizabeth Wollaston, died Oct. 13,
    1833, age 52 years.
Jonathan Byrnes died July 6, 1845, age 77 years.

Daniel Byrnes and Rachel (Bull) Byrnes were
    married April 12, 1804 in Baltimore;
    Rachel died December 1810, Wilmington.

Jonathan Byrnes was born April 2, 1805, Hanover
    Street opposite the Market House.
Eleanor Byrnes was born November 30, 1807 in
    Baltimore.
Eleanor Byrnes died January 14, 1845 at age 35
    years, 1 month and 16 days in Doylestown -
    buried at Buckingham Meeting, Bucks Co., Pa.
Daniel Byrnes died July 12, 1851, age 79 years,
    at the residence of his niece Elizabeth
    Stroud, Wilmington, Del.
Esther Fussell Byrnes died March 21, 1853, age
    78 years, 4 months and 21 days, at the
    residence of her niece Elizabeth Stroud,
    Wilmington, Del.

Jonathan Byrnes died February 26, 1879, age
73 years and 2 months.

Daniel Byrnes and Esther Fussell were married
May 9, 1816 at Friends Meeting House,
Wilmington, Del.

Esther Fussell, now Byrnes, was born Sept. 1,
1779 in Wilmington.
Jacob F. Byrnes was born April 19, 1821 in
Wilmington, Del.
Jacob Fussell Byrnes died August 15, 1905 at
1803 Canal St., Philadelphia, leaving as
widow Mary (Wilson) Byrnes and two daughters:
Sarah Palmer and Esther Fussell Byrnes. No
descendants. Buried in Fairhill Friends
Cemetery, 8th and Cambria St., Phil.
Mary Wilson, wife of Jacob Fussell Byrnes, died
at her summer home, Camden's Neck, South
Wilport, Mass., in the arms of her daughter,
Esther, July 15, 1925; age 84 years, 6 months
and 16 days. Buried July 18th at Fairhill.

- - - - - - - - - -

Daniel Byrnes emigrated from County Wicklow,
Ireland, about 1730. He lived in Philadelphia for
awhile but later moved to Jones Creek, Delaware,
about 1764. Children:
    Joshua Byrnes, born in Ireland; married
        Ruth Woodcock.
    Charles, died 5-12-1794, age 74 years.
    Elizabeth, m. William Woodcock.
    Rachel, married B. Wilson, 1762.
    Daniel, married Dinah Hichen.
    Caleb, married Mary Davis.

Joshua Byrnes became a sea captain, crossed
the ocean 70 times. Died 1777. Owned a tavern
and ferry over the Schuykill River. After his
death, his wife, Ruth, lived at Christiana Bridge,
then moved to Wilmington, where she kept a school
and later with her son, Samuel, lived in Baltimore.
She had four children:
    Rachel Byrnes - never married.
    Samuel Byrnes, married Hannah Woodnut of
        Salem, N.J.
    James Fitch Byrnes - never married.

Thomas Byrnes, married Sarah Pancoast of Philadelphia.

Samuel Byrnes learned to be a carpenter and joiner with Ziba Ferris and worked with Mr. White in Wilmington. Opened an Iron Mongery and also kept Post Office. Moved to Baltimore in 1796, milling business at Jones' Fall. Children of Samuel and his wife, Hannah Woodnut:
Ruth, born in Wilmington - never married.
Caleb, born in Baltimore.
Sarah
Elizabeth
Thomas
Woodnut

Thomas Byrnes was born in Delaware, February 1766; died July 8, 1798 in Wilmington. He was a silversmith and worked with his uncle, Bancroft Woodcock, in Wilmington. Married Sarah Pancoast of Philadelphia on July 10, 1795. Children:
Hannah, born July 29, 1796; married
    Edwin Lowns, October 1816; died
    June 4, 1820. Hannah Lowns was
    born May 12, 1820; married William
    Ellis, August 1842.
Thomas, born 1798.

Elizabeth Byrnes married William, son of Robert and Rachel Bancroft. Children:
William Woodcock and Rebecca

Rachel Byrnes Wilson's children:
Elizabeth, married Elias Carl.
Benjamin

Daniel Byrnes married Dinah Hickens in Newark Meeting, 1751. Children:
William Byrnes, born 7-22-1759; m.
    Anna Shipley, daughter of Thomas
    Shipley, and they had a son, Thomas,
    born 9-14-1787; m. Sarah Townsend:
    son Joseph, born 1840; m. Lydia Jones.
Rebecca Byrnes, born 3-6-1761; died young.
Joshua Byrnes, born 7-3-1762 - single.
Lydia, born 7-19-1767; m. John Poultney
    and had: Sarah, Ann, Daniel, Lydia.
Joseph, born 12-16-1769; m. had 3 children.

Caleb, born 9-21-1771 and lived in France - 1 daughter.

Daniel Byrnes was a recommended minister in Society of Friends. He had a mill during the Revolutionary War. Invented an instrument, later made of brass by D. Rittenhouse for taking lunar observations. Lived on the Post Road in White Clay Creek Hundred, Del. In 1791 he bought a mill near Newburg, Orange Co., New York, where he died June 29, 1797. Buried at New Cornwall. His wife died later.

Caleb Byrnes, son of Daniel, was born 1732 - after the arrival of the family in America. Was a chairmaker; married Mary Davis at Plymouth Meeting near Philadelphia. Caleb died January 11, 1794; Mary died January 5, 1794. Children:
Susannah, born 11-22-1760 - died young.
Tacy, born 3-27-1763.
Martha, born 4-18-1765.
Jonathan, born 4-16-1768.
Rachel, born 3-4-1771; d. 1804.
Daniel, born 3-17-1773.

Daniel Byrnes, son of Caleb and Mary (Davis) Byrnes, was born March 17, 1773 at Stanton, Del. He was living at Mill Creek Mill at Stanton when George Washington and his American Army were camped there. He married Rachel Bull on April 12, 1804 in Baltimore. They had:
Jonathan, born 4-2-1805.
Eleanor, born 11-30-1807; died 1-14-1835.

Daniel married 2nd Esther Fussell, May 19, 1816, and they had:
Jacob F. Byrnes, born 4-19-1821.

Chart - next page.

1.
Daniel Byrnes   2.
m.   Joshua; m. Ruth Woodcock
_____   Charles, b. 1794
                 Elizabeth
                 Rachel
                 Daniel   3.
                 b.   1. William, b. 1759
                 d. 6-29-1797   2. Rebecca, b. 1761
                 m. 1751   3. Joshua, b. 1762
                 Dinah   4. Joseph, b. 1769
                 Hichens   5. Caleb, b. 1771

                 Caleb
                 b. 1732   1. Susanna, b. 1760
                 d. 1-11-1794   2. Tacy, b. 1763
                 m.   3. Martha, b. 1765
                 Mary Davis   4. Jonathan, b. 1768
                 d. 1-5-1794   5. Rachel, b. 1771
                               6. Daniel
                                  b. 3-17-1773
                                d. 7-12-1851
                         1st m. 3-12-1804
                                Rachel Bull
                                d. 12-1810
                         2nd m. 5-19-1816
Jacob Fussell   Esther Fussell
m.   d. 3-21-1858
Esther

     4.
1. Jonathan, b. 4-2-1805; d. 2-26-1879
2. Eleanor, b. 11-30-1807; d. 1-14-1843
3. Jacob F. Byrnes
   b. 4-19-1821
   d. 8-15-1905
   m.
   Mary Wilson
   d. 7-15-1925

     5.
1. Sarah Byrnes
2. Esther

CANTWELL FAMILY - NEW CASTLE CO.

Edmund Cantwell (1) was one of the large landowners of Appoquinimink Hd. He lived near Odessa, then called Cantwell's Bridge. He also owned a big tract between Haugnaris Branch and Blackbird Creek, containing 2,200 acres. At his death he had 1,500 acres of land highly improved called "Redcliff."

Offices held: Capt. Edmund Cantwell, Deputy Gov. 1675-1676, Pa. Archives, 2nd Ser., p. 609, 613, 615.
    Sheriff, Aug. 12, 1672; Nov. 1676.
    Commissioner to appraise Island of Tinicum 3-2-1673, p. 616.
    Governor's Council, p. 623; 1683-4.
    Sheriff, 1682.
    Justice of Peace, 8-22-1684.
    Surveyor of Customs from Christiana Creek to Lewistown, 1742?
    Surveyor, 1672-77, under Gov. Lovelace, N.Y., Doc. v 12, p. 496.
Will dated 10-28-1679; prob. 1-17-1685, p. 7.
Wife - Mary DeHass. She m. 12-12-1686, Richard Hallowell of N.C. Co. Children: Richard, Elizabeth.

2nd Generation

Will of Richard Hallowell (2); Merchant, dated 12-4-1716; proved 12-17-1719, p. 22.
    Wife - not mentioned - probably dead (Mary Dyer).
    Richard and Mary Cantwell, children of Richard Cantwell
    Richard, Edmund and Cantwell Garretson, sons of Henry Garretson Hallowell and Bridget Garretson, son and daughter of said Henry. Mary Garretson, daughter of Henry.
    4 Godchildren: Jasper, Yeats Jr., Wm. Bedford and Priscilla Robinson.
    Brother - Thomas Halliwell and his daughters: Bridget and Mary.
    Elizabeth Garreston, widow.
Offices held: Justice of Common Pleas, N.C. Co.
    Sheriff under W. P. Hight.

3rd Generation

Richard Cantwell (3), b. 1690; d. 1750; m. Eleanor Peterson, daughter of Andrew and Lydia William-neering. Children:
1. Richard Cantwell (4); m. Sarah Goodwin, no issue.
   Richard died 1787; Sarah died 1801.
2. Edmund - unmarried.
3. Lydia; m. John Jones - see Milligan family, v. 9.

Offices: Justice of Peace King's Court, N.C.Co. (Court of Oyser Terminer).
Justice of Common Pleas, Ref. Gov. Reg. p. 11.

Edmund
Cantwell   1. Richard Cantwell
d. 1685   1. Richard Cantwell
Mary deHass   m.   1. Richard
m.   Andrew   m. Sarah
Richard Hallowell   Eleanor   Goodwyn
                                Peterson   2. Edmund
William Dyer   Lydia   3. Lydia m.
          Mary Dyer   John Jones
Mary
                               2. Mary Cantwell
                                  m.
          2. Johanna, d.y   Henry Lowe
                                1. Richard
                                   Garretson
          3. Elizabeth   2. Edmund
             Cantwell   3. Cantwell
             m.   4. Hallowell
             Henry Garrettson   5. Bridget
                                6. Mary

BIBLE OF THOMAS CARTMELL -
BRANDYWINE HUNDRED, DELAWARE

(Printed by Mathew Carey, No. 118 Market St., Philadelphia, October 20, 1801. Record given by Mrs. Charles D. Bird.)

Family Records

Births

Thomas Cartmell was born April 10, 1769.
Margret Cartmell was born August 2, 1768.
Mary Cartmell, daughter of Thomas C. and Margret Cartmell, was born May 15, 1794.
Thomas Cartmell, son of Thomas and Margret Cartmell, was born November 13, 1796.
Joseph Cartmell, son of Thomas and Margret Cartmell, was born November 9, 1799.
John Cartmell, son of Thomas and Margret Cartmell, was born July 17, 1803.
Sarah Ann Cartmell, daughter of Thomas and Margret Cartmell, was born February 21, 1806.
George Cartmell, son of Thomas and Margret Cartmell, was born August 25, 1808.
John B. Cartmell, son of George and Rebecca Ann Cartmell, was born July 30, 1840.
Margaret Ellen, daughter of George T. and Rebecca Ann Cartmell, was born September 12, 1845.
Thomas B. Cartmell, son of George T. and Rachel H. Cartmell, was born January 28, 1854.

Deaths

Joseph Cartmell, son of Margaret and Thomas Cartmell, died August 16, 1829, age 29 years, 9 months and 7 days - drowned.
Thomas Cartmell died February 9, 1838, age 68 years and 10 months.
Margaret Cartmell, his wife, died December 24, (?)
Sarah Ann Cartmell, daughter of Thomas and Margaret Cartmell, died April 22, 1852.
John Cartmell, son of Thomas and Margaret Cartmell, died (no dates shown).
George T. Cartmell, son of Thomas and Margaret Cartmell, died February 21, 1858, age 49 years.
Mary Cartmell, daughter of Thomas and Margaret Cartmell, died January 1, 1868.
Thomas Cartmell, son of Thomas and Margaret Cartmell, died September 4, 1872.
Rebecca Ann, wife of George T. Cartmell, died July 4, 1851, age 36 years.
John B. Cartmell, son of George T. Cartmell, died March 20, 1867, age 26 years.
Rachel H. Cartmell, wife of George T. Cartmell, died January 23, 1895, age 84 years.

Thomas B. Cartmell, son of George T. and Rachel H. Cartmell, died June 16, 1921, new time, age 67 years. He died June 15, standard time, 11:45 P.M.

Thomas Cartmell Chart

1.
Thomas Cartmell
b. 4-10-1769
d. 2-9-1838
m.
Margret
b. 8-2-1768
d. 12-24-?

2.
1. Mary Cartmell
   b. 5-15-1794
2. Thomas
   b. 11-13-1796
   d. 9-4-1872
3. Joseph
   b. 11-9-1799
   d. 8-16-1829
4. John
   b. 7-17-1803
   d. 3-20-1867
5. Sarah
   b. 2-21-1806
   d. 4-22-1852
6. George
   b. 8-25-1808
   d. 2-21-1858
   m. 1st
     Rebecca
   b. 1815
   d. 7-4-1851

   m. 2nd
     Rachel
   b. 1811
   d. 1-23-1895

3.
1. John B..
   b. 7-30-1840
2. Margaret
   b. 9-12-1845

1. Thomas
   b. 1-28-1854
   d. 6-15-1921

GEORGE CASEY & CATHERINE MILLER

(Bible published by A. J. Holman, 1222 Arch St., Philadelphia. 1885. Owned by Miss Lena A. Casey, Claymont, Delaware. 1957. Record given by Mrs. Charles D. Bird.)

Marriages

George Merritt Casey and Catherine Walker Miller were married May 7, 1884 at the residence of J. S. Miller, in presence of Ella Smith et al.

Births

George Merritt Casey, son of Robert and Mary Ellen Casey, was born July 27, 1858.
Catherine Walker Casey, wife of George M. Casey and daughter of John Savage and Anna Mary Miller, was born June 19, 1862.
Mary Ellen Casey, daughter of George Merritt and Catherine Walker Casey, was born Nov. 16, 1884.
John Miller Casey, son of George Merritt and Catherine Walker Casey, was born June 6, 1886.
George Merritt Casey, Jr., son of George M. and Catherine W. Casey, was born April 24, 1888.
Cora Rebecca Casey, daughter of George M. and Catherine W. Casey, was born March 5, 1890.
Lena Elva Casey, daughter of George M. and Catherine W. Casey, was born Sept. 5, 1892.
Anna Archer Casey, daughter of George M. and Catherine W. Casey, was born June 12, 1894.
Mildred Jane Casey, daughter of George M. and Catherine W. Casey, was born May 17, 1896.
Amy Estelle Casey, daughter of George M. and Katherine W. Casey, was born Sept. 10, 1897.
Adelaide Roberta Casey, daughter of George M. and Katherine W. Casey, was born July 2, 1899.
Ethel May Casey, daughter of George M. and Katherine W. Casey, was born April 5, 1901.
Katherine Winifred Casey, daughter of George M. and Katherine W. Casey, was born Jan. 10, 1905; died January 28, 1957.

Mary Estelle Tayntor, daughter of Charles Lawrence and Mary E. Tayntor, was born Feb. 4, 1906.
James Elliott Casey, son of John M. Casey and Virginia Casey, was born July 20, 1910.
Lena Virginia Casey, daughter of John M. and Virginia Casey, was born Feb. 25, 1912.
Helen Marie Casey, daughter of John M. and Virginia Casey, was born Sept. 21, 1913.
Martha Marian Casey, daughter of John M. and Virginia Casey, was born April 4, 1915.

John Miller Casey, son of John M. and Virginia
    Casey, was born October 11, 1916.
Mildred Frances Casey, daughter of John M. and
    Virginia Casey, was born April 12, 1918.

CHASE RECORD

(Daily texts with Verses of Hymns; published by
the American Tract Company, New York. It is a
tiny book - 2 x 2 inches; belonged to Laura Dailey
Bird, wife of Charles D. Bird, Wilmington, Del.
Owned and record was given by Mrs. Charles D.
Bird, Wilmington, Del.)

Kate Montgomery was the original owner.

George M. Chase was born January 10, 18--?
Mrs. Phebe C. Johnson was born February 7, 1827 -
    (when you read this think of one that writes
    it. She is sick and can't get out and she
    sits here often alone to think of past days
    gone).

Mary B. Chase was born September 22, 1814.
Peter Dailey was born November 28, 1836.
James T. Chase was born June 17, 1838.
Mary E. Chase was born October 8, 1839.
Emily B. Chase was born November 30, 1848.

Laura E. Dailey was born April 16, 1862.
Joseph Dailey was born June 18, 1871.

JOHN S. CLARK - SARAH E. CONWELL

(Bible is dated 1812 and is owned by a sister of
Mrs. Hannah Alta (Lank) Mellick, LaCrosse, Kansas.
Record given by Mrs. D. A. Potter.)

Susan R. Conwell's Book - Susan Riley
Susan R. Pepper her book
Elizabeth Couston her book - June 10, 1812.

Sarah S. Conwell was born January 27, 1828.
John S. Clark was born October 25, 1832.

Asbury Conwell and Susan R., his wife, were married February 6, 1834.
    Edward W. W. Conwell was born December 27, 1834.
    Sarah S. Conwell was born January 27, 1838;
      m. John Clark.
    Martha C. Conwell was born January 29, 1841
      (my grandmother).
Susan R. Pepper was born May 18, 1810 - wife of
    Asbury.

Deaths

Edward W. Conwell died June 18, 1839.
Asbury Conwell died May 20, 1857 in Galesburg, Ill.
Susan S. Clark died November 17, 1862, at
    Galesburg.
Susan R. Conwell died December 4, 1873.

Parents

John Conwell died February 22, 1840, age 66.
Sarah Conwell, his wife, died December 30, 1841.

John Conwell
b. 1774
d. 2-22-1840
m.
Sarah
d. 1841

Asbury Conwell
b. 4-18-1811
d. 5-20-1857
m. 2-6-1834

Susan R. Pepper
b. 5-18-1810
m. 2-6-1834
d. 12-4-1873

1. Edward W. Conwell
   b. 1834
   d. 1839
2. Sarah S.
   b. 1836
   d. 1862
   m.
   John S. Clark
3. Martha S. Conwell
   b. 1841

LOT & REBECCA CLOUD BIBLE

(Bible was Stereotyped and Published by C. Alexander & Co., Philadelphia, Pa. 1839. From the estate of Anne Lodge Parrish from Mrs. Josiah Titzell. Now owned by the Delaware Historical Society, Wilmington, Del. Copied by Mrs. Alban Shaw.)

Family Record

Births

Elmira Cloud, daughter of Lot and Rebecca Cloud, was born April 11, 1837.
Joel Cloud, son of Lot and Rebecca Cloud, was born August 13, 1838.
George Lodge Cloud, son of Lot and Rebecca Cloud, was born October 31, 1839.
Ann Mary Cloud, daughter of Lot and Rebecca Cloud, was born September 3, 1841.
Charity Cloud, daughter of Lot and Rebecca Cloud, was born November 26, 1843.
William Cloud, son of Lot and Rebecca Cloud, was born August 7, 1845.
Maria Elizabeth Cloud, daughter of Lot and Rebecca Cloud, was born April 19, 1848.

THE WILLIAM CLOUD BIBLE

(Bible printed and sold by Isaac Collins of Trenton, N. J. Published 1793. From the estate of Anne Lodge Parrish, from Mrs. Titzell, January 25, 1947. Now in the Delaware Historical Society, Wilmington, Del. Copied by Mrs. Alban Shaw.)

Births

Ann Cloud, daughter of William and Ann Cloud, was born September 30, 1802.
Maria Cloud, daughter of Wm. and Ann Cloud, was born January 31, 1805.
Lot Cloud, son of William and Ann Cloud, was born August 9, 1811.
Abner Cloud, son of William Cloud, was born born March 6, 1797.

Joel Cloud, son of William and Ann Cloud, was
    born September 10, 17 8?
Charity Cloud, daughter of William and Ann Cloud,
    was born January 5, 1801.

CONELLY RECORDS

(Bible was printed by William Harding, 326 Chestnut St., Philadelphia, Pa. 1865. Now in possession of Mrs. Gerald L. Montague, a member of Caesar Chapter, N.S.D.A.R., Wilmington, Del. Record given by Mrs. Clara W. Bird, Wilmington.)

Marriages

James Connelly and Poly Mary Nutgrass were married
    June 17, 1824. Head of the family.
Jesse Connelly and Rhoda Rush were married
    April 20, 1845.
Edna Connelly and William Collings were married
    December 9, 1846.
James Harvey Connelly and Elizabeth Johnson were
    married September 17, 1850.
Sarah Ann Connelly and John Collings were married
    September 18, 1850.
Gray Connelly and Mary Jane Stout were married
    April 7, 1852.
Mary T. Connelly and Rev. Alvah Dooley were
    married April 7, 1852.
Elizabeth Connelly and James Stark were married
    December 17, 1857.
Nancy D. Connelly and William P. Swaim were
    married October 11, 1860.
Eliza Connelly and Thomas Lanning were married
    October 17, 1866.

Births
James Connelly was born October 12,   )
    1801 in Shelby Co., Kentucky.   ) Head of
Polly Mary Nutgrass Connelly was   ) the family
    born May 28, 1807 in Virginia.   )

Jesse Connelly was born October 20, 1825 in
    Shelby Co., Ky.

Harrison Connelly was born January 23, 1827 in
    Shelby Co., Ky.
James H. Connelly was born May 7,1828 in
    Shelby Co., Ky.
Edna N. Connelly was born May 13, 1830 in
    Shelby Co., Ky.
Sarah Ann Connelly was born October 5, 1831 in
    Shelby Co., Ky.
Gray Connelly was born February 26, 1833 in
    Shelby Co., Ky.
Mary J. Connelly was born July 28, 1835 in
    Shelby Co., Ky.
Elizabeth Connelly was born May 25, 1837 in
    Shelby Co., Ky.
Nancy D. Connelly was born December 14, 1840
    in Shelby Co., Ky.
Lucinda Connelly was born April 7, 1843 in
    Parke Co., Ind.
David Connelly was born March 27, 1845 in
    Parke Co., Ind.
Eliza Jane Connelly was born September 28, 1848
    in Parke Co., Ind.
Susan Frances Connelly was born April 12, 1839
    in Shelby Co., Ky.

Deaths

Susan Frances Connelly died December 27, 1846.
Lucinda Connelly died January 28, 1848.
David Connelly died September 30, 1851.
Polly Connelly died April 23, 1870 (Matson).
James Connelly died September 14, 1876.
Infant son Connelly (stillborn) February 8, 1847.
Jesse Connelly died August 10, 1889.
James H. Connelly died January 15, 1900.
Edna N. Connelly Collings died April 5, 1891.
Nancy D. Connelly died February 8, 1903.
Harrison Connelly died April 3, 1904.
Mary Thatcher Connelly Dooley died Jan. 1, 1907.
Sarah Ann Connelly Collings died March 26, 1907.
Gray Connelly died March 2, 1916.
Elizabeth Connelly Stark died January 28, 1917.
Eliza J. Connelly Lanning died August 31, 1926.
Nancy D. Connelly, daughter of James and Polly
    Nutgrass Connelly, was born December 14,
    1840; died February 8, 1903. Married William
    P. Swaim of Parke Co., Ind. 10-11-1860.

Their children were all born in Bellmore, Ind.:
- Mary Emily Swaim, born April 22, 1862; died 5-13-1943.
- David Howard Swaim, born February 28, 1864; died 5-19-1941.
- Addie Ellen, born February 23, 1866; died 6-8-1947.
- Alice Edna, born February 23, 1866; died 6-21-1944.
- Lottie Ann, born March 8, 1876.
- Fred Harrison, born January 17, 1878.
- Carrie Amelia, born February 8, 1881.
- Col. John E. Swaim, born Oct. 19, 1882.

Carrie Amelia Swaim, daughter of Nancy D. Connelly and Wm. P. Swaim, married George Duncan Neal, who was born November 27, 1879; died Feb. 20, 1949. They were married December 27, 1905 in Bellmore, Indiana. Children:

1. Joseph Duncan Neal, born Sept. 27, 1906 in Parke Co., Ind.; m. Jan. 25, 1925 Louise McCarns in Delaware County, Pa. and they had 2 sons:
    Joseph Wm. Neal, born 6-7-1925; d. 11-3-1928.
    George Duncan Neal, born 6-17-1928; m. Ruth Weichardt 1-27-1951 and had:
        Deborah Lynn Neal, born 11-10-1951.
        Donna L. Neal, born 11-16-1955.

2. John Edwin Neal, son of Carrie A. and George D. Swaim, was born Feb. 12, 1914 in Parke Co., Ind. Married Della Lois Hopkins from Maryland on Sept. 25, 1935. Children:
    Nancy Carrie Neal, born Feb. 13, 1946.
    David John Neal, born Jan. 3, 1950.
    Susan May Neal, born May 26, 1952; died JUne 26, 1954.

3. Edith Neal, daughter of Carrie Amelia Swaim and George Duncan Swaim, was born Jan. 29, 1922 in Parke Co., Ind. Married June 15, 1946, Gerald Laurence Montague; born Sept. 3, 1916 in Landenberg, Pa. Their daughter:
    Patricia Neal Montague, born April 10, 1951.

(Patricia is a member of the Blue Hen's Chicken Chapter of N.S.C.A.R.)

Connelly Chart

1.
James Connelly
b. 10-12-1801
d. 9-14-1876
m. 6-17-1824
Polly M. Nutgrass
b. 5-28-1807
d. 4-23-1870

2.
1. Jesse, b. 10-20-1825
d. 9-10-1889
m. 4-20-1845
Rhoda Rush

2. Harrison, b. 1-23-1827
d. 4-3-1904

3. James, b. 5-7-1828
d. 1-15-1900
m. 9-17-1850
Elizabeth Johnson

4. Susan, b. 4-12-1839
d. 1846

5. Edna, b. 2-13-1830
d. 4-5-1891
m. 12-9-1846
William Collings

6. Sarah, b. 10-5-1831
d. 3-26-1907
m. 9-18-1850
John Collings

7. Gray, b. 2-26-1833
d. 3-2-1916
m. 4-7-1852
Mary J. Stout

Connelly Chart cont'd.

8. Mary J., b. 7-28-1835
d. 1-1-1852
m. 4-7-1852
Rev. Alvah Dooley

NOTE: The typist noticed the dates of death and marriage of Mary J. If she died January 1, 1852, she could not have been married April 7, 1852 - so there is an error in one of these dates.

9. Elizabeth, b. 5-25-1835(?)
d. 1-28-1917
m. 12-17-1857
James Stark

10. Nancy, b. 12-14-1840
d. 2-8-1903
m. 10-11-1860
William P. Swaim

3.
1. See Below

11. Lucinda, b. 1843
d. 1848

12. David, b. 3-27-1845
d. 9-30-1851

13. Eliza, b. 9-28-1848
d. 8-31-1926
m. 10-17-1866
Thos. Lanning

                                  3.
1. Mary, b. 4-22-1862
2. David, b. 2-28-1864
3. Addie, b. 2-23-1866
4. Alice, b. 2-23-1866
5. Lottie, b. 3-8-1876
6. Fred, b. 1-17-1878
7. Carrie, b. 2-8-1881
m. 12-27-1905
George D. Neal
b. 11-27-1879
d. 2-20-1949
8. Col. John, b.
b. 10-19-1882

Connelly chart cont'd.

3.
Carrie A. Connelly
b. 2-8-1881
m. 12-27-1905
George D. Neal
b. 11-27-1879
d. 2-20-1949

1. **Joseph Neal**
   b. 9-27-1906
   m. 1-25-1925
   Louise
   McCarns

   5.
   1. Joseph
      b. 1925
      d. 1928
   2. **George**
      b. 6-17-1928
      m. 1-27-1951
      Ruth
      Weichardt

2. **John Neal**
   b. 2-12-1914
   m. 9-25-1935
   Della
   Hopkins

   1. Nancy
      b. 1946
   2. David
      b. 1950
   3. Susan
      b. 1952
      d. 1954

3. **Edith Neal**
   b. 1-29-1922
   m. 6-15-1946
   Gerald L. Montague
   b. 9-3-1916

   Patricia
   b. 4-10-1951

6.
1. Deborah
   b. 1951
2. Donna
   b. 1955

JANE CORD RECORD

(From a book belonging to H. Ernest Conwell, Milton, Delaware. Entitled, A Collection of Memorials concerning Divers deceased Ministers and others of the People called Quakers, in Pennsylvania, New Jersey and Parts adjacent, from nearly the first Settlement thereof to the year 1787. With some of the last expressions and exhortations of many of them. Philadelphia. Printed by Joseph Cruikshank, Market Street between Second and Third Streets. MDCCLXXXVII.)

Written on a fly leaf:
    Jane Cord Her Book
    Jane Cord was born 1733
    Elizabeth Robbins

Written in back:
    Jane Cord her Book got of Dan--- (torn, could be Daniel) Heavelow got in the year 1788. Price 5 shillings and 6 pence.

On next page:
    Jane Cord her Book. God gave her grace there in (faded) but not to look but understand.

Jane Cord, wife of Joseph Cord, was born
    August 28, 1733.
Joseph Cord, husband of Jane Miers, died
    January 17, 1787, age about 60 years.
Miers Cord, son of Joseph Cord and Jane his wife,
    died March 17, 1787.
Isair Cord, son of Joseph Cord and Jane his wife,
    died January 12, 1795.
Mary Cord, wife of William Cord, died February 14,
    1796.
Samuel Cord, son of Joseph Cord and Jane his wife,
    died February 12, ?
William Cord, son of same, died June 15, 1803.

Written on back of fly leaf:
    Jane Cord was born August the twenty eight
        day 1733.
    Joseph Cord was born 1726 and departed this
        life 1787 January the seventeen day.

On back page:
> Jane Cord being the daughter of John Miers and Jane his wife was born 8 mo. and 28 day 1733.

Jane Cord departed this life 1787 January the seventeen day.

In front:
> Joshua R. Bowman, 3 mo. 1821

Presented to his cousin Ann Robins 1826 hoping that she may derive the same pleasure and information from it that he has done. Signed: J.B. 10 mo 23rd 1826.

In back:
> Ann C. Robbins her Book from J.B.
> Ann C. Conwell.

WILLIAM COULTER BIBLE

(Bible bought of William Dixon at Christeen Bridge, later was Charles McCullough's Bible. Owned by the Delaware Historical Society, Wilmington, Del. Record given by Mrs. Glenn S. Skinner, Newark, Del.)

William Coulter and Edith (Clark) his wife were married February 27, 1796.
William Coulter was born January 1, 1798 and was Baptized by Parson Barr at Christiana Bridge on May 9, 1798.
George Coulter was born August 7, 1800 and Baptized by Parson Shelly at Christiana, December 12, Bridge in the meeting house.
Mary Coulter was born February 3, 1802 and Baptized by John Jatta in our own house June 3, 1802.
Ingebor Bryon Coulter was born February 20, 1805 and was Baptized in Christiana Meeting House on May 10 by the Rev. John Latta.

William Coulter died February 23, 1818, age 69 years, 6 months and 14 days.

Edith Coulter, wife of William Coulter, died
   January 11, 1841, age 69 years.
George Coulter died January 19, 1841, age
   40 years.

- - - - - - - - - - -

Peter B. Vandever was married to Catherina
   McCullough on December 19, 1843.
Charles McCullough Vandever, their son, was born
   October 26, 1844.
Henry Harvey Vandever was born July 26, 1846.

Charles McCullough was born August 19, 1819.
Catharina McCullough was born November 29, 1821.
Mary McCullough was born October 27, 1823.
John McCullough was born September 29, 1825.
Sarah Ann McCullough was born September 8, 1827.

Charles McCullough died May 19, 1828.
Charles McCullough, son of Charles and Mary
   McCullough, died October 19, 1848 at
   Mobile, Alabama.
Charles McCullough, son of Mary E. and Charles
   McCullough, died February 19, 1848(?).
Henry H. Vandever died January 25, 1854.

Written on a page in the Bible:
   William Coulter, February 23, 1818; age
   69 years, 6 mos. 14 d.
   (Very faint): Nathaniel Clark 1851 - 27.

COVINGTON RECORD

(The Holy Bible, published by the American Bible
Society, New York. 1850. Old and New Testaments.
Owned by Mrs. Samuel Hollis Morris, daughter of
the original owner, Royston Covington. Mrs.
Morris lives in Newark, Delaware. Record given by
Mrs. Rees S. Jarmon, Newark, Del.)

Marriages

Royston Covington and Nancy Wilson were married
   December 15, 1840.

Royston Covington and Martha Jane Hargis were
    married January 5, 1860 by Rev. James Hargis.
Southey Taylor and Sallie Elizabeth Covington were
    married April 6, 1864.
Algey T. Covington and Margaret E. Davis were
    married (no dates shown).
Charles W. Tull and Virginia Covington were
    married January 19, 1882.
William R. Covington and Kitty Jones were married
    February 22, 1882.
Hester Ann Covington and Samuel Hollie Morris were
    married January 27, 1909 in New Church, Va.
Hester Morris and Roy T. Walton were married
    November 30, 1933.

Births

Royston Covington, son of James and Mary
    Covington, was born September 23, 1816.
Nancy Wilson, daughter of William and Nancy
    Wilson, was born March 17, 1815.
Martha Jane, daughter of Jacob and Comfort Waples
    Hargis, was born September 15, 1825.
Algey Thomas Covington, son of Royston and Nancy,
    was born January 25, 1842.
Henry M. Covington, son of Royston and Nancy, was
    born February 11, 1844.
Sallie E., daughter of Royston and Nancy
    Covington, was born February 3, 1846.
George Washington, son of Royston and Nancy, was
    born September 28, 1844?
Charlott Matilda Covington, daughter of Royston
    and Nancy, was born January 5, 1851.
James Rider, son of Royston and Nancy was born
    February 9, 1853.
William Royston, son of Royston and Nancy, was
    born October 2, 1855.
Mary Anna, daughter of Royston and Nancy
    Covington, was born January 28, 1858.
Jacob Hargis, son of Royston and Martha Jane
    Hargis Covington, was born May 11, 1861.
Francis A., son of Royston and Martha Jane
    Covington, was born March 24, 1863.
John James, son of Royston and Martha Jane
    Covington, was born September 1, 1865.
Hester Ann, daughter of Royston and Martha Jane
    Covington, was born November 24, 1869.

Samuel Hollie Morris was born May 5, 1865.
Hester Morris, daughter of Hester A. and
    Samuel Hollie Morris, was born February 20,
    1912.
Roy T. Walton was born February 27, 1910.

Deaths

Henry M. Covington, son of Royston and Nancy
    Covington, died June 6, 1850.
James Rider Covington, son of Royston and Nancy
    Covington, died October 17, 1866, age 13
    months and 17 days.
Charlott M. Covington, daughter of Royston and
    Nancy Covington died December 23, 1907.
Nancy Wilson Covington, wife of Royston Covington,
    died September 3, 1858.
Sarah Elizabeth Covington Taylor died February 13,
    1867.
Royston Covington died June 11, 1880.
Martha Jane Hargis Covington, 2nd wife of Royston
    Covington, died August 25, 1893.
Samuel Hollie Morris died November 27, 1938.

1.
James Covington
b.
d.
m.
Mary
 	
William
Wilson
m.
Nancy
 	
Jacob
Hargis
 	
Comfort
Waples
	2.
	Royston Covington
	b. 9-23-1816
	d. 6-11-1880
	m. 1st
	12-15-1840
	
	Nancy Wilson
	b. 3-17-1815
	d. 9-3-1858
	
	m. 2nd
	1-5-1860
	Martha J. Hargis
	b. 9-15-1825
	d. 8-25-1893
		See 3. next
		page.
		
		1. Jacob H.
		    b. 5-11-1861
		2. Francis A.
		    b. 3-24-1863
		3. John
		    b. 9-1-1865
		*4. Contd. next
		    page.

Covington Chart cont'd.

*4. Hester Ann Covington
     b. 11-24-1869
     m. 1-27-1909   See 4.
     Samuel H. Morris
     b. 5-5-1865
     d. 11-27-1938

              3.
1. Algey
    b. 1-25-1842
    m. Margaret Davis
2. Henry
    b. 2-11-1844
    d. 1850
3. Sallie
    b. 2-3-1846
    d. 1867
    m. Souhey Taylor
4. George W.
    b. 9-28-18
5. Charlott
    b. 1-5-1851
    d. 1907
6. James R.
    b. 2-9-1853
    d. 1866
7. William
    b. 10-2-1855
    m. Kitty Jones
8. Mary
    b. 1-28-1858

       4.
Hester Morris   5.
b. 2-20-1912   Jane Walton
m. 11-30-1933   Max
Roy T. Walton   Peggy
b. 2-27-1910

ESAU COXE BIBLE RECORD

(Bible is owned by the Delaware Historical Society, Wilmington, Del. Record given by Mrs. Glenn S. Skinner, Newark, Del.)

Marriages

Esau Coxe and Eliza McKain were married in 1805.
Ellen Coxe and Charles Bush were married
    March 12, 1829.
Edward Coxe and Sarah Sparks were married
    November 15, 1832.
James M. Coxe and Charlott Warlow were married
    September 7, 1836.
Martha Ann Coxe and Robert Lloyd were married
    December 15, 1836.
Louis H. Coxe and Mary Seely Gibson were married
    July 9, 1846 by Rev. Anthony Atwood.

Births

Ellen Coxe was born January 6, 1806.
James Coxe was born August 24, 1808.
Edward Coxe was born November 13, 1810.
Martha Ann Coxe was born October 3, 1812.
Thomas Coxe was born September 8, 1815.
Esau Lyon Coxe was born October 12, 1818.
Rebecca Coxe was born May 28, 1821.
Eliza McKain was born November 23, 1785.
Louis Henry Coxe was born on Easter morning
    April 18, 1824.
Elizabeth Coxe was born November 12, 1826.
Albert Fisher Coxe was born November 4, 1828.

Grandchildren

Elizabeth McCain Bush was born September 22, 1830.
Samuel Bush was born 1832. Children of Ellen and
    Charles Bush.
David Potter Bush was born March 22, 1834.

Ellen Coxe was born November 4, 18331 daughter of
    Edward Coxe.
E. J. (?) was born January 27, 1836.
Elizabeth Cox was born July 22, 1837, daughter of
    Edward Coxe.

Rebecca Coxe was born September 15, 1837, daughter of James McK. Coxe.

Deaths

Thomas Coxe, son of Esau and Eliza Coxe, died
    August 22, 1816, age 11 months and 18 days.
Mary Clungis died October 27, 1820.
Ann McKain died December 27, 1825.
James McKain, son of James and Ann McKain, died
    August 4, 1826.
Elizabeth McKain Coxe, daughter of Esau and
    Elizabeth Coxe, died July 23, 1832, age
    5 years and 8 months.
Ann Sperry, formerly wife of Thomas Coxe, died
    May 4, 1833, age 87 years.
John Robinson died November 1834.
James Cocren died March 30, 1835.
Henry Robinson died May 1836.
Sarah P. Bush, formerly wife of James McKain,
    died April 28, 1836.
Esau L. Coxe died January 10, 1879.
Catherine Rumford died July 22, 1837.
Eliza Lyon died March 31, 1839.
Rebecca Lyon died April 13, 1840.
Samuel Rumford died August 1840.
John Lyon died August 18, 1840.
James M. Coxe, son of Esau and Eliza Coxe,
    died March 11, 1841.
Albert Fisher Coxe died March 13, 1855.

- - - - - - - - - -

Thomas Coxe was born 1748 and died February 27,
    1801.
Ann Patterson, his wife, married 1774 and died
    May 4, 1833.
Esau Coxe, only son of above, was born 1783; died
    May 18, 1850
Eliza McKain was born November 23, 1785 and died
    (no dates shown) - was married July 1805.
Louis Henry Coxe was born April 18, 1824.
Mary Gibson (no dates shown) ...
    Above is from a letter written by A. R.
Stiles of Springfield, N..J., July 29, 1919,
grandson of James Coxe.

Mary married George Burns.
Margaret married Samuel Rumford.
Catherine married Thomas Rumford; she died
    July 22, 1827.

1.
Thomas Coxe
b. 1748
d. 2-27-1801
m. 1774
Ann
Patterson
d. 5-4-1833

2.
Esau Coxe
b. 1783
d. 5-18-1850
m. 7-1805

3.
1. Ellen, b. 1806;
   m. Charles Bush
2. James, b. 1808;
   m. Charlott
   Warlow
3. Edward, b. 1810;
   m. Sarah Sparks
4. Martha, b. 1812;
   m. Robert Lloyd
5. Thomas, b. 1815
6. Esau, b. 1818
7. Rebecca, b. 1821
8. Louis, b. 1824;
9. Elizabeth
   b. 1826
10. Albert, b. 1828

James McKain
m.

Eliza McKain
b. 11-23-1785

THE DAVID CRANE BIBLE

(Printed by D. Fanshaw for the American Bible Society, 1843. Now owned by Mrs. W. David R. Straughn (Henrietta Crane), Westover Hills, Wilmington, Del., a member of the Casesar Rodney Chapter, N.S.D.A.R. Record given by Mrs. Harriett Shaw of Caesar Rodney Chapter.)

The earliest records cannot be read.

Marriages

Stephen M. Crane and Mary E. Hicks were married
    July 24, 1838.
Stephen M. Crane and Josephine Trenchard were
    married December 12, 1847.
William H. Crane and Margaret R. Lucas were
    married March 6, 1862.

Thomas H. Crane and Annie E. Hickman of Accomac
    County, Eastern Shore of Virginia, were
    married March 26, 1864.
John C. Crane and Mary L. Moffett were married
    December 3, 1873 by Rev. George P. Leakin.
George T. Crane and Clara M. Washington were
    married May 7, 1872.

Births

Stephen P. Crane, son of Annie and Thomas H.
    Crane, was born June 3, 1866.
William H. Crane was born September 6, 1840.
Stephen M. Crane, Jr. was born February 5, 1842.
Thomas H. Crane was born August 24, 1843.
John C. Crane was born December 9, 1844.
Jonathan Crane was born April 14, 1846.
George T. Crane was born March 22, 1850. (Son
    of Stephen W. Crane and Josephine T. Crane).
George O. T. Crane, son of Josephine and Stephen
    M., was born September 5, 1847.
Mary P. Crane was born December 15, 1862.
William K. Crane was born October 3, 1864.

Deaths

Jonathan Crane died August 6, 1846.
Mary E. Crane, wife of Stephen M. Crane, died
    October 17, 1846.
George O. T. Crane died December 23, 1848.
Mary P. Crane died July 7, 1863.
William H. Crane died July 27, 1864.
William K. Crane died October 5, 1864.
Stephen R. Crane died September 16, 1866.

PETER C. & REBECCA DAILEY

(Brown's Self Interpreting Bible. Published by
Johnson Fry & Co., 27 Beekman St., New York.
Owned by Charles Weatherby. Record given by Mrs.
Charles D. Bird, Wilmington, Del.)

Parents

Peter C. Dailey and Rebecca E. Dailey.

Peter C. Dailey and Rebecca E. Dailey were married
    August 11, 1859.

Peter C. Dailey was born November 28, 1836; died
    June 17, 1903.
Rebecca E. Dailey was born June 6, 1839; died
    January 4, 1905.

Children

Edistina M. Dailey was born June 26, 1860;
    married December 15, 1881.
Laura E. Dailey was born April 16, 1862;
    married December 21, 1882; died
    September 24, 1939.
Elenora Dailey was born February 26, 1864;
    died June 20, 1864.
Samuel J. Dailey was born June 6, 1866; died
    December 22, 1867.
Joseph L. Dailey was born June 18, 1871;
    married November 15, 1894; died April 7,
    1905.
Charles D. Bird was born August 6, 1862; died
    January 16, 1935.
Alfred D. Bird was born March 13, 1885; married
    December 7, 1912; died April 13, 1937.
Charles D. Bird, Jr. was born August 10, 1889;
    married December 2, 1915; died October 25,
    1957.

NOTE: Charles D. Bird married Laura E. Dailey
        and had 2 sons - Alfred and Charles D., Jr.
        Both sons married and had no children.

DARBY - LOFLAND BIBLE

(Bible is owned by Mr. and Mrs. Harry A. Darby,
Milford, Delaware.)

Marriages

Eliza Jain Lofland and Alex Burtin Darby were
    married May 9, 1861.
Evva G. Darby, daughter of A.B. Darby and Eliza
    his wife, and Geo. F. Boyer were married
    September 30, 1890.
Amandus B. Darby, son of A.B. Darby and Eliza
    his wife, married Emily F. Foster (no dates).

Births

Amandus B. Darby, son of Burtin and Eliza his
    wife, was born May 2, 1862.
Rachel Lizzie Darby, daughter of Burtin and
    Eliza his wife, was born September 18,
    1866 or 1865.
Harry A. Darby, son of Alex and Eliza his wife,
    was born March 2, 1870.
Evva G. Darby, daughter of Alex B. and Eliza J.
    his wife, was born November 18, 1872.
Clarence A. Darby, son of Alex B. and Eliza J.,
    was born January 31, 1875.

Deaths

Rachel Lizzie Darby, daughter of Burtin and Eliza
    his wife, was born September 18, 1866; died
    April 11, 1869, age 3 years, 6 months and
    7 days.
Alexander Burton Darby, son of William and Nacy M.
    Darby, died December 27, 1883, age 42 years,
    5 months and 19 days.
Nancy M. Darby, wife of William Darby and mother
    of Alexander Burton Darby, was born Nov. 15,
    1808; died September 29, 1892, age 83 years,
    11 months and 17 days.
Elza May Darby, daughter of Alex B. and Eliza J.,
    was born September 26, 1877.
Eliza J. Darby, wife of A. B. Darby, died
    February 27, 1909.
Evva G. Boyer died March 1949, age 76 years.

William Darby	Alexander Burton Darby	
Nancy M.	b.	Amandus B., b. 1862
b. 11-15-1808	d. 12-27-1883	Rachel Lizzie,
d. 9-29-1892	m. 5-9-1861	b. 1865
	Eliza J.	Harry A., b. 1870
	Lofland	Evva G., b. 1872
	d. 2-17-1909	m. George Boyer
		Clarence, b. 1875
		Else May, b. 1877

DAVIDSON RECORD

(Bible was published by the Bible Society of Philadelphia. 1816. Owned by Herbert Downing, Wilmington, Del. 1956. Record given by Mrs. Charles D. Bird.)

Francis Davidson was born February 1767.
Mary Davidson was born November 15, 1772.

Francis Davidson, Sr., died May 16, 1848, age 81 years.
Mary Davidson, Sr., died October 24, 1849, age 76 years and 11 months.

Francis Davidson, Jr., was born March 8, 1813.
Esther Davidson was born October 28, 1816.
Elizabeth Davidson was born January 23, 1819.
Rachel Davidson died November 2, 1814.
Francis Davidson, Jr., died November 7, 1834.
John Davidson died April 15, 1837.
William Davidson died August 3, 1868, age 69 years and 10 months.
Jane Davidson died September 18, 1874, age 70 years and 7 months.
Robert Davidson died May 21, 1885, age 89 years, 5 months and 17 days.
Mary Davidson died November 29, (no year shown), age 88 years, 3 months and 23 days.

Robert Davidson, son of Francis and Mary Davidson, was born December 4, 1795.
Grizelda Davidson was born July 9, 1797.
William Davidson was born November 22, 1798.
Mary Davidson was born August 6, 1800.
John Davidson was born May 27, 1802.
June Davidson was born March 26, 1804.
James Davidson was born Ocober 12, 1805.
Ratchel Davidson was born December 30, 1807.
Isaac Davidson was born October 6, 1809; died October 18, 1810.
Isaac Davidson was born August 18, 1811.

Davidson Chart

Francis	Robert	Jane	b. 3-26-1804
Davidson	b. 12-4-1795		d. 9-18-1874
b. 2-1767	d. 5-21-1885	James	b. 12-30-1807
d. 5-16-1848	Grizelda	Isaac	b. 10-6-1809
m.	b. 7-9-1797		d. 1810
Mary	William	Isaac	b. 8-8-1811
b. 11-15-1772	b. 11-22-1798	Francis	b. 3-8-1813
d. 10-24-1849	d. 8-3-1868	Esther	b. 10-28-1816
		Elizabeth	b. 1-23-1819

DAWSON FAMILY RECORD

(This is a collection of Family Records with Biographical Sketches and other data of various families and individuals bearing the name of "Dawson" and other names. Compiled by Charles C. Dawson. Owned by Mrs. Lillian R. Slaughter, of Felton, Delaware. Albany, New York, Joel Munsell, 82 State St., N.Y. 1874.)

William Dawson, a Quaker in England according to tradition, fled thence to America to escape persecution with his wife Isabella and 11 children. They were both dead when Elisha married a second time in 1821. William Dawson and Isabella's children:

1. John, born May 24, 1754; died in Caroline Co., Md., 1826. Married Anna Harris, daughter of William and Anna Harris and had 3 children.
2. Elizabeth, born July 17, 1755; married Mr. Wilson.
3. William, born April 13, 1757; died in Kentucky about 1815. Married and had 8 children.
4. Margaret, born June 13, 1758; married Mr. Perry.
5. Jonas, born May 31, 1760.
6. Edward, born December 9, 1761 - no further record.
7. Elizah, born March 9, 1764; lived in Kent Co., Delaware; married Catharine Broadway, daughter of

          Robert and Sarah Russum Broadway and had 2 children.
8. Elisha, born January 20, 1766; died near Camden, N.J., May, 1837. Married Lydia Harris (born 1-4-1771), daughter of William and Anna Harris.
9. Shadrach H., born April 23, 1768; died in Lancaster, Pa. May 24, 1838. Married Ann Callahan and had 10 children.
10. Frederick, born July 29, 1770; was a soldier in War of 1812; went to Missouri.
11. Joseph, born in Carolina Co., Md., January 26, 1773; died in Kent Co., Delaware either November or January 1824, near Mt. Moriah, Del. Married Mary Carter, widow of Edward Carter and daughter of Robert and Sarah Russum Broadway, and had 5 children. Mary B. Carter Dawson was born March 4, 1762; died July 5, 1833.

NOTE: Sarah Russum Broadway later married Rev. Edward Callahan and had 3 children. A daughter Ann; married Shadrach H. Dawson.

Children of Joseph Dawson and Mary B. Carter Dawson:

1. William Dawson died at 8 years of age.
2. Sarah, born Dec. 14, 1795; died an infant.
3. Mary, born Dec. 14, 1797; died young.
4. Robert, born Aug. 30, 1799; died in his 28th year; married Maria Cooper - no issue.
5. Mary, born June 19, 1801; resided in 1873 near Mt. Moriah, Del.; married June 21, 1822 to Isaac Gruwell. He was born June 12, 1792 and died April 8, 1849, son of John and Rachel Gruwell.

Children of Mary Dawson and Isaac Gruwell:

1. Elizabeth, born October 7, 1824; died age 2 months.

2. Joseph D., born March 19, 1828; resided in Kent Co.; married Jan. 1852 to Caroline Lewis, daughter of John and Susan Cooper Lewis, and had 8 children.
3. Eliza Ann, born October 7, 1831; married Dec. 31, 1861 to Meredith. He was born Jan. 18, 1809, and lived at Marydel, Md. in 1873.
4. John, born August 8, 1833; resided in Kent Co., Del.; married Dec. 25, 1855 to Elizabeth A. Lewis, sister of wife of Joseph D. Gruwell, and had 6 children:
    William   Mary Emily
    Walter   Henry
    Joseph Edward   Watson
5. William, born September 28, 1839.

Note by Mrs. Slaughter: Many of the Gruwell family live in and around Felton, Delaware. Elizah and Joseph Dawson are brothers and they married sisters. Shadrach, a brother, married half sister to the girls. I descend from Elijah Dawson, born 1766. Levin Caulk (L.D. Caulk & Co.) of Milford is also descended from Elijah Dawson, born 1766.

<u>William Dawson</u>
   England   John, born 1754; m. Anna Harris
<u> Isabella   </u> Elizabeth, born 1755; m. Mr. Wilson
William, born 1757
Margaret, born 1758; m. Mr. Perry
Jonas, born 1760
Edward, born 1761
Elizah, born 1764; m. Catherine
                          Broadway
Elisha, born 1766; m. Lydia Harris
Shadrach, born 1768; m. Ann Callahan
Frederick, born 1770
Joseph, born 1773; m. Mary Broadway
                          Carter

DAY FAMILY - BRANDYWINE HUNDRED, DELAWARE

(These records were taken from an old ledger now owned by Elmer W. Day, Gordon Ave., Hillcrest, Delaware. 1957. Record given by Mrs. Charles D. Bird, Wilmington, Del.)

Some entries are typed and others are hand written. This one was neatly typed:
    Memorial of the Day Family
        by Lewis B. Day, Sharon Hill, Pa.
        May 9, 1915

Benjamin Day, son of Francis and Mary Day, born April 12, 1780; died October 2, 1860.
Priscilla Kellam, wife of Benjamin Day, was born April 28, 1781; died February 19, 1866.
John Day, son of Benjamin and Priscilla Day, was born December 9, 1813; died November 4, 1894.
Matilda Bird, wife of John Day, was born February 25, 1823; died March 15, 1857; married July 4, 1844.
Eliza M. Day, born May 23, 1845; died March 20, 1911.
Lewis F. Day, born August 1, 1846; died October 14, 1846.
Priscilla Day, born August 19, 1847.
John B. Day, born November 12, 1848; died December 13, 1913.
George W. Day, born December 8, 1850; died April 14, 1923.
Sarah E. Day, born September 17, 1852; died March 11, 1940.
Mary Ida Day, born April 6, 1854; died April 14, 1927.
Benjamin H.(?) Day, born June 11, 1855.
Eunice Bird, second wife of John Day, was born December 12, 1825; married December 17, 1857; died February 22, 1907.
William S. Day, born September 16, 1858; died September 26, 1922.
Alfred Day, born June 4, 1860; died April 27, 1924.
Lewis B. Day, born April 4, 1862; died September 24, 1923.
Harry C. Day, born May 30, 1864.
Maggie E. Day, born June 15, 1866; died September 10, 1924.

Following was written in lead pencil, probably by Wm. S. Day, as the record starts with his marriage:
William S. Day, born September 16, 1858; married
    March 3, 1882.
Hannah Mary Day, born March 3, 1862; married
    March 3, 1882.
    (Elmer W. Day, her son, said her maiden name
    was Williams)
George Bayard Day, born September 12, 1882.
Anna Margaret Day, born February 17, 1884.
Addie May Day, born May 28, 1887; died
    March 25, 1888.
William Cleveland Day, born March 18, 1889.
Harry Lore Day, born December 18, 1890.
Harry John Day, born January 4, 1895.
Elmer Watson Day, born August 2, 1899.

Anna M. Day Callahan, born February 7, 1884;
    married September 24, 1904.
Francis Frederick Callahan, born May 6, 1878.
Freddie Wm. Callahan, born October 1, 1905.
Haddie May Callahan, born August 17, 1907.
George LeClarice Callahan, born May 6, 1911.

Joseph Bird   ) Parents of Matilda and Eunice
Rebecca Bird) Bird, buried at New Ark Union.

John Palmer - Susan - wife of John buried at New
    Ark Union.
Martha Jane Palmer
Rebecca Palmer
Elizabeth Bird, born November 11, 1816; died
    April 9, 1887.
Thomas Talley, daughter Leah (?)
Mary Bird
Kirk Bullock
Matilda Bird, born February 25, 1823; died 1857.
William R. Mousley
John Maxwell, born May 19, 1823; died
    March 16, 1914.
Sarah Maxwell, born September 9, 1808; died
    April 12, 1888.
Benjamin Maxwell, born July 16, 1846; died
    January 26, 1893.
Sarah Maxwell, born November 28, 1848; died
    May 29, 1864.
Mary Maxwell, sister of John B., born
    September 27, 1833; died August 7, 1911.

Gean Callahan, born January 30th year ? 20 ?.
Sam Callahan, born September 22, ?
Author Callahan, born February 26, ?
Mary Day, born August 15, 1800.
William Mousley
Harriett Day, born July 1, 1802.
John Boycxe
Elica Day, born October 15, 1805; died at
    age 37 years.
Sarah, born September 9, 1808; died
    April 12, 1888.
John Day, born December 9, 1813; died
    November 4, 1894.
John Maxwell, born May 19, 1823; died
    March 16, 1914.
William I. Simon, born May 28, 1864; married
    November 27, 1889.
Maggie E. Simon, born June 15, 1866; married
    November 27, 1889.
Ida E. Simon, born May 11, 1891.
Elsie M. Day, born May 23, 1845; died
    March 20, 1911.
(Born Eliza).

BENJAMIN DEACON'S BOOK

(Printed and sold by Collins & Co., N.Y. 1816.
Present owner: Baldwin Book Barn, R.D. 5, West
Chester, Pa. June 27, 1962. Copied by Clara
Wallace Eyre for D.A.R. Bible Records, v. 10.)

Family Record

Benjamin Deacon, son of John and Hanna Deacon, was
    born February 11, 1793.
Hannah Heulings Deacon, daughter of Joseph and
    Keturah Heuling, was born November 1, 1795;
    died June 10, 1835.
Joseph H. Deacon, son of Benjamin and Hannah
    Deacon, was born January 20, 1818.
Sarah H. Deacon, daughter of Benjamin and Hannah
    Deacon, was born October 2, 1819; died
    April 13, 1865.
John E. Deacon, son of Benjamin and Hannah Deacon,
    was born February 17, 1822.

Ann Deacon, daughter of Benjamin and Hannah, was
    born November 3, 1824.
Benjamin F. Deacon, son of Benjamin and Hannah
    Deacon, was born July 19, 1826.
Charles T. Deacon, son of Benjamin and Hannah
    Deacon, was born January 13, 1829.
George H. Deacon, son of Benjamin and Hannah
    Deacon, was born November 2, 18??

Deaths

Hannah H. Deacon died October 26, 1835.
Sarah H. Deacon died April 13, 1845.
Benjamin Deacon died August 15, 1874.
Charles T. Deacon died January 24, 18??, age
    53 years.
Ann D. Wills died May 14, 1892, age 68 years.
Benjamin F. Deacon died February 9, 1908,
    age 82 years.
Mary M. Deacon, wife of Benjamin D. Deacon, died
    December 9, 1921 at Mt. Holly, N.J., age
    89 years and 9 months.

J. W. DENNISON BIBLE

(Owned by Adaline Louise Matthews, Rodney Court
Apts., Wilmington, Del. Printed for the American
and Foreign Bible Society by the Bible Association
of Friends in America. 1846. Philadelphia.)

Marriages

Rev. J. W. Denison, son of Tho. Denison of Albany
    N.Y. to Miss M. W. Briggs, daughter of Prof.
    A. Briggs of Waterville College, Maine,
    October 19, 1846.

Married the second time, August 3, 1859 to Miss
    Eliza B. Lewis, daughter of Nathan C. Lewis
    of Seekonk, Mass., whose wife, Louise, was
    sister of Prof. A. Brigg's wife, so that
    the aforesaid Eliza B., usually called
    Lissie, was own cousin to the first wife,
    Mary W. Briggs.

Mary Louise Denison and Thomas Hooker of New Have, Conn., were married June 27, 1872.

Julia P. Denison and Rev. Albert M. Duboc of Rochester, N.Y. were married June 25, 1874.

Said Mary and Julia were each married at the house of their father in Denison, Iowa.

Maria Louisa Denison and William C. Matthews were married June 24, 1885 at Denison, Iowa.

Percy W. Denison and Isobelle Stimmel of Columbus, Ohio, were married 1907.

Births

J. W. Dennison was born Albany, N.Y., April 9, 1818.
1. Mary Denison, his wife, was born Waterville, Main, January 1, 1822.
Mary Louise Denison was born December 5, 1848, Fairfield, Herkimer, N.Y.
Julia Porter Denison was born July 19, 1851, Rock Island, Ill.

2. Eliza B. Lewis, 2nd wife of J. W. Denison, was born October 24, 1834, Seekonk, Mass.
William Sprague Denison was born Feb. 1, 1862, Denison, Crawford Co.
Jesse Lewis Denison was born May 13, 1876, Denison, Iowa.
Maria Louisa Denison was born August 17, 1866, Denison, Iowa.
Percy Nightingale Denison was born January 19, 1882, Denison, Iowa.

William Chipman Matthews was born May 31, 1861; died September 30, 1928; married Maria Louisa Denison; born August 17, 1866; died March 15, 1945.

Children

Adaline Louise Matthews was born April 7, 1886 at Des Moines, Iowa.
Margaret Matthews was born September 18, 1889 at Denver, Colorado.

Paul Denison Matthews was born January 21, 1896 at
Denver, Colorado; married Mildred McCardell
in Wilmington, Delaware.

Children

Paul Denison Matthews, Jr., was born December 17,
1918, Wilmington, Delaware; married Cecilia
Riley in Wilmington, Delaware. Children:
David Cameron Matthews, born
October 4, 1939, Wilmington, Del.
Claire Louise Matthews, born
August 31, 1940, Wilmington, Del.
Elaine Matthews, born August 1, 1943.

Deaths

Jesse Wood Denison died October 1, 1881 in
Denison, Iowa.
Mrs. Mary W. Denison died December 27, 1855 at the
house of her father in Rock Island, Ill.,
age 33 years, 11 months and 26 days.
Jesse Lewis Denison died April 1, 1877.
Percy W. Denison died June 5, 1946, Santa
Monica, Calif.
William C. Matthews died March 13, 1945,
Wilmington, Del.
Eliza B. Denison died May 31, 1931, Wilmington,
Del.
William S. Denison died April 8, 1929,
Des Moines, Iowa.

Copied by Harriett A. Shaw for Caesar Rodney
Chapter, D.A.R.

DERICKSON FAMILY

Married August 26, 1879 by the Rev. Daniel
Birtwell, 515 Kelsh Street, Chester, Pa., Jacob
Derickson and Mary E. Husbands of Brandywine Hd.,
Delaware.

Mary E. Derickson was born October 28, 1884,
   Brandywine Hd., Delaware.
Isabella A. Derickson was born January 5, 1887,
   Brandywine Hd., Delaware.
John H. Derickson was born November 7, 1890,
   Brandywine Hd., Delaware; died December 24,
   1896.
William C. Derickson was born April 21, 1892,
   Brandywine Hd., Delaware.
Bessie A. Derickson was born May 28, 1895,
   Brandywine Hd., Delaware.
Jane Derickson was born May 16, 1906,
   Brandywine Hd., Delaware.

Deaths

Jacob Derickson, father, died September 28, 1911,
   Brandywine Hd., Delaware. Buried Oct. 2,
   1911.
Mary E. Derickson, mother, died December 4, 1929,
   Brandywine Hd., Delaware. Buried Dec. 7,
   1929.
Jacob Derickson, brother, died October 30, 1929.
   Buried Nov. 2, 1929, Brandywine Hd., Delaware.

(Record given by Mrs. Clara W. Bird.)

1.
Jacob Derickson
b.
d. 9-28-1911
m. 8-26-1879
Mary E. Husbands
b.
d. 12-4-1929

2.
1. Hannah
   b. 4-1-1880
2. Jacob
   b. 9-15-1881
   d. 11-2-1929
3. Joseph H.
   Derickson
   b. 6-15-1883   1. William J.
   m. 1-5-1921   **SEE

William M. Webster   Viola Webster   NEXT
b. 12-23-1863   b. 6-15-1893   PAGE
m. 7-22-1886
Lottie Edwards
b. 12-9-1863
d. 5-1-1942
dau. of James &
Mary Edwards

Derickson Cont'd.

    4. Mary E.
       b. 10-028-1884
    5. Isabella
       b. 1-5-1887
       d. 12-24-1896
    6. William C.
       b. 4-21-1892
    7. Bessie A.
       b. 1895
    8. Jane
       b. 5-16-1906

**1. William J.
    b. 10-6-1923   Nancy
    m.   b. 19?9
    Mary   Joseph
                         b. 1956
  2. Vesta C.
     b. 5-31-1930
  3. Willard
     b. & d. 5-27-1934
  4. Mary
     b. 1-27-1925

ABSALOM DODD BIBLE

(Copied by Mrs. Elsie Robinson, 9-29-1960. Bible published by Eugene Cummiskey, 1840. Stereotyped by J. Howe. Owned by Mrs. S? Dodd Watson, daughter and widow of John A. Watson, RFD Gils Neck Road, Lewes, Del.)

    Mrs. Watson stated that her father, Absalom Dodd, had no brothers or sisters. His father died when he was less than two years old. He was raised by Jim Coverdale, who was a brother to George Coverdale of Coolspring, Del. Mr. and Mrs. Coverdale were thought of as parents by Absalom Dodd and he adopted the Coverdale relatives as his own, rather than his own Dodd relatives. Mrs. Watson did not seem to know why the mother gave Absalom up so completely. She does not remember any Messick relatives either.

Matrimonial page is missing.

Births

Hannah Hand, daughter of Nehemiah Hand and Alety his wife, was born March 14, 1820.
James McKay, son of George McKay and Elizabeth his wife, was born February 6, 1807.
Absalom Dodd, son of Absalom Dodd and Hannah his wife, was born February 24, 1855.
Eliza Jane Messick was born May 29, 1861.

Children of Absalom and Eliza Jane (Messick) Dodd:

Annie Dodd, daughter of Absalom and Eliza Dodd, was born May 17, 1886.
Effie Dodd, daughter of Absalom and Eliza Dodd, was born April 15, 1887.
Carrie Lee Dodd, daughter of Absalom and Eliza Dodd, was born April 7, 1890.
James Ralph Coverdale Dodd, son of Absalom and Eliza Dodd, was born February 24, 1892.
John Paynter Dodd, son of Absalom and Eliza Dodd, was born December 17, 1893.
Pernel Norman Dodd, son of Absalom and Eliza Dodd, was born July 26, 1895.
Hannah Marshall Dodd, daughter of Absalom and Eliza Dodd, was born May 29, 1898.
Frank Wiltbank Dodd, son of Absalom and Eliza Dodd, was born May 8, 1900.

Deaths

James McKay died June 5, 1846.
Absalom Dodd died September 17, 1856.
Absalom Dodd died November 17, 1921/2?
Eliza J. Dodd died December 10, 1903.

Mrs. Effie Steele died October 15, 1927.
John Dodd died June 27, 1943.
P. Norman Dodd died November 4, 1949.
John A. Watson died August 9, 1946; born June 20, 1885.

JOSEPH DODD BIBLE

(The Holy Bible, Old and New Testaments, with Marginal References, printed for Thomas Dobson at the Stone House, 41 S. 2nd Street, Philadelphia, Pa. 1799. Owned by William A. B. Dodd, Rehobeth Beach, Delaware. Record given by Mrs. D. Anthony Potter, Lewes, Del.)

On the flyleaf: THE JOSEPH DODD BIBLE
    Sunday morning Oct. 11, 1863 (ink blurred)
       Joseph Holland 1863

William Dodd, son of Wm. Dodd and Elizabeth his wife, was born September 14, 1775.
Eleanor Bruce, daughter of Alexander Bruce and Ester (Jacobs) his wife, was born May 29, 1778.

Eliza Turner Dodd, daughter of Wm. Dodd and Eleanor his wife, was born September 17, 1779 (in ink and corrected to 1799 in pencil).
Maria Dodd, daughter of Wm. Dodd and Eleanor his wife, was born October 24, 1801.
Comfort Bruce Dodd, daughter of Wm. Dodd and Eleanor his wife, was born February 11, 1804.
Hannah Dodd, daughter of Wm. Dodd and Elener his wife, was born December 25, 1805.
Elenor Bruce Dodd, daughter of Wm. Dodd and Elenor his wife, was born April 14, 1808.
Joseph Hazlett Dodd, son of Wm. Dodd and Elenor his wife, was born October 6, 1810.
Amy Dodd, daughter of Wm. Dodd and Elenor his wife, was born April 22, 1814.
William Alexander Dodd, son of Wm. Dodd and Elenor his wife, was born August 11, 1820.

On next page:

Ebenezer Holland and Eliza T. Dodd were married May 3, 1826.

Hannah N. Lank, daughter of Ebenezer Holland and Eliza his wife, died December 24, 1859, age 26 years, 9 months and 2 days.

On third page from front of Bible:
Ebenezer, son of John Holland and Elizabeth his wife, was born September 4, 1801.
Maria Holland, daughter of Ebenezer Holland and Eliza T. Holland his wife, was born June 18, 1827.
Ann Robbins Holland, daughter of Ebenezer Holland and Eliza his wife, was born Jan. 7, (or 11, writing very poor), 1829.
Hetty Elenor Holland, daughter of Ebenezer Holland and Eliza his wife, was born June (?) 21, 1831.
Hannah Newbold Holland, daughter of Ebenezer Holland and Eliza his wife, was born March 22, 1833.
Joseph Holland, son of Ebenezer Holland and Eliza his wife, was born September 12, 1835.
Tabitha Holland, daughter of Ebenezer Holland and Eliza his wife, was born February 11, 1837.
William Dodd Holland, son of Ebenezer Holland and Eliza his wife, was born March 22, 1839.
John Paynter Holland, son of Ebenezer Holland and Eliza his wife, was born August 6, 1841.
Albert Bruce Holland, son of Ebenezer Holland and Eliza his wife, was born January 4, 1846.

Hannah N. Lank, daughter of John C. Lank and Hannah his wife, was born November 14, 1859.

In back of Bible:

Births

John R. White, son of Wallace W. White and Tabitha his wife, was born August 21, 1863 (? faded).
Clara C. White, daughter of Wallace W. White and Tabitha his wife, was born August 26, 1865.
Benjamin B. White, son of Wallace W. White and Tabitha his wife, was born February (? faded) 19, 1868.
Louizzie May White, daughter of Wallace W. White and Tabitha his wife, was born September 22, 1870.
Katie C. White, daughter of Wallace W. White and Tabitha his wife, was born December 16 (?), 1874.

Annie E. Holland, daughter of John P. Holland and Maggie his wife, was born September 25, 1866.

Mary H. Holland, daughter of John P. Holland and
   Maggie his wife, was born July 14, 1868.

Marriages

Wallace W. White and Tabitha Holland were married
   December 24, 1862.
John P. Holland and Maggie A. White were married
   December 29, 1865?

Deaths

Maggie A. Holland, wife of John P. Holland, died
   August 18, 1869.
Mary H. Holland, daughter of John P. Holland and
   Maggie his wife, died July 10, 1869?

WILLIAM A. DODD'S BOOK

(Harding's Medium Edition. The Holy Bible. Old
and New Testaments, translated out of the
original Tongue and containing the Apocrypha,
Concordance and Psalms with the former translations
diligently compared and revised. The Text conformable
to the Oxford Edition in the Year of our Lord
1610, and the American Bible Society's original
Standard Edition of 1816. Jesper Harding and Son,
Philadelphia, 1857. Owned by Mrs. Hannah (Dodd)
Thompson, Midway, Del. Record given by Mrs. D.
Anthony Potter, Lewes, Del.)

David Miller, son of Ester Miller, was born
   September 13, 1848.
Rodney K. Prettyman, son of Joshua Prettyman and
   Jannette his wife, was born March 30, 1848.
Sarah J. Prettyman, daughter of Joshua and
   Jannette his wife, was born March 2, 1852.
Joseph, son of Samuel Stewart and Lydia his wife,
   was born April 22, 1857.
George E. L. Prettyman, son of Joshua Prettyman and
   Janette his wife, was born August 14, 1854.
James Waples, son of Ann Waples, was born
   September 30, 1860.
Richard McIlvain, son of Handy McIlvain and
   Harriet his wife, died February 25, 1857
   age 11 years, 11 months and 25 days.

Sarah T. Prettyman, daughter of Joshua and Janette his wife, died April 9, 1863, age 11 years, 1 month and 7 days.
David Miller, son of Esther Miller, died November 28, 1899.

NOTE: The Dodds say the above were all colored slaves.

Marriages

William A. Dodd and Ella S. Lank were married January 7, 1885.

Births

William Dodd, son of Wm. Dodd and Elizabeth his wife, was born September 14, 1775.
Eleanore Bruce, daughter of Alexander Bruce and Esther his wife, was born May 26, 1778.
Eliza Turner Dodd, daughter of Wm. Dodd and Eleanor his wife, was born September 17, 1799.
Maria Dodd, daughter of Wm. Dodd and Eleanor his wife, was born October 24, 1801.
Comfort Bruce Dodd, daughter of Wm. Dodd and Eleanor his wife, was born February 11, 1804.
Hannah Dodd, daughter of Wm. Dodd and Eleanor his wife, was born December 25, 1805.
Eleanor Bruce Dodd, daughter of Wm. Dodd and Eleanor his wife, was born April 14, 1808.
Joseph Haslett Dodd, son of Wm. Dodd and Eleanor his wife, was born October 6, 1810.
Amy Dodd, daughter of Wm. Dodd and Eleanor his wife, was born April 22, 1814.
William Alexander Dodd, son of Wm. Dodd and Eleanor his wife, was born August 11, 1820.

Ella S. Lank, daughter of James Lank and Maria his wife, was born July 26, 1851.

William Alexander Bruce Dodd, son of William A. Dodd and Ella S. his wife, was born November 18, 1885.
Hannah Maria Dodd, daughter of William A. Dodd and Ella S. his wife, was born November 26, 1886.
Eleanor Comfort Dodd, daughter of William A. Dodd and Ella S. his wife, was born March 16, 1892.

Deaths

William Dodd, son of Wm. Dodd and Elizabeth his
    wife, died March 31, 1838.
Eleanor Dodd, daughter of Alexander Bruce and
    Esther his wife, died April 3, 1840.
Maria Rust, daughter of William Dodd and Eleanor
    his wife, died May 31, 1858.
Eleanor Bruce Holland, daughter of Wm. Dodd and
    Eleanor his wife, died July 26, 1863.
Eliza T. Holland, daughter of Wm. Dodd and Eleanor
    his wife, died August 13, 1865.
Amy Rust, daughter of Wm. Dodd and Eleanor his
    wife, died October 7, 1868.
Joseph H. Dodd, son of William Dodd and Eleanor
    his wife, died April 10, 1883.
Comfort B. Holland, daughter of William Dodd and
    Eleanor his wife, died October 18, 1883.
Hannah Dodd, daughter of William Dodd and Eleanor
    his wife, died June 30, 1884.
William A. Dodd, son of William Dodd and Eleanor
    his wife, died July 8, 1896.
Ella S. Dodd, daughter of James Lank and Maria
    his wife, died June 14, 1927.
William G. Dodd, son of Joseph H. Dodd and Ann B.
    his wife, died October 29, 1926.

James Newbold died August 25, 1831.
Hannah Newbold died August 14, 1825.

DRAGOO BIBLE

(Copied by Rev. Albert Bell, Delaware Historical
Society.)

The Dragoos came to Delaware from Michigan.

Chart, next page.

Dragoo Chart:

John C. Dragoo
b. 5-27-1828
d. 1-19-1901
   age 71
m. 11-22-1849
Rebecca Ann
Boron
b. 9-26-1829
d. 4-17-1905
   age 75

1. Sarah E. Dragoo
   b. 7-31-1851
   m. Higgins
2. M.H.
   b. 4-1-1853
3. Henryetta
   b. 9-25-1855
4. Alice
   b. 3-22-1858
   m. Samis

     1. Annemary
       b. 3-11-1871
     2. Merit Elmer
       b. 3-2-1874

     1. Ida May
       b. 6-30-1875
     2. Frankie
       b. 7-18-1877
     3. Julia
       b. 10-10-1879

5. Emma G.
   b. 9-15-1860
   m. Levi Lewis Gray
   b. 5-31-1881
6. James Ezekiel
   b. 1-23-1865
7. Elmer Elsworth
   b. 9-22-1865
8. Ida Romilda
   b. 12-13-1868 (Millie)
   m. 5-4-1888,
   Samuel Cubbage
9. John Adelbert
   b. 8-22-1871
10. Martha Adella
   m. 12-19-1895
   James B. Hatfield

James B.
Hatfield
b. 10-30-1870
Martha A.
Dragoo

1. Lanah E.
   Hatfield
   b. 1-13-1896
   m.
   12-24-1913
   Lincoln, Del.
   Charles Benson
   b. 6-7-1889
   Georgetown,
   Del.

     1. Herman Roach
       Benson
       b. 2-9-1915
     2. Ruth Adella
     3. Edythe Louise
       b. 6-6-1919
     4. Janet
       b. 11-25-1927

Ella Marie Wilkins, b. 2-27-1910;
   daughter of Martha A. Dragoo.

DUFF BIBLE RECORD

(Printed in London in 1712. Now owned by the
Delaware Historical Society, Wilmington, Del.
Record copied by Mrs. Glenn S. Skinner, Newark.)

Richard Duff was born July 10, 1757.
Ann Duff was born November 5, 1758.
Henry Duff died September 14, 1762.
John Pickles and Ann Davis were married
   April 2, 1749.
Richard Pickles was born January 31, 1750.
Sarah Pickles, daughter of John and Ann, was
   born November 5, 1751.
John Pickles died September 3, 1755.
Richard Pickles died November 10, 1756.

Martha ----? Rachel Moore was born March 1(?),
   1763.
Mathew Moore was born March 31, 1765.

Ann Moore died July 21, 1765, age 38 years.
Sarah Williams died October 30, 1730.
Edwin Thomas died April 11, 1722, age 54 years.
John Pickles, Sr., died December 24, 1736.
Richard Pickles died November 10, 1756.
Martha Moore died September 1772.

Ann Flower, December 12, in her 24th year.

Col. Thomas Duff died 1807; married Jane Williams
   1751. He was a soldier, churchman, Major in
   the Militia. Commanded forces in Trenton,
   Princeton and Brandywine. Was a member of
   the Vestry at St. James Episcopal Church at
   Santon, Del. Land papers 1760-76, etc.
   Children:
   1. Ann Duff, born May 24, 1752; died
      March 16, 1780.
   2. Dr. Edward Duff, born March 17,
      1755; died April 2, 1785. He was
      a surgeon in Col. Samuel
      Patterson's Flying Camp. Received
      cerificate in anatomy and Surgery
      at U. of Pa. 1780.

3. John Duff, born March 24, 1757; died August 12, 1759.
4. Capt. Henry Duff, born June 15, 1759; died February 8, 1785; ensign in Col. Hall's Regiment; a member of the Cincinnati Society.
5. Jane Duff, born April 15, 1763; died March 1, 1788.
6. Thomas Duff, born September 27, 1766; Revolutionary War soldier.

From a paper found in the Duff Bible:

JOHN ALLEN

My grandfather, John Allen, was born in the year sixteen hundred and ninety four and on the third day of the eighth month old stile and on the fourteenth day of the tenth month new stile. 8-3-1694.

My grandfather, John Allen, departed this life the sixteenth day of the ninth month in the year one thousand seven hundred and seventy one, age 70 years, 11 months, 2 days. 9-16-1771.

My grandmother, Emey Allen, departed this life the thirteenth day of the ninth month one thousand seven hundred and seveny eight. 9-13-1778.

My father, William Allen, was born the third day of the eighth month old stile and on the fourteenth day of the tenth month new stile in the year one thousand seven hundred and thirty. 8-3-1730.

My mother, Sarah Allen, was born the fifteenth day of the ninth month old stile and on the twenty sixth day of the eleventh month new stile in the year one thousand seven hundred and thiry eight. 9-15-1738.

My sister, Jane Allen, was born the twentieth of the fifth month in the year one thousand seven hundred and fifty nine. 5-20-1759.

John Allen, son of William Allen and Sarah, was born the twenty seventh day of the eleventh month in the year one thousand seven hundred and sixty five. 11-27-1765.

My mother, Sarah Allen, departed this life the twenty fifth day of the tenth month in the year one thousand seven hundred and seventy five. 7-25-1775.

My half-brother, William Allen, was born the ninth day of the eighth month in the year one thousand seven hundred and eighty. 8-9-1780.

My half-brother, Ellie Allen, was born the twenty seventh day of the seventh month in the year one thousand seven hundred and eighty three.

My uncle, Benjamin Allen, departed this life the twenty third day of the ninth month in the year 1792, aged about 50. 9-23-1792.

Ant Hannah Allen, wife of Benjamin Allen, departed this life the twenty ninth day of the first month one thousand eight hundred and twelve.

Uncle Joseph Allen born the twelfth day of the seventh month old stile seventeen hundred and thirty three.

My sister, Jane Cloud, departed this life the twenty sixth day of the fifth month eighteen hundred and fourteen. Aged fifty five years and six days. 5-26-1814.

The above wrote by me, John Allen.

JOHN EASTWICK RECORD

(Record is owned by Mrs. Edward Zebley, Foulk Road, Wilmington. Given by Mrs. Charles D. Bird, Wilmington, Del.)

John Eastwick was born 1752 and lived in Newton, Bucks Co., Pa. until about 1787, when he came to Philadelphia and then moved to New Castle County, Delaware.

He first married Sarah Smith at St. Michael's and Zion Lutheran Church, Philadelphia, October 18, 1773.

He married his second wife, Rebecca Cherry, January 17, 1795, by whom he had no children.

There were 8 children by his first wife, viz:
    Letitia Eastwick; married 1789,
        John Wright, had 14 children.
    Thomas Eastwick, born August 30, 1775;
        died November 1816; married
        Margaret McCalla, June 19, 1797
        and had 7 children.
    Stephen Eastwick, married Elizabeth Cale
        of Egg Harbor, N.J., 7 children.
    Mary Eastwick, married Abram Vickers,
        April 21, 1791 and had 2 children.
    Rachel Eastwick, married Wm. Burnett -
        no issue.
    Wm. Smith Eastwick - unmarried.
    Hannah Eastwick, born March 21, 1789;
        died June 16, 1870; married
        Nicholas Grubb, July 15, 1812 and
        had 8 children.
    John Eastwick, born August 7, 1793; died
        September 8, 1793.

Stephen Eastwick, son of John and Sarah Smith
    Eastwick, died 1852; married Elizabeth Cale.
    Children:
        Mary, born 1802; died 1893; married
            Isaac Weer and had 11 children.
        John, married Elizabeth Warmick and
            had 7 children.
        Eliza, married John Sutton.
        Emeline, married John Wolverton.
        Matilda, born 1817; died 1887; married
            John Wible and had 5 children.
        Hannah, married Henry Tyson and had
            2 children.
        Thomas, married Kate Mason and had
            2 children.
        Sarah, born 1806; married Ruben Mousley.

NOTE: Mrs. Zebley was Bessie G. McGlaughlin,
        daughter of George and Esther A. (Weer)
        McGlaughlin; granddaughter of Isaac and
        Mary (Eastwick) Weer.

Tombstone Record in the Bethel Methodist Churchyard on Foulk Rd.

JOHN EASTWICK
Born 1752, Bucks County, Pa.
Died 1834 in Brandywine Hd.
Sergeant in 5th Regiment
Continental Troops   1776-1777
Stone erected by his Descendants
1916

Eastwick Chart

1.
John Eastwick   2.
b. 1752   1. Letitia
d.   m.
m. 1st   John Wright
10-18-1773
Sarah Smith   2. Thomas
m. 2nd   b. 8-30-1775
1-17-1795   d. 11-1816
Rebecca   m. 6-19-1797
Cherry   Margaret McCalla

                      3. Stephen   3.
                         d. 1852   1. Mary   4.
                         m.   b. 1802   Esther
                         Elizabeth   d. 1893   Weer
                         Cale   m. Isaac   m.
                                             Weer   George
                                                             McClaughlin

                      4. Mary
                         m. 4-21-1791
                         Abram Vickers
                                          2. John, m.
                                             E. Warmick
                      5. Rachel   3. Eliza, m.
                         m.   John Sutton
                         Wm. Burnett   4. Emeline, m.
                                             John Wolverton
                                          5. Matilda, m.
                      6. William S.   John Wible

- 122 -

Eastwick Chart Cont'd.

7. Hannah
b. 3-21-1789
d. 6-16-1870
m. 7-15-1812
Nicholas
Grubb
8. John
b. & d. 1793

6. Hannah, m.
Henry Tyson
7. Thomas, m.
Kate Mason
8. Sarah, m.
Ruben Mousley

5.
Bessie McGlaughlin
m.
Edward Zebley

EDWARDS - LAWSON RECORD

(Bible published by Andrus, Judd and Franklin, Hartford, Conn. 1838. Owned by Mrs. Leslie Bamberger (Alice Peters), now living in West Point, Georgia. 1956.)

Marriages

Richard Edwards and Mary A. Lawson were married
    June 11, 1854.
Frank J. Peters and Charlotte M. Edwards were
    married April 6, 1881.

NOTE: Mrs. Bamberger said that her father's name was John Franklin Peters.

Albert L. Edwards and Susan Bailey were married
    April 6, 1887.
John F. Veale, Jr. and Isabella R. Edwards were
    married May 9, 1889.
William L. Cloud and Mary E. Edwards were married
    April 11, 1898.

Births

Albert L. Edwards was born August 2, 1855.
Charlotte M. Edwards was born November 27, 1859.
Lorena W. Edwards was born June 29, 1864.

Isabella R. Edwards was born December 4, 1867.
Mary E. Edwards was born June 19, 1870.
Alice L. Edwards was born November 21, 1872.

Sons and daughters of William and Mary Lawson:
    Jane Lawson was born July 25, 1808.
    Francis Lawson was born January 21, 1811.
    William Lawson was born December 20, 1812.
    Charlotte Lawson was born November 18, 1816.
    Rebecca Lawson was born November 11, 1819.
    John Lawson was born July 20, 1823.
    Craven Lawson was born June 18, 1827.
    Ellen E. Lawson was born November 5, 1829.
    Mary Ann Lawson was born April 29, 1833.

Deaths

Luke Lawson died December 15, 1815, age 38 years.
Robert Lawson died May 4, 1834.
George Lawson died 1847.
John Lawson died 1848.
William Lawson died June 30, 1852, age 74 years.
Robert C. Lawson died May 28, 1858, age 31 years.
Mary Lawson died January 14, 1873, age 82 years.
William Lawson, Jr., died November 29, 1883, age 71 years.
Alice L. Edwards died October 29, 1884.
Lorena W. Edwards died June 21, 1886.
Mary A. Edwards died November 19, 1898.
Rebecca Williams died March 29, 1902 at Claymont, Delaware. (Was Rebecca Lawson.)
J. Franklin Peters died December 19, 1913.
Richard W. Edwards died December 16, 1915.

<u>William Lawson</u>
b. 1778
d. 6-30-1852
m.
<u>Mary</u>
b. 1791
d. 1-14-1873

1. Jane Lawson
   b. 7-25-1808
2. Francis
   b. 1-21-1811
3. William
   b. 12-20-1812
   d. 11-29-1883
4. Charlotte
   b. 11-18-1816
5. Rebecca
   b. 11-11-1819
   d. 1902
   m. Williams

Edwards-Lawson Chart Cont'd.

    6. John
       b. 7-20-1823
    7. Craven
       b. 6-18-1827
    8. Ellen
       b. 11-5-1829
    9. Mary Ann Lawson   1. Albert L.
       b. 4-29-1833   b. 8-2-1855
       d. 1898   m. 4-6-1887
       m. 6-11-1854   Susan Bailey
       Richard Edwards 2. Charlotte
                           b. 11-27-1859
                           d. 1955
                           m. 4-6-1881
                           Frank J. Peters
                           d. 12-19-1913
                    3. Lorena
                       b. 6-29-1864
                       d. 6-21-1886
                  4. Isabella
                       b. 12-4-1867
                       m. 5-9-1889
                       John Veale, Jr.
                  5. Mary
                       b. 6-19-1870
                       m. 4-11-1894
                       Wm. Cloud
                  6. Alice
                       b. 11-21-1872
                       d. 1884

ELDER - FOSTER RECORD

(The Holy Bible. Based upon the Authorized Version of the Old and New Testaments. Published by The S.A. Mullikin Company, Marrietta, Ohio. The owner is Early Joy, Brookneal, Virginia.)

Llewllyn Elder, son of Oliver Elder and Martha
    Jones Elder, was born October 9, 1825.
Martha Ann Foster was born March 21, 1833.
John Wesley Elder, son of Llewellyn Elder and
    Martha Ann Foster Elder, was born August 26,
    1852; married Anna Bettterton.

Nannie Witt Elder, daughter of Llewellyn and
    Martha Elder, was born November 20, 1856;
    married Inman Suddith.
William Henry Elder, son of Llewellyn and Martha
    Elder, was born August 9, 1857; married
    Edna Monroe.
Roxana Elder, daughter of Llewellyn and Martha
    Elder, was born April 6, 1859; married
    Charlie Monroe.
Sylvester Elder, son of Llewellyn and Martha
    Elder, was born July 2, 1860; married
    Nannie Estella Dowdy.
Emma Elder, daughter of Llewellyn and Martha
    Elder, was born November 1, 1863; married
    Thomas Mason.
Robert Lee Elder, son of Llewellyn and Martha Elder,
    was born May 8, 1865; married Nannie Stephens.
Lucy Elnora Elder, daughter of Llewellyn and Martha
    Elder, was born October 4, 1867; married
    Burrues E. Pool.
George Washington Elder, son of Llewellyn and Martha
    Elder, was born April 5, 1869; married
    Anna Watts.
Charles Oliver Elder, son of Llewellyn and Martha
    Elder, was born June 17, 1872; married
    Lula Francis.
Rosa Holmes Elder, daughter of Llewellyn and Martha
    Elder, was born March 15, 1872; married
    Charlie Hunter.
Samuel Bunyan Elder, son of Llewellyn and Martha
    Elder, was born August 28, 1877; married
    Lula Elder.

Marriages

Ephriam Elder and Martha Patsy Matthews of
    Campbell Co., Va. were married July 9, 1787.
Oliver Elder and Martha Jones, daughter of
    Lewellyn Jones, were married in Campbell Co.,
    Va. in 1815.
Llewellyn Elder and Martha Ann Foster of Campbell
    Co., Va. were married April 24, 1851.
Sylvester Elder and N. Estella Dowdy of Campbell
    Co., Va. were married March 22, 1893.

Deaths

Ephriam Elder died in 1800 in Campbell Co., Va.

Martha (Patsy) Elder Moore died January 6, 1846
    in Campbell Co., Va.
Oliver Elder died in 1867 in Campbell Co., Va.
Llewellyn Elder died October 2, 1906 in Campbell
    Co., Va.
Martha Ann Foster Elder died May 2, 1917 in
    Campbell Co., Va.
Estella Elder died June 26, 1928 in Campbell
    Co., Va.
Sylvester Elder died December 25, 1944 in
    Campbell Co., Va.

Children of Sylvester Elder and Estella Dowdy
Elder:
    Martha Ann Elder was born February 12, 1896.
    William Lee Elder was born November 9, 1897.
    Josephine Elder was born August 3, 1899.
    Russell Burns Elder was born October 6, 1902.
    Alma Royall Elder was born April 9, 1905.
    Virginia Gillem Elder was born November 14,
        1908.
    Mary Elizabeth Elder was born April 27, 1913.
    Louise Estella Elder was born November 14,
        1917.

ELLIS FAMILY RECORD

(Printed by M'Carty & Davis, 171 Market Street,
Philadelphia, Pa. 1834. Now owned by Mr. Harry
Ellis, Lewes, Delaware.)

Family Record

Marriages

Isaiah Ellis and Hetty P. Townsend were married
    April 10, 1844.

Births

Hetty P. Ellis, daughter of John Townsend and
    Hetty his wife, was born February 17, 1821.
John S. Ellis, son of Isaiah and Hetty P. Ellis,
    was born April 17, 1845.
Martin L. Ellis, son of Isaiah and Hetty P. Ellis,
    was born January 15, 1848.

Isaiah M. Ellis, son of Isaiah and Hetty P. Ellis,
    was born March 8, 1854.
Martha E. Ellis, daughter of Isaiah and Hetty P.
    Ellis, was born June 8, 1858.
Mary H. T. Ellis, daughter of Isaiah and Hetty P.
    Ellis, was born August 23, 1864.

Lovey Ellis, daughter of Stephen and Mary Ellis,
    was born June 5, 1813.
Stephen Ellis, son of Stephen and Mary Ellis, was
    born November 10, 1814.
Levin Ellis, son of Stephen and Mary Ellis, was
    born December 26, 1816.
Martha Evans, daughter of Stephen and Mary Ellis,
    was born June 2, ?
Sally Dirickson, daughter of Stephen and Mary
    Ellis, was born September 8, 1821.

John B. Dirickson, son of Nathaniel M. Dirickson
    and Elizabeth his wife, was born November 21,
    1829.
Stephen E. Dirickson, son of Nathaniel and
    Elizabeth Dirickson his wife, was born
    December 16, 1830.
Stephen Ellis, son of William and Elizabeth Ellis,
    was born December 16, 1772.
Mary Ellis, wife of Stephen Ellis, was born
    October 14, 1778.
Nathaniel Ellis, son of Stephen and Mary Ellis,
    was born January 15, 1801.
Elizabeth Dirickson, daughter of Stephen and Mary
    Ellis, was born June 27, 1805.
John T. Ellis, son of Stephen and Mary Ellis, was
    born May 13, 1807.
William Ellis, son of Stephen and Mary Ellis, was
    born August 20, 1809.
Isaiah Ellis, son of Stephen and Mary Ellis, was
    born November 11, 1811.

Deaths

John S. Ellis, son of Isaiah and Hetty P. Ellis,
    died October 6, 1852, age 7 years, 5 months
    and 19 days.
Lovey Ellis, daughter of Stephen and Mary Ellis,
    died December 14, 1813.
Stephen Ellis, son of Stephen and Mary Ellis, died
    July 6, 1827.

Levin Ellis, son of Stephen and Mary Ellis, died
    June 29, 1834.
Martha Evans, daughter of Stephen and Mary Ellis,
    and wife of N. W. Evans, died November 10,
    1867, age 48 years, 3 months and 8 days.
Sally Dirickson, daughter of Stephen and Mary
    Ellis, and wife of J. B. Dirickson, died
    August 1, 1885.
John B. Dirickson, son of Nathaniel M. Dirickson
    and Elizabeth, died September 11, 1834.
Stephen E. Dirickson, son of Nathaniel M.
    Dirickson and Elizabeth, died January 10,
    1851, shot by Peter M. Dirickson.
Stephen Ellis, son of William and Elizabeth Ellis,
    died January 28, 1834, age 61 years, 1 month
    and 12 days.
Mary Ellis, daughter of Wm. and Nanny Taylor
    widow of Stephen Ellis, died February 7,
    1859, age 81 years, 3 months and 24 days.
Nathaniel Ellis, son of Stephen and Mary, died
    August 30, 1854, age 53 years, 7 months
    and 15 days.
Elizabeth Dirickson, wife of Nathaniel M.
    Dirickson, died January 3, 1831.
John T. Ellis, son of Stephen and Mary Ellis,
    died June 18, 1825, age 18 years, 2 months
    and 5 days.
William Ellis, son of Stephen and Mary Ellis,
    died June 23, 1824, age 14 years, 10 months
    and 3 days.
Isaiah Ellis, son of Stephen and Mary Ellis, died
    November 23, 1886, age 75 years and 18 days.

Wm. Ellis			
	Stephen Ellis	1.	Nathaniel
Elizabeth	b. 12-16-1772	2.	Elizabeth
	d. 1-28-1834		b. 1805; d. 1831;
Wm. Taylor	m.		m. Nathaniel
	Mary Taylor		Derickson
Nannie	b. 10-14-1778	3.	John, b. 1807
	d. 2-7-1859	4.	William, b. 1809

Ellis Chart Cont'd. next page.

Ellis Chart Con'd.
        5. Isaiah
             b. 1811; d. 1886;
             m. Hetty P.
                Townsend
        6. Lovey
             b. 1813; d. 1813
        7. Stephen
             b. 1814; d. 1827
        8. Levin
             b. 1816; d. 1834
        9. Martha
             d. 1867; m.
             N. W. Evans
       10. Sally
             b. 1821; d. 1885;
             m. J. B. Derickson

ENTRIKIN FAMILY

(Ref. Pennock Family Genealogy by G. V. Massey.
Pennock Family by Charles Rudolph. Data at Del.
Hist. Soc.)

Christopher
Pennock   1. John
                     b. 6-24-1665 Cork Friends Mt.
m. 1st   2. Hannah
Dorothy   3. Sarah
Harwood   4. Elizabeth
d. 5-4-1671   5. Ann
m. 2nd   6. Joseph Pennick
Mary
Coolett   m.   William Pennick

                Mary Levis   Phoebe Pennick

                Wm. Mendenhall   Alice Mendinhall

                                      Jacob Way

Chart cont'd next page.

- 130 -

Annie Way
Caleb
Entrikin

Emmer Entrikin
b. 10-20-1803
d. 9-28-1879
Susanna Bennett
b. 2-14-1807
d. 10-9-1875
m. 12-16-1828

John King

Hannah
Chaney

Eli T. King

Mary L.
Mendinhall

1. Franklin Wayne Entrikin
   b. 7-27-1830;
   d. 5-13-1897;
   m. 10-1-1852
   Sarah Lyon
2. James Bennett Entrikin
   b. 3-6-1832;
   d. 7-12-1887;
   m. 2-14-1861;
   Martha McGarven
3. Caleb Barton Entrikin
   b. 7-27-1835;
   d. 4-28-1903;
   m. 1-20-1859;
   Anna M. King
4. Ann Amanda Entrikin
   b. 8-30-1837;
   d. 1909
5. Emmor Elwood Entrikin
   b. 4-12-1840;
   d. 1-30-1884;
   m. 5-3-1863;
   Mary Jane Chisholm
6. Ferdinand
   b. 8-30-1842;
   d. 5-29-1869
7. Edwin
   b. 8-27-1846;
   m. 2-14-1878
   Ursula Berleda
   Carpenter
   Ursula, b. 6-29-1855

Edwin Entrikin
b. 8-27-1846

m. 2-14-1878
Ursula
Burleda
Carpenter
b. 6-29-1855

1. Albert Entrikin
   b. 9-24-1879;
   m. 7-2-1910;
   Nellie Carter -
   Zela Alberta Entrikin
   b. 2-22-1916
2. Laura Edna Entrikin
   b. 8-7-1880;
   m. 8-24-1910
   Armour M. Gilbert
   son of Marien Francis

Chart cont'd. next page.

3. Malvern Edwin
   b. 10-8-1883;
   m. Stella VanBibber,
   dau. of Geo. & Julietta
   Ch: Ellwood, b. 3-10-1910; d. 1910
       Richard Dean, b. 9-14-1911;
       m. Frances McClure 8-14-33 and
       Raeburn Lamb, b. 9-2-1913.

4. <u>Grace Anna Entrikin</u>
   b. 11-15-1885   1. Beula Ruby Orr
   m. 10-23-1904   b. 8-25-1905
   <u>Clarence Orr</u>   2. Viola Ursula
                            b. 12-15-1906
                            m. Ellis G.
                               Martin
                         3. Mary Elizabeth

                         <u>See below</u>:

   3. Mary Elizabeth
      b. 12-20-1909   1. Paul Eugene
      m. 2-15-1930   Lotz
         Don Lotz   b. 7-7-1931
                         2. Teresa Joan
                            Lotz
                            b. 9-5-1933

   4. Edwin Clarence Orr
      b. 5-25-1912

5. <u>Mary Ruby Entrikin</u>
   b. 9-25-1887
Wm. C.   m. 5-1-1917
<u>Hilliard</u> <u>DeWitt T. Hilliard</u>

<u>Vesta Albite</u>

ESTELL FAMILY BIBLE

(The Self-Interpreting Holy Bible. Published by American Bible Publishing Co., No. 22 Park Place, New York. 1873. Owned by Mr. Harry Estell, Lewes, Delaware.)

<u>Marriages</u>

John Black Estell and Anna Mary Henderson were
   married November 8, 1860.

- 132 -

Howard Estell and Anna Whartnaby were married
    June 29, 1907.
Harry Howard Estell and Emma Davidson were married
    April 19, 1932.

Births

Frank Stephens Estell was born August 25, 1861.
Thomas Estell was born January 17, 1863.
John B. Estell was born February 5, 1865.
Harry Esttell was born August 29, 186(7?).
John Vedder Estell was born January 20, 1871.
Howard Estell was born March 19, 1873.
Morris Leslie Estell was born August 24, 1875.
William Raymond Estell was born January 24, 1878.

Grandchildren:

Beatrice Estell was born February 14, 1904.
Harry Howard Estell was born December 29, 1908.

John B. Estell was born July 4, 1832.
Annie M. Estell was born December 20, 1836.

NOTE: In this Bible was a small Family Register, taken from some other Bible:

    Parents names: Husband: Howard Estell, born March 19, 1873, son of John B. Estell and Anna May Estell.
    Wife: Anna B. Whartnaby, born May 17, 1882, daughter of Ellen F. Whartnaby and Joseph Whartnaby.

Howard Estell was born March 19, 1873.
Anna B. Estell was born May 17, 1882.
Harry Howard Estell, son, was born December 29, 1908.
Robert Clark, son, was born April 20, 1914.
Westley Orcutt Estell, son, was born May 31, 1921.
Elizebert Anna Estell, granddaughter, was born April 13, 1933.
Anna May Estell Henderson was born December 20, 1836.
John Black Estell was born July 4, 1832.

Joseph (spelled Joesph) Whartnaby was born
December 15, 1848.
Ellen F. Whartnaby was born August 27, 1853.

Deaths

Frank Stephens Estell died September 8, 1862, age
1 year and 14 days.
Thomas Estell died July 29, 1863, age 6 months and
12 days.
John B. Estell, Jr. died July 6, 1868, age 3
years and 5 months.
Morris Leslie Estell died October 24, 1882, age
7 years and 2 months.
Beatrice Estell died February 3, 1905.
Harry Estell died January 3, 1939, age 72 years
and 4 months.
Elizabert Anna Estell died at birth April 13, 1933.
William Raymond Estell died November 6, 1940; age
62 years.
My father died January 1, 1881, John B. Estell.
Anna B. Estell died May 1, 1946; age 64; wife of
Howard Estell born 1882 in Philadelphia, Pa.

Mother - Anna Mary Estell, died 1906, age 70; wife
of John Black Estell.
Annie Estell died February 12, 1947, age 76; wife
of Harry Estell born 1870.
My mother - Anna Estell, died January 22, 1874,
age 73 years, 3 months and 6 days.
My father - William Estell, died July 20, 1862,
age 60 years.
Mother Ellen F. Whartnaby died June 10, 1931.
Father Joseph Whartnaby died January 24, 1920.
Son Westley Orcutt Estell died June 22, 1921.
Son Robert Clark died April 20, 1914.
Granddaughter Elizebert Anna Estell doed April 13,
1933.
Mother Anna M. Estell died October 6, 1906.
Father John B. Estell died January 1, 1881.

Estell Chart on next page.

Estell Chart

John Black
Estell
b. 7-4-1832
d. 1-1-1881
m. 11-8-1860
Annie M.
Henderson
b. 12-20-1836
d. 1906

Howard Estell
b. 3-19-1873
m. 6-29-1907

Harry H. Estell
b. 12-29-1908   Elizebert
m. 4-9-1932   Estell
Emma   b. and d.
Davidson   4-13-1933

Joseph
Whartnaby
b. 12-15-1848
d. 1-24-1920
m.
Ellen F.
b. 8-27-1853
d. 6-10-1931

Anna Whartnaby
b. 1882
d. 5-1-1946

JOHN AND ESTHER FARRA

(Bible published by American Bible Society, New York. 1856. Owned by Herbert Downing, Wilmington, Delaware. 1956. Record given by Mrs. Charles Bird.)

"John and Esther Farra from their affectionate
    Sister, Lizzie Davidson."

Births

John M. Farra was born November 13, 1813.
Esther Farra was born October 28, 1816.
George D. Farra, son of John and Esther Farra,
    was born October 11, 1841.
John W. Farra was born February 15, 1843.
Mary J. Farra was born December 25, 1844.
Sarah E. Farra was born August 4, 1847.
Louisa A. Farra was born April 24, 1850.
Emma V. Farra was born January 5, 1855.
Hannah M. Farra was born October 30, 1860.
Wilmer R. Farra was born October 7, 1877, son
    of John and Maggie Farra.

Deaths

John M. Farra died September 5, 1881, age 68 years.
Esther Farra died August 5, 1899, age 82 years
and 10 months.
George D. Farra died (no dates shown).
J. Worthington Farra died December 1914.
Emma V. Downing died January 27, 1905.
Louisa A. Farra died February 19, 1930.

Downing - Farra

(Bible published by Keystone Publishing Co.,
Harrisburg, Pa. 1872. Owned by Herbert Downing,
Wilmington, Del. 1956. Record given by Mrs.
Charles Bird.)

This is to certify that Elijah J. Downing and Emma
V. Farra were united By Me in Holy Matrimony, at
1236 S. 4th Street, Philadelphia, on the Twentieth
day of December in the year of our Lord 1882. In
the presence of T. W. Downing and H. M. Farra.
                              Enoch Stubbs.

Marriages

Herbert E. Downing and Ellen A. Allen were married
   June 16, 1909.
Leslie (Leslie) F. Downing and Elsie M. Sheldon
   were married October 14, 1914.

Births

Elijah J. Downing, son of John R. and Rebecca, was
   born February 15, 1852.
Emma V. Downing, daughter of John M. and Esther
   Farra, was born January 5, 1855.
Ethel V. Downing, daughter of Elijah J. and Emma
   V. Downing, was born August 28, 1884.
Herbert E. Downing, son of Elijah J. and Emma V.
   Downing, was born June 8, 1886.
Mildred L. Downing, daughter of Elijah J. and
   Emma V. Downing, was born May 10, 1890.
Leslie F. Downing, son of Elijah J. and Emma V.
   Downing, was born January 17, 1894.

Deaths

Ethel V. Downing died October 24, 1886.

Emma V. Downing died January 27, 1905.
Elijah J. Downing died April 27, 1927.
Mildred Downing died June 21, 1950.

John M. Farra
b. 11-13-1813
d. 9-5-1881
m.
Esther
d. 8-5-1899
	1. George D.
	  b. 10-11-1841
	2. John W.
	  b. 2-15-1843
	  d. 1914
	  m. Maggie
	3. Mary T.
	  b. 12-25-1844
	4. Sarah
	  b. 8-4-1847
	5. Louisa A.
	  b. 4-24-1859;
	  d. 1930
		Wilmer R.
		b. 10-7-1877

John R.
Downing
m.
Rebecca
	6. Emma V.
	  b. 1-5-1855
	  d. 1-27-1905
	  m. 12-20-1882
	  Elijah J.
	  Downing
	  b. 2-15-1852
	  d. 4-27-1927
	7. Hannah
	  b. 1860
		1. Ethel V.
		  b. 1884;
		  d. 1886
		2. Herbert
		  b. 6-8-1886
		  m. 6-16-1909
		  Ella Allen
		3. Leslie
		  b. 1896
		  m.
		  Elsie Sheldon
		4. Mildred
		  b. 1890

FENEMORE - DONOHO BIBLE

Births

John Fenemore was born April 14, 1786.
Sarah Lord was born March 4, 1786.
A. Elizabeth Fenemore, daughter of John and Sarah
    Fenemore, was born November 23, 1810.
James Lord Fenemore, son of John and Sarah
    Fenemore, was born December 18, 1812.
Sarah J. Fenemore, daughter of John and Sarah
    Fenemore, was born February 7, 1815.
Keria Ellen Fenemore, daughter of John and Sarah
    Fenemore, was born January 28, 1818.

Mary Rebecca Fenemore, daughter of John and
    Sarah Fenemore, was born January 25, 1820.
John Ford Fenemore, son of John and Sarah
    Fenemore, was born August 3, 1825.

Mathew Edgar Donoho, son of Joseph and A----
    Donoho, was born December (?) 22, 1838.
John Pemberton, son of Joseph and A. E. Donoho,
    was born May 21, 1843.
Joseph Franklin, son of Joseph and A. E. Donoho,
    was born December 3, 1845.
William Randall, son of Joseph and A. E. Donoho,
    was born July 16, 1848.
Harriet George, daughter of Joseph and A. E.
    Donoho, was born April 20, 1851.
George Smith, son of Joseph and A. E. Donoho,
    was born August 11, 1852.
Attalus, son of Joseph and A. E. Donoho, was
    born January 28, 1856.
James E. Donoho was born February 10 (?), 1866.
Carrie A. Groff, daughter of Abram Groff and
    S. E. Groff, and wife of Attalus Donoho, was
    born July 10, 1859.

Deaths

James L. Fenemore, son of John and Sarah Fenemore,
    died March 13, 1876.
Keria Ellen Fenemore, daughter of John and Sarah
    Fenemore, died in her fourth year, 1822.
John Ford Fenemore, son of John and Sarah
    Fenemore, died August 27, 1825.
M. Edgar Donoho, son of James and A. Elizabeth
    Donoho, died March 22, 1850.
Harriet Donoho, daughter of Joseph and A. E.
    Donoho, died August 31, 1851.
J. Pemberton Donoho, son of Joseph and A. E.
    Donoho, died November 26, 1884.
Ann Elizabeth Donoho, wife of Joseph Donoho,
    died October 12, 1889, age 79 years.
Joseph Donoho, husband of Ann Elizabeth Donoho,
    died March 1, 1891, in 75th year.
Joseph F. Donoho, son of Joseph and Ann Elizabeth
    Donoho, died December 19, 1907.
William Randall Donoho, son of Joseph and Ann
    Elizabeth, died March 5, 1914.
Anna R. Donoho, wife of William Randall Donoho,
    died September 12, 1920.

Carrie A. Donoho, wife of Attalus Donoho, died
June 11, 1920, age 61 years.

1.
John
Fenemore
b. 4-14-1786
d.
m.
Sarah Lord
b. 3-4-1786

2.
1. A. Elizabeth
b. 11-23-1810
d. 10-12-1889
m.
Joseph Donoho
d. 3-1-1891
2. James Lord
b. 12-18-1812
d. 3-13-1876
3. Sarah J.
b. 2-7-1815
4. Keria E.
b. 1-28-1818
d, 1822
5. Mary R.
b. 1-25-1820
6. John F.
b. 8-3-1825
d. 8-27-1825

Abram Groff
m.
S. E. ?

3.
1. Mathew E. Donoho
b. 12-22-1838
d. 3-22-1850
2. John Pemberton
b. 5-21-1843
d. 11-26-1884
3. Joseph Franklin
b. 12-3-1845
d. 12-19-1907
4. William Randall
b. 7-16-1848
d. 3-5-1914
m.
Anna R.
d. 9-12-1920
5. Harriett George
b. 4-20-1851
d. 8-31-1951
6. George Smith
b. 8-11-1852
7. Attalus
b. 1-28-1856
d.
m.
Carrie A. Groff
b. 7-10-1859
d. 6-11-1920

GEORGE W. FIELDS BIBLE

(From the Bible belonging to Ira T. Fields, 19
Marshall St., Milford, Del. Published by Globe
Bible Publishing Co., 723 Chestnut St., Phil., Pa.)

Marriages

George W. Field and Sarah E. Walls were married
    December 22, 1879. Will be 76 years old
    December 2, 1935.

Ira T. Fields and Rosa May Behles were married August 7, 1904 by Rev. Howard T. Twigg in Georgetown, Del.

Births

Ira T. Fields was born December 2, 1880.
George E. Fields was born June 16, 1882.
Joseph H. Fields was born February 27, 1884.
Bessie J. Fields was born November 12, 1885.

Sarah E. Walls was born December 2, 1859.

Verna Fields, daughter of Ira T. and Rosa M. Fields, was born December 1, 1906.

Rosa M. (Behles) Fields was born October 18, 1883.

Deaths

Matilda Walls died March 3, 1905.
Mary Fields died February 22, 1889.
Sarah E. Blizzard died August 11, 1905 (Bessie's daughter.

Additional data given by Mr. and Mrs. T. Fields:

Ira's full name is: Ira Thomason Fields.
Verna Fields married Paul W. Baumgardner - no issue.
George W. Fields and wife are buried in Odd Fellows Cem., Milford, Del.
George W. Fields parents are buried in Slaughter Neck Cem.
Rosa M. (Behles) Fields is the daughter of George and Catherine Behles who came to the U.S.A. from Germany and settled in Sussex Co., Del.

FLICKWIR - WOOD

(Bible record at Bookstore at 18th & Sansom Sts., Philadelphia, Pa.)

Marriages

Frank W. Wood and Rebecca W. Flickwir were married January 27, 1875 at 226 German Street, Philadelphia, Pa., by Rev. J. Burk.
Frank Willard Wood, Jr. and Martha E. McArdle were married November 11, 1908 at the residence of the bride, 41st & Parrish Sts., Philadelphia.

Births

Joseph Flickwir Wood was born April 11, 1876; baptized November 1, 1876 at St. Peters Church by Dr. Davis.
Frank Willard Wood, Jr., was born August 28, 1879; baptized February 7, 1880 at St. Peters Church by Dr. Davis.

Deaths

Frank Willard Wood died November 27, 1899; born March 21, 1847; interred at Woodlands, December 1, 1899.
Frank Willard Wood, Jr. died April 4, 1930; interred at Woodlands, April 7, 1930.

WILLIAM J. & MAGGIE T. FORD

(S.S. Teacher's Combination Bible - first 10 or 15 pages are missing. Record was copied by Mrs. Charles D. Bird.)

Husband, William J. Ford, was born September 1, 1877.
Wife, Maggie T. Ford, was born April 27, 1879.

Married August 15, 1896.

Children:

John W. Ford was born May 6, 1898.
Ernest C. Ford was born August 6, 1900.
Chester K. Ford was born December 12, 1904.
Muriel J. Ford was born March 14, 1907.
Margaret E. Ford was born September 3, 1908.

GEORGE FAMILY

George line of Cecil County, Maryland.

Sampson George married Elizabeth ____? Their children:

1. John B., died May 22, 1755; m. Mary ?
2. Sampson, died November 4, 1739.
3. Mary, married William Currier December 26, 1713.
4. <u>Nicholas</u>, died August 8, 1760.

Nicholas George, son of Sampson and Elizabeth, died August 8, 1760; married Mary ___? Their Children:
1. Rebecca, born June 1, 1727; married William Mainly.
2. <u>Sampson</u>, born October 3, 1729.
3. Ann, born December 10, 1731.
4. John, born March 27, 1734; died September 10, 1735.
5. Nicholas, born November 3, 1738; married Mary ____?
6. Elizabeth, married George Loman.

Sampson George, son of Nicholas George and his wife Mary, was born October 3, 1729; died July 13, 1760; married Sarah Currier, daughter of William and Mary (George) Currier. Sarah was born February 17, 1734 or 1735. Their children:
1. <u>John George</u>, born November 30, 1753.
2. Mary
3. Rachel
4. Ann

John George, son of Sampson George and his wife Sarah (Currier) George, was born November 30, 1753. Married March 8, 1778 to Frances Clark, daughter of John and Tabitha Clark. Frances was born April 19, 1761; died March 20, 1815. Their children:

1. John, Jr.
2. Abby
3. Sampson
4. **Stephen**
5. William
6. Weston
7. Joseph
8. Millicent
9. James
10. Jacob
11. Frances

Stephen George, son of John George and Frances, was born January 18, 1787; died 8-24-1854; married 1-13-1808 to Mary Simpers, daughter of John and Margaret (Crouch) Simpers. She was born November 8, 1790 at Northeast, Cecil Co., Md., died September 13, 1854. Their children:

1. John S., born 1808; died 1888; married Mary S. Whittington.
2. **Ann**, born 1809; died 1907; married Daniel M. Reese.
3. William, S., born 1821; died 1888.
4. Mary, born 1814; died 1884; married Charles Shipley.
5. Stephen, born 1816; died 1887; married Mary ____?
6. Charles W., born 1818; died 1874; married Ann Pennington.
7. Joseph, born 1820; died 1829.
8. Thomas, born 1822; died 1833.
9. Martha, born 1824; died 1826.
10. Alfred, born 1926; died 1867.
11. Margaret, born 1828; died 1904; married Theodore Mottes.
12. Sophia, born 1830; died 1918 - single.
13. Eliza Jane, born 1833; died 1886 - single.
14. Sarah F., born 1838; died 1888 - single.

See McNeal - Reese for children of Ann George and Daniel M. Reese.

GIBBONS FAMILY

John
Gibbons, III
b. Wiltshire,
Eng.
d. 1721
Bethel,
Chester Co.,
Pa.

Margery

1. Mary
   bur. 1684
2. John
   Gibbons
   b. 1675
   d. 1706
   m.

   7-24-1700
   Sarah
   Howard

   George Pearce

   Ann Gayner

1. Rebeccae
   m. 1725
   John Carton
2. John
   Gibbons   1. *
              See
              Below
   b. 1690
   d. 1732
   m.

   Ann Pearce

   m. 2nd
   Wm. Pim

   1. * James **below
   2. Joseph - 7 Ch. #below
   3. Mary Gibbons
      m. John Hannum - no
      children

**
James Gibbons
b. 1710/11
d. 1745
m. 8-10-1734
Jane Sheward
b. 1715
d. 1-12-1798

1. James Gibbons, d.10-27-1823 -
   Scholar
2. Wm. Gibbons - Col. Rev. d. age 66
   m.
   Susannah Ashbridge
3. Thomas Gibbons

\#
Joseph Gibbons
b. 8-24-1712
d. 1782
m. 3-23-1734
Hannah Marshall
dau. of Abraham
& Mary Hunt

1. John Gibbons
   m. Martha Griffiths
2. Joseph Gibbons   1. John H.
   m. 5-9-1759   m.
   Mary Hannum   Mary Heysham
   dau. of John   2. Wm. d. unm.
   & Jane Neild   3. Jane
                        m. Robert
                        Monckton
                        Malcolm and
                        Thomas Vernon

(Joseph m. Sarah Milhous
Hanna m. Edward Bonsall)

- 144 -

Gibbons Chart Cont'd.

    3. <u>Abraham Gibbons</u> 1. Wm. m. Jane
       b.   Massey -Mary m.
       d.   Mathew Ash
       m. Lydia   2. Joseph d. y.
          Garrett   3. Jame d. u.
       m. <u>Mary Canby</u>   4. Ann d. y. **See
                                           below ..
                              5. Hannah d. y.
                              6. Lydia
                              7. <u>Abraham</u>
                              8. Hannah m.
                                 Benjamin Ferris
                            9. Mary

**James m. Margaret Garrett
Joseph m. Lydia Dicks
Hannah m. Enoch Harlan
Marshall d.y.
Ann m. Robert Pennell
Eliz. m. Isaac Lloyd
Sarah m. Samuel Clarkson
Geo. W. m. Eliz. Cladden
Rebecca m. Abishai Clark

<u>Thomas</u>   Canby
             <u>Oliver</u>
<u>Mary Oliver</u>
            <u>Eliz. Shipley</u>

    4. Jacob Gibbons
    5. <u>James Gibbons</u>   1. Alice, d.y.
       b. 1735   2. Joseph, d.y.
       d. 7-18-1810   3. Hannah d.y.
       m.   4. Samuel, b. 5-28-1764
       <u>Deborah Hoopes</u>   5. Ann, d.y.
                            6. Mary, m. 4-26-1787
                               John Kendall, Wilm.
                          7. James, d.y.
                          8. James, b. 1772
                          8.(?) Daniel, 1775-1853
                          9. Rebecca, m. Wm. Daniel,
                             son of Andew & Hannah.

Chart continued next page.

Gibbons Chart Cont'd.

6. <u>Mary Gibbons</u>
   b. 2-15-1742
   d. 1827
   m.
   John Hill

   1. Wm. Hill, m.
      Anna Gibson
   2. Joseph, d. y.
   3. Humphrey, m.
      Alice Howard
   4. Hannah, m.
      Dell Pennell
   5. Anna, m.
      Isaac Hibberd
   6. Rachel, m. Wm. Gray;
      m. Nathan Sharpless
   7. Mary Hill, m.
      Thomas Steel
   8. Lydia, m.
      Amos Sharpless;
      m. Isaac Lowery
   9. Tacy Hill, m.
      Nathan Yearsley
   10. John Hill, m.
       Esther Mendenhall
   11. Deborah Hill m. Dr.
       Ralph C. Marsh
   12. Sidney Hill, m.
       Edward E. Temple
   13. Norris Hill, d.y.

7. Ann Gibbons m. Isaac Lloyd
   1. Richard m. Mary Diehl
   2. Hannah m. Isaac Oakford
   3. Mary m. Benjamin Tyson
   4. Joseph
   5. Isaac m. Elizabeth Gibbons,
      dau. of Jos. & Mary Hannum
   6. James d. - no issue

8. Jacob m. Jane Gibbons, dau. of James and
   Eleanor (Peters) Gibbons.

9. Hanna m. Norris Jones
   1. Marshall Jones
   2. Joseph
   3. Rachel
   4. Norris
   5. Hannah

10. Rachel Gibbons m. John Hunt.
    b. 4-26-1760; d. 2-15-1845; m. 11-29-1777.

ARTHINGTON GILPIN BIBLE

(Bible printed by John Arch Deacon, printer to the University and sold by John Beecroft, John Rivington, Benjamin White and Edward Dilly, in London and T. & J. Merrill in Cambridge. 1775 - Cum Privilegio.

Mary Arthington to her Granddaughter Mary Dilworth, 9th mo. 1789. Present owner: Baldwin Book Barn, R.D. 5, West Chester, Pa., June 27, 1962. Copied by Clara Wallace Eyre for D.A.R.)

Henry Dilworth Gilpin was born in Lancaster, England, April 14, 1801; died '56.
Sarah Lydia Gilpin was born in Frankford, in Pennsylvania, August 21, 1802; died April 15, 1894 at Norristown, N.J.
Elizabeth Gilpin was born in Philadelphia, March 27, 1904; died 1892.
Jane Gilpin was born in Philadelphia, January 2, 1806; died February 19, 1806.
Thomas William Gilpin was born in Philadelphia, December 3, 1806.
Mary Gilpin was born in Philadelphia, August 23, 1810; died May 20, 1889.
Richard Arthington Gilpin was born at Yealand Conyers, in Lancashire, England, November 21, 1812; died May 15, 1887.
William Gilpin was born at Yealand Conyers, in Lancashire, England, October 4, 1814; d. January 20, '94.
Henry Dilworth Gilpin and Eliza Johnston were married at Kentmere, in Delaware, September 3, 1835.
Elizabeth Gilpin married Martin? or Maury?
Mary H. Maury
James Fontain Maury married Kaye Brown.
    2 children - Fountain and Alfred Blake
Richard Arthington Gilpin married Mary E.C. Watmough at Burlington, N.J., August 5, 1854; died September 1919.
William Gilpin married Mrs. J. Dickerson - 3 children - died January 20, 1894.
Richard Arthington Gilpin died at ..... thwaite, Del. Co., Pa., May 15, 1887.
Mary L. Gilpin died at Galveston, Texas, May 20, 1889.

Alfred Coxe was born 1812; died 1891.
Laurette deT Coxe born 1821; died Dec. 1885.

Children of R. A. and E. C. Gilpin:
    Arthington Gilpin was born at Houghton,
        Chester Co., Pa., June 24, 1855;
        m. Caroline Coxe, April 17, 1884.
    Maria Julianna was born May 2, 1858 at
        Houghton, Chester Co., Pa.
    B... Georgianna was born Houghton, Chester
        Co., Pa.; m. Thomas Lynch Montgomery,
        October 16, 1889.
    Sarah Elizabeth was born at Houghton.
    Henry Edmund; m. Helen Church.
        Children:
            B... Watmough b. March 1892;
                m. Brener Root - 1 child:
            Gilpin Church Root.
            Henry Edmund
            Richard Church
    Richard William
    William Bernard

- - - - - - - - - -

1st: 3113 Delaney Place - 2nd: 1344 Pine Street -
3rd: 219 W. John St., Gtn. - 4th: 242 School Lane.

- - - - - - - - - -

Children of A. and C. C. Gilpin:
    Arthington Gilpin 2nd, born Ardmore, Del.
        Co. Pa., August 4, 1885.
    Alfred Cox Gilpin, born Phila., Nov. 12,
        1888.
    Edmund Watmough, born Phila., January 31,
        1894; m. Nancy P.

William S. Goodley

(Bible was published by Wm. W. Harding, Philadelphia. 1860. Owned by Rev. Geo. W. Goodley, Denton, Md. 1957. Record was given by Mrs. Charles D. Bird, Wilmington, Del.)

Bible was presented to Wm. S. Goodley by the pupils of Sandy Bank School. William S. Goodley and Matilda B. Walter Goodley were school teachers.

Marriages

William S. Goodley and Matilda B. Walter were married April 30, 1863.
Horace Goodley and Lillian Hutton were married April 1892.
Charles Pusey Goodley and Laura Wilkinson were married December 31, 1891.
John C. Merion and Bertha Goodley were married March 23, 1893.
George M. W. Goodley and Etta Fritz were married February 8, 1911.
Samuel Goodley, Jr. and Lottie Anne Swain were married Sept. (?) 11, 1912.

Births

Horace Greely Goodley, first son of William S. and Matilda B. Goodley, was born in Haverford Township, Delaware Co., Pa. on July 26, 1864.
Charles Pusey Goodley, second son of William S. and Matilda B. Goodley, was born in Bethel Township, Delaware Co., Pa., on November 3, 1867.
Matilda Goodley, first daughter of William S. and Matilda B. Goodley, was born in Bethel Township, Delaware Co., Pa., on November 4, 1870.
Bertha Goodley, second daughter of William S. and Matilda B. Goodley, was born in Bethel Township, Delaware Co., Pa., on September 15, 1872.
Samuel Goodley, son of William S. and Matilda B. Goodley, was born July 19, 1876.
George M. Walter Goodley, son of William S. and Matilda B. Goodley, was born September 16, 1877.
Egbert S. Goodley, son of Charles P. and Laura Goodley, was born October 8, 1892.
Harold E. Goodley, son of Charles P. and Laura Goodley, was born November 8, 1895.
Charles P. Goodley, son of Charles P. and Laura Goodley, was born February 2, 1899.

Sarah W. Goodley, daughter of Charles P. and Laura
    Goodley, was born September 28, 1900.
Matilda B. Goodley, daughter of Horace and Lillian
    Goodley, was born December 11, 1892.
Lydia May Goodley, daughter of Horace and Lillian
    Goodley, was born August 19, 1894.

William Goodley Merion, son of John C. and Bertha
    G. Merion, was born March 18, 1894.
John Merion, son of John C. and Bertha G. Merion,
    was born April 18, 1896.

George Walter Goodley, first son of George W. and
    Etta L. Goodley, was born June 11, 1912.
Lawrence Elbert Goodley, second son of George W.
    and Etta L. Goodley, was born April 8, 1914.
Lillian May Goodley, first daughter of George W.
    and Etta L. Goodley, was born January 23,
    1916.
Marian Esther Goodley, second daughter of George
    W. and Etta L. Goodley, was born January 13,
    1918.
Edward Calmer Goodley, third son of George W. and
    Etta L. Goodley, was born July 27, 1920.
Bertha Claire Goodley, third daughter of George W.
    and Etta L. Goodley, was born April 2, 1923.
Samuel Alvin Goodley, fourth son of George W. and
    Etta L. Goodley, was born March 8, 1925.

Deaths

Matilda Goodley, first daughter of William S. and
    Matilda B. Goodley, died in Bethel Township,
    Delaware Co., Pa., on March 23, 1873, age 2
    years, 4 months and 19 days.
Charles Pusey Goodley died January 26, 1910, age
    42 years, 2 months and 23 days.
Matilda W. Goodley died June 28, 1915.
John C. Merion, Jr., died November 11, 1915.
John C. Merion died April 22, 1947.

GORDON FAMILY RECORD

(Printed by Wanzer Foote & Co., Rochester, N.Y. 1850. This Bible was given by Wilson Gordon of Cavendish, Vermont to his daughter Jerusha Gordon. She was the daughter of Lydia Pratt and her husband Wilson Gordon.)

James Gordon was born March 1752 at Leeds, Perthshire, Scotland. He was the son of Kastron Davis and James Gordon. James Gordon, born 1752, came to America with the British Forces under Burgoyne. He later joined the Continental Army and served in the Revolutionary War.

James Gordon married Jerusha Tarbell of Groton, Mass. Their children:
1. Thomas
2. Kastron
3. James
4. Tarbell
5. William
6. John
7. Wilson
8. Samuel

Births

Wilson Gordon was born 6-4-1794; died 2-27-1879.
Lydia (Pratt) Gordon was born ?; died 8-29-1859.

Children of Lydia and Wilson Gordon:
1. Orson W. G. Gordon, born 9-30-1826; died 1-14-1864.
2. Sophia Gordon, born 9-23-1818.
3. Thomas L. Gordon, born 9-11-1824; died 1-24-1864.
4. Jerusha Gordon, born 9-22-1822; died 9-30-1895 at Rochester, N.Y.

Wilson Gordon married 2nd Paulina Walker - no issue.

Jerusha Gordon's family: Jerusha Gordon married Ira Newell McCall, born 8-3-1821 at Rushford, N.Y.; died 8-9-1892. Their children:

1. Orson Gordon McCall, born 2-14-1844
2. William Wallace McCall, born 2-7-1846
3. James Wilson McCall, born 1-21-1851
4. Ella Sophia McCall, born 5-28-1853
5. Della Maria McCall, born 5-28-1853
6. Frank Erwin McCall, born 10-3-1858
7. Corvie Ellsworth McCall, born 2-20-1861

All were born at Rushford, Allegheny Co., N.Y.

Frank Erwin McCall married Elizabeth Rycraft; b. 3-25-1858; died 11-20-1943. Their children:
1. Ira Newall McCall, born 12-20-1884; died 2-15-1943.
2. Genieve J. McCall, born 11-14-1886.
3. John Erwin McCall, born 1-6-1890; died 5-12-1932.
4. Ethel Della McCall, born 7-21-1892.
5. Gordon A. McCall, born 4-1-1894; died 4-12-1950.

- - - - - - - - - -

James McCall Bible:

Benajah McCall was born 9-12-1743 at Lebanon, Conn. He married 1st, Abigail Comstock; married 2nd Naomi Crampton - no issue; married 3rd Mrs. Lois Brinsmade.

Benajah McCall died 12-18-1824 at Walton, N.Y.

Children of Abigail and Benajah McCall:
1. James, born 1-5-1775; married Elizabeth Dye of Princeton, N.J. Their children:
   1. Sophia, born 9-27-1800 at Ovid, N.Y.
   2. Milton McCall, born 9-22-1801, Ovid, N.Y.
   3. Mathilda, born 4-16-1803 at Seneca Co., N.Y.
   4. Emila, born 5-2-1805 at Seneca Co., N.Y.
   5. Seneca McCall, born 10-18-1807 at Seneca Co., N.Y.
   6. Nelson McCall, born 3-25-1810 at Seneca Co., N.Y.
   7. Mariah McCall, born 2-20-1812 at Seneca Co., N.Y.

8. Ansel McCall, born 3-1-1814.
9. Naomi McCall, born 10-5-1815 at Rushford, N.Y.
10. Eliza Ann McCall, born 1-25-1817 at Rushford, N.Y.
11. James McCall, born 7-23-1820 at Rushford, N.Y.
12. Ira Newall McCall, born 8-3-1821 at Rushford, N.Y.
13. Catherine Janette McCall, born 10-10-1822 at Rushford, N.Y.
14. Jacob N. McCall, born 4-12-1824.

Marriages

James McCall and Elizabeth Dye were married 12-19-1799.
Sohpia McCall and Richard S. Goff were married 5-24-1823.
Milton McCall and Lucy R. Searl were married 5-24-1823.
Mathilda McCall and Ebenezer K. Howell were married 5-5-1823.
Emila McCall and David Searl were married 6-14-1821.
Seneca McCall and Sarah Rappleye were married 1-15-1839.
Mariah McCall and Rev. Absalom Miner were married 12-1-1830.
Eliza Ann McCall and Almond Benjamin were married 6-21-1835.
Nelson McCall and Rosinal Bell were married 8-?-1833.
James McCall married 2nd Mrs. Lydia Washburn, 6-2-1836.
Ansel McCall and Mary Griffith were married 3-11-1837.
Catherine J. McCall and James Rappleye were married 10-1839.
Ira Newall McCall and Mary Jane McCall were married 6-17-1846.
Naomi McCall and Ezra Chase were married 1842.

Deaths

Benajah McCall died 12-18-1824.
James Clark McCall, son of James, died 8-3-1820.
Elizabeth (Dye) McCall, wife of James, died 7-3-1833.
Lydia Washburn McCall died 3-6-1850.

James McCall died 3-24-1856.
Mariah McCall Miner died 7-26-1847.
Seneca McCall died ?
Milton McCall died 3-7-1890.
Della McCall died 2-13-1884 at Rochester, N.Y.
Ira Newall McCall died 8-9-1892.
Jerusha McCall died 9-30-1895.
Frank McCall died 1-25-1899.
Orson Gordon McCall died 6-19-1907 at Brooklyn, N.Y.
William Wallace McCall died 7-2-1893 at Olean, N.Y.

RALPH P. GORDON - SARAH BRERENTON BIBLE

(Public Archives, Dover, Delaware.)

Births

Sarah Brerenton, daughter of Henry Brerenton, was
    born March 15, 1776.
Ralph P. Gordon, son of Jonathan and Sarah, was
    born 3-17-1801, Philadelphia, Pa.
Hetty Gordon, daughter of Jonathan and Polly his
    wife, was born September 25, 1789.
Nathaniel Gordon, son of Jonathan Gordon and Rutha
    his wife, was born March 23, 1795.
Henery Gordon, son of Jonathan Gordon and Sally
    his wife, was born September 10, 1797.
Polly Gordon, daughter of Jonathan Gordon and
    Sally his wife, was born April 9, 1799.
Thomas Gordon, son of Jonathan and Sally his
    wife, was born February 1, 1811.

Deaths

Jonathan Gordon died at age 77 years, 9 months
    and 18 days.

Jonathan Gordon
 m. **Polly, 1st** Hetty Gordon

 m. **Rutha, 2nd** Nathaniel

Henry Brerenton

 m. **Sally, 3rd** Henery
       Polly
       Ralph P.
       Thomas

GRING BIBLE

(Holy Bible in German, now owned by Mrs. J. A. Seebach, Marian, Pa. Printed by J. Howe. 1830.)

I, Daniel Gring, was born in the year 1799, the 25th of November 1799.

Births

Israel Gring was born March 31, 1825.
Catherine Gring was born July 13, 1826.
Fanny was born December 19, 1827.
Suphyah was born September 19, 1829.
Daniel was born January 4, 1831.
John was born March 30, 1832.
Eliza Ann was born February 10, 1834.
My wife was born December 2, 1802; died 11-23-1836.
Rebecca was born May 4, 1835.
Daniel was born November 8, 1836.
A daughter was born March 7, 1839.
A son was born July 23, 1849 and named David
  Martain Gring.

Deaths

Daniel died June 4, 1833; age 2 years, 5 months.
Daniel died ? November 1839; age ?
Catherine died December 3, 1844, age 18 years,
  4 months and 20 days.
John died October 12, 1852, age 20 years, 6 months
  and 12 days.
Daniel Gring died September 14, 1860, age
  60 years, 9 months and 20 days.

GRUBB FAMILY BURYING GROUND

(Records were copied by Mrs. Alban Shaw, Wilmington, Delaware.)

This Family Cemetery is in Brandywine Hundred, New Castle Co., Delaware. It is near Grubb's Corner on Grubb's Road. It is sometimes called Harvey Road. This Burying Ground was a part of a Plantation of William Grubb who was born November 16, 1713. He was the son of John Grubb 2nd and his wife Rachel (Buckley) Grubb. It is by the side of the road in his garden which he devised forever as a burial ground. It is half an acre in size. The records were copied by Mrs. Shaw on July 9, 1941. Some markers were so worn that they were very hard to read. The grounds are in splendid shape. The stone of William Grubb, the owner, states that he was in his 65th year.

1. William Grubb 2-3-1775 - 65 years.
    "Build not your house too high
    But always have before your eyes
    That you were born to die."

2. Lydia Grubb 2-27-1774 (wife of William).

3. B. R. (very old head and foot stone of field stone).

4. Samuel Grubb died 1-21-1769; 47 years.

5. Rebekah Grubb died December 6, 1760; 32 years (1st wife of Samuel).

6. Isaac Grubb died November 5, 1831; 82 years.
    "Death Thou hast conquered me
    I by Thy darts am slain
    But Christ has conquered thee
    And I shall rise again."

7. His wife, Margaret, died March 27, 1825; 72 years.

8. Deborah Grubb died 1830; 39 years.

9. Mary Robinson died February 21, 1769; age 24 years.

10. Adam Buckley died 10-29-1760; 64 years.

11. Beulah Pyle, October 10, 1794' 44 years.
"Farewell vain world
As thou hast been to me
Dust and a shadow
Is all I leave thee."

HAMILTON BIBLE

(Family Bible of John Hamilton, owned by Delaware Historical Society, Wilmington, Delaware.)

John Hamilton 1791 - May 1st.
Thursday, August 21, 1749.
Martha Hamilton was born November 18, 1751.
Mary Hamilton was born ?

Martha Hamilton, now Martha Simpson, died
    July 16, 1786, age 37 years.
Susannah Hamilton, now Susannah Cann, died
    August 10, 1787, age 25 years and 4 days.
James Hamilton was born January 25, 1755.
Robert Hamilton was born April 22, 1756; died
    July 22, 1826.
Susannah Hamilton was born February 12, 1758.
Richard Hamilton was born March 24, 1759.
David Hamilton was born November 27, 1760.
Susannah Hamilton was born August 6, 1762.
Charles Hamilton was born April 15, 1764; died
    August 7, 1829.

Robert and Ann Hamilton were married October 11,
    1779. Ann died September 1, 1825.

John Hamilton, son of Robert and Ann Hamilton,
    was born July 6, 1780; died January 23, 1828
    at Liverpool, England.
Archbald Hamilton, son of Robert and Ann Hamilton,
    was born January 23, 1782.
James Hamilton, son of Robert and Ann Hamilton,
    was born January 12, 1784; died at sea
    July 10, 1826.

Charles Hamilton, son of Robert and Ann Hamilton,
    died at Havannah in the Island of Cuba,
    July 8, 1825.
James, son of Robert and Ann Hamilton, died at sea
    on his passage from Liverpool, July 10, 1826.
John, son of Robert and Ann Hamilton, died in
    Liverpool, England, January 23, 1828.

James Hamilton married Eliza Anderson,
    July 27, 1813.
Maria Louisa Hamilton, their daughter, was born
    June 13, 1814.
William Penn Hamilton, their son, was born
    April 17, 1819.
James Henry Hamilton, son of James and Eliza
    Hamilton, was born July 17, 1821.

Maria Louisa and Daniel Trotter were married
    October 2, 1832.
William Hamilton, son of Daniel and Maria Louisa
    Trotter, was born December 31, 1833.

William Penn Hamilton died in Cincinnati, Ohio,
    October 28, 1832.
James Henry Hamilton died in Cincinnati, Ohio,
    October 13, 1834.

Maria Louisa, wife of Daniel Trotter, died
    March 22, 1835.

Charles Hamilton, son of Robert and Ann Hamilton,
    was married August 1820 to Eliza C. Palmer.
Ann Elizabeth, their daughter, was born
    July 8, 1821.

Alexander Hamilton, son of Robert and Ann Hamilton,
    died August 13, 1835.

Archibald Hamilton, son of Robert and Ann Hamilton,
    died October 4, 1841.
Anna Hamilton, daughter of Robert and Ann Hamilton,
    died March 16, 1844.

Ann Elizabeth Hamilton and Mahlon Hutchinson, Esq.
    of Bordertown, N.J., were married March 24,
    1844.
Mary Eliza, daughter of Mahlon and Ann Elizabeth
    Hutchinson, was born February 1, 1845;
    died July 13, 1845.

Ann Elizabeth Hutchinson, wife of Mahlon
    Hutchinson, died August 2, 1845.

Susan Hamilton, daughter of Robert and Ann Hamilton,
    died December 19, 1850.
Mary Hamilton died November 19, 1879.
Ann Hamilton died February 11, 1881.

Isaac Hamilton, son of Robert and Ann Hamilton, was
    born February 23, 1786.
Susanna Hamilton, daughter of Robert and Ann
    Hamilton, was born February 22, 1788.
Charles Hamilton, son of Robert and Ann Hamilton,
    was born January 19, 1790; died at Havanna
    July 8, 1825.
Mary Hamilton, daughter of Robert and Ann Hamilton,
    was born April 4, 1792.
Anna Hamilton, daughter of Robert and Ann
    Hamilton, was born August 8, 1794.
Sarah Hamilton, daughter of Robert and Ann
    Hamilton, was born January 16, 1797.
Robert Hamilton, son of Robert and Ann Hamilton,
    was born October 31, 1800; died April 9,
    1801, age 5 months, 10 days.
Alexander Hamilton, son of Robert and Ann Hamilton,
    was born January 30, 1804.

Ann Hamilton, wife of Robert Hamilton, died
    September 1, 1825.
Robert Hamilton died July 22, 1826.

HANBY FAMILY

(Bible published by William W. Harding, 326 Chestnut
St., Philadelphia, Pa. 1869. Owned by Harry S.
Hanby, Wilmington, Del. 1956. Record given by
Mrs. Charles Bird.)

Marriages

Samuel Larkin, son of Jacob K. and Esther Ann
    Hanby, and Nellie V. Pierce were married
    March 29, 1887.
Willard Saulisbury, son of Jacob K. and Esther
    Ann Hanby, and Susie A. Talley were married
    March 18, ---?

Levenia Humphrey Larkin, daughter of Jacob K. and Esther Ann Hanby, and William L. Barlow were married March 17, 18??

Births

Jacob Klough Hanby was born October 25, 1839.
Esther Ann Larkin was born November 30, 1842.
Samuel Larkin, son of Jacob K. and Esther Ann Hanby, was born November 13, 1863.
Willard Saulisbury, son of Jacob K. and Esther Ann Hanby, was born May 3, 1866.
Levenia Humphrey Larkin, daughter of Jacob K. and Esther Ann Hanby, was born August 17, 1868.
Edward Larkin, son of Jacob K. and Esther Ann Hanby, was born September 1, 1870.
Jacob Benjamin, son of Jacob K. and Esther Ann Hanby, was born September 4, 1873.
Arthur, son of Jacob K. and Esther Ann Hanby, was born December 6, 1875.
Ann Eliza, daughter of Jacob K. and Esther Ann Hanby, was born July 6, 1880.
Harry Sharpley, son of Jacob K. and Esther Ann Hanby, was born April 11, 1884.
Charlotte Prince, daughter of Jacob K. and Esther Ann Hanby, was born April 11, 1884.

Deaths

Edward Larkin, son of Jacob K. and Esther Ann Hanby, died February 13, 1871.

HANNUM-WALTER BIBLE

(Bible published by G & C. Merriman, Springfield, Mass. Owners: Norris M. and Susanna Y. Hannum's Book - December 23, 1848. Present owner, Baldwin Book Barn, R. 5, West Chester, Pa. Copied by Clara Wallace Eyre, for D.A.R.)

Marriages

Norris M. Hannum and Susanna Y. Walter were married September 29, 1847.

- 160 -

Benjamin Sharpless of Birmingham, Chester Co., and
   Annie T., daughter of Norris and Susanna Y.
   Hannum, were married June 5, 1873.

Births

Norris M., son of Esau P. and Elizabeth Y. Hannum,
   was born January 2, 1819.
Susanna Y., daughter of John and Abagail H. Walter,
   was born November 14, 1825.
Abagail H., daughter of Norris M. and Susanna Y.
   Hannum, was born July 23, 1848.
Annie T. Hannum was born December 1, 1851.
Margaret G. Hannum was born July 29, 1853.
Henry W. Hannum was born October 18, 1856.

Deaths

Abagail H., wife of John Walter, died November 21,
   1832.
Maggie G. Hannum died May 5, 1857, age 3 years,
   9 months and 6 days.
Benjamin, son of Benjamin and Annie T. Sharpless,
   died August 1, 1877, age 1 year and 4 months.

Esau P. Hannum
                    Norris M. Hannum
Elizabeth   b. 1819
                                Annie T. Hannum
John Walter
                    Susanna Walter
Abagail   b. 1825
                                Benjamin Sharpless

JAMES HARRIS BIBLE

(Bible was published by John B. Perry, No. 198
Market St., Philadelphia, Pa. Given to the
Delaware Historical Society by Hilda Harris
Stevens, daughter of Annie E. and Harry F.
Stevens, 9-22-1959.)

Marriages

James Harris and Martha A. Reynolds were married
   September 4, 1846.

Herbert Haynes and Mary Emma Harris were married
    December 24, 1868.
John S. Latomis and Martha E. Harris were married
    March 15, 1887.
John ? Harris and Amelia Kiruso (?) were married
    September 11, 1872.
Joseph C. Raisin and Sallie C. Harris were married
    February 20, 1889 by Rev. L. E. Barrett in
    Wilmington.
Annie E. Harris and Harry F. Stevens were married
    February 24, 1892.

Births

Joshua Harris, son of James Harris and Mary his
    wife, was born May 21, 1818.
Elizabeth Harris, daughter of James Harris and
    Mary his wife, was born September 14, 1820.
James Harris, son of James Harris and Mary his
    wife, was born December 21, 1822.
John B. Harris, son of James and Mary his wife,
    was born April 21, 1821.
Temperance Harris, daughter of James Harris and
    Mary his wife, was born November 13, 1831.
Benjamin C. Harris, son of James Harris and Mary
    his wife, was born January 21, 1835.
George W. Harris, son of James Harris and Mary
    his wife, was born June 24, 1842.

Lulu H. Haynes, daughter of Herbert Haynes and
    Mary Emma his wife, was born January 13,
    1875.
Arrabell Haynes was born of the same parents
    March 11, 1877.
Jennie M. Haynes was born October 18, 1879.
Eva M. Haynes was born October 10, 1883.
Martha E. Haynes was born November 1, 1886.
Annie H. Haynes was born October 1, 1887.
Sallie C. Haynes was born May 10, 1889.

John R. Harris, son of James Harris and Martha
    his wife, was born November 26, 1848.
Mary Emma Harris, daughter of James Harris and
    Martha his wife, was born June 14, 1851.
Anna Catherine Harris, daughter of James Harris
    and Martha his wife, was born March 7, 1854.
Sarah Cole Harris, daughter of James Harris and
    Martha his wife, was born December 8, 1855.

Alfanza Kate Harris, daughter of James Harris and
    Martha his wife, was born December 14, 1857.
Martha Evalin Harris, daughter of James Harris and
    Martha his wife, was born February 7, 1859.
Lily M. Harris and Josephine Harris, daughters of
    James Harris and Martha his wife, were born
    August 28, 1760?

HAY - BACON RECORD

Andrew S. Hay was born in Morayshire, Scotland in
    1832. He died 1917. He married Anne C.
    Stuart, who was born in Banffshire, Scotland
    in 1842. Died 1903. Their son:
William Stuart Hay was born in Morayshire,
    Scotland in 1866; died 1942. He married
    Mary Elizabeth MacKenzie, daughter of
    Alexander and Elizabeth (Stone)
    MacKenzie. She was born 1866 in Keith,
    Banffshire, Scotland; died 1926. Their
    children:
    1. William
    2. Mary, married William C. Scroggis.
    3. Alexander
    4. Ann (Dollie)
    5. Jean
    6. James, married Millie Frances Bacon.
    7. Albert
James Hay, son of William S. Hay and his wife
    Elizabeth, was born September 27, 1897 in
    Keith, Scotland. He married July 8, 1923 in
    Philadelphia, Millie Frances Bacon, daughter
    of George W. Bacon and Amelia (Scales) Bacon.
    She was born September 18, 1897 in Norwich,
    England. Their children:
    1. Edith MacKenzie Hay, born 2-9-1924
            in Philadelphia.
    2. Mary Jean, born May 18, 1934; m.
            William N. Flowers, April 19,
            1953; they have a daughter,
            Elizabeth Ann, born 1-24-1954.

Edith MacKenzie Hay, daughter of James Hay and
   Millie F. (Bacon) Hay, was born in
   Philadelphia, 2-9-1924. She was married
   April 3, 1948 in Ambler, Pa., to Daniel R.
   McNeal, Jr., son of Daniel R. McNeal and
   Clara Louise (Berlin) McNeal. He was born
   August 20, 1920. Their children:
   1.   Daniel R. III, born 9-11-1949;
            died 4-15-1951.
   2.   Debra Jeanne, born 11-24-1952.

(See McNeal record)

HAY - BARNITZ - SEEBACH

(Bible is owned by Mrs. J. Arthur Seebach, Marian, Pennsylvania.)

Marriages

John Hay and Julian Moul were married - no date.
Jacob Hay and Mary Rudisill were married - no date.
Adam Ebert and Gloria Hoke were married
   October 18, 1785.
John Hay and Eliza Ebert were married May 5, 1818.
Charles Barnitz and Anna Barbara Miller were
   married - no date.
Jacob Barnitz and Mary McClean were married
   September 23, 1784.

David Grier was born June 27, 1741 O.S.; died
   June 3, 1790; married Janett McPherson, born
   May 11, 1752; died May 5, 1813.
Charles A. Barnitz was born August 7, 1787; died
   March 8, 1850; married Margaret Grier, born
   December 1, 1785; died April 2, 1857.
Charles A. Hay and Sarah Rebecca Barnitz were
   married in York at the residence of Charles
   A. Barnitz, Esq., by Rev. Lockman.
John William Hay, M.D. was married August 3, 1871
   to Miss Sarah Jane Welty of Gettysburg, Pa.,
   daughter of Solomon and Jane Welty.
John Andrew Himes A.M., was married June 30, 1874
   to Miss Mary Jane Hay.

Edward Grier Hay A.M. and Miss Laura Ella Buchanan
were married September 16, 1879.
Charles Ebert Hay A.M. was married May 10, 1881
to Miss Florence Eugenia, daughter of Rev.
Albert Galatin Dole and Maria (Jefferis).
Frances Eliza Hay was married February 10, 1885
to Rev. M. L. Heisler.

Note: All of the above were married by Charles A.
Hay, beginning with John William Hay M.D.

Julius Frederick Seebach and Margaret Rebecca
Himes were married November 15, 1897.
Julius F. Seebach, Jr. married 1st, Mary Esther
Hare, June 1920. Married 2nd Helen Phillips.
Mary Esther Seebach and Thomas Dheridan Knapp were
married - no date.
Julius Frederick Seebach, III - ?
J. Arthur Seebach and Beth Hefelbower were married
July 2, 1935.

Births

Children of Jacob and Mary Hay:
Henry, born February 4, 1787
Michael, born July 29, 1788
Charles, born May 31, 1790
John, born June 23, 1793
Sarah, born November 25, 1796
Charles, born December 28, 1798
Jacob, born July 28, 1801
Mary Ann, born December 2, 1803
Eliza, born May 6, 1806

Children of Jacob and Mary Barnitz:
Anna Maria, born December 17, 1785
Charles A., born August 17, 1787;
died March 8, 1850.
Anna Maria, born August 5, 1789
Rebecca, born October 16, 1791
Jacob, born August 28, 1793
William, born November 23, 1795
George Washington, born June 18, 1798
Samuel McClean, born October 21, 1800
Alexander Hamilton, born July 14, 1804

Children of Charles and Mary Barnitz:
　Jane Grier, born August 23, 1812; died
　　August 3, 1840.
　Mary McClean, born August 23, 1812;
　　died October 14, 1886.
　David Grier, born June 20, 1816.
　Ann Grier, born September 5, 1818.
　Charles Jacob, born September 10, 1820.
　Sarah Rebecca, born April 4, 1824; died
　　May 5, 1895.
　McPherson, born April 26, 1826.

Children of John and Eliza Hay:
　William Ebert, born February 8, 1819.
　Charles Augustus, born February 11, 1821.

Children of Charles A. and Sarah H. Hay:
　Frances Eliza, born February 25, 1846.
　John William, born April 15, 1847.
　Charles Barnitz, born August 6, 1848.
　Margaret Rebecca, born June 28, 1850.
　Charles Ebert, born October 8, 1851.
　Mary Jane, born June 1, 1853.
　Edward Grier, born May 4, 1856.
　George Washington, born February 13, 1861.

Children of John A. and Mary J. Himes:
　Margaret Rebecca, born July 5, '75.
　Edwin Hay, born September 11, '88.
　Mary Hay, born June 26, '90.

Children of Julius and Margaret Seebach:
　Julius Frederick, Jr., born August 29, 1898.
　John Arthur, born July 8, 1902.

Children of Julius and Esther Seebach:
　Mary Esther, born April 14, 1921.
　Julius Frederick, III, born May 24, 1923.

Children of Julius and Helen Seebach:
　Joan Phillips, born July 8, 1932.
　Helen Fleming, born March 8, 1938.

Children of Mary Esther and Thomas Knapp:
　Rebecca Jane, was born July 7, 1946.

Children of Edward and Ella Hay:
　Edward Buchanan, was born June 24, 1881.

Children of Arthur and Beth Seebach:
   John Arthur, Jr., was born May 17, 1938.

Children of John W. and Sallie J. Hay:
   Rebecca Jane, was born August 25, '72.
   William Welty, was born May 1, '76.
   Bessie Barnitz, was born May 25, '78.
   Charles Livingston, was born October 15, '81.
   Martin Luther, was born October 23, '83.
   Ruth Stevenson, was born October 11, '84.
   Nellie McKnight, was born March 16, 1886.
   Mary, was born December 26, 1889.
   John DeYoe, was born June 10, 1892.

Children of Charles E. and F. E. Hay:
   Lillian Jeffries, was born September 25, 1882.

Deaths from tombstones in York:

   In memory of William G. McPherson, who died January 8, 1810, aged 22 years and 6 months.
   In memory of John Grier, native of County Arnagh, Ireland; for many years a respectable inhabitant of this borough, who departed this life on the 20 of August in the year 1813, aged 53 years.

Edwin Hay Himes, at Gettysburg, September 19, 1869.
Charles Augustus Hay, D.D., at Gettysburg, June 26, '93.
Sarah Rebecca Hay, at Gettysburg, May 5, 1895.

John Andrew Hay, August 11, 1923.
Mary Jane Himes, January 18, 1929.

John Hay, November 21, 1821.
William E. Hay, July 14, 1823.
Charles A. Barnitz, March 8, 1850.
Sally Ebert, April 26, 1852.
Margaret Barnitz, April 2, 1857.
Eliza Hay, February 16, 1862.
Jane Grier Barnitz, August 3, 1840.
Charles Barnitz, at Hanover, Pa., March 22, 1849.
Margaret Rebecca Hay, at Harrisburg, July 17, 1850.
George Washington Hay, at Harrisburg, June 23, 1861.

Rebecca Jane Hay, at Harrisburg, November 1876.
William Welty Hay, at Gettysburg, September 19, 1884.
Ruth Stevenson Hay, at Harrisburg, July 25, 1885.
John DeYoe Hay, at Harrisburg, February 5, 1893.
Mary McClean Barnitz, at Gettysburg, October 14, 1886.

Memorandum from Judge Russell:

    David Grier, born June 27, 1741; died June 2, 1790.
    Jannet Grier, born March 10, 1742; died May 3, 1813.

William G. McPherson, died June 8, 1810; age 22 years and 6 months.
Mary Grier, daughter of David and Jannet, born May 29, 1781; died July 20, 1806.
Jane Grier, born August 10, 1783; died August 30, 1842.
Nancy Agnes Grier, died January 20, 1845 (?)
Jane (Barnitz) Lewis, born August 23, 1812; died August 1, 1840.

HEFFLEBOWER - GRING

(Original Bible in possession of Mrs. J. A. Seebach, Marian, Pa. Printed by Jesper Harding and Son. 1857.)

Marriages

Samuel Hefflebower and Miss Anna E. Gring were married October 16, 1855.

Births

Samuel Hefflebower was born July 13, 1821.
Anne E. Gring was born February 10, 1834.
Alice Kate Hefflebower was born March 26, 1861.
Samuel Gring Hefflebower was born November 11, 1871.

Newspaper clippings in this Bible - The Altar -

Married on the 14th by the Rev. J. C. Owens,
    Mr. John Frick of Cumberland Co., to
    Miss Susannah Beecher.

At the residence of Mr. Jacob Holt, near
    Shippensberg on Tuesday morning the 16th inst
    by the Rev. T. T. Titus, Mr. Robert L. Barr
    of Newberg, Pa., to Miss Ellen Nora Markward
    of Richland Co., Ohio.

On Tuesday the 25th ult by J. A. Murray, Mr.
    William A. Spahr to Miss Lydia B. Hursh,
    all of Dillsburg.

On the 9th inst by the Rev. J. S. Bucher, Mr.
    Ruben Enck to Miss Jane Catherine Witmore,
    all of Monroe Twp.

On the 11h inst by the Rev. J. Evans, Mr.
    Levan H. Orris of Frankford to Miss
    Nancy A. Westler of Mifflin.

On the same day by the same Mr. Benjamin Brennesser
    of Frankford to Miss Elizabeth J. Failor of
    West Pennsborough.

On the 16th by the same Mr. Samuel Hefflebower to
    Miss Anne E. Gring both of West Pennsborough
    Township.

DAVID HILL'S BOOK

("A Key to Reeve's New Practical Decimal
Arithmetic" by Shepherd A. Reeve. Printed for the
author by Dennis Heartt, Philadelphia, Pa. 1812.)

On the front fly leaf:
    Kendall B. Crockett
    Thomas Knowles
    Nancy Knowles

On top of Preface:
    David Hill's Book

On back fly leaf:
   James Jenkins
   Minos T. Connaway his name

On reverse of back fly leaf:
   Bought of Genl. Jesse Green
   Price one dollar.
And sold to Richard V. Coard or Combs.
Now the property of Kendall B. Crockett
Wrote by David Hill, this 10th day of February
   Anno domino 1824.

On inside back cover:
   Phillip W. Knowles, the son of Isaac Knowles
   and Elizabeth Knowles, and Nancy Ann H. Hill,
   the daughter of Elezey and Nancy Hill, was
   married and also joined their heart and hand
   in marriage the 22th of August 1832.

- - - - - - - - - -

JEFFERSON BIBLE

(The Holy Bible, New York - American Bible Society. 1852.)

<u>Family Record</u>

Lydia O. Jefferson, daughter of William Bagwell
   and Ann his wife, was born June 22, 1809.
James K. P. Jefferson, son of (faded) Jefferson
   and Lydia his wife, was born (faded, looks
   like February) 7 or 17, 1847.
Virginia F. Jefferson, daughter of (faded)
   Jefferson and Lydia (faded), was born
   (faded) 12, 1845.
James K. P. Jefferson, son of of Thomas P. (?)
   Jefferson and Lydia his wife, was born
   February 7, 1847.
Mary J. Johnson, daughter of Benton H. Johnson
   and Lydia his wife, was born Sept. 16, 1849.

<u>Births</u>

1873 our litle babe, son of James K. P. Jefferson
   and Jennie his wife, was born April 30, 1873.

Death 1873, our litle babe, son of James K. P.
    Jefferson and Jennie his wife, died May 1,
    1873, age 40 hours.
James K. P. Jefferson and Mary J. Johnson were
    married January 25, 1871.

HARRY HINKSON & VILETTA P. HANBY

(An Edition of Brown's Family Bible by A. J.
Holman & Co. 1872. Owned by Harry Hinkson,
Wilmington, Delaware. 1957. Record copied by
Mrs. Charles D. Bird.)

Marriage Certificate

Harry C. Hinkson and Viletta P. Hanby married at
    Siloam Parsonage on the Twenty Fourth day of
    December in the year of our Lord One Thousand
    Eight Hundred and Sixty Eight.
            By W. W. McMichael

Family Record

Harry C. Hinkson
Viletta P. Hinkson
Lewis W. Hinkson
Sallie E. Hinkson
V. Emma Hinkson
Mattie R. Hinkson
L. Jennie Hinkson
Ella C. Hinkson
Harry M. Hinkson
Thomas L. Hinkson

Marriages

Henry C. Hinkson and Viletta P. Henry were married
    December 24, 1868.
Lewis W. Hinkson and Jessie P. Valentine were
    married April 23, 1891.
George E. Morley and Sallie E. Hinkson were
    married November 15, 1893.
Orlando F. Carter and V. Emma Hinkson were married
    November 21, 1894.
Howard D. Talley and L. Jennie Hinkson were
    married March 29, 1899.

I. Howard Forwood and Ella C. Hinkson were married
   November 23, 1904.
Harry M. Hinkson and Mary Ingram were married
   March 4, 1908.
Thomas L. Hinkson and Emma Wilson were married -
   no date.

Births

Harry C. Hinkson was born September 2, 1844.
Viletta P. Hinkson was born November 22, 1846.
Lewis W. Hinkson was born August 17, 1870.
Sallie E. Hinkson was born March 9, 1872.
V. Emma Hinkson was born September 26, 1873.
Mattie R. Hinkson was born August 5, 1876.
L. Jennie Hinkson was born November 25, 1878.
Ella C. Hinkson was born September 10, 1880.
Harry M. Hinkson was born October 3, 1884.
Thomas L. Hinkson was born May 18, 1888.

Deaths

Mattie R. Hinkson died November 23, 1877.
Harry C. Hinkson died April 28, 1904.
Viletta P. Hinkson died December 13, 1925.
Lewis W. Hinkson died January 1927.
Emma Carter died August 28, 1943.
Sara E. Morley died January 25, 1948.

HITCH FAMILY BIBLE RECORD

(Owned by Harold W. T. Purnell, Georgetown, Del.
Copied from a photostat.)

Births

Levin Hitch, son of Levin Hitch, was born
   October 15, 1800.
Eleanor Fooks, daughter of Benjamin Fooks,
   was born February 26, 1803.
Samuel Benjamin Hitch was born May 12, 1824.
Levin Hitch was born September 1, 1825.
Ellen Mitchell Woolten, daughter of George M.
   Woolton, was born May 13, 1834.

Benjamin Franklin Hitch was born January 15, 1860.
George Washington Hitch was born October 9, 1861.
Ellen Fooks Hitch was born December 11, 1868.

HORNER FAMILY

Elijah and Elizabeth Coles Horner were natives and lifelong residents of Gloucester County, New Jersey. Elijah Horner was born 1790; died 1872, age 82 years. His father, George Horner, was also born in Gloucester Co., in 1764; died 1847, age 83 years.

Thomas Coles, the maternal grandfather, was a prominent farmer, a mill owner and influential citizen in Harrisonville, New Jersey.

Children of Elijah and Elizabeth Horner:
    Martha, married Robert Kirkbride; born 1817; died July 10, 1897, age 80.
    Caroline, married Samuel Guant.
    Alice, married 1st, Joseph Harker; married 2nd, --- Stratton.
    Eliza
    George, born 1825.
    Mary Ann, married Jacob Kirby; she was born 1828.
    Elma, married Chalkey Duel.
    Thomas - twin of Mary Ann.

1.
George Horner
b. 1764
d. 1847
m.

Thomas Coles

2.
Elijah Horner
b. 1790
d. 1872
m.
Elizabeth Coles

3.
Mary Ann Horner
b. 1828
d.
m.

Chart continued next page.

Horner Chart Cont'd.

    John Kirby
    m.   Jacob Kirby
    Hannah
    Bassett

4.
Edwin
Elizabeth
Chalkey
George*
Emily
Ida
Bassett

5.
*George Kirby   6.
b.   Eleonora Kirby   7.
d.   b.   Edna Edwards
m.   d.   m.
Sarah Bishop   m   George M.
                    Sherman   Shaffer
                    Edwards

8.   9.
Elenora Shaffer   Rebecca Lamborn
m.   and
R. Louis Lamborn   Patricia Lamborn

SAMUEL C. HUGHES & AMY E. LONGFELLOW

(Bible published by National Publishing Co., Phil., Pa. 1886. Owned by Mrs. Royal E. Smith, Gordon Heights, Wilmington, Del. Record copied by Mrs. Charles D. Bird, Wilmington, Del.)

Marriage Certificate

Samuel C. Hughes of Kent County, Delaware, and
    Amy E. Longfellow of Caroline County,
    Maryland, were married on December 30, 1885
    at Felton, Delaware, by Rev. I. Jewel.

Births

Samuel C. Hughes was born November 28, 1860.
Amy E. Longfellow was born October 26, 1868.
Edward Hughes was born April 20, 1887.
James H. Hughes was born January 9, 1889.
S. Carl Hughes was born March 14, 1891.

Amy Catherine Hughes, daughter of Carl and Amy his wife, was born May 14, 1894.
Rebecca, daughter of S. Carl Hughes and Amy E. his wife, was born March 15, 1898.
Paul Bryan, son of S. Carl Hughes and Amy E. his wife, was born August 9, 1896.
Nellie Esther, daughter of S. Carl Hughes and Amy his wife, was born February 15, 1900.

Deaths

James P. Longfellow died May 23, 1870.
Catherine M. Cooper died July 25, 1884.
Susan Nellie Smith died February 19, 1886.
Rebecca Hughes died March 12, 1900.
Samuel Carl Hughes died August 20, 1936.
James H. Hughes, Jr. died July 3, 1938.

HUSSEY FAMILY OF DELAWARE

(Data from Dr. A. A. Knapp given to Delaware Historical Society. By Mrs. Clara W. Bird, January 1960.)

Ref.: "Immigration of Irish Quakers into Pa." page 233. Delaware Deed Book B, page 88 - John Hussey bought from Charles Rumsey of Christiana Creek 300 acres; operated a mill. Newark Meeting: John and son applied to visit eastern part of New England, 1722.

John Hussey of Dorking, England, died 1638;
married 12-15-1593 Mary Wood, who died
6-16-1660. Children:
2. John Hussey, born 1592; died 1597.
3. Christopher, born 1599, Dorking, Eng.,
went to Holland; died 1695, age 87;
shipwrecked on the east coast of
Florida and was drowned.

3. Christopher Hussey married 1st, Theodate
Batchelder, daughter of Rev. Stephen
Batchelder. She died 1649. Children:
4. Stephen Hussey, born 1622; died
4-2-1718; married Martha Bunker,
daughter of George and Jane Bunker,
10-8-1676.
5. John Hussey, born 1635; died 1707.
6. Mary, born 3-1637; died 1-21-1733;
married 1st, 2-2-1664 Thomas Page;
married 2nd, 3-10-1691, married
3rd, 11-10-1704 Henry Dow.
7. Theodate, born 8-20-1640; died 10-20-1645.
8. Hulda, born 1643; died 8-16-1740;
married 2-26-1667, John Smith.
9. Joseph, died 1672; name may have been
Joshua.

Christopher came to New England from Southampton,
England with John Winthrop and 1700 passengers
on 11 ships. Rev. Stephen Batchelder would
not consent to their marriage unless he would
remove to N.E. so, with his wife and widowed
mother, he arrived in Lynn, Mass. 1630 where
Stephen was born - 2nd white child born
there. He moved to Newberg 1630, and filled
several important offices. (Note: Annals
of Lynn, Mass. state that he moved 1636).
Much is written of Rev. Batchelder (Bachiler)
in the Annals of Lynn, Mass. He died in
England, age 100.

5. John Hussey, son of Christopher and Theodate
(Batchelder), was born 1635 at Hampton,
N.H.; moved to New Castle, Del., 1692;
died 1707 or 11; will was made
2-18-1707; married Rebecca Perkins,
daughter of Isaac Perkins, 9-2-1659.
Children:

10. Theodate, born 6-2-1660; married
    Benjamin Sweet.
11. Rebecca, born 3-10-1661; married
    Samuel Collins.
12. Mary, born 11-18-1665; married
    Moses Sweet, son of Benjamin.
13. Susannah, born 9-7-1667; married
    Richard Otis.
14. Ann, born 54-14-1669; married
    James Sternegen.
15. Hulda, born 7-16-1670; married
    Nathaniel Ware.
16. Bethsheba, born 9-21-1671; married
    Thomas Babb (See Babb Family).
17. Christopher, born 10-16-1672;
    married Sarah - children:
        Eliakin
        Judith, m. John Sloop
18. Hope, died young.

HUTSON BIBLE RECORD

Births

Harry Carl Hutson was born March 20, 1880.
Edgar L. Hutson was born September 13, 1888.
Edna Belle Hutson was born August 28, 1890.
Charles James Hutson was born October 1, 1892.
Arla Thomas Hutson was born August 20, 1894.
Reuben Jester Hutson was born June 5, 1897.
Ray Hutson was born January 4, 1900.
Earl Riggle Hutson was born December 16, 1901.
George B. Hutson was born April 30, 1855.
Martha J. Hutson was born September 9, 1868.

Edna M. Hudson was born September 5, 1900.
Harlie W. Hudson was born June 25, 1892.
Orbourne W. Hudson was born January 21, 1919.
Preston J. Hudson was born April 6, 1923.
Ruth Hudson was born April 25, 1927.

MARY JANE HYATT BIBLE

(Original owner of this Bible was Mary Jane Hyatt, daughter of Mary E. (Thatcher) Hyatt and Benjamin Merrit Hyatt, son of Samuel and grandson of Capt. Peter Hyatt of St. Georges Hundred. The present owner of this Bible is Mrs. Edward Hyatt Porter, 1102 Brandon Lane, "Westover Hills", Wilmington, Delaware. Bible published by John E. Potter & Co., Philadelphia, Pa. 1866.)

Marriages

Morrison D. White and Mary Jane Hyatt, both of Wilmington, Delaware, were married on December 20, 1860 by Rev. Wm. H. Brisband at Wilmington, Delaware.
William Frank Porter and Eva E. White, both of Wilmington, Delaware, were married on October 28, 1884 by Rev. Turner at Philadelphia, Pa.
Homer M. White and Rhea W. Larkin, both of Wilmington, Delaware, were married March 20, 1902 by Rev. O. G. Duddington at Wilmington, Delaware.
Albert Hyatt White and Jeanette Y. Leary, both of Wilmington, were married September 27, 1905 by Rev. T. S. McCurdy.

Births

Mabel White was born September 17, 1861.
Florence H. White was born June 21, 1863.
William M. White was born January 4, 1865.
Eva Estella White was born June 11, 1868.
Homer M. White was born July 26, 1871.
Mary Thatcher White was born December 31, 1874.
Albert Hyatt White was born December 15, 1878.
Mabel Hyattt Porter was born December 1, 1885.
Morrison D. White was born August 27, 1835.
Mary E. Thatcher Hyatt was born December 11, 1809.
Mary Jane Hyatt was born April 6, 1839.

Deaths

Mabel White died September 18, 1861.
Florence H. White died August 21, 1863.
William Morris White died April 21, 1869.

Mary Thatcher White died October 25, 1877.
Mabel H. Porter died July 20, 1886.
Morrison D. White died July 5, 1895.
Mrs. Eva E. Porter, wife of W. Frank Porter, died April 29, 1916.
Mary Jane White died February 21, 1926.

Memorandum:

    Eva E. White was baptized in Delaware Avenue Church by Rev. J. M. Haldeman, February 5, 1892, and was taken in or received the Right Hand of Fellowship, March 5, 1892.

    Charles Edward Hyatt Porter was baptized in Second Baptist Church by Rev. F. F. Briggs on April 10, 1904.

Copied by Harriett A. Shaw for Caesar Rodney Chapter D.A.R., 11-19-1959.

<u>Capt. Peter Hyatt</u>
St. Georges Hd.

    Samuel <u>Hyatt</u>

        Ben. Merritt <u>Hyatt</u>

            Mary Jane <u>Hyatt</u>
            b. 4-6-1839 1. **
        Mary E. d. 2-21-1926
        <u>Thatcher</u> m.
        b. 12-11-1809
        d. 2-14-1897
            Morrison D. <u>White</u>
            b. 8-27-1835

1.** from above:
    1. Mabel
    2. Florence
    3. Wm. M.
    4. Eva E.
    5. Homer M.
    6. Mary T.
    7. Albert H.

Chart continued next page.

Hyatt Chart Cont'd.

Eva Estella White
b. 6-11-1868
d. 4-29-1916
m. 10-28-1884   Edward Hyatt Porter

Wm. Frank Porter

Homer M. White
b. 7-26-1871
d.
m. 3-20-1902
Rhea W. Larkin

Albert Hyatt White
b. 12-15-1878
d.
m. 9-27-1905
Jeanette Y. Leary

JAMISON - VANDERGRIFT - MCWHORTER

(Old and New Testament, Hartford, Conn. B. White and Hutchinson Ducise. Owned by Agnes Golden Hackenburg, Philadelphia, niece of Mrs. Florence Jamison Posey, 1011 West 8th St., Wilmington, Delaware.)

Marriages

Abraham Vandergrift and Mary Bowman were married
    March 17, 1818.
Mary Ann Vandergrift and Thomas Jamison were
    married April 24, 1837.
Agnes Jamison and Charles Henry McWhorter were
    married September 6, 1865.
Laura Jamison and John Thomas McWhorter were
    married - no date.
Clarence Jamison and Margaret McWhorter were
    married April 27, 1876.
Agnes Irene McWhorter and Albert Golden were
    married January 26, 1899.
Albert Vandergrift Jamison and Ella Lacey were
    married April 10, 1904 in Philadelphia, Pa.

Florence Vane Jamison and Albert W. Posey were
married October 17, 1917 at home in
St. Georges, Delaware.

Births

Thomas Jamison was born December 12, 1809.
Mary Ann Vandergrift, daughter of Abraham and
Mary Bowman Vandergrift, was born
March 24, 1819. Children of Thomas and
Mary Ann Jamison:
  Albert Jamison, son of Thomas and Mary Ann
    Jamison, was born October 18, 1839.
  Mary Jamison, daughter of Thomas and Mary Ann
    Jamison, was born December 9, 1841.
  Anna Jamison, daughter of Thomas and Mary Ann
    Jamison, was born December 13, 1843.
  Agnes Jamison, daughter of Thomas and Mary Ann
    Jamison, was born February 18, 1845.
  Laura Jamison, daughter of Thomas and Mary Ann
    Jamison, was born July 29, 1849.
  Edgar Jamison, son of Thomas and Mary Ann
    Jamison, was born 1851.
  Oliver Jamison, son of Thomas and Mary Ann
    Jamison, was born 1856.
  Clarence Jamison, son of Thomas and Mary Ann
    Jamison, was born March 17, 1857.

Children of Clarence and Margaret Jamison:
  Charles Henry was born April 18, 1877.
  Albert Vandergrift was born August 24, 1879.
  Raymond Leslie was born June 5, 1881.
  Florence Vane was born September 1, 1884.
  Clarence Lee was born May 30, 1887.

Deaths

Mary B. Vandergrift, wife of Abraham Vandergrift,
  died November 12, 1820, age 23 years.
Mary Jamison (Houston), mother of Thomas Jamison,
  died March 2, 1852.
Albert Jamison, son of Thomas and Mary Ann
  Jamison, died July 6, 1854.
Mary Ann Vandergrift, wife of Thomas Jamison, died
  October 9, 1862.
Our father, Thomas Jamison, died December 12, 1864.
Sarah Janvier, second wife of Abraham Vandergrift,
  died December 15, 1871, age 82 years.

Abraham Vandergrift died December 2, 1872.
Agnes Jamison McWhorter died May 6, 1927.
Laura Jamison McWhorter died January 9, 1930.
Oliver Jamison died 1932.
Clarence Jamison died September 9, 1935.
Margaret McWhorter Jamison, wife of Clarence
    Jamison, died December 12, 1941.
Raymond Leslie Jamison died February 4, 1917.
Charles Henry Jamison died August 10, 1932.
Clarence Lee Jamison died August 3, 1933.
Albert Vandergrift Jamison died June 6, 1944.

WILLIAM JARDEN & MARY YOEST

William Jarden and Mary Yoest were married
    September 25, 1802.

Births

Christianna Jarden, daughter of William and Mary
    his wife, was born December 10, 1803.
A son was born December 20, 1805.
Alexander Jarden was born October 11, 1806.
Charles Jarden was born June 26, 1809.
Mary Jarden was born August 6, 1812.
Margaret Jarden was born June 5, 1815.
Samuel Jarden, son of Wm. and Mary his wife,
    was born January 19, 1818.

Robert Jarden was born July 20, 1730.
Christianna, wife of Robert, was born 1738.
Mary Jarden was born November 18, 1765.
Margaret Jarden was born October 23, 1768.
Samuel Jarden was born June 10, 1770.
Alexander Jarden was born May 6, 1773.
William Jarden was born May 4, 1778.

Deaths
A son of Wm. and Mary his wife, died December 22,
    1805, age 2 days.
Alexander Jarden died July 6, 1808, age 1 year,
    8 months and 27 days.
William Jarden died November 14, 1823, age 46
    years, 6 months and 12 days.

Mary Jarden died January 18, 1850, in her
   17 year (77?).
Robert Jarden died December 20, 1803, age
   73 years and 5 months.
Christianna Jarden died 24 or 6 (should it be
   24 or 6?) 1814, age 76 years.
Samuel Jarden died 1817, age 47 years.
Alexander Jarden died April 1809, age 36 years.

Robert Jarden
b. 7-20-1730   William Jarden
                b. 5-4-1778
Christianna   d. 11-14-1802   Christianna
b. 1738   m. 11-14-1823   b. 1803
                                 Alexander b. 1806
Christopher   Charles b. 1809
Yoest   Mary, b. 1812
b. 1738   Mary Yoest   Margaret, b. 1815
                b. 5-31-1782   Samuel, b. 1818
Hannah   d. 1-18-1850

JOHNS FAMILY BIBLE RECORD

(Bible now owned by the Delaware Historical
Society. Record given by Mrs. Glenn S. Skinner,
Newark, Delaware.)

Fidelia Johns, daughter of Kensey and Anne Johns -
   late Anne - was born January 18, 1785.
Anne Johns, daughter of Kensey and Anne Johns,
   was born September 10, 1787.
Susanna Johns, daughter of Kensey and Anne Johns,
   was born December 16, 1789.
Kensey Johns, son of Kensey and Anne Johns, was
   born December 10, 1791.
John Johns, son of Kensey and Anne Johns, was
   born July 10, 1796.
Vandyke Johns, son of Kensey and Anne Johns, was
   born November 5, 1798.
Vandyke Johns died February 15, 1801.
Henry Vandyke Johns, son of Kensey and Anne Johns,
   was born October 23, 1803.

Anne Johns, wife of Kensey Johns, died October 21,
   1839, age 71 years and 2 months.

Hon. Kensey Johns, our father, own hand wrote the above.

Henry Vandyke, son of Kensey and Anne Johns, died April 22, 1859, age 55 years and 6 months.
Kensey Johns, eldest son of Kensey and Anne Johns, died March 28, 1857, age 66 years.
Susan Johns, third daughter of Kensey and Anne Johns, and wife of Doctor David Stewart, died December 5, 1862, age 72 years, 11 months and 19 days.
Fidelia Johns, eldest daughter of Kensey and Anne Johns, and wife of Major Thomas Stockton, died February 20, 1871, age 86 years, 1 month and 2 days.
Kensey Johns, Sr., died December 21, 1848, age 90 years; buried at Immanuel Chruchyard, New Castle, Delaware.

ANDREW M. JOHNSON BIBLE

(Copyright July 1, 1886. Owned by Clifford E. Johnson, Rodaline Ave., Lewes, Delaware.)

Certificate of Marriage

This is to certify that Andrew M. Johnson of Angola, and Maggie E. Pettyjohn of Georgetown, were joined together by me in the bonds of Holy Matrimony at Georgetown, on the 22nd day of December in the year of our Lord 1829.

Marriages

Tilleta E. Johnson and Walter L. Warrington were married July 27, 1917 at the Nassau Parsonage by Rev. G. S. Allen.

Births

Annie Mary Johnson was born April 13, 1891.
William Perry Johnson was born April 29, 1894.
Tilleta Emily Johnson was born December 3, 1895.
Maggie Susan Johnson was born August 8, 1897.
Ebe Tunnell Johnson was born May 5, 1899.
Clifford Edward Johnson was born January 24, 1901.

Clifford Edward Johnson married Lida May Steele on
December 19, 1921. Their children:
Clifford Edward Johnson, Jr. born 2-14-1930
Mary Elizabeth Johnson born 7-29-1926
Margaret Johnson born 3-10-1923
Phyllis Lillian Johnson born 6-20-1934

Deaths

William Perry Johnson died June 21, 1901.
Andrew Manship Johnson died February 3, 1925.
Maggie Emma Johnson died February 10, 1937.
Ebe Tunnell Johnson died October 1938.
Anna Mary Johnson died May 15, 1945.

From a card in the above mentioned Bible:

William A. Pettyjohn died June 13, 1938.

JOHNSTON FAMILY

(Original record is owned by Genealogical Society
of Pennsylvania. This record is on a slip of
paper in the Kirby Bible.)

Births

John Johnston, born 1781.
Caroline Snyder, his wife, born June 29, 1803.

James Gardner Johnston, born June 2, 1826.
John Johnston, Jr., born September 23, 1827.
Thomas Johnston, born July 7, 1829.
Mary Ann Elizabeth Johnston, born February 6, 1831.
Caroline White Johnston, born June 28, 1832.
Margaretta Johnston, born November 6, 1833.

George S. Warren, born October 7, 1836.
Charles Henry Ball Warren, born March 25, 1838.
Caroline W. Warren, born March 25, 1838.

Shreve Warren, born January 25, 1795.
Christina Dickinson, born July 30, 1819.

Deaths

John Johnston died March 17, 1834, age 53 years.
George S. Warren died November 7, 1836, age 1 mo.
Caroline White Johnston died September 17, 1837.
Margaretta Johnston died September 30, 1837, age
    4 years.
Charles Henry Ball Warren died July 14, 1838.
Caroline Williamson Warren died July 17, 1838,
    age 4 months.
Caroline Warren died November 13, 1838, age
    35 years.
James Gardner Johnston died June 5, 1840, age
    14 years.
John Johnston, Jr. died February 2, 1849, age
    22 years.
Shreve Warren died October 2, 1849, age 55 years.
Thomas Johnston died May 1, 1861.

On another sheet of paper in Kirby Bible:

Sarah Warren was born January 1, 1768.
William Warren was born April 1, 1770.
Isaac Warren was born October 1, 1771.
John Warren was born November 12, 1773.
Eunice Warren was born October 12, 1776.
Jacob Warren was born December 31, 177?.
Priscilla Warren was born October 1, 1781.
William Warren was born January 16, 1784.
Mary Warren was born September 8, 1786.
Rebecca Warren was born September 28, 1788.
Elizabeth Warren was born November 12, 1790.
Ann Warren was born December 9, 1792.
Shreve Warren was born January 25, 1795.

Above are the children of Jacob and Rebecca Warren.

JOYCE BIBLE

(Bible was printed by W. Young, Bookseller, Phil.
1790. Presented to the Delaware Historical
Society, Wilmington, Del., November 12, 1946 by
Mr. F. H. Clymer, Wilmington. Record was given by
Mrs. Glenn S. Skinner, Newark, Del.)

Thomas R. Joyce, son of Garret Joyce, was born December 21, 1767 in Dublin. He married Rebecky R. _____, who was born 1768 and who died September 16, 1833. Their Children:
1. Nancy R. Joyce, born July 10, 1792; died April 24, 1797.
2. Thomas R. Joyce, born November 18, 1794; died August 5, 1832.
3. Betsy R. Joyce, born November 23, 1796.
4. Samuel R. Joyce, born June 17, 1798 at Lewistown.
5. Nelly R. Joyce, born September 8, 1800.
6. Liddy R. Joyce, born September 8, 1802 at Brandywine.
7. Rebecky R. Joyce, born March 20, 1807; married James Horton and they had a son: Thomas Horton; died Sept. 2, 1832.
8. Phillip R. Joyce, born February 25, 1809; died August 14, 1810.
9. Anney R. Joyce, born March 10, 1812.
10. Patty R. Joyce, born September 20, 181?

KELSO & FRIEDEL BIBLE

(Bible was owned by John Kelso, grandfather of Rev. John Mason Kelso. Now owned by Mrs. John M. Kelso, Richardson Park, Wilmington. Record copied by Mrs. Clara W. Bird.)

William T. H. was born September 13, 1836.
Elizabeth Kelso was born August 2, 1828.
Jane Fipps Kelso was born August 12, 1832; died June 4, 1851.
John Mitchell was born September 23, 1838.
Sofia Kelso was born May 22, 1816.
John Kelso was born June 21, 1818.

Susan Jane Mason was born July 15, 1845.
John M. Kelso was born February 23, 1878, Evergreen Farm, Virginia.

Note: Susan J. Kelso was mother of Rev. John M. Kelso.

Children of John and Susan Kelso:
  Rev. Hugh Klair Kelso
  Rev. John Mason Kelso; married Rachel Adel
    Friedel of Viola, Del., 3-25-1908;
    born 12-22-1879.
  Annie Kelso, married William Edward Moore.
  Jane Kelso, married Charles Sledd Diggs.
  Etruria McKay Kelso, married Rev. Richard B.
    Wells.

Rev. John M. Kelso died May 19, 1950 at Dover,
  Del. Children:
  John Friedel Kelso, born May 20, 1909 at
    Viola, Del.
  Frederick Kelso, born June 15, 1911 at
    Queenstown, Md.
  Rose Mary Kelso, born January 19, 1914 at
    Nassau, Del.
  Margaret Jane Kelso, born August 2, 1918 at
    Crapo, Md.

- - - - - - - - - -

(Frederick Friedel and Rosanna (Heyd) Bible was published by John E. Potter & Co., Phil. Original owner was Frederick & Rosanna Friedel; present owner Mrs. J. M. Kelso, Wilmington, Del.)

Marriages

Frederick Friedel and Rosanna Heyd were married
  March 11, 1875.
Reuben Franklin Friedel and Martha H. Dacis were
  married November 15, 1906.
Rachel Adella Friedel and John M. Kelso were
  married March 25, 1908.
Mary Ellen Friedel and Dallas C. Moore were
  married November 18, 1908.

Births

Frederick Friedel was born March 5, 1850;
  died July 2, 1937.
Rosanna Heyd Friedel was born December 29, 1849;
  died December 18, 1935.
John Jacob Friedel was born January 22, 1876;
  died September 17, 1876.

Reuben Friedel was born December 4, 1877; died
    September 6, 1920.
Rachel Adella was born December 22, 1879.
Mary Ellen was born February 8, 1882.

KENDALL BIBLE - 1831

(Bible in the possession of Edwin Sawdon, 4172
21st St., Wilmington, Delaware. 1954.)

Marriages

Jesse Kendall and Mary Kellam were married
    August 10, 1819.
Jesse Kendall and Elizabeth Forwood were
    married April 13, 1837.
James Kendall and Elenor Balys were married
    May 27, 1841.
Samuel Baylis and Sarah Kendall were married
    May 12, 1842.
Henry Kendall and Elizabeth Booth were married
    December 21, 1848.
Benjamin F. Hanby and Martha Kendall were married
    February 7, 1850.
John J. Martin and Mary E. Kendall were married
    November 20, 1865.

Births

Jesse Kendall was born April 10, 1793.
Mary Kendall was born May 16, 1799.

James Kendall was born June 22, 1820.
Susan Kendall was born January 19, 1822.
Sarah H. Kendall was born August 31, 1823.
Rebecca Kendall was born August 6, 1825.
Henry R. Kendall was born December 18, 1827.
Margaret L. Kendall was born October 9, 1830.
Martha C. Kendall was born September 15, 1831.

Elizabeth Kendall was born December 28, 1801.

Mary Emma Kendall was born December 18, 1838.
Lydia Kendall was born January 8, 1841.

Lillie C. Martin was born November 14, 1866
(Mrs. Lillie Barnes).

On a loose piece of paper in this Bible:

Mary Emma Hanby, b. May 24, 1851.
Jesse H. Hanby, b. 6-11-1853.
Lotie D. Hanby, b. Feb. 7, 1857.
Clara Hanby, b. April 7, 1859.
James, b. July 15, 1861.
B. Frank, b. Dec. 5, 1863.
Charles Hanby was born Oct. 7, 1874.

Mabel R. Hanby died June 18, 1867; b. 1-28-1865.
Mabel Hanby died July 5, 1873; b. 7-24-1871.
Arthur S., b. 12-15-1867.

Note: Mary Kellam has bro. and sisters: Richard, David, Margaret, Elizabeth, Eveline, Sarah, Ann and Rebecca.

Note: Commodore MacDonough's sister was Frank's grandmother on his father's side (Lydia).

Jesse Kendall
b. 4-10-1793
d. 7-10-1874
   Age 81-3m.
m. 8-10-1819
Mary Kellam
b. 5-16-1799
d. 8-11-1835
m. 4-13-1837
Elizabeth
Forwood
b. 12-28-1801
d. 12-12-1869

1. James Kendall
   b. 6-22-1820
   d. 6-21-1871
   m. 5-27-1841
   Elenor Balye

2. Susan Kendall
   b. 1-18-1822
   d. 10-19-1822

3. Sarah H. Kendall
   b. 8-31-1823
   d.
   m. 54-12-1842
   Samuel Baylis

4. Rebecca
   b. 8-6-1825
   d. 6-5-1828

Chart continued next page.

Kendall Chart Cont'd.

5. Henry R. Kendall
   b. 12-18-1827
   d.
   m. 12-21-1848
   Elizabeth Booth

6. Margaret Kendall
   b. 10-9-1830
   d. 10-24-1830

7. Martha C. Kendall
   b. 9-15-1831
   d.
   m. 3-7-1850
   Benjamin F. Hanby

8. Mary Emma Kendall
   b. 12-18-1838
   d.   Lillie C. Martin
   m. 11-2-1865
   John J. Martin

9. Lydia
   b. 1-8-1841

KINSEY - WHITEMAN

David Kinsey, of the Parish of Nantmeal County, Radnor, Wales, carpenter, purchased 100 acres of land in Pennsylvania - date of purchase as recorded in Phila., Deed Book was June 19 and 20, 1682.

From the records of the Board of Property we learn that a tract of 300 acres was laid out to David Kinsey in Radnor Township in the Welsh Tract and the Town Lot to which he was entitled was laid out on Chestnut Street - a part of which is the present site of Independence Hall.

He was a member of the Society of Friends. In a list of "Burials at Burying Place of Harverford West side of Scoolkill" is the following record:

"David Kinsey buried ye 7th day of 7th month, 1687."

On the 16th day of November 1689, letters of administration were granted by the Register General at Phil., to Magdalen Kinsey, relict and widow of David Kinsey, late of ye township of Radnor in the County of Phil., Yeoman, deceased, on the estate of her said husband. (Adm. Docket A, p. 98).

Patents were issued for the 300 acres in Radnor to Magdalen Kinsey and her son, John.

On the 20th day of the 9th month 1690, Magdalen Kinsey, widow, married Howell James, widower. Her son, John, was a witness. Her maiden name is unknown. She died before 4-25-1715 as Howell James then married Phebe Moor (More). He later moved to New Castle Co., Delaware.

The records of Newark Monthly Meeting (which later became Center Meeting), 5th month 3rd, 1798, show that Howell James appeared and produced a letter from his wife's son, Edmund Kinsey, asking certificate of this meeting of his clearance in relation to marriage and at the following meeting a certificate was signed for Edmund Kinsey to Woodbridge Meeting in order for his marriage to Sarah Ogborn. She was the daughter of Jane Fitzrandolph.

This record was taken from "Early Friends of Upper Bucks Co., Pa." by Roberts.

Samuel Kinsey was the son of Sarah Ogborn and Edmund Kinsey. He was born near Woodbridge, N.J., October 20, 1710. He moved with his parents to Buckingham in 1715 and died there in December 1776. He married July 1733, Elizabeth Crewe, of a New Jersey family and had 11 children, all of whom raised families.

John Kinsey was the son of Samuel and Elizabeth
(Crewe) Kinsey. He was born in Buckingham in
1749 and died in Chester Co., Pa., January 13,
1834, is buried in the Friend's Burying Ground
at Little Britain. He married at Buckingham
Meeting, May 21, 1777, Margaret Kitchen,
daughter of Thomas Kitchen of S---bury. They
lived at Buckingham until 1811 when they moved
to Chester Co., Pa., taking a certificate to
New Garden Monthly Meeting, 4th month 9th,
1811.

KINSEY - WHITEMAN

(This record was found after Vol. VII of "Delaware
Bible Records" was written. See that Vol. for
"Kinsey" data. Record was given by Mary Irene
Kinsey, Librarian of Richland Library, Quakertown,
Pa. It was compiled by her father.)

David Kinsey, the founder of the Kinsey family in
America, came from Bristol, England, with a
brother, John Kinsey. John settled in New
Jersey; was very active in the Government at
that time. A book entitled "John Kinsey"
describes his activities.

David Kinsey carried his Certificate from Bristol,
England, dated June 26, 1682. He died 1688.
He had two sons:
 Edmund Kinsey
 John Edmund Kinsey

Edmund Kinsey married Sarah Ogborn, daughter of
Jane Fitzrandolph Ogborn.

John Edmund Kinsey married Sarah ---; settled in
Bucks Co., Pa. He purchased 500 acres around
Buckingham Meeting and became a very
prominent Minister of that Meeting. He was
previously a member of Woodbridge, New Jersey
Meeting. He is buried at Buckingham Meeting.

1st: David Kinsey; died 1688; wife Magdalene
2nd: Edmund Kinsey; wife Sarah Ogborn.
3rd: Samuel Kinsey; wife Elizabeth Crewe.
4th: John Kinsey; wife Margaret Kitchen.

Children of John and Margaret (Kitchen) Kinsey:
1. Elizabeth, born April 25, 1778; married John Ballance.
2. Rachel, born November 6, 1779; married Jonathan Swayne.
3. Nathaniel, born July 13, 1781; married Nov. 12, 1812 to Hannah Griffith.
4. Margaret, born October 9, 1783; married Moses White.
5. Mary, born October 27, 1785; unmarried.
6. Martha, born March 10, 1787; married James Buckingham of New Castle Co., Del. (See Vol. VII). Died January 30, 1858.
7. Mary (2nd), born June 5, 1789; married Joseph Iliff of Bucks Co., Pa.
8. Abigail, born May 30, 1791; died Nov. 10, 1856; married John G. Griffith.
9. John, Jr., born October 18, 1794; died Jan. 24, 1864; married 1st Elizabeth Foulke; married 2nd Margaret Woodward.
10. Anna, born March 8, 1798 in Greenville, Bucks Co., Pa., now called Holicong; died Jan. 3, 1875; married Henry Whiteman.

Joseph Iliff was a Methodist Minister of Bucks Co., Pa. Children of Mary 2nd and Joseph Iliff:
1. John K. Iliff
2. George Washington Iliff; married Mary Hibbard of Willistown, Chester Co., Pa., and moved to Richmond, Ind. Their children were:
    1. Elizabeth
    2. Carrie
    3. Lydia
    4. Josephine
3. Margaret Iliff
4. John Wesley Iliff

5. Joseph Iliff married a niece of Mary
   Hibbard's 1st, 2nd married Tillie---?
   Their children were:
   1. Ella
   2. Minnie (lived in Media, Pa.)

Children of Abigail Kinsey and John G. Griffith, a coachmaker of Quakertown, Pa.:
1. Edward K. Griffith, born September 24, 1816; died February 1854; married --- Roth.
2. Margaretta Griffith, born December 6, 1818; married ? Pracket. Children:
   1. Abby
   2. Maggie
   3. Gertrude

3. Jane, born December 29, 1820; died 1872.
4. Hannah, born January 25, 1823; died January 16, 1892.

Anna Kinsey, born 3-8-1798 in Greenville, Bucks Co., Pa., now called Holicong; died 1-3-1875; married Henry Whiteman, a German, born April 19, 1791; died Feb. 20, 1855.

Children of Anna Kinsey and Henry Whiteman:
1. John Kinsey Whiteman, born 9-18-1817; married Margaret ---. Children:
   1. Florence   5. Anna   9. Emma
   2. Henry   6. Louis   10. Jefferson
   3. Sarah   7. Belle   11. Clara
   4. Levenia   8. Laura

2. George Washington Whiteman, born 1-11-1825.
3. Henry Whiteman, born 9-29-1827; married Sallie Ann Moore, 5-7-1857.
4. Kicel Whiteman, born 4-3-1830; died 4-12-1831.
5. Gilberyt, born 2-14-1833; married Emma Moore. Children:
   1. Bessie; married Thadeus Montgomery.

6. Andrew Jackson Whiteman, born 12-16-1835; married 1st, Mary Elizabeth Moore; married 2nd, Susanna Moore (sisters of Jacob Moore). Children:
    Arthur Whiteman
    Bertha; married William Trayner
    Jesse, married Samuel Pearson
    Irma; married B. Whiteman
7. Margaret Jane, born 10-26-1838; married Jacob Moore.
8. (Should be 2nd) Sarah Ann Whiteman, born 10-19-1819; married --- Chambers and had a son:
    Joseph, who married Rachel Moore, sister of Jacob, Sallie, etc.
9. (Should be 3rd) Lemuel Whiteman, born 12-23-1821; married twice and had:
    William
    Molly, married --- Past and had Molly Past.
    Children by 2nd wife:
    Amos
    Enos
    George
    Louise

KIRBY FAMILY RECORD

(This record was given by Eleanora Shaffer Lamborn, West Chester, Pa.)

    Recompense Kirby of Sandwich, Mass., first appears on the records of New England in 1636, as an inhabitant of Lynn, Mass. In 1637, together with William Wood and others of Lynn, he moved to Cape Cod and began the settlement of the town of Sandwich. He is mentioned as the neighbor of Thomas Gampton of Sandwich in his will, dated 1638 and, the same year, he with others was fined for having swine unringed.

    He shared his division of the new lands in 1641. His name appears in the list made in August 1634 of the 68 inhabitants of Sandwich who were able to bear arms.

He is one of the 11 male members whose names are found in the first recorded list of members of the Puritan Church of Sandwich.

In 1651 he was presented, with others, with notice of non-attendance of public worship. There was trouble at this time in the Church between the Rev. Leveridge and his people and Recompense Kirby may have simply stood off from the contestants. In the Autumn of 1656, Nicholas Upsall (Upsaill), a Puritan of Boston who had been exiled from protesting against imprisonment of Mary Fisher, the first Quaker to appear in Boston, found a temporary refuge in Sandwich.

The Plymouth Records of this time contain a complaint that Nicholas Upsaill, Richard Kirby and the wife of John Newland, and others did frequently meet together at the home of William Allen on the Lords Day and other times. They used to protest against Magistrates and Ministers to "dishonor" God and Contempt of Government (Plymouth Court Orders III, page 105). So far as we know, the names contained above are the first persons in this country to embrace Principles of the Friends.

The name of the wife of Richard Kirby, Sr. is not known. Her first name was probably Jane. There is a Sandwich record that Jane Kirby had twin children, Increase and Abigail, born February 1650; they died soon after. Jane was buried together with her son, Richard, March 23, 1650. The mention of her son, however, throws some doubt upon the matter and suggests that she might have been the wife of Richard Kirby, Jr. Nevertheless, the circumstances of having two living children of the same name is unprecedented and a daughter of Richard Kirby, Jr. was named Jane.

This daughter was married in September 1651, it is probable her mother married before 1635 in Lynn, Mass.

The children of Richard Kirby were:
1. Jane; died before July 21, 1707; married July 12, 1651 to Theodore Saunders of Sandwich.
2. Sarah, born 1638; died after July 21, 1707; married Matthew Allen.
3. Richamath, died after July 21, 1707.
4. Patience Gilford, widow of Abigail Howland.
5. Recompense, died 1720; married Rebecca A--------.

It is quite probable that John Kirby of Middletown; Joseph of Harford; Richard of Sandwich, were related - perhaps brothers.

It is highly probable that John and Joseph were brothers - from various records and incidents. Both came from Warwickshire, England and both were at Hartford near the time of the settlement. The tradition in both families claim they were brothers. There is also reason for this belief that John was a brother of Richard of Sandwich too.

John came to New England in the "Hopewell," Captain Hobb Master. It sailed from London for New England, September 11, 1635. His name is found registered among those of the other passengers as "jo Kirby, age 12 years" and it is the only Kirby named.

It is reasonable to believe that he came in care of "husb" William Wood, aged 27 years. William Wood seems to have settled in Lynn, as early as 1629, sailed for London August 15, 1633, and returned to Lynn September 11, 1635. In 1637 he went with 50 people and commenced a settlement at Sandwich, Mass. Ref.: "History of Lynn" by Lewis & Newhall. He says on page 113, that William Wood wrote an interesting work entitled "New Englands Prospect" which contains a fine account of the early settlements.

Since Richard Kirby was at first a resident of Lynn and afterward accompanied William Wood to Sandwich, we may suspect that John Kirby, aged 12 years, was in the care of William Wood to be conveyed to his brother, Richard.

Children of Richard Kirby (III):
Mary   Jonathan   A child born
Recompense   Joseph   after Oct. 14,
Richard   John   1733.

Joseph Kirby of New Hanover, N. J. was born October 1751. He married Anne -----, born 1752. Their children:
Abraham
Isaac
Jacob Kirby, who was a Revolutionary soldier
    (Ref: Register of New Jersey soldiers).

Isaac Kirby was born September 23, 1756 in New Jersey; married 1st Hannah Haines; married 2nd Phoebe Haines. He was a soldier before he married. After the Revolution he removed to Pennsylvania and settled in Greene County, where he died 1852, age 96 years. Children by his 1st wife:
Samuel S. Kirby, born September 16, 1794 in
    Greene Co.; married Elenor Haines.

* * * * * * * * *

Richard Kirby (1st) came to America 1634, and settled in Lynn, Mass. He married Sarah Allen (?); he died 1688. Their children:
Recompense
Richard, died 1740.

Recompense married Rebecca. Died 1720 at Burlington Co., New Jersey. Their children:
William
Rebecca
Benjamin
Richard

Richard Kirby, son of Recompense and Rebecca Kirby, married Elizabeth (? Anne). Their children:
Mary
Jonathan, born 1752
Amos, born 1757; died 1795, 38 years.
John
Joseph
Jacob

Amos Kirby, son of Richard and Elizabeth Kirby, married Ann Haines, who was born 1755; died 1838. Their children:

Richard, born 1782; died 1845, age 53 years.
William, born 1783; died 1787, age 4 years.
Hannah, born 1784; died 1852, age 72 years.
Job, born 1788; died 1872, age 84 years.
John, born 1789; died 1832, age 43 years.
Amos, born 1791; died 1814, age 23 years.
Elizabeth Ann (Guant), born 1792; died 1869, age 77 years.
Deborah, born 1794; died 1878; age 84 years (Somers).

Job Kirby, son of Amos and Ann Kirby, was born 1788; died 1872; married May Varnon. Their children:
Enoch, born 1808; died 1861, age 53 years.
Charles, born 1810; died 1883, age 73 years; married Martha.
Amos, born 1814; died 1900, age 86 years.
William, born 1816; died 1887, age 71 years.
David, born 1818.
Asa M., born 1821; died 1822, age 1 year.
Elizabeth, born 1823; died 1846, age 23 years.

Amos Kirby, son of Job and May Kirby, married Rachel ---, lived at Mullica Hill, New Jersey. Their children:
Elizabeth, married --- Rudgway.
Maggie P., married --- Iredell.
Mary, married 1st --- Coless; married 2nd --- Iredell.
George
Christina, married --- Edwards.
Clayton J.
Edward
Frank

(Note: Belle Owen's great grandmother was Mercy Kirby. This family dates back to 1625 when they came from Wales.)

John Kirby, son of Amos and Ann Kirby, was born 1789; died 1832; married March 2, 1815 Hannah Bassett. Their children:
Ebenezer, born April 24, 1816; married Martha Somers. Children:
Sara, married Joel Borton
Hanna, married (Fitchcraft)

Emily, born August 1, 1818; died young.
Ruth, born July 6, 1820; died young.
Chalkey, born December 6, 1822; married
   Malissa ---. Children:
   Jacob
   Rachel
   Deborah, married Richard Somers.
   Chalkey
   Jane

Jacob, born June 16, 1825; died 1-30-1890;
   married Mary Ann Horner 2-22-1849. Their
   children:
   Edwin C., b born 6-26-1850; died 1933.
   Elizabeth H., born 8-3-1852; died 1914.
   Chalky, born 9-11-1854.
   George H., born 12-11-1857.
   Emily R., born 1-21-1860.
   Ida, born 2-16-1865.
   Bassatt, born 3-25-1867.

Jacob Kirby, son of John and Hannah Kirby, was born June 16, 1825; died January 30, 1890; married Mary Ann Horner 2-22-1849, before William Pimm, Harrisonville, N.J. She was born 12-16-1828; died 1-29-1915. Their son, Edwin C., was born 6-26-1850; died 1933; married Caroline Dickinson (1855-1913). Children:
   Viola Matilda Kirby, 1876-1878.
   Verna Black, born 1879; married Frank
     Garrigues. Children:
     Ruth Alta Garrigues; married
       Charles McFadden. Children:
       Charles McFadden, III
       Alice Alta
       Frank G.
   Frances B., married Francis G. Tumbelty.
     Children:
     Francis G. Tumbelty
     Rhoda Ashcraft
     Betty Ann
     Franklin, died when a baby.
   Alice Richman, born 1887; married
     Maxwell H. Bunting.

Afer the death of Caroline H. Dickinson, wife of Edwin C. Kirby, he married a widow, Francena Doane Worthington, 1915.

Elizabeth Horner Kirby, daughter of Jacob and Mary
    Ann Horner Kirby, was born 8-3-1852; died
    1914, age 62 years. She married Samuel Moore.
    Their children:
    Wilbert Jacob, married 1st Mary Mancill;
        married 2nd Mae Sheppard. Children of
        Jacob and 1st wife:
        Legrand W., married Helen Clark.
        Martha E., married Henry Hunt.
        Samuel M., married Ruth Simpson.
     Children of Jacob and 2nd wife:
        Florence H., married Horace Wiley and
            had:
            Elizabeth M., married Donald W. Adams.
            David W., married Marjorie Biedert.
        Carlton E., married Mabel Andrews and
            had:
            Carlton, married Sara Edwards.
            Caroline (deceased).
            Elizabeth.
    Mary Kirby, married George R. Shinn and
        had:
        Verna Florence
        Wilbert Rollen

Chalkey Kirby, son of Jacob Kirby and Mary Ann
    Horner Kirby, was born 9-11-1854; died 1922,
    age 68 years. He married Emaline Wood.
    Their children:
    Thomas
    Arlene Louise
    Granville, married Ellen Harris and had:
        Jean
        Granville, Jr.
        William
        Harris
The 2nd wife of Chalkey Kirby was America.
The 3rd wife of Chalkey Kirby was Jennie Doane.

George Horner Kirby, son of Jacob and Mary Ann
    (Horner) Kirby, was born 12-11-1857; died
    1926, age 69 years. He married Sarah Bishop.
    Their children:
    Elsie (deceased)
    Elizabeth, married her 2nd cousin,
        Jacob Horner. Children:
        Erna, married Lloyd McJunken.
        Gladys, married Thomas Carroll.

     Joan, married Walter Nordquist.
     Kirby, married Mary.
     Cora.
    Eliza B., married Alfred Webester and had:
     Alice, married Cecil Chaney.
     Edith
     Ruth
     Audrey
     Edna (deceased)
     Bassett
     John (deceased)
     Melvin (deceased)

4. Amos B. Kirby, married Florence Paulding and had:
    Theophils, married Mary Peters.
    George, married Beatrice.
    Horace, married Grace.
5. Hannah, married Charles Feyhl.
6. <u>Eleonora, married Sherman Edwards</u> - both deceased. Children:
    Sherman Edwards, Jr. - deceased.
    <u>Edna, married George M. Shaffer</u>.
    Children:
     Eleonora M., married Louis
      Lamborn
     George M. Shaffer, Jr.
    John Jacob, married Hazel Jones and had:
     Marian
     Emily Ruth
     Dorothy

52. Emily Ruth Kirby, born January 21, 1869; died October 12, 1924, age 64 years.

53. Ida Kirby, born 1864; married Cooper Coles and had:
   William M. Coles, married 1st Sara Colson and had:
    Frances Vera and William.
   Married 2nd Margaret Hough and had:
    Mary Elizabeth Coles
    Marjorie.
   Jacob Kirby Coles
   Edwin C. Coles, married Eleanor DeMaris and had:
    Edwin and Merton.

       Frances Willard, married Frank Pettit
       and had:
          Elizabeth
          Marian
          Emily Ruth
          Elmer
       Oliver Hammond Coles, married Frances
          Hudson.

54. Bassett Kirby, son of Jacob Kirby and Mary Ann (Horner) Kirby, was born 3-25-1867; died ?; married Rhoda Ashcraft.

KIRBY RECORD

(Bible printed and published by M. Carey, 121 Chestnut St., Philadelphia, Pa. 1817. Now owned by The Genealogical Society of Pennsylvania.)

Marriages

Richard Kirby was born March 10, 1780; married December 22, 1806 to Mary Champney's, who was born March 27, 1780.

Robert Kirby was born April 7, 1731; married Mary Ann Bloyke on February 22, 1757, who was born August 9, 1736.

Richard Kirby, son of Robert, who was born June 5, 1769, was married July 8, 1783 to Eliz Crowninshield, who was born May 3, 1764.

Reginald W. Kirby married Wilhelimina Zimmerman on April 1, 1898 by Rev. Jessie Williams.

Edward Warren Kirby married Annette Thorington Conde, daughter of Joseph and Annette Norman Conde, in 1899. Born to them a son, Dunne Wilson Kirby on October 15, 1901.

Births

Maria Kirby, daughter of Richard Kirby and Mary his wife, was born October 24, 1807.

Rebecca Kirby, daughter of Richard Kirby and Mary his wife, was born June 17, 1809.

John Kirby, son of Richard Kirby and Mary his wife, was born February 10, 1811.

Mark M. Kirby, son of Richard and Mary, was born
   January 12, 1812.
Elizabeth Kirby, daughter of Richard Kirby and
   Mary his wife, was born August 30, 1814.
John Smith Kirby, son of Richard Kirby and Mary
   his wife, was born February 18, 1819.

Mary Ann Kirby, daughter of Richard Kirby and Ann
   his wife, was born February 1, 1820.
Hannah T. Kirby, daughter of Richard Kirby and Ann
   his wife, was born January 20, 1822.
Richard Kirby, son of Richard Kirby and Ann his
   wife, was born July 23, 1824.

Ann Kirby, daughter of Jacob and Rebecca Warren,
   and wife of Richard Kirby, was born
   December 9, 1792.
Robert Kirby, son of Richard, was born Sept. 15,
   1758.
Winnifred Kirby, daughter of Richard Kirby and
   Mary his wife, was born March 12, 1787.

Elizabeth Kirby, wife of John Kirby, died
   November 1, 1815, age 65 years.
Mary Kirby, wife of Richard Kirby, died
   July 16, 1818.
Richard Kirby Sr. died December 25, 1823.
Rebecca Warren died February 18, 1827.
Jacob Warren died August 7, 1836.
John Kirby, son of Richard Kirby and Mary
   his wife, died February 13, 1811.
Elizabeth Crowninshield Kirby died April 3, 1821.
Richard Kirby, who was born June 5, 1760, died
   November 25, 1816.
Robert Kirby, who was born September 15, 1758,
   died July 28, 1817.
Alice, wife of Robert Kirby, died September 2,
   1823.

In this Bible was another Bible Record torn out:

Marriages

In Calvary Church by Rev. Jos. H. Smith, Jr., on
   February 16, 1854, Richard Kirby - who was
   born July 23, 1824 - married Isabell Debell -
   who was born (deliberately cut out).
John Benjamin Hench was married October 15, 1843
   to Mary Ann Kirby, who was born Feb. 1, 1820.

By the Rev. Lewis Baker on August 12, 1877,
Reginald W. Kirby - who was born Jan. 1,
1855 - married Anna R. McDonald - who was
born October 18, 1858.
In Trinity M. E. Church by Rev. Chas. Nagle on
July 18, 1893, William Shreve Warren Kirby
married Sara L. Robinson.

Births

Reginald Warren Kirby, son of Richard Kirby and
Isabel his wife, was born January 1, 1855.
William Shreve Warren Kirby, son of Richard Kirby
and Isabel his wife, was born October 19,
1856.
Bellville Kirby, son of Richard Kirby and Isabel
his wife, was born September 12, 1860.
Elizabeth Drake Kirby, daughter of Reginald W.
Kirby and Ann his wife, was born July 9, 1878.
Edward Warren Kirby, son of Reginald W. Kirby and
Ann his wife, was born May 1880.
William Channing Hench, son of John B. Hench and
Mary Ann his wife, was born August 6, 1844.
Edward Warren Hench, son of John B. and Mary Ann
his wife, was born February 9, 1846.
Alice Caroline Hench, daughter of John B. and Mary
Ann his wife, was born April 6, 1857.
John Benjamin Hench, son of John B. and Mary Ann
his wife, was born August 14, 1854.

Deaths

Isabel Kirby, wife of Richard Kirby, died
September 17, 1860.
Bellville Kirby, son of Richard and Isabel
Kirby, died June 9, 1861.
Ann Warren Kirby, wife of Richard Kirby, died
April 9, 1877.
Richard Kirby, son of Richard and Ann Warren
Kirby, died November 17, 1888.
Hannah Thorne Kirby, daughter of Richard Kirby
Sr. and Ann his wife, died February 13, 1908.
Reginald Warren Kirby, husband of Wilhelmina
Kirby, died January 9, 1923,

LACEY FAMILY RECORD

(The Holy Bible. Published by John B. Perry, 198 Market Street, Philadelphia, Pa., and for sale by J. W. Bradley, 48 North Fourh Street, W. A. Leary, 138 North 2nd Street, New York, Nafis & Cornish. 1850. Owned by Mrs. Agnes (Lacey) Hazzard, Milton, Delaware. Record given by Mrs. D. Anthony Potter, Lewes, Delaware. 1957.)

Marriages

Robert L. Lacey and Priscilla, his wife, were
    married December 11, 1848.
Robert L. Lacey and Hester A. P. Simpler, his wife,
    were married May 3, 1856.
John Fletcher Lacey and Katherine Morse were
    married April 30, 1904 in St. Louis, Mo.
Chas. Franklin Lacey and Hannah E. Black were
    married July 1, 1889 in Milton, Del.
Agnes Lacey and John B. Hazzard were married
    January 18, 1919 in Philadelphia, Pa.
Franklin W. Hazzard and Thelma Townsend were
    married June 4, 1941 in Elkton, Md.

Pasted in by the marriage page:

Robert Louis Lacey, son of Spencer Lacey
    and Elizzabeth his wife, was born May 28,
    1815.
Priscilla Shepherd Hudson, daughter of Daniel
    Hudson and Louvenia his wife, was born
    February 5, 1820.
Hester Ann Parker Simpler, daughter of Peter R.
    Simpler and Louvenia his wife, was born
    September 11, 1827.
Hester A. P. Lacey-Houston, daughter of Peter R.
    Simpler and Louvenia his wife, died
    March 30, 1912.
Mary Boone Lacey, daughter of Hester Simpler and
    Robert L. Lacey, died September 17, 1951,
    age 94 years.
Franklin William Hazzard, son of Agnes Lacey and
    John Benjamin Hazzard, died October 26, 1952,
    age 31 years.

On a loose family record page from a much smaller Bible, placed here:

Marriages

Married April 8, 1834, Johnson Ellingsworth to Caroline Hudson, daughter of Daniel and Lavenia Hudson, both of Sussex Co., Del. by the Rev. Rogers, pastor of the Baptist church of the same place.

Births

Johnson Ellingsworth was born 1810.
Caroline Hudson, daughter of Daniel and Levenia Hudson, was born December 25, 1815.
Ann Eliza, daughter of Johnson and Caroline Ellingsworth, was born June 27, 1835.
John Henry, son of Johnson and Caroline Ellingsworth, was born January 23, 1838.
James Wise, son of Johnson and Caroline Ellingsworth, was born September 21, 1839.
Henry Smith, son of Johnson and Caroline Ellingsworth, was born July 2, 1842.

Deaths

Johnson Ellingsworth died August 22, 1844.
Ann Eliza, daughter of Johnson and Caroline Ellingsworh, died January ?, 1837.
John Henry, son of Johnson and Caroline Ellingsworth, died July 10, 1838.

(End of the small Bible record.)

Continuing in the large Bible:

Births

William Henry Lacey, son of Robert L. Lacey and Priscilla his wife, was born October 23, 1849.
James Emery Lacey, son of Robert L. Lacey and Priscilla his wife, was born June 25, 1851.
Charles Franklin Lacey, son of Robert L. Lacey and Priscilla his wife, was born September 21, 1853.
Mary Boone Lacey, daughter of Robert L. Lacey and Priscilla his wife, was born March 1, 1857.

George Robert Lacey, son of Robert L. Lacey and
   Hester A. P. Lacey his wife, was born
   June 16, 1862.
John Fletcher Lacey, son of Robert L. Lacey and
   Hester A. P. Lacey his wife, was born
   September 30, 1865.

Agnes Lacey, daughter of Charles F. Lacey and
   Hannah Eliza his wife, was born December 29,
   1890.
Dorothy Lacey, daughter of John Fletcher Lacey and
   Katherine Morse Lacey his wife, was born
   January 22, 1906.
Elizabeth Lacey, daughter of John Fletcher Lacey
   and Katherine Morse Lacey his wife, was born
   October 15, 1913.

Franklin William Hazzard, son of Agnes Lacey and
   John B. Hazzard, was born July 31, 1921.
Barbara Lacey Hazzard, daughter of Thelma Townsend
   and Franklin William Hazzard, was born
   December 30, 1946.
Nancy Johnson Hazzard, daughter of Thelma Townsend
   and Franklin William Hazzard, was born
   July 27, 1949.
John Franklin Hazzard, son of Thelma Townsend and
   Franklin William Hazzard, was born March 10,
   1953.

Deaths

James Emery Lacey, son of Robert L. Lacey and
   Priscilla his wife, died March 9, 1852.
Priscilla S. Lacey, wife of Robert L. Lacey,
   died February 5, 1855.
George Robert Lacey, son of Robert L. Lacey and
   Hester A. P. Lacey his wife, died October 14,
   1865.
Robert L. Lacey, son of Spencer Lacey and
   Elizabeth his wife, died January 27, 1869.
William Henry Lacey, son of Robert Lacey and
   Priscilla his wife, died Sept. 3 (?), 1914.
Charles Franklin Lacey, son of Robert L. Lacey and
   Priscilla his wife, died January 23, 1924.
John Fletcher Lacey, son of Robert L. Lacey and
   Hester his wife, died February 26, 1937.

On a small sheet of paper:

Curtis S. Houston and Hester A. P. Lacey, his wife,
were married May 9, 1870.

Clipping:

Obituary of John Fletcher Lacey - died at his
home in Tavares, Fla., and gives his age
and members of his family, etc.

1.
Spencer Lacey
m.
Elizabeth   2.
      Robert L.   3.
      b. 5-28-1815 1. William H.
      d. 1-27-1869   b. 10-23-1849
   1st m. 12-11-1848 d. 9-3-1914
Daniel Hudson Priscilla S. 2. James E.
m.   Hudson   b. 6-25-1851
Louvenia   b. 2-5-1820   d. 3-9-1852
      d. 2-5-1855   3. Charles F.
   2nd m. 5-3-1856   b. 9-21-1853
               m. 7-1-1889
Peter R.   d. 1-23-1924
Simpler   Hannah Black
m.   Hester A.
Louvenia   Simpler   4. Mary B.
      b. 9-11-1827   b. 3-1-1857
      d. 3-30-1912   d. 9-17-1951
      m. 5-9-1870
      Curtis Houston 5. George R.
               b. 6-16-1862
               d. 10-14-1865
             6. John F.
               b. 9-30-1864 **
**Dorothy, b. 1-22-1906   m. 4-30-1904
 Elizabeth, b. 10-15-1913   d. 2-26-1937
               Katherine Morse
4.
Agnes Lacey 5.   6.
b. 12-29-1890 Franklin W. 1. Barbara L.
m. 1-18-1919 Hazzard   Hazzard
John B. Hazzard b. 7-31-1921   b. 12-30-1946
      d. 10-26-1952 2. Nancy J.
      m. 6-4-1941   b. 7-27-1949
      Thelma   3. John F.
      Townsend   b. 3-10-1953

LANE - GALBRAITH

(From a Bible in the Freeman Auction Room, Philadelphia, Pa.)

Married August 21, 1845 by Rev. Henry Tullings, William Steel Lane, son of James and Martha S. Lane, to Elizabeth Ann Galbraith, daughter of John and Amy A. Galbraith.

December 28, 1880 by Rev. Richard Newton, D.D., Amy A. Lane and John Arthur.

Births

Amy Augusta Lane born July 26, 1846.
John Galbraith Lane born November 6, 1848.
Marion Lane born September 12, 1850.
William Brashear Lane born September 20, 1853.
Annie Lane born October 5, 1855.
Charles B. Lane born July 9, 1860.
Florence G. Lane born June 19, 1867.

Deaths

John Galbraith Lane died May 1849.
Annie Lane died December 1855.
Marion Lane died March 20, 1895.
Charles B. Lane died March 20, 1896.

James Lane
             William S. Lane
Martha
             m. 8-21-1845   Amy A. Lane
                                         b. 7-26-1846
John Galbraith   m. 12-28-1880

             Elizabeth Galbraith

Amy A.   John Arthur

LAWSON BIBLE RECORD

(A copy of a handwritten account in the Bible of Alfred DuPont Bird and Ellen E. (Lawson) Bird.)

Alfred DuPont Bird married Ellen Elizabeth Lawson on December 11, 1850 at Philadelphia, Pa.

Copied by Clara Wallace Bird, 6-1-1956.

Births

1. Jane Lawson, born July 25, 1808
2. Francis Lawson, born January 21, 1811.
3. William Lawson, born December 20, 1812.
4. Charlotte Lawson, born November 18, 1816.
5. Rebecca Lawson, born November 14, 1819.
6. John Lawson, born July 20, 1823.
7. Craven Lawson, born June 18, 1827.
8. Ellen E. Lawson, born November 5, 1829.
9. Mary Ann Lawson, born April 29, 1833.

CAPTAIN JOHN LOCKTON BIBLE

(This record was taken from a Bible presented to the Delaware Historical Society, Wilmington, Delaware. Record was copied by Mrs. Glenn S. Skinner, Newark, Delaware.)

Note: This old volume was the Family Bible of Captain John Lockton, whose wife, Elizabeth, and whose daughter, Mary, were the sincere friends of Captain John Cooper and his family by whom they were held in the highest esteem, and it came into my possession as Executor of Miss Mary Lockton's estate.
    Signed: Edward E. Law

John Lockton died April 30, 1768. He married October 30, 1754. Children:

1. First child was born dead October 12, 1756.

2. Thomas was born April 2, 1758; died August 13, 1762, age 4 years and 10 days.
3. John was born December 2, 1759; married November 30, 1779 to Elizabeth McCulloch. Their daughter, Mary, was born November 2, 1780.
4. James was born December 25, 1762; died July 30, 1763, age 7 months and 2 days.
5. Robert was born June 24, 1765; died August 27, 1765, age 2 months and 3 days.
6. A son was born dead February 4, 1767.
7. John was born December 2, 1769; died August 1769, age 8 months and 7 days.
8. A son was born dead September 5, 1777.

John Lockton's wife was Martha Jaquet, died September 14, 1778.
John Lockton was drowned.

SAMUEL LODGE & TALITHA SOMERS

(Bible published by Kimber & Sharpless, 93 Market Street, Philadelphia, Pa. 1824. Owned by Mrs. William Dawson, Holly Oak, Delaware. Record given by Mrs. Charles Bird.)

Marriages

Samuel Lodge and Talitha Somers were married December 15, 1808.

Samuel Lodge, Sr., was born September 10, 1783.
Talitha Somers was born March 5, 1786.

Births

Hiram H. Lodge born November 17, 1809.
John S. Lodge born October 15, 1812.
Joseph P. Lodge born August 25, 1815.
Samuel W. Lodge born May 26, 1818.
Elizabeth Ann Lodge born December 18, 1821.

Charles L. Lodge born October 26, 1825.
Alfred J. Lodge born May 5, 1828.
Anna Maria Lodge born July 8, 1833.

COL. ARMWELL LONG BIBLE

(Data taken from Family Bible in old English, original Greek translations, printed for Mathew Carey, 118 Market St., Philadelphia. Oct. 20, 1801. By special Command of King James I of England.)

Col. Armwell Long, born Feb. 17, 1754; died Nov. 22, 1834; married Elizabeth Robinson July 27, 1773.
Elizabeth Robinson Long was born April 29, 1754; died December 6, 1826.
Children:

    Leurander C. Long, born May 27, 1774; died December 1, 1844.
    James Long, born March 17, 1776; died March 2, 1839.
    John Long, born March 24, 1778; died July 1, 1846.
    Jeremiah Long, born Augus 15, 1780.
    Isaiah Long, born August 31, 1783; died July 29, 1832.
    Elam Long, born December 10, 1785; died December 18, 1839.
    Lydia Long, born October 15, 1790.
    Elizabeth Long, born December 15, 1790; died February 21, 1838.
    Martha Long, born May 2, 1793.
    Hester Long, born May 10, 1795.
    William Long, born January 3, 1797.

Lydia Long married Ebe Gray.

    Son, George Gray, born April 26, 1833.

Long Chart next page.

Long Chart:

David Long
    Col. Armwell Long
    b. 2-17-1754
    d. 11-22-1834   Lydia Long
    m. 7-27-1773   b. 10-15-1790
    Elizabeth   d.
    Robinson   m.
                    Ebe Gray

                    Elizabeth Long
                    b. 12-15-1790
        ?   d. 2-21-1838   **See
                    m. 7-9-1809   Below
                    Noah Lockwood

**Maria Long Lockwood
                1. Katherine
                   m. John Fleetwood
                2. Sarah Pauline
Wm. R. Taylor   m. Godfrey, Jos. C.
                3. Lucinda
                   m. McCabe, Dr. Ed.
                4. Arena
                   d. unm.
                5. Louise
                   d. unm.
                6. Joseph B. Taylor
                7. Mary
                   m. Hudson, Peter

Data sent by Pauline C. Godfrey
Caesar Rodney Chapter D.A.R.
1720 Washington Street
Wilmington, Del.

LUNT FAMILY OF MAINE & DELAWARE

(Present owner is Buford Lunt, 227 Chestnut St., New Castle, Delaware. Record given by Mrs. Charles D. Bird, Wilmington.)

Belongs to Lunt Family of Oldtown, Maine; brought
to New Castle, Delaware by Ira Lunt, grandfather of present owner, Buford Lunt, more
than 83 years ago. Mr. Lunt lives in his
grandfather's old house.

Buford Lunt is the son of Charles C. Lunt and
Harriett Frazier, a Delaware girl. She died
February 1958, age 89 years, but is not
mentioned in these records.

Births

Joshua Lunt, born August 4, 1776; died March 21,
1863, age 86 years 8 months.
Abigail Lunt, born October 8, 1780; died
May 6, 18--?
Abigail Lunt, born February 3; died April 6,
1883; born 1798.
Joshua Lunt, Jr., born August 24, 1799; died
November 23, 1843, age 44 years, 3 months.
John Lunt, born June 10, 1801; died November 1825,
age 24 years and 6 months.
Mary Lunt, born June 28, 1803; died December 1824,
age 22 years and 6 months.
Hannah Lunt, born December 20, 1805; died March
1849, age 44 years and 9 months.
Margaret Lunt, born October 1, 1807; died ??
Elmira Lunt, born April 16, 1810; died August 3,
1879, age 69 years.
William Lunt, born October 23, 1808; died
January 6, 1880, age 71 years, 2 months
and 14 days.
Abraham Lunt, born May 31, 1812.
Susan Lunt, born July 10, 1814.
Grace Lunt, born May 22, 1816; died April 10, 1882.
Olive Lunt, born June 10, 1817.
Francis Lunt, born October 9, 1821; died
December 3, 1913 in Boston.

Marriages

Joshua Lunt, Jr. married Jerusha W. Winslow on
February 4, 1828? (?); died November 23, 1843.
Ira Lunt and Thankful L. Flagg were married
November 17, 1853.
Ira Lunt and Rebecca Winslow were married
May 10, 1861.

Births

Julia F. Lunt, born December 27, 1861; died
    May 27, 1936, age 74 years and 5 months.
Fannie M. Lunt, born September 17, 1863; died
    October 9, 1935, age 72 years and 23 days.
Flora A. Lunt, born June 11, 1865; died
    September 5, 1952, age 87 years, 2 months
    and 25 days.
Charlie C. Lunt, born November 27, 1866; died
    July 24, 1902.
Emily F. Lunt, born September 24, 1891; died
    May 8, 1925, age 34 years.
Eva M. Lunt, born July 23, 1868; died June 22,
    1956, age 87 years.
Norma M. Lunt, born January 11, 1870; died
    September 17, 1941, age 71 years,
    8 months and 6 days.
Ozra S. Lunt, born June 26, 1871.
Hannah A. Bee Lunt, born September 22, 1870; died
    March 3, 1939, age 68 years, 5 months and
    9 days.

- - - - - - - - - -

Lucy A. Lunt, born November 7, 1832; died
    July 22, 1848; age 16 years.
Melinda B. Lunt, born November 14, 1834; died
    July 24, 1853, age 18 years.
Isaac Lunt, born April 18, 1839; died June 19,
    1913.
Phebe Jane Lunt, born July 15, 1843; died
    August 22, 1865, age 22 years.

Benjamin C. Winslow married Rebecca A. Howes
    June 8, 1848.

Deaths

Joshua Lunt, Jr. died November 23, 1843; age
    44 years and 3 months.
Joshua M. Lunt died August 14, 1877; age 72
    years and 11 months.
Lucy A. Lunt died July 22, 1848, age 16 years
    and 4 months.
Melinda B. Lunt died July 24, 1853, age 18
    years and 4 months.

Phebe Jane Lunt died August 22, 1865, age 22
   years and 1 month.
Jerusha M. Lunt died August 14, 1877, age
   73 years.

Births

Buford Thomas Lunt, born August 19, 1898 at
   Denver, Colorado (owner of the Bible).
Jessie Wilson Lunt, born April 9, 1901 at
   Philadelphia, Pa. (wife of Buford T. Lunt).
Ira Charlie Lunt, born November 30, 1937 at
   Wilmington, Del.
Ruth Christine Lunt, born February 3, 1927 at
   Wilmington, Del.

Benjamin C. Winslow, born January 5, 1824;
   died January 14, 1857, age 33 years.
Rebecca A. Howse, born January 29, 1831.
Ira Lunt, born January 28, 1831; died
   July 15, 1915, age 84-6-17.
Thankfull L. Flag, born 1836; died March 1860.
Clara J. Winslow, born January 23, 1850;
   died March 30, 1896, age 46 years.
Hannah B. Winslow, born April 15, 1852; died
   January 12, 1908, age 57 years..
Frank W. Winslow, born September 7, 1855; died
   January 26, 1936, age 81-4-9.

LUNT FAMILY
JOSHUA LUNT, JR. & JERUSHA M. WINSLOW

(Bible was published by Luther Roby, Concord, N.H.
1845. Owned by Buford Lunt, New Castle, Del.
Record given by Mrs. Charles D. Bird, Wilmington,
Delaware.)

Ira Lunt, born January 28, 1831.
Lucy A. Lunt, born November 7, 1832.
Melinda B. Lunt, born November 14, 1835.
Isaac L. Lunt, born April 18, 1839.
Phebe J. Lunt, born July 15, 1843.

Lucy A. Lunt died July 22, 1844.
Melinda Lunt died July 24, 1853.
Isaac Lunt died January 19, ----?
Phebe J. Lunt died August 22, 1865.

Marriages

Joshua Lunt, Jr. and Jerusha M. Winslow were married October 19, 1828 (?); died November 23, 1843.
William Kingsley and Jerusha M. Winslow were married February 4, 1845; Jerusha died August 14, 1877 at New Castle, Delaware.

Jerusha M. Winslow was born September 3, 1804.
Jerusha M. Winslow died August 14, 1877.

Joshua Lunt, Jr. was born August 24, 1799, died November 23, 1843.
Gersham Howes and Jane Dunlap were married December 11, 1823.
Gersham Howes was born November 18, 1801.
Jane Howes was born September 21, 1798.
Henry Howes was born December 8, 1824.
Eliza J. Howes was born February 1, 1829.
Rebecca Howes was born January 29, 1831.
Catherine Howes was born March 12, 1833.
Mary J. Howes was born February 16, 1835.
Jane Howes was born September 21, 1839.
Lorenzo Howes was born January 11, 1841.
Eliza J. Howes died May 13, 1832; age 3 years and 3 months.
Susan Howes was born December 27, 1837.

LUNT CHART

1.
Joshua Lunt
b. 8-4-1776
d. 3-21-1863
m.
Abigail
b. 10-8-1780

   2.
1. Joshua, Jr.
   b. 8-24-1799
   d. 11-23-1843
   m. 1828
   Jerusha M.
   Winslow
   b. 9-3-1804
   d. 8-14-1877
2. John
   b. 6-10-1801
   d. 11-1825
3. Mary
   b. 1803
   d. 12-1824

   3.
1. Ira Lunt
   b. 1-28-1831
   d. 7-15-1915
   m. 11-17-1853
   Thankfull
   Flagg
   b. 1836
2. Lucy A.
   b. 1832
   d. 1848
3. Melinda
   b. 1835
   d. 1853

Chart continued next page.

Lunt Chart Continued.

    4. Hannah   4. Isaac
        b. 1805   b. 1839
        d. 1849   d. 1913
    5. Margaret   5. Phoebe
        b. 10-1-1807   b. 1843
    6. William   d. 1865
        d. 1-6-1880
    7. Elmira
        b. 4-16-1810
        d. 8-3-1879
    8. Abraham
        b. 5-31-1812
    9. Susan
        b. 7-10-1814
  10. Grace
        b. 5-22-1816
        d. 4-10-1882
  11. Olive
        b. 6-10-1818
  12. Francis
        b. 10-9-1821
        d. 12-3-1913

4.
1. Julia   5.   6.
   b. 12-27-1861   <u>Buford Lunt</u>   <u>Ira C. Lunt</u>
   d. 5-27-1936   b. 8-19-1898   b. 11-30-1937
2. Fannie   m.   m.
   b. 9-17-1863   Jessie   <u>Ruth   </u>
   d. 10-9-1935   <u>Wilson </u>
3. Flora   b. 4-9-1901
   b. 6-11-1865
   d. 9-5-1952
4. <u>Charlie Lunt</u>
   b. 11-27-1866
   d. 7-24-1902
   m.
   <u>Harriett Frazier</u>
   d. 2-1958

MACKENZIE - HAY RECORD

Alexander MacKenzie was born 1840, Sutherlandshire, Scotland; died 1900. He married Elizabeth Stone, who was born 1842 in Keith, Banshire, Scotland; died 1904.

Their daughter, Mary Elizabeth MacKenzie, was born 1866 in Banffshire, Scotland; died 1926. She married William Stuart Hay, son of Andrew S. Hay and Anne C. (Stuart) Hay. He was born 1866 in Morayshire, Scotland; died 1942.

Their son, James Hay, was born September 27, 1897 in Keith, Scotland. He married July 8, 1922 in Philadelphia, Millie Frances Bacon, who was born September 18, 1897 in Norwich, England.

Their daughter, Edith MacKenzie, was born in Philadelphia on February 9, 1924. She married April 3, 1948, Daniel R. McNeal, Jr., son of Daniel R. McNeal and Clara Louise (Berlin) McNeal, grandson of H. W. McNeal and Myrtie V. (Reese) McNeal.

    Their children:
        1. Daniel R. III, born 9-11-1949; died 4-15-1951.
        2. Debra Jeanne, born 11-24-1952.

    (See McNeal Record)

THOMAS E. MALIN & ELLA WEBSTER

(Bible published by William W. Harding, Phil., Pa. 1873. Owned by Anna Mary Malin, Shipley Road, Wilmington, Delaware. 1956. Record given by Mrs. Charles D. Bird.)

Marriages

Thos. Elmer Malin, son of Elmer and Rachel (Haines) Malin, married Ella, daughter of Henry and Priscilla Webster.

Births

Florence Anna Malin, born May 22, 1875.
Adda Emma Malin, born July 29, 1877.
Ella Bertha Malin, born September 21, 1878.
Alice Matilda Malin, born October 25, 1881.
Anna Mary Malin, born February 2, 1886.

Deaths

Adda Emma Malin died September 2, 1877.
Florence Malin Clay died December 4, 1950.
Ella Bertha Malin died February 22, 1954.
Thomas E. Malin died March 26, 1925.
Andrew H. Shellhorn died February 22, 1949.

Skippy, October 8, 1956.

MESSICK BIBLE

(A Bible record copied from an Episcopal Psalm Book by Mrs. Clara (Messick) Jerschied, which she had owned but recently has given to Edwin Messick of Milford, Delaware.)

Births

George Messick, son of Minos and Comfort Messick, was born November 1, 1781; died January 8, 1841.
Nellie Pusey, daughter of William and Betsy Pusey, was born February 22, 1782. (Was this Betty Saunders)?

George Messick and Nellie Pusey were married January 7, 1805. They had 9 children as follows:
   1. Comfort Messick, born February 2, 1806.
   2. Jane Messick, born December 29, 1808.
   3. John Hall Messick, born November 8, 1810.
   4. George Miller Messick, born February 21, 1813.
   5. Minos Messick, born May 17, 1807. (Was this the Minos who married Levina Truitt) 12-8-1836?

6. Ellener Messick, born March 2, 1816.
7. Elizabeth Messick, born June 4, 1818.
8. Sallie Messick, born June 8, 1820.
9. William Messick, born December 26, 1823.

Note by Roland Messick:
   Minos and Comfort Messick, my great-great-grandparents.
   George and Nellie Pusey, my great-grandparents.
   George Miller and Sarah (Kollock) Messick, my grandparents.
   Geo. Roland and Lina (Swain) Messick, them's us.

KOLLOCKS

Phillip Kollock was born 1752 and Penelope Rodney Kollock.
John Kollock, born 1785 and Polly Scott Kollock.

John Kollock, 1st son of John and Polly Kollock, was born 12-10-1810; died 11-10-1811.
Mary Fields, daughter of John and Polly Kollock, was born 11-17-1812; died 2-16-1879.
*Sarah S., daughter of John and Polly Kollock, was born 11-17-1814; died 6-21-1859.
Nancy, daughter of John and Polly Kollock, was born 3-4-1816; died 1820.
John 2nd son of John and Polly Kollock, was born 12-5-1817; died 10-6-1836.
Mira, daughter of John and Polly Kollock, was born 11-17-1819; died 1820.
Hetty, daughter of John and Polly Kollock, was born 7-17-1825; died 8-31-1911.
Hannah, daughter of John and Polly Kollock, was born 1-2-1826; died 9-17-1907.
Adeline, daughter of John and Polly Kollock, was born 5-20-1830; died 7-5-1944 (?)

*Sarah S. Kollock was my grandmother - Roland.

MESSICK-PUSEY RECORD

(The Holy Bible containing the Old and New Testaments but of the original tongues and with the former translations diligently compared and revised. Philadelphia. Towar, J. & D.M. Hogan and Hogan & Co., Pittsburgh. C. Sherman & Co. Printers. 1830.)

Marriages

George Messick and Nelly Pusy were married
    January 17, 1805.

Births

George Messick, son of Minas Messick and Comfort
    his wife, was born November 1, 1731.
Nelly Pusey, daughter of William Pusey and Betsy
    his wife, was born February 22, 1782.

Comfort Messick, daughter of George Messick and
    Nelly his wife, was born February 2, 1806.
Minas Messick, son of George Messick and Nelly his
    wife, was born May 17, 1807.
Jane Sandres Messick, daughter of George Messick
    and Nelly his wife, was born December 29,
    1808.
John Hall Messick, son of George Messick and Nelly
    his wife, was born November 8, 1810.
George Miller Messick, son of George Messick and
    Nelly his wife, was born February 22, 1813.
Ellonder Messick, daughter of George Messick and
    Nelly his wife, was born March 2, 1816.
Betsey Miller Messick, daughter of George Messick
    and Nelly his wife, was born June 4, 1818.
Sally Thoroughgood Messick, daughter of George
    Messick and Nelly his wife, was born
    June 8, 1820.
William Messick, son of George Messick and Nelly
    his wife, was born December 26, 1823.

John William Messick, oldest son of George M.
    Messick and Sarah his wife, was born
    March 1, 1845.
George Mitchel Messick, youngest son of George M.
    Messick and Sarah his wife, was born March 1,
    1845.

Deaths

George Messick, Sr. died January 8, 1841.
George Miller Messick, son of George and Nelly
    Messick, died December 19, 1845, age 32 years,
    9 months and 28 days.
William Messick, son of George Messick and Nelly
    his wife, died November 28, 1865.

Written on back page of Bible:

Edward P. Morris and Eleanor A. Messick were
    married December 28, 1840 by Rev. H. Frieze.
E. P. Morris died December 24, 1892.
Eleanor A. Morris died August 31?, 1897.
Comfort Hudson died May 16, 1887.
John P. Hudson died November 17, 1863.

John P. Hudson and Comfort Messick were married
    December 14, 1826.
William Messick and Mary E. White were married
    July 28, 1850.

Wm. Messick died November 28, 1865.
Mary E. Messick, his wife, died 1855.

Written on a small piece of paper:

Elenor Messick died April 24, 1855.

Minas Messick

	George Messick	
Comfort	b. 11-1-1781	1. Comfort Messick
	d. 1-8-1841	b. 2-2-1806
		d. 5-16-1887
Wm. Pusey		m. 12-14-1826
	Nelly Pusey	John P. Hudson
Betsy		d. 11-17-1863
		2. Minas
		3. Jane
		4. John Hall
		5. George Miller **See
		m. Sarah Below
		6. Ellonder
** 1. John William Messick		m. E.P. Morris
b. 1842		12-28-1840
2. George Michel Messick		
b. 1845		

- 225 -

Messick Chart Continued:

                                      7. Betsey Miller
                                      8. Sally Thoroughgood
                                      9. William Messick
                                          m. 7-28-1850
                                          Mary E. White
                                          d. 1855

MARTIN MILLER AND ANN JUSTISON

(Bible published and sold by Kimbler & Sharpless, Philadelphia, 50 Norh Fourth Street. Stereotype Edition. Property of Martin and Ann Miller. Owned by Mrs. Walter Jones (Georgie Miller), Wilmington, Delaware. Record given by Mrs. Charles D. Bird.)

Marriages

Martin Miller and Ann Justison were married
    September 27, 1832.
Charles Miller and Charlote Way were married
    (no dates).
Lewis M. Miller and Annie E. Barlow were married
    September 12, 1871.
Robert C. Fraim and Eliza Jane Miller were married
    May 1, 1851.
Curtis M. Talley and Anna Mary Miller were married
    (no dates).
George W. Hanby and Emma A. Miller were married
    (no dates).

Births

Martin Miller, son of George and Sarah Miller,
    was born November 9, 1802.
Anna Justison, daughter of John and Rebecca
    Justison, was born January 23, 1811.
Eliza Jane Miller, daughter of Martin and Anna
    Miller, was born July 6, 1833.
Sarah Miller, daughter of Martin and Anna Miller,
    was born April 17, 1836.
Hannah Ann Miller, daughter of Martin and Anna
    Miller, was born April 5, 1838.

George Hiram Miller, son of Martin and Anna Miller, was born September 28, 1841.
Charles Miller, son of Martin and Anna Miller, was born December 25, 1843.
Angeline Miller, daughter of Martin and Anna Miller, was born April 13, 1846.
Anna Mary Miller, daughter of Martin and Anna Miller, was born October 12, 1847.
Lewis Miller, son of Martin and Anna Miller, was born September 10, 1849.
Emma Amanda Miller, daughter of Martin and Anna Miller, was born February 22, 1853.

Theodore O. Fraim, son of Robert C. and Eliza Jane Fraim, was born (no date shown).
Laura Fraim, daughter of Robert C. and Eliza Jane Fraim, was born (no date shown)
Martin F. Fraim, son of Robert C. and Eliza Jane Fraim, was born March 14, 1856.
Eugene F. Fraim, son of Robert C. and Eliza Jane Fraim, was born January 10, 1859.
Martha Ann Fraim, daughter of Robert C. and Eliza Jane Fraim, was born August 28, 1860.
Robert Franklin Fraim, son of Robert C. and Eliza Jane Fraim, was born December 21, 1866.
Ida Jane Fraim, daughter of Robert C. and Eliza Jane Fraim, was born September 3, 1868.
Charles F. Fraim, son of Robert C. and Eliza Jane Fraim, was born February 7, 1875.

Laura V. Talley, daughter of Curtis M. and Anna M. Talley, was born (no date shown).
Mary Talley, daughter of Curtis M. and Anna M. Talley, was born (no date shown).
Linda Talley, daughter of Curtis M. and Anna M. Talley, was born (no date shown).

Ida Jane Hanby, daughter of George and Emma Amanda Hanby, was born May 19, 1871.

Sarah Elva Miller, daughter of Charles and Charlotte Miller, was born August 27, 1871.
Anna P. Miller, daughter of Charles and Charlote Miller, was born February 2, 1874.

Albert M. Miller, son of Lewis M. and Annie E. Miller, was born March 28, 1873.
Albert M. Miller died December 1928.

Frank C. Miller, son of Lewis M. and Annie Miller, was born May 27, 1875.
Frank C. Miller died August 27, 1922.

Ulyses M. Hanby, son of George W. and Emma A. Hanby, was born March 25, 1873.
Georgie N. Miller, daughter of Lewis M. and Anna E. Miller, was born October 1, 1877.
L. Martin Miller, son of Charles Miller and Charlotte Miller, was born July 27, 1876.
Josephine Gebhart was born December 11, 1865.
Elizaann Justison was born September 27, 1826.

Deaths

George Miller, father of Martin Miller, died August 1851.
Sarah Miller, mother of Martin Miller, died August 4, 1859.
Martin Miller died March 8, 1891.
Anna Miller died December 27, 1891.
Emma Hanby, wife of George W. Hanby, died December 6, 1891.
Sarah Miller, daughter of Martin and Ann Miller, died March 8, 1840.
Hannah Ann Miller, daughter of Martin and Ann Miller, died November 26, 1842.
George Hiram Miller, son of Martin and Ann Miller, died December 28, 1842.
Angiline Miller, daughter of Martin and Ann Miller, died August 4, 1846.

Marriages

Georgine N. Miller and Walter S. Jones were married November 25, 1896.
Anna Elizabeth Jones was born April 25 and died January 11, 1919.
Frank C. Miller and Mary Elizabeth Hinkson were married October 1895.
  Helen G. Miller was born December 9, 1897.
Helen G. Miller and Joseph C. Kavanagh were married June 19, 1920.
  Elizabeth Kavanagh was born September 25, 1922 (Anna E.).
  Joseph Charles Kavanagh was born February 18, 1924, died at birth.
  Janet Louise Kavanagh was born March 5, 1927.
  Joan Miller Kavanagh was born March 14, 1931.

Albert M. Miller and Mary M. Hanby were married
   May 24, 1894.
   Albert LeRoy Miller was born April 17, 1900.
Albert LeRoy Miller and Frances Titus were married
   1922.
   Carolyn Mae Miller was born November 11, 1927.
   Mary Ellen Miller was born September 6, 1929.
Carolyn Mae Miller and Frank McGarry were married ?
   Michael McGarry was born July 28, 1948.
   Carol Lynne McGarry was born April 21, 1952.
Mary Ellen Miller and Gordon LaHue were married ?
   Virginia LaHue was born November 1950.
Anne Elizabeth Kavanagh and Gerald Montaigue, Jr.
   were married November 6, 1948.
   Gerald Montaigue III, was born January 4,
      1951.
   Joseph Fenwick Montaigue was born July 9,
      1952.
Joan Miller Kavanagh and Charles Hugh Daniels were
   married June 16, 1951.
   Charles Joseph Daniels was born April 20,
      1954.
   Hugh Miller Daniels was born March 14, 1957.

The following was written on the blank page in
back of Bible:
                    Union Church
      was dedicated on Saabbath January 4, 1846
               by Samuel Kiner Cox
      94.00 Collection, Ninety four dollars.

      Protracted Meeting commenced September 20, 1846.
      Preachers in attendance: Rev. Edward T. Fraim
                               Rev. Christian I. Page
      The first sister converted was Sarah Wilson.
         "They that seek shall find
          The door of Mercy free
          For God is good and Kind
          To those who bow the knee."

The above refers to Newark Union Methodist Church,
Brandywine Hundred, Delaware, near Carrcroft, on
Carr Road.

Miller Chart:

1.
George Miller
b.
d. 1851
m. **Sarah**
d. 8-4-1859

2.
Martin Miller
b. 11-9-1802
d. 3-8-1891
m. 9-27-1832

John Justison
m.
Rebecca

Ann Justison
b. 1-23-1811
d. 12-27-1891

3.
1. **Eliza J.**
b. 7-6-1833
m. 1851
Robert Fraim

4.
1. Theodore
2. Laura
3. Martin, b. 1856
4. Eugene, b. 1859
5. Martha, b. 1860
6. Robert, b. 1866
7. Ida,   b. 1868

2. Sarah
   b. 4-17-1836
   d. 3-8-1840

8. Charles, b. 1875

3. Hannah
   b. 4-5-1838
   d. 11-26-1842

4. George
   b. 9-28-1841
   d. 12-26-1842

5. **Charles**
   b. 12-25-1843
   m.
   Charlotte Way

1. Sarah,   b. 1871
2. Anna,   b. 1874
3. L. Martin, b. 1876

6. Angeline
   b. 4-13-1846
   d. 8-4-1846

7. **Anna M.**
   b. 10-12-1847
   m.
   Charles Talley

1. Laura
2. Mary
3. Linda

Miller Chart Cont'd.

8. Lewis
b. 9-10-1849
m. 1871
Annie Barlow

   1. Albert
   b. 1873
   d. 1928
   m. 1894
   Mary Hanby
   2. Frank
   b. 1875
   d. 1922
   m. 1895
   Mary Hinkson
   3. Georgie N.
   b. 1877
   m. 1896
   Walter B. Jones

9. Emma
b. 2-22-1853
d. 12-6-1891
m. Geo. M. Hanby

   1. Ida,   b. 1871
   2. Ulyses, b. 1873

MAURICE - VAN BUSKIRK

(Pages of Family Records removed from the old Family Bible of Luke VanBuskirk and Mary E. (Boys) Maurice. Owned by Mrs. Ralph McCloskey, Hillcrest, Delaware. Record given by Mrs. Charles D. Bird, Wilmington, Delaware. Both are members of Caesar Rodney Chapter, Wilmington.)

Marriages

Lucas V. B. Maurice and Alvina Boys were married October 19, 1843.
Lucas V. B. Maurice and Mary E. Boys were married October 2, 1854.
J. Otis McClune and Jennie F. Maurice were married January 22, 1891.
John S. T. Bearsdale and Cora A. Maurice were married December 31, 1895.
Mary E. Bearsdale and Ralph A. McCloskey were married March 12, 1919.
Cora M. McClune and Ralph W. Lear were married September 2, 1919.

Henry Maurice McCloskey and Annie Lizenia Slusher were married February 7, 1941.
John Ralph McCloskey and Mary Anne McGinnes were married June 18, 1943.
Vaughn Arthur McCloskey and Elizabeth Anne Wessells were married November 6, 1948.

A number of original marriage certificates:

1. Mr. John Barber of New Castle Co., State of Delaware and Miss Ellen Benge of New Castle Co., State of Delaware, married July 31, 1874 by Geo. W. Lybrand, Minister of the Gospel. Wit: Kate C. Lybrand, Rachel Benge.
2. Luke V. Maurice of Ithaca, State of New York and Mary E. Boys of Ithaca, State of New York, married October 2, 1854 by C. D. Burritt, Minister of the Gospel. Wit: Almon I. Boys, Charlotte Boys.
3. Samuel F. Bearsdale of Twp. of Southfield and Co. of Oakland and State of Michigan - aged 24 years, and Phebe Codington, of the same place - aged 18 years, were married at Southfield on May 12, 1847, and that Benjamin F. Foster of Southfield and Edward Ervin of Farmington Co., of Oakland, Michigan, witnessed the bans. J. T. Stevens, Justice of Peace.
4. William McCloskey of New Castle Co., Delaware and Emma Barber of New Castle Co., Delaware, married at the Minister's home in Newark on March 11, 1894. J. L. Vallandingham, Minister of Gospel.
5. December 31, 1895 at Ithaca, New York, John S. L. Beardslee and Cora A. Maurice, in accordance with the Ordinance of God and the Methodist Church and the Laws of New York State. Thereon Cooper, Minister. Wit: Charles W. Mabee, Josie Culligan.

Births

Lucas V. B. Maurice, born March 20, 1820.
Alvina Boys, born May 14, 1825.
Eugene B. Maurice, born November 6, 1847.
Frances Ella Maurice, born February 25, 1850.
Mary Eliza Boys, born August 13, 1835.
Edgar Lucas Maurice, born September 12, 1855.
Albert Henry Maurice, born February 5, 1857.

Cora Amelia Maurice, born January 15, 1860.
John Franklin Maurice, born July 31, 1862.

Cora M. McClune, born February 24, 1893.
Mary E. Beardslee, born August 11, 1899.
John Ralph McCloskey, born May 18, 1920.
Henry Maurice McCloskey, born April 20, 1921.
Harold Fowler McCloskey, born May 1, 1924.
Vaughn Arthur McCloskey, born January 27, 1926.

Carolyn Ann McCloskey, born to Henry & Anne McCloskey, December 17, 1941.
Beverly Jane McCloskey, born to John Ralph and Mary Ann McCloskey, July 18, 1944.

Deaths

Frances Ella Maurice died July 11, 1850.
Alvina Maurice died August 25, 1851.
Edgar L. Maurice died April 6, 1857.
Albert Henry Maurice died September 10, 1858.
Lucas V. B. Maurice died April 14, 1890.
Mary E. Maurice died November 9, 1912.
J. Otis McClune died March 20, 1925.
Jennie F. McClune died March 25, 1925.
Harold F. McCloskey died May 31, 1925.
Eugene B. Maurice died March 1, 1934.
John F. Maurice died May 1930.
Cora A. M. Beardslee died December 23, 1934.
John S. T. Beardslee died January 20, 1939.

MILLIGAN RECORD

George Milligan, only son of Robert Milligan, Esq., of Gelnein Ayreshire, Scotland, was born in Scotland 1721; came to Maryland and married 1745, Catherine, daughter of Col. John Baldwin and Catherine. He died at Bohemia, January 17, 1784-5. Their children:
  1. Mary, married James Christie, Esq. of Doris, Fifshire. Their only child was the father of Mary Christie Wilson.

2. Robert, born 8-11-1754; died 1806;
    married about 1789, Sarah Jones, born
    1768; died 2-1-1796. Their children:
    1. Catherine, married Hon. Louis McLane.
    2. George Baldin, married Mary Urguhard.
    3. Lydia, married Joseph Sims, Jr.
    4. John Jones, married Martha Mary
       Anne Levy.

Judge John Jones Milligan was born December 10,
    1795 at Bohemia Manor, Cecil Co., Md., died
    in Phildelphia 1875. Married February 5,
    1820 in Philadelphia, Martha Mary Anne Levy,
    who was born July 13, 1798; died February
    1889.

Robert Milligan of Bohemia Manor was born June 11,
    1754; died 1806; married 1789, Sarah Cantwell
    Jones of New Castle County, Delaware; who was
    born 1768; died February 20, 1796.

1.
John Jones Milligan   2.
b. 12-10-1795   George B. Milligan   3.
d. 1875   b. 8-13-1825   Elisa Milligan
m. 2-5-1820   d. 2-24-1889   m
Martha Levy   m. 2-5-1852
b. 7-13-1798   Sophia Carroll   R. H. Bancroft
d. 2-1-1889   b. 4-13-1824
                           d. 5-13-1881

4.
Elizabeth H. Bancroft   5.
m.   Alexander Winsor
Alexander Winsor   Elise
                           Robert

MARY LEVY MILLIGAN'S JOURNAL

(As arranged by Mrs. Glenn S. Skinner, Newark, Delaware.)

"This book was given to me by Robert Bancroft with a request that I should enter in it any reminiscences of members of our family which I can collect or remember to have heard from my grandmother or other elderly relatives."
Signed: Mary L. Milligan

Of my father's aunt, who died in Philadelphia in 1795(?), published in one of the Journals of the day--

On Thursday last, died Miss Peggy Milligan, after a short illness and on Saturday last her remains were attended to Gray's (Ferry?) by a number of very respectable citizens and thence conveyed to Maryland to be deposited in the family burial ground. The order of Society throws the virtue of the female character in the _____ but on so melancholy an occasion as this their display may be excused and a public tribute to departed excellence cannot by unacceptable. Miss Milligan's mind was cast in the happiest mould, etc.

There is a miniature of this lady (Margaret Milligan) painted by her friend, Mrs. Charles Carroll of Carrollton, who was Harriett Chew of Philadelphia, granddaughter of Chief Justice Chew of Pennsylvania. Her husband was the Hon. Charles Carroll of Carrollton, one of the Signers of the Declaration of Independence. This miniature is in the possession of her grand-neice, Martha Elizabeth Milligan.
April 10, 1899.

Copy of a letter to my grandfather, Robert Milligan, telling him of his election to the Senate of Maryland.

"In Senate, Dec. 17, 1796

Sir:

    I have the honor to inform you that you are elected a member of the Senate of this State in the place of General Lloyd who has resigned. As it is uncertain whether the Session will continue beyond the 25th instant, it is the desire of the Senate if you cannot make it convenient to attend during the present session that you would signify by a letter to me, your acceptance of a seat in the Senate. I am, Sir, with great Respect yr Obedient Servant.

President of the Senate."

My grandfather accepted this seat in the Senate of the State of Maryland and retained it until 1799 when he sent in his resignation December 1, 1799.

    My grandmother, Mary Levy, after whom I am named, was the eldest daughter of Henry Ward Pearce, Esq. of Maryland, who had a plantation on the shores of the Chesapeake Bay. She was born there and lived there until her marriage and frequently has told me incidents of her life there which occurred during the Revolutionary War. As her father belonged to a League which refused to use any imported articles, they were put to great inconvenience for the necessaries of life. For years they had to use thorns and gather them with great care from the Black thorn hedges surrounded the grounds. When they snipped a dress, to alter or repair it, they drew out each stitch and never cut the silk with which it was sewed as they had to use it again.

    She loved to describe the French Fleet under Count DeEsting, coming up the Chesapeake which she said was a superb sight. The anchorage was in sight of her father's house and their arrival was the occasion of many festivities.

She remembered being called up in the night to see a messenger who brought the news of the surrender of Cornwallis at Yorktown. He was Col. Tilghman, an aide of General Washington's who rode through the country stopping at the principal houses to tell the glad news.

My grandmother's mother was Anastasia Carroll, daughter of Dominick Carroll and Mary Sewall.

Her mother, Mrs. Dominick Carroll, married, when a widow, Col. John Baldwin, High Sheriff of Cecil Co., Md., who was my father's step great grandfather by a previous marriage.

1.
Dominick
Carroll
m.
Mary
Sewall

Col. Benj.
Pearce
b. 1712
d. 1756
m.
Margaret
Ward
dau. of
Henry & Ann
(Herman)

2.
Anastasia
Carroll
b. abt. 1736
m.
Henry W. Pearce
b. 12-6-1736
d. 1-6-1759

3.
Mary Pearce
b. 10-22-1762
d. 6-21-1791
m. Moses Levy
b. 6-1-1728
d. 1792

4.
Martha M. Levy
b. 7-7-1798
d. 2-1889
m. 1820
John J. Milligan

Ann Marie Herman was the daughter of Augustine Herman and she married 1st Henry Ward.

The Pearce family came from England to Maryland 1660 and settled in that portion of Kent, which was given to Cecil in 1674 and returned to Kent 1706. (See "Old Kent" p. 160 & 380).

MONTGOMERY RECORD

(Bible was printed in Edinburgh by Mark and Charles Kerr, His Majesty's Printers. MDCCXCIII. Owned by Mrs. Clara Guest Eastburn. Record given by Mrs. James Marsey, Yorklyn, a member of Captain William McKennan Chapter, N.S.D.A.R.)

Ages of Robert and Jean Montgomery's children:
    William Montgomery, born February 22, 1784.
    John Montgomery, born May 29, 1785.
    Ann Montgomery, born October 109, 1786.
    Robert Montgomery, born June 24, 1789.
    Martha Montgomery, born December 4, 1790.
    Thomas Montgomery, born January 5, 1794.
    James Montgomery, born November 4, 1795.
    George Montgomery, born June 25, 1797.
    Sarah Montgomery, born August 14, 1800.

Record of the ages of George and Mart T. Montgomery's children:
    Robert Montgomery, born May 1, 1833.
    Rachele Montgomery, born April 28, 1834.
    Anna Jane Montgomery, born November 28, 1836.
    Sarah Montgomery, born October 8, 1838.
    John Herman Montgomery, born November 27, 1840.
    George Franklin Montgomery, born April 22, 1843.

Record of the ages of John H. and Mary J. Montgomery's children:
    Jennie Herdman Montgomery, born January 29, 1872.
    John Herdman Montgomery, born July 16, 1877.

Children of George F.C. and Mary E. Montgomery:
    Rebecca Springer Montgomery, born September 14, 1867.
    Anna Mary Montgomery, born October 20, 1869.
    George C. Montgomery, born November 23, 1873.

Birth of children of Anna J. and Palmer Guest:
    Mary Lizzie Guest, born November 9, 1856.
    George Willie Guest, born August 22, 1858.
    Lydia Amanday Guest, born December 5, 1859.
    Everett Guest)
    Irvine W. Guest) twins, born January 26, 1862.

C. Edgar Guest, born April 26, 1865.
William P. Guest, born March 18, 1867.
Mary R. Guest, born June 3, 1870
Lewis B. Guest, born March 20, 1872.
Clara R. Guest, born February 13, 1879.
    Her son:
        Joseph Buford Eastburn, born
        September 1, 1904.

Ages of Jonathan and Ann Graves children:
Samuel Graves, born December 12, 1804.
Robert Graves, born August 9, 1806.
Ann Graves, born March 13, 1809.
Jean Graves, born July 16, 1811.
Hayes Graves, born January 9, 1814.

      * * * * * * * * * *

<u>EASTBURN BIBLE</u>

(Printed in New York by A. J. Johnson, 276 Mulberry Street. 1869. Owned by Mrs. Clara Eastburn.)

Maud N. Barrett, born July 3, 1880.
Joseph P. Barratt, born April 28, 1884.
Anna Barratt, born August 23, 1886.
Alice C. Barratt, born May 17, 1888.

Joseph Buford Eastburn, born September 1, 1904.
Doris Ann Eastburn, born April 6, 1928.
Patricia Jane Eastburn, born September 23, 1946.
Roxanna Lee Eastburn, born February 23, 1950.

Nathan Guest and Lydia Mendenhall were married.
Palmer Guest, son of Lydia and Nathan, was born
    October 15, 1853; died October 23, 1887.
Elizabeth Guest, born 1831.

Palmer Guest married Anna J. Montgomery on
    January 8, 1856.

ROBERT I. MORROW & LYDIA ANN BARLOW

(Bible was published by Jesper Harding, Philadelphia. 1854. Owned by Mrs. Lewis P. Talley, Naaman's Rd., Delaware. 1956.)

Marriages

Robert I. Morrow and Lydia Ann Barlow were married November 8, 1855.
R. J. Morrow and Mary Russell were married on January 3, 1869.
Hannah Ella Morrow and George A. Willis were married (no date shown). They lived in Centerville, Del. She died June 26, 1939 and both she and George A. Willis are buried at Siloam at Booth's Corner on Foulk Road.
Eliza Eva Morrow and Willard Talley Galbreath were married December 11, 1877.

Births

William Harry Morrow, born September 3, 1856.
Eliza Eva Morrow, born July 8, 1858.
Mary Emma Morrow, born November 10, 1859 in Chadsford, Delaware County, Pa.
Ida Lizzie Morrow, born April 6, 1860 in Delaware.
Hannah Ella Morrow, born February 25, 1862 in Delaware.

Deaths

Chester - Lydia A. Morrow died January 29, 1867, age 30.
Tanguy, Penn. - Robert I. Morrow died at his home in his 87th year. Buried at Siloam.
William Harry Morrow was burned to death when his home burned down February 5, 1927. He is survived by a son, William, of California. Was buried in Fernwood Cemetery, Phila., Pa.
William I. Galbreath died July 11, 1923, age 67.
Eliza Eva Galbreath died January 1, 1951, age 93. Both are buried in Chester Bethel Cemetery, Foulk Road, Brandywine Hundred, Delaware.

MURPHY, SIMPKINS, FRENCH, DAVID, MORGAN

(From Diary - owner unknown.)

Marriages

Joseph E. Murphy and Miss Wiliamina Jackson, both of Cecil Co., Md., were married (no date shown) by Rev. Oram.
William Simpkins and Miss Margaretta Finley, both of N.C. Co., Del. were married (no date shown) by Rev. S. W. Thomas.
Joseph Henry French, of Middleown, Del., and Miss Annie Atkinson were married March 31, ---- in New Jersey.
Elisha David and Martha Hersey were married March 27, 1826.

Births

Elisha David was born July 24, 1766.
David Morgan was born October 8, 1787.
Martha Anderson was born January 13, 1773.
Mary David, daughter of Elisha David and Rebecca, was born May 30, 1795.
Margaret David, daughter of Elisha David and Rebecca, was born December 26, 1797.
Elishua Morgan, daughter of David Morgan and Margaret his wife, was born January 2, 1827.
Mary Ann Morgan, daughter of David Morgan and Margaret his wife, was born June 20, 1828.
Elisha D. Morgan, son of David Morgan and Margaret his wife, was born September 4, 1830.
Evan F. Morgan, son of David Morgan and Margaret his wife, was born November 18, 1831.
Emly Sophiah Morgan, daughter of David Morgan and Margaret his wife, was born April 28, 1833.
Charlote Jane Morgan, daughter of David Morgan and Margaret his wife, was born December 9, 1834.
Anderson Jackson Morgan, son of David Morgan and Margaret his wife, was born August 10, 1836.

Deaths

Rebecca David, wife of Elisha, died October 24, 1823.
Elisha David died August 4, 1828.
Mary David died June 12, 1816.

David Morgan died December 25, 1837.
Evan F. Morgan died August 31, 1850.
Mary A. Morgan died February 2, 1853.
Anderson J. Morgan died December 26, 1864.
Elishua Morgan, daughter of David Morgan and
    Margaret his wife, died January 5, 1827.
Elisha D. Morgan, son of David Morgan and
    Margaret his wife, died August 3, 1831.
Emley Sopher Morgan, daughter of D. and M. Morgan,
    died March 30, 1834.
Charlotte Jane Morgan, daughter of David Morgan
    and Margaret his wife, died March 7, 1836.
Martha David died February 8, 1849.

THE McCRONE FAMILY, FARNHURST, DELAWARE

John
McCrone, Sr.   1. James
b. c. 1756   McCrone, Jr.
   Ireland   b. 12-1-1788   1. Ann Jane McCrone
d. 4-16-1848   d. 10-25-1863   b. 11-12-1818
   age 90   m. 2-13-1838
m. 1786   m. 3-7-1816   Leontine
                     Hannah Farmer   McWhorter
                     d. 3-8-1834
                                        2. John III
                     m. 2nd   1821-1863
                        9-17-1835
                     Elizabeth   3. Wm. Brooks
                     (Ellen)   1841-1862
                     Hinsley
                     b. 12-3-1793   4. George P.
                     d. 12-22-1861   1843-1862

                                        5. John Hanibal
                                           1845-1865
                                        6. Hannah Mary
                                           b. 4-25-1825
                                           d. 2-16-1881
                                           m. 4-2-1846
                                           Alexander Jones
                                        7. Margaret McCrone
                  2. Sarah   b. 8-8-1830
                     McCrone   m. 12-29-1857
                     b. 5-8-1800   Dr. James
                     d. 3-23-1870   Ridgeway Andre
                                            (Andrew)

JOHN & ELEANOR (BYERLY) McCULLOUGH

(Bible record is in possession of Genealogical Society of Pennsylvania. Front page is missing.)

Marriages

John McCullough and Eleanor Byerly were married June 14, 1815 by the Rev. Robert Graham.

Births

John McCullough, son of Thomas and Hannah, was born January 10, 1793.
Eleanor McCullough, daughter of John and Mary Byerly, was born January 21, 1798.
Eliza, daughter of John and Eleanor, was born March 9, 1816.
Thomas McCullough, son of John and Eleanor, was born June 7, 1818.
Charles McCullough, son of John and Eleanor, was born October 6, 1820.
John B. McCullough, son of John and Eleanor, was born February 13, 1823.
George W. McCullough, son of John and Eleanor, was born January 11, 1825.
Mary Ellen McCullough, daughter of John and Eleanor, was born September 18, 1827.
Margaret Carey McCullough, daughter of John and Eleanor, was born October 10, 1829.
William McCullough, son of John and Eleanor, was born December 1831.
Matilda McCullough, daughter of John and Eleanor, was born July 16, 1833.

Deaths

Thomas McCullough died at 1914 Brandywine St., Philadelpia, March 9, 1894, age 75 years.
John B. McCullough died at Chester Heights, Del. Co., Pa., July 25, 1894, age 71 years.
Eliza McCullough died July 15, 1818, age 2 years.
William McCullough died December 1831, age 3 hours.
John McCullough died January 16, 1834, age 41 years.
Mary Ellen McCullough died August 23, 1837, age 11 years.
Matilda McCullough died October 2, 1837, age 4 years.

Charles McCullough died May 31, 1872, Columbia, Pa., age 50 years.
Eleanor McCullough died in Germantown, Phil., Pa. February 19, 1884, age 86 years.
George W. McCullough died December 22, 1891, age 66 years.

Thomas McCullough

Hannah

John Byerly

Mary

John McCullough
b. 1-10-1793
d. 1-16-1834
m. 6-14-1815

Eleanor Byerly
b. 1-21-1796
d. 2-19-1884

Eliza
Thomas
Charles
John B.
George
Mary Ellen
Margaret
William
Matilda

McDADE - BLACK RECORD

James McDade was born in Belfast, Ireland. He married Elizabeth _____, who was born in Belfast, Ireland. Their children:
1. Sarah Jane McDade, born December 22, 1829.
2. Elizabeth, born 1831
3. James
4. John
5. William

Sarah Jane McDade, daughter of James and Elizabeth McDade, was born December 22, 1829 in Pittsburgh, Pa.; died January 1, 1908 in Wilkinsburg, Pa. She married 1st ---- McCracken; married 2nd Thomas J. Black. Their children:
1. Clara Amanda Black, born December 25, 1855.
2. John Wesley, born February 23, 1858.
3. Ida Jane, born September 4, 1860.
4. Thomas Howard, born August 3, 1863.
5. Kate Young, born April 6, 1869.
6. Minnie M., born November 18, 1871.

Clara Amanda Black, daughter of Thomas J. and
Sarah Jane, was born December 25, 1855; died
June 2, 1936 in Pittsburgh. She married
George W. Berlin on June 24, 1880 in
Pittsburgh. He was the son of Joseph Berlin
and Jane Braden Schall, born December 20,
1846 at Latrobe, Pa.; died June 22, 1928.
Their daughter:
Clara Louise Berlin, born June 5, 1892 in
   Pittsburgh; married Daniel Raymond
   McNeal, son of H. W. McNeal and
   Myrtie V. (Reese) McNeal. Their son:
   Daniel Raymond McNeal, Jr., was born
   August 20, 1920; married April 3, 1948
   Edith MacKenzie Hay, daughter of James
   Hay and Millie Frances (Bacon) Hay.
   Their children:
   1. Daniel R. III
   2. Debra Jeanne

(See McNeal, Berlin, Brinker Record)

McNEAL FAMILY

(Warner Family Record of Newark, Delaware.)

Thomas McNeal was born August 4, 1804 in Maryland.
He married Hannah Davis on September 12, 1827
in New Castle Co., Delaware. She was born
January 18, 1805 in New Jersey. Thomas McNeal
died October 13, 1874 and was buried in the
Methodist Cemetery in Elkton, Cecil Co., Md.
His wife, Hannah, died May 2, 1872 and is
also buried in the Methodist Cemetery in
Elkton.

A marriage bond was issued for Thomas McNeal
and Hannah Davis in New Castle Co., Del. on
September 12, 1827. (Reference: Delaware
Archives, Vol. 10, page 70, Archives, Dover).
Bondsmen were: Thomas McNeal and William
Slack. The marriage bonds of this period
supply no personal information about the
contracting parties.

Thomas McNeal and Hannah (Davis) his wife left no will; but Administration Accounts give the distribution of the estate as share and share alike: to Lydia McNeal; Amos E. McNeal; Joseph H. McNeal; Susan J. Wright; Anna M. Henry; Mary C. Dunbar and George W. McNeal.

Reference: Libro R.D.F. #2, Vol. 33; folio 368 in Elkton Court House, Elkton, Cecil Co., Md.

The dates of Thomas McNeal and Hannah (Davis) McNeal are from their tombstones; also information on Thomas McNeal and his wife Hannah was furnished by Mrs. Harvey T. Alexander, Elkton, Md.

Children of Thomas McNeal and Hannah Davis McNeal:
1. Amos E., born 1831; m. Lizzie Gladfelter.
2. Joseph Henry, born August 11, 1833; m. Anne J. Logan.
3. Susan J., born 1836; m. William Wright.
4. Thomas
5. Annie, born January 1839; died Feb. 1916; m. W. F. J. Henry.
6. George Washington, born January 9, 1842; m. Indiana T. Logan.
7. Mary C. "Pink" born 1845; m. Morris Dunbar.
8. Lydia married John T. McNeal of Penn.

Joseph Henry NcNeal, son of Thomas McNeal and Hannah his wife, was born at Belle Hill, Md., on August 11, 1833; married Anne Jane Logan, daughter of Samuel Logan and his wife Sarah Reed, April 7, 1857. Anne was born in Charlestown, Md. on January 4, 1837. Joseph McNeal died in Washington, D.C., February 7, 1907; buried in the Methodist Cemetery in Elkton.

Anne Logan McNeal died in Metheun, Mass., July 16, 1916 and was also buried in Elkton.

The Deed for the Belle Hill property is found in Libro J.S. 40, Vol. 16, Folio 312 in Elkton Court House, Md. The property was bought from William H. Gilpin and his wife Margaret Ann Gilpin for the sum of $805.00 in January 1838. Deed was recorded January 13, 1838. In the Census of 1850, this property was valued at $1500.00.

Children of Joseph Henry McNeal and Anne Jane Logan McNeal:
1. Hiram Rudolph McNeal, born March 2, 1858.
2. Eliza S., born October 24, 1859.
3. George V., born December 27, 1864.
4. Minnie T.)
5. May Belle) twins, born January 2, 1868.
6. Henry Warner, born March 7, 1879; m. Myrtie V. Reese.
7. Sarah M.)
8. Mary H.) twins, born January 9, 1872.
9. Bertha Brown, born November 22, 1873.
10. LeRoy Cooling, born April 26, 1877; died April 17, 1950.

Henry Warner McNeal, son of Joseph Henry McNeal and Anne Jane Logan, was born at Belle Hill, Md., March 7, 1870. He married Myrtie Virginia Reese, daughter of Daniel Webster Reese and Maryland V. Pattison, on November 4, 1891 at Kensington, Maryland. Myrtie V. Reese was born in Baltimore, Md., February 14, 1869. Henry W. McNeal died July 29, 1939 at Mantoloking, New Jersey. He was buried in Cemetery of Head of Christiana Presbyterian Church near Newark, Delaware.

His wife Myrtie V. McNeal died in Wilmington, Delaware on December 27, 1951 and is also buried at Head of Christiana Church. Their children:
1. Daniel Raymond McNeal, born September 5, 1892.
2. Mildred Stoek, born May 27, 1894.
3. Helen Louise, born June 3, 1897.
4. Elizabeth Reese, born November 2, 1901.
5. Dorothy Warner, born June 10, 1905.

Daniel Raymond McNeal, son of Henry Warner McNeal and Myrtie Virginia Reese, was born at Belle Hill, Md., September 5, 1892. He married Clara Louise Berlin, daughter of George Washington Berlin and Clara A. Black, October 15, 1919 in Pittsburgh, Pa. She was born June 5, 1892 in Pittsburgh, Pa. Their children:
1. Daniel Raymond McNeal, Jr., born August 20, 1920.

2. Joan Pattison, born February 22, 1927
at Abington, Pa.; died Sept. 26,
1937 at Abington, Pa. and was
buried in Whitemarsh Memorial Park,
Prospectville, Pa.

Daniel Raymond McNeal, Jr., son of Daniel Raymond McNeal and Clara Louise Berlin, was born August 20, 1920 in Philadelphia, Pa. He married Edith MacKenzie Hay, daughter of James Hay and Millie Frances Bacon, April 3, 1948 in Ambler, Pa. She was born in Philadelphia, February 9, 1924. Their children:
    1. Daniel Raymond McNeal, III, born
       September 11, 1949 in Evanston,
       Ill.; died April 15, 1951 in
       Evanston and was buried in
       Whitemarsh Memorial Park,
       Prospectville, Pa.
    2. Debra Jeanne, born November 24, 1952
       in Philadelphia.

During World War I, 1917-1919, Daniel Raymond McNeal served as 2nd Lieutenant in Battery C - 330th Field Artillery, 85th Division; Saumur Artillery School, Saumur, France.,

During World War II, 1942-1946, Daniel Raymond McNeal, Jr. served as Ensign (Lieutenant Junior Grade) Engineering Watch 2nd Division Officer on U.S.S. Cabot and U.S.S. Little Rock.

Mildred Stoek McNeal, daughter of H. Warner McNeal and Myrtie V. Reese, was born May 27, 1894. She married April 7, 1917, 1st: Carl Richard Lind. Children:
    1. Carl, Jr., born and died January 25,
       1918.
    2. Warner, born January 25, 1919; died
       February 2, 1921.

She married 2nd: Dr. William Yuckman.

Elizabeth Reese McNeal, daughter of H. Warner McNeal and Myrtie V. Reese, married Francis A. Jennings, December 30, 1939.

* * * * * * * * * *

LOGAN - McNEAL

Samuel Logan, Methodist Minister, known as "Bishop Logan", was born 1808; died December 20, 1892 at Liberty Grove, Maryland. He was buried at Charlestown, Md. He married Sarah Reed. Their children:
1. <u>Anne Jane Logan</u>, born January 4, 1837; died July 16, 1916 at Meheun, Mass. Buried at Elkton, Md.; married Joseph Henry McNeal, April 7, 1857. He was born in Charlestown, Md.
2. Indiana Townsend Logan, born April ___; married George Washington McNeal.
3. Samuel, Jr.

(See McNeal Record)

FRANCIS L. McSORLEY AND ANNA MARIA LODGE

(Bible published by J. B. Lippincott and Co., Philadelphia. 1859. Owned by Mrs. William Dawson, Holly Oak, Delaware. 1956. Record given by Mrs. Charles Bird.)

FAMILY RECORD

Frank Leland McSorley, born May 31, 1861.
Samuel Lodge McSorley, born July 19, 1863.
Wilfred Earl McSorley, born March 10, 1866.
Clarence Stewart McSorley, born March 3, 1868.
Ida Alice McSorley, born January 26, 1870.
Everett Newton McSorley, born March 15, 1872.
Ellis Alvin McSorley, born September 27, 1876.
Ralph Leonard McSorley, born August 8, 1878.
Francis L. McSorley, born ?
Anna Maria McSorley, born July 8, 1833.

Alfred Whartenby and Ida McSorley were married January 8, 1895.
Edna Ellis Whartenby was born September 8, 1896.
Marion Leiter Curzon Whartenby was born August 23, 1898.

Edith Lodge Whartenby was born October 26, 1901.
Alfred Whartenby was born October 26, 1901; died
the same day.

Anna Maria McSorley died September 5, 1884.
Francis McSorley died January 30, 1889.
Ellis Alvin McSorley died January 3, 1899.
Clarence Stewart McSorley died October 23, 1920.
Wilfred Earl McSorley died March 19, 1922.
Ida Alice McSorley died December 1, 1940.
Samuel Lodge McSorley died May 1949.
Frank Leland McSorley died ?

Alfred Whartenby, son of Robert J. and Elizabeth
   Whartenby, was born in Philadelphia on
   April 13, 1864.
Edna Ellis Whartenby married William Percifer
   Dawson, June 24, 1916. They had one
   daughter:
      Ida Frances, born March 2, 1922.
Ida Frances Dawson married Herbert Earl Stouffer
   June 4, 1945 and had:
      Shirley Dawson, born January 23, 1952.
      Herbert William, born April 25, 1956.

Edith Lodge Whartenby married Horace L. Malin.

Robt. J.
Whartenby   Alfred
m.   Whartenby
Elizabeth   b. 4-13-1864   1. Edna
             m. 1-8-1895   Whartenby   **Ida
             Ida A. McSorley   b. 9-8-1896   Frances
             b. 1-26-1870   m. 6-24-1916   See
                               Wm. Dawson   Below
                            2. Marion
                            3. Edith
                            4. Alfred

**Ida Frances
   b. 3-2-1922
   m. 6-4-1945
   Herbert Stouffer

Children of Ida and Herbert Stouffer:
   Shirley, born 1952
   Herbert, born 1956

MCWHORTER, JAMISON, FERRIS, ETC.

(Holy Bible, Old and New Testament. Published by John B. Perry, Philadelphia, Pa. Owned by Mrs. Albert W. Posey, Wilmington, Delaware.)

Marriages

Leontine N. McWhorter and Ann Jane McCrone were married February 13, 1838.
Charles Henry McWhorter and Agnes Jamison were married September 6, 1865 at St. Georges, Del.
John Thomas McWhorter and Laura Jamison were married (no dates shown).
Margaret McWhorter and Clarence Jamison were married April 27, 1876 at the Homestead.
Caroline H. McWhorter and Charles E. Ferris were married January 30, 1889 at the Presbyterian Church.
Emerson H. McWhorter and Jennie D. Craighead were married (no dates shown) at Pittsburgh, Pa.
Emerson H. McWhorter and Therese Ralston Slicer, 2nd wife, were married (no dates shown).
Mary E. McWhorter and William G. Janvier were married December 16, 1896 at the Presbyterian Church.

Births

Leontine N. McWhorter, son of Thomas and Rachel P. McWhorter, was born June 25, 1807.
Ann Jane McCrone was born November 12, 1818.

Charles Henry, 1st son of Leontine and Ann Jane McWhorter, was born December 24, 1838.
Mary Elizabeth, 1st daughter of Leontine and Ann Jane McWhorter, was born June 24, 1840.
Emma Frances, 2nd daughter of Leontine and Ann Jane McWhorter, was born March 5, 1842.
John Thomas, 2nd son of Leontine and Ann Jane McWhorter, was born July 25, 1846.
Leontine James, 3rd son of Leontine and Ann Jane McWhorter, was born October 28, 1848.
Ella Olivia, 3rd daughter of Leontine and Ann Jane McWhorter, was born April 14, 1850.
(Maggie) Margaret McCrone, 4th daughter of Leontine and Ann Jane McWhorter, was born January 5, 1853.

Emerson Hopkins, 4th son of Leontine and Ann Jane
    McWhorter, was born October 9, 1855.
Caroline (Carrie) Hurlock, 5th daughter of
    Leontine and Ann Jane McWhorter, was born
    June 28, 1859.
Mary Emeretta, 6th daughter of Leontine and Ann
    Jane McWhorter, was born April 2, 1864.

Deaths

Rachel Packard McWhorter, beloved wife of Thomas
    McWhorter, died February 4, 1824, age
    39 years.
Thomas McWhorter died October 3, 1858, age 80
    years and 8 months.
Emma Frances McWhorter, daughter of Leontine and
    Ann Jane McWhorter, died July 20, 1842.
Mary Elizabeth McWhorter, daughter of Leontine and
    Ann Jane McWhorter, died October 6, 1843.
Ella Olivia McWhorter, daughter of Leontine and
    ann Jane McWhorter, died July 26, 1854.
Charles Henry McWhorter died in Wilmington, Del.,
    December 3, 1895, the eldest child of
    Leontine and Ann Jame McWhorter.
Jennie Craighead McWhorter, wife of Emerson H.
    McWhorter, died June 11, 1894 in Allegheny
    City, Pa.
Ann Jane McWhorter, our dear Mother, died
    October 19, 1899 at Kirkwood Place in her
    home, St. Georges, Del. Intered in St.
    Georges Cemetery, October 21, 1899.
Our dear Father, Leontine N. McWhorter, died
    April 11, 1900 at his old home Mt. Hope.
    Intered at St. Georges Cemetery, April 14.
Emerson H. McWhorter, son of Leontine and Ann
    Jane McWhorter, died in 1937.
Theresse McWhorter, wife of Emerson McWhorter,
    died (no dates shown).

NORMAN BIBLE RECORD

(Bible published by Charles Eyre and William
Strahan, Printers to the King's Most Excellent
Majesty. London. Owned by Mrs. Lenora (Norman)
Long, Lewes, Delaware. Record given by Mrs. D.
Anthony Potter. Old pages sewed in - browned,
stained and writing faded.)

Purnal P. Norman, son of Thomas and Mariane
   Norman, was born January 18, 1816.
Mary H. White, daughter of Benjamin and Hannah
   White, was born July 16, 1817.

John Clifton and Mary H. White were married
   March 6, 1834.
Purnal B. Norman and Mary H. Clifton were married
   October 17, 1838.
Purnal B. Norman, Jr. and Helen M. Maull were
   married September 3, 1872.

Births

Hannah W. Clifton, daughter of John and Mary
   Clifton, was born January 9, 1835.
Cecelia Bennett Norman, daughter of Purnal B. and
   Mary H. Norman, was born July 26, 1839.
Benjamin White Norman, first son of P.B. and Mary
   H. Norman, was born March 14, 1841.
William James DeWolfe, second son of P.B. and
   Mary Norman, was born January 11, 1843.
Thomas, son of P.B. and Mary Norman, was born
   November 22, 1844; died January 7, 1845.
John White, son of P.B. and Mary Norman, was born
   October 18, 1845.
Mary, daughter of P.B. and Mary H. Norman, was
   born October 29, 1847.
Martha, daughter of P.B. and Mary H. Norman, was
   born October 29, 1847; died November 13,
   1847.
Purnal B. Norman, son of P.B. and Mary H. Norman,
   was born October 10, 1848.
Geo. Francis, son of P.B. and Mary H. Norman, was
   born May 7, 1851; died April 17, 1852.
Wrexham, son of P.B. and M. H. Norman, was born
   February 6, 1853.
Fanny Helen, daughter of P.B. and M. H. Norman,
   was born April 23, 1855; died July 16, 1855.
Thomas, son of P.B. and Mary H. Norman, was born
   April 22, 1857.

Cecelia B. Norman
   Presented by her father.

THOMAS NORMAN BIBLE

(Copied from Bible owned by Miss Fannie C. Norman, "The Embassy" 21st & Walnut Sts., Philadelphia. Record given by Mrs. D. Anthony Potter, Lewes, Delaware.)

"Thomas Norman's Bible presented to him by his friend, O. Dudley - A. O. Master Sergeant in the 32nd Regiment, U. S. A. 1814."

Marriages

Thomas R. Norman and Mariam Bennett were married June 17, 1798.

Births

Thomas R. Norman, son of John and Anner Norman, was born October 22, 1774.
Mariam Bennett, daughter of Pernal and Mariam Bennett, was born February 20, 1779.
John B. Norman, son of Thomas and Mariam Norman, was born November 18, 1799.
Mills R. Norman, son of Thomas and Mariam Norman, was born August 4, 1801.
Joshua L. Norman, son of Thomas and Mariam Norman, was born December 10, 1807 (?)
Patience Norman, daughter of Thomas and Mariam Norman, was born February 20, 1805.
Annes ? Norman, daughter of Thomas and Mariam Norman, was born September 30, 1808.
Eliza Norman, daughter of Thomas and Mariam Norman, was born September 22, 1810.
Mary Norman, daughter of Thomas and Mariam Norman, was born April 18, 1813.
Purnal Norman, son of Thomas and Mariam Norman, was born January 18, 1816.
Mary Norman, daughter of Thomas and Mariam Norman, was born April 29, 1818.

Note: There is another birth following the above, but it isn't readable.

Deaths

Mary Norman, daughter of Thomas and Marian Norman, died September 18, 1814.

Judge Thomas L. Norman, son of Thomas and Mariam
   Norman, died July 11, 1823.
Thomas R. Norman died March 27, 1863.
M. B. Norman died September 27, 1857.
George Orton, son of William and Hannah Orton,
   died February 5, 1830.

Note: See "Some Records of Sussex County, Del."
   by C. H. B. Turner, page 340, which gives
   above with some differences.

NORMAN RECORD

(Bible printed by Virtue & Co., City Road and Ivy
Lane, London. Owned by Mrs. Lenora (Norman) Long,
Lewes, Delware. Record given by Mrs. D. Anthony
Potter.)

FAMILY RECORD

Marriages

William J. Norman and Emma A. Marshall were married
   February 14, 1883.
Handy M. Long and Lenora L. Norman were married
   June 24, 1914.

Births

William J. Norman, son of P.B. Norman and Mary H.
   Norman, was born January 11, 1843.
Emma A. Marshall, daughter of David J. and Eliza
   Marshall, was born July 7, 1851.
Wilber T. Norman, son of W. J. and Emma A. Norman,
   was born November 21, 1883.
Lenora L. Norman, daughter of W. J. and Emma A.
   Norman, was born March 12, 1887.
Edwin Connor Marshall, son of Thomas C. and Essie
   Marshall, was born April 11, 1877.

Deaths

William J. Norman died January 31, 1921; buried
   February 2, 1921.
Emma A. Norman, wife of Wm. J. Norman, died
   June 3, 19--?

Wilber T. Norman, son of W. J. and Emma A. Norman, died August 9, 1889.
Catherine F. Carpenter, wife of Thomas Carpenter, died June 29, 1869, age 33 years. Buried in St. Louis, July 10, 1869 in Belle Fountin (?) Cemetery.
David J. Marshall died December 28, 1882, age 71 years, 1 month and 18 days.
John Maull died October 9, 1843, age 68 years, 8 months and 17 days.
Sarah Maull, wife of John Maull, died April 18, 1850, age 70 years.
Mary Jane Maull, daughter of John and Betsey Maull, died August 28, 1860, age 28 years, 4 months and 17 days.

Miscellaneous Notes:

David J. Marshall, son of William and Kitty, was born November 10, 1811.
Eliza Ann Maull, daughter of John and Sarah Maull, was born March 13, 1813.
Catherine Franklin Marshall, daughter of David and Eliza Ann Marshall, was born December 26, 1835.
William M. Marshall, son of David and Eliza Ann Marshall, was born September 16, 1838.
Sarah Rowland Marshall, daughter of David and Eliza Ann Marshall, was born July 8, 1842.
John M. Marshall, son of David and Eliza Ann Marshall, was born February 2, 1845.
Thomas Griswold Connor Marshall, son of David and Eliza Ann Marshall, was born April 12, 1848.
Emily Annie Marshall, daughter of David and Eliza Ann Marshall, was born July 7, 1851.
Louis Marshall Carpenter, son of Thomas and Catherine Carpenter, was born October 5, 1859.
Mary M. Carpenter, daughter of Thomas and Catherine Carpenter, was born August 25, 1861.
Annie Eliza Carpenter, daughter of Thomas and Catherine Carpenter, was born September 24, 1863.
Thomas H. Carpenter, son of Thomas and Catherine Carpenter, was born August 19, 1866.

Deaths

William M. Marshall, son of David and Eliza
    Marshall, died March 19, 1916 in Silver
    City, New Mexico; buried St. Louis,
    March 1916.
John M. Marshall, son of David and Eliza Marshall,
    died July 2, 1917 in Chicago, Ill. Buried
    in Chicago, July-17.
Thomas Connor Marshall, son of David and Eliza
    Marshall, died in Lewes, Del., Doc.
    Dec. 20; buried Dec. 22nd, 1928, age 80
    years.
Eliza Anne Marshall, daughter of Sarah and John
    Maull, died March 1, 1912 in Lewes, Del.
    Burial March 5, 1912, age 99 years.
Emily Anne Norman died June 3, 1930.

JACOB Z. ORR AND SARAH A. MAXWELL

(Bible was published by Gately and Fitgerald, 1025
Market St., Philadelphia. Owned by Mrs. George
Bigger, Claymont, Delaware. 1957. Record copied
by Mrs. Charles Bird, Wilmington, Del.)

Presented to Sarah Orr by her husband, Jacob Z.
    Orr, April 1894. The original Marriage
    Certificate was in the Bible.

Jacob Z. Orr of Wilmington, Delaware, and Sarah A.
    Maxwell, also of Wilmington, Delaware, married
    at Asbury Parsonage on November 13, 1888 by
    J. E. Bryan, Minister.

Marriages

Lillie Orr and Wm. Frederick Hadley were married
    at Brandywine M. E. Parsonage by Rev. F. F.
    Carpenter on June 1, 1914.
Sarah Elizabeth Orr and George S. Bigger were
    married in Harrison M. E. Church by the Rev.
    G. T. Alderson on April 11, 1917.
Margaret Orr and Wm. Ives Bradbury were married in
    Harrison Street M. E. Church by the Rev.
    G. T. Alderson on April 12, 1919.

Dollie Barden Hammond and Jacob Orr were married
in Harrison Street, M. E. Church by Rev.
W. E. Habbart on June 17, 1922.

Births

Children of Jacob Z. and Sarah Annie Orr:
    Margaret Orr, Baptized by Rev. J.D.C. Hanna,
        was born October 26, 1889.
    Lillie Orr, Baptized by Rev. H.A.G. Westerfield,
        was born June 3, 1892.
    Saraelizabeth Orr, Baptized by Rev. H.A.G.
        Westerfield, was born April 25, 1895.
    Robert Winfield Orr, Baptized by Rev. H.A.G
        Westerfield, was born November 26, 1898.
    Jacob Orr, Baptized by Rev. H.A.G. Westerfield,
        was born September 22, 1900.

Winfield Scott Orr, born July 17, 1861.
Robert Orr, born October 25, 1863.
Jacob Zebley Orr, born March 22, 1867.
Joseph Carr Orr, born March 24, 1869.
William Smith Orr, born September 3, 1825.
Sarah E. Orr, born March 9, 1832.

Deaths

Jacob Z. Orr died August 14, 1906.
Sarah Annie Orr died February 20, 1925.
Margaret Kromer died February 10, 1922; buried
    Riverview Cemetery, February 13, 1922.
Wm. Ives Brad (not finished?) died February 14,
    1886, Brandywine Hundred, Delaware
    October 24, 1886.

MEMORANDUM

Wm. Frederick Jr., son of Lillie Orr and Wm. F.
    Hadley, born March 10, 1915; died May 16,
    1917.
Margaret Elizabeth Hadley, born December 10, 1918.
Virginia Orr Hadley, born July 7, 1921.
Donald Hale Hadley, born April 9, 1927.

Children of Jacob Orr and Dollie H. Orr:
    Barbara Orr, born February 10, 1924.
    Willard Jacob Orr, born July 29, 1925.
    Marjorie Jean Orr, born December 18, 1926.

Richard Maxwell Orr, born February 27, 1928.
Roger Cooper Orr, born December 25, 1929.

Deaths

Sarah E. Orr died May 29, 1873, age 41 years.
William S. Orr died October 28, 1882, age 57 years.

Married at Marcus Hook Parsonage by Rev. C. J.
   Crouch, William S. Orr and Sarah E. Orr
   January 12, 1860.

Amor P. Orr was born October 2, 1877.

Photograph of headstone, in the Bible:

ORR
Joseph Orr died Jan. 26, 1859
Elizabeth Orr, His Wife
Samuel Orr died Dec. 8, 1862
Robert Orr died Nov. 1888
Jane Orr died Mar. 19, 1878
Margaret Orr died Feb. 18, 1892
Eliza Ann Orr died Feb. 1859
Albanas Phillips died May 1893.

ROBERT ORR AND MARGARET LATIMER

(Bible printed by Mathew Carey, 118 Market Street, Philadelphia. 1802. Owned by Mrs. Margaret (Orr) Bradbury, Wilmington, Delaware. 1957. Record given by Mrs. Charles Bird, Wilmington.)

   "Bible of Robert Orr Anno Domini, 1802"
Price Five Dollars or one pound seventeen shillings and six pence.

Marriages

Robert Orr intermarried with Margaret Latimer.
   1773.
Joseph Orr intermarried with Elizabeth Smyth
   December 11, 1815.
Samuel Walker intermarried with Margaret Orr
   June 15, 1820.

Births

Samuel Orr, son of Robert and Margaret Orr, was born December 11, 1776.
Samuel Orr, son of Joseph and Elizabeth Orr, was born May 3, 1817.
Robert Orr was born November 7, 1819.
Jane Orr was born November 9, 1821.
Margaret Orr was born March 22, 1823.
William Orr was born November 3, 1825.

— — — — — — — —

Robert Orr, son of Robert and Margaret Orr, was born March 10, 1740.
Margaret Orr, daughter of Joseph and Jane Latimer and wife of Robert Orr, was born April 15, 1751.
Elizabeth Ann Orr was born May 2, 1827.

Deaths

Samuel Orr, son of Robert and Margaret Orr, died May 6, 1802, age 25 years, 5 months and 11 days.
Margaret Orr, sister of Samuel Orr, died August 5, 1802, age 65 years.
Jane Orr, daughter of Robert and Margaret Orr, died October 29, 1815.
Robert Orr died January 5, 1819.

WILLIAM S. ORR AND SARAH E. ZEBLEY

(Bible published by E. A. and T. T. More, Dayton, Ohio. 1857. Owned by Mrs. Margaret (Orr) Bradbury, Wilmington, Delaware. 1957. "The Property of Sarah E. Zebley, presented to her by her brother, Joseph Zebley" 1859. Record given by Mrs. Charles Bird.)

Marriages

Married at Marcus Hook Parsonage by the Rev. C. J. Crouch, William S. Orr and Sarah E. Zebley, January 12, 1860.

Married at Asbury M. E. Parsonage by the Rev.
J. E. Bryan, Jacob Zebley Orr and Sarah Annie
Maxwell, November 13, 1888.
Married at 1208 N. 6th Street, Philadelphia, Pa.,
Pastor's Home by J. Hervey Beale, Robert Orr
and Anna Edna Weaber, November 22, 1905.
Married at Mt. Pleasant Parsonage by Rev. C. H.
Wiliams, J. C. Orr and Sarah E. McCrea,
January 28, 1896.

Births

Winfield Scott Orr, son of William S. and Sarah E.
Orr, born July 17, 1861.
Robert Orr, son of William S. and Sarah E. Orr,
born March 22, 1867.
Joseph C. Orr, son of William S. and Sarah E. Orr,
born March 24, 1869.

William S. Orr, born September 3, 1825.
Sarah E. Orr, born March 9, 1832.

Margaret Orr, daughter of Jacob Z. and Sarah A.
Orr, born October 26, 1889.
Lillie Orr, daughter of Jacob Z. and Sarah A. Orr,
born June 3, 1892.
Sarah Elizabeth Orr, daughter of Jacob Z. and
Sarah A. Orr, born April 25, 1895.
Robert Winfield Orr, son of Jacob Z. and Sarah A.
Orr, born November 26, 1898.
Jacob Orr, son of Jacob Z. and Sarah A. Orr, born
September 22, 1900.
Helen Elizabeth Orr, daughter of Joseph C. and
Sarah Ellen Orr, born June 22, 1897.
Alice Barbara Orr, daughter of Joseph C. and Sarah
Ellen Orr, born May 1898.

Deaths

Sarah E. Orr, wife of William S. Orr, died
May 29, 1873, age 41 years.
William S. Orr died October 28, 1882, age 57 years.
Jacob Zebley Orr, son of William S. and Sarah E.
Orr, died August 14, 1906, age 39 years.
Robert Orr, son of William S. and Sarah E. Orr,
died October 31, 1935, age 72 years.
Winfield Scott Orr, son of William S. and Sarah E.
Orr, died January 20, 1946, age 85 years.

Helen Elizabeth Orr, daughter of Joseph C. and
    Sarah E. Orr, died October 4, 1897.
Alice Barbara Orr, daughter of Joseph C. and
    Sarah E. Orr, died June 8, 1918.
Sarah Ellen McCrea Orr, wife of Joseph Carr Orr,
    died May 17, 1951; born October 19, 1870.

On a slip of paper in the Bible was the following:

    Jane Orr died March 19, buried 22nd, 1878.
    Robert Orr, born Nov. 7, 1819; died
        Dec. 1888, age 69.
    Margaret Orr, born March 22, 1823; died
        Feb. 19, 1891, age 68.
    William Orr, born Nov. 3, 1825; died
        Oct. 28, 1882, age 57.

NOTE: Mrs. Bradbury, owner of the Bible, said
    that the above are 2 sisters and 2 brothers.
    The William Orr is William Smyth Orr.

Wm. S. Orr	Jacob Z. Orr	1. Margaret
b. 9-3-1825	b.	b. 10-26-1889
d. 10-28-1882	d. 1906	2. Lillie
m. 1-12-1860	m. 11-13-1888	b. 6-3-1892
Sarah E. Zebley	Sarah Maxwell	3. Sarah
b. 3-9-1832		b. 4-25-1895
d. 5-29-1873	Winfield Orr	4. Robert
	b. 7-17-1861	b. 11-26-1896
	d. 1-20-1946	5. Jacob
		b. 9-22-1900
	Robert Orr	
	b. 3-22-1867	
	d. 10-31-1935	
	m. 11-22-1905	
	Anna E. Weaber	
	Joseph C. Orr	1. Helen E.
	b. 3-24-1869	b. 6-22-1897
	m. 1-28-1896	d. 1897
	Sarah E. McCrea	2. Alice
	b. 10-19-1870	b. 5-1898
	d. 5-17-1951	d. 6-8-1918

JOSEPH F. OUTTEN - MARY A. BRYAN

(The Holy Bible, published by A. J. Holman & Co., 1020 Arch St., Philadelphia, Pa. 1880. Owned by Mrs. Elmer Dickerson, Milton, Delaware. Record given by Mrs. D. A. Potter, Col. David Hall Chapter, Lewes, Delaware.)

This Certifies that the Rite of Holy Matrimony was celebrated between Joseph F. Outten and Mary A. Bryan, both of Milton, Delaware on the Thirtieth Day of December 1880 at Milton, Delaware by the Rev. George Sears Gassner M. M. E. C.
    Wit: Henry P. Burton, Eunice Burton

Marriages

Andrew Bryan and Mary C. Willey were married January 7, 1846.
Thomas Lee Dickerson and Ruth Edna Holston were married February 20, 1943.

Births

Joseph F. Outen, son of Seth L. and Elizabeth Outten, born December 16, 1850.
Mary C. Bryan, daughter of George A. and Mary Bryan, born March 27, 1853.
George Andrew, son of Andrew Brian and Mary his wife, born August 9, 1848.
Mary C. Brion (Bryan), born April 13, 1815.
Sallie A. Bryan, born September 5, 1857.

Deaths

Mary Elizabeth Outten died September 14, 1935, age 83 years, 5 months and 17 days.
Captain Joseph Frank Outten died May 9, 1933, age 83 years.
Andrew Bryan, son of William and Sarah Brine (Bryan) his wife, died January 25, 1853.
Mary C. Bryan died July 6, 1891.
Sallie A. Bryan died July 19, 1909.
George Andrew Bryan died February 27, 1928, age 79 years.

Wm. Brine
m.   Andrew Brian   1. George A. Bryan
Sarah   b.   b. 8-9-1848
        d. 1-25-1853   d. 2-27-1928
        m. 1-7-1846   2. Mary E. Bryan
        Mary C. Willey   b. 3-27-1853
        b. 4-13-1815   d. 9-14-1935
        d. 7-6-1891   m.

        Seth Outten   Capt. Jos. F. Outten
        m.   b. 12-16-1850
        Elizabeth   d. 54-9-1933

                           3. Sallie A.
                             b. 9-5-1857

PAINTER FAMILY RECORD

(Bible was printed and published by Mathew Carey, 122 Market Street, Philadelphia, Pa. 1812. Owned by Wilbur S. Corkran, Rehobeth Beach, Delaware. Record given by Mrs. D. Anthony Potter, Lewes, Del.)

Marriages

William Painter and Phebe Churchman were married
     November 18, 1807.
Samuel Painter and Mary H. Hoopes were married
     December 12, 1832.
Davis H. Hoopes and Mary W. Painter were married
     (no dates shown).
Edward Painter and Louisa Gilpin were married
     (no dates shown).
Darwin Painter and Sarah B. Pierce were married
     (no dates shown).
Manuel Eyre and Eliza Painter were married
     October 8, 1840.
John Painter and Hannah Hannum were married
     May 5, 1847.
Milton Painter and Sarah Ann Hickson were married
     October 24, 1849.
William Pyle and Margaret C. Painter were married
     September 30, 1851.
Charles Painter and Margaret H. Hickson were
     married September 15, 1853.

Births

Samuel Painter, born February 29, 1752.
Elizabeth Painter, born February 14, 1751.

Children of Samuel and Elizabeth Painter:
  Sarah Painter, born November 14, 1778.
  John Painter, born April 5, 1780.
  Cidney Painter, born May 1, 1782.
  William Painter, born April 12, 1785.
  Milton Painter, born August 27, 1787.

Children of William and Phebe Painter:
  Mary W. Painter, born September 22, 1808.
  Samuel Painter, born September 5, 1810.
  Edward Painter, born November 29, 1812.
  Milton Painter, born (month faded) 7, 1815.
  Charles Painter, born October 10, 1817.
  Darwin Painter, born March 12, 1820.
  Eliza Painter, born March 24, 1822.
  John Painter, born December 17, 1824.
  Margaret Painter, born October 4, 1828.
  Sarah D. Painter, born July 19, 1790 –
    and after this is added: "Nee
    Darlington, wife of John Painter."

Deaths

Samuel Painter died January 17, 1802 (or 3?).
Milton Painter died August 22, 1801.
Hannah Painter, daughter of John Painter, died
  (no dates shown).
Jane Painter, daughter of John Painter, died
  (no dates shown).
Sarah Painter died May 12, 1818.
Sarah Parks died June (?) 21, 1817 – Relict of
  John Painter – married J. Parks.
Sarah Painter died June 8, 1819 – spinster.
William Painter departed this life full of days
  of righteousness at one o'clock in the
  morning of the 6th day of the seventh month
  1854; aged seventy years.

His life was spent in usefulness and his end was
   marked with Peace - 7th month 6th day Anno
   Domini
                    MDCCCLIV
Charles Hoopes died March 24, 1848.
He now reaps the reward of his Sweetness and
   Innocence during life.
                    MDCCCXLVIII
John Painter died June 9, 1824.

PASSMORE BIBLE RECORDS

(Bible published by American Bible Society, New
York. 1890. Owned by Pusey Passmore, Wilmington,
Delaware. 1956. Record given by Mrs. Charles
Bird, Wilmington, Delaware.)

Marriages

William P. Passmore and Crphia Pusey were married
   December 1, 1848.
Harry C. Passmore, son of William and Orphia, and
   Sarah N., daughter of Joseph and Hannah
   Mitchell, were married December 13, 1883.

Births

William P. Passmore, son of Carleton and Mary
   Passmore, was born January 17, 1813.
Orphia Pusey, daughter of David and Naomi Pusey,
   was born December 21, 1817.
Wills Passmore, son of William P. and Orphia
   Passmore, was born September 23, 1849.
Edward B. Passmore, son of William P. and Orphia
   Passmore, was born November 6, 1851.
Harry C. Passmore, son of William P. and Orphia
   Passmore, was born January 12, 1854.
Thomas H. Passmore, son of William P. and Orphia
   Passmore, was born September 15, 1858.

To Harry C. and Sarah N. Passmore:
   Thomas Hoopes, born April 3, 1885.
   Hannah Mitchell, born June 17, 1888.
   Mary Bertolett, born October 3, 1890.
   Pusey, born October 30, 1897.

Edward B. Passmore and Emma Sharpless were married
(no dates shown). Born to them:
Samuel S.
Sarah
Helen
Lydia

Deaths

Thomas H. Passmore, son of William P. and Orphia
    Passmore, died December 17, 1877, age
    19 years, 3 months and 2 days.
William P. Passmore died September 28, 1886, age 74.
Orphia P. Passmore died September 19, 1896, age 79.
Wills Passmore, son of William P. and Orphia
    Passmore, died August 8, 1912, age 63.

PATTISON RECORD

William Pattison, son of William Pattison, was a
    sea captain. He died June 11, 1851, although
    the date of his death is listed in Mt. Olivet
    Cemeery Records as March 27, 1851. He
    married Ann Jones, January 26, 1832. She
    died May 30, 1880 and is buried in Mt. Olivet
    Cemetery, Baltimore, Md. She had a brother,
    Ezekiel.

Children of William Pattison and Ann Jones:
    1. Maryland Virginia Pattison
    2. Sallie Ann Elizabeth
    3. William
    4. George

Maryland Virginia Pattison was born 1844; died
    March 23, 1888. She married Daniel Webster
    Reese, May 9, 1865. Their daughter:
    Myrtie Virginia Reese; married H. W. McNeal.

NOTE: Date of marriage of William Pattison and
    Ann Jones is from Clerks Office in
    Cambridge, Maryland.

        (See McNeal Record for children of
        Myrtie V. Reese and H. W. McNeal)

PATTON BIBLE RECORD

(Bible was published by Harper and Brothers, 82 Cliff Street, New York, New York. 1846. Now owned by Joseph L. Patton, Lyndalia, Delaware.)

Marriages

Alexander Patton and Laetitia V. Jackson were
    married July 13, 1831.
Alexander N. Patton and Mary Jane Maxwell were
    married September 17, 1861. (Son)
James R. Patton and Mary E. Sullivan were
    married December 18, 1862. (Son)
Joseph D. Patton and Martha E. Hallman were
    married March 29, 1866. (Son)
Edmund R. Patton and Mary E. Burns were married
    October 12, 1871. (Son of A. and L. Patton)
J. Walter Hollingsworth and Letitia L. Patton were
    married June 14, 1893. (Daughter of Jas. and
    Mary E.)
Leslie H. Patton and Julia Grubb Bird were married
    February 1899.

Births

William Jackson Patton was born April 27, 1833.
Alexander Nesbit Patton was born August 19, 1835.
Mary Elizabeth Patton was born July 31, 1837.
James Rice Patton was born December 29, 1840.
Joseph Davis Patton was born May 2, 1843.
Thomas Nesbit Patton was born July 22, 1845.
Edmund Richardson Patton was born April 25, 1848.
Elizabeth Virtue Jackson was born October 11, 1789.

- - - - - - - - - -

Jas. Franklin Patton (Grandson) was born June 16,
    1862 (son of A. N. and M. J. P.).
Wm. Alexander Patton (Grandson) was born
    October 22, 1863 (son of J. R. andc M. E. P.
Lettie S. Patton (Granddaughter) was born
    January 3, 1866 (daughter of Janey and M. E.
    Patton).
Lizzie J. Patton, daughter of Joseph and Martha,
    was born April 13, 1868.
Leslie Patton, son of Joseph and Martha, was born
    September 25, 1870.

Alexander Patton, son of Edmund and Mary, was born
   February 14, 1873.
Harvey Burns Patton, son of Edmund and Mary E.,
   was born December 31, 1880.

Deaths

William Jackson Patton died January 29, 1837, age
   3 years, 9 months and 2 days (son).
Mary Elizabeth Patton died September 4, 1838, age
   one year, 1 month and 4 days (daughter).
Eliza Martin died December 3, 1843, age 40 years
   (cousin to Lettie).
Elizabeth Virtue Jackson died June 11, 1845, age
   57 years (mother to Lettie).
Thomas Nesbit Patton died October 29, 1846, age
   1 year, 3 months and 7 days (son).
Alexander Patton, husband to Lottie V. Patton,
   died March 21, 1854, age 45 years.
Wm. Alexander Patton died February 1866, age
   2 years and 4 months (grandson of Lettie
   and Elex., son of James Patton).
Letitia V. Patton died October 2, 1889, age
   79 years.
J. Frank Patton, son of Alex. N. and Mary Jane
   Patton, died January 19, 1896, age 33 years
   and 7 months.
Alexander Nesbit Patton, husband of Mary G. Patton,
   died December 10, 1908, age 73 years.
Hannah Patton, sister of Alexander Patton, Senior,
   died May 14, 1893, age 83 years.
Mary Jane Patton, wife of Alexander Nesbit Patton,
   born March 29, 1838; died February 19, 1919.

- - - - - - - - -

Births

Lizzie Jackson Patton was born April 13, 1868.
Leslie Hallam Patton was born September 28, 1870.

- - - - - - - - -

Martha Hallam Patton was born January 26, 1900.
Joseph Leslie Patton was born July 27, 1901.

- - - - - - - - -

James Leslie Patton was born July 20, 1939.

Deaths

Martha E. Patton died January 4, 1920.
Joseph D. Patton died May 15, 1926.
Elizabeth J. Patton died December 2, 1933.
Martha Hallam Pyle died December 29, 1937.

PENNINGTON BIBLE RECORDS

(Bible was printed and published by Kimber & Sharpless at their bookstore, No. 93 Market St., Philadelphia, Pa. 1824. It was rebound about 1900, by Martin Johnson, Book Binder of No. 420 Shipley St., Wilmington, Delaware. Now owned by Mrs. Sara Pennington Evans, Newark, Delaware. The Bible originally belonged to Ann Mercer Pennington and she gave it to Laurence H. Pennington, father of Mrs. Evans. Record was given by Mrs. Sara Evans, Regent of Captain William McKennan Chapter N.S.D.A.R. 1959.)

Marriages

John Mercer and Mary Copes were married July 14, 1804 by the Rev. John Derborough.
John Mercer and Ann Lambdin were married December 19, 1819 by the Rev. William Williams.
John B. Pennington and Ann Mercer were married October 4, 1838 by the Rev. John B. Magany.
James Mercer Pennington and Mary L. Brooks were married December 29, 1864. (James M. was the eldest son of John B. and Ann Mercer Pennington).
Lawrence Hipple Pennington, eldest son of James Mercer and Mary L. Brooks, and Emma Walker were married February 20, 1895.
Ann Mary Pennington, second daughter of James M. and Mary B. Pennington, and Leslie Derickson were married April 14, 1897.

THOMAS PEPPER-RACHEL LAWLES BIBLE

(In possession of Thomas B. Pepper, September 7, 1960. H. E. Phinneys stereotype edition. The Holy Bible containing the Old and New Testament, together with the Apyocrypha. Translated out of the original tongue and with the formed translations diligently copied and revised. Cooperstown, N.Y. Printed and published by H. E. Phinney. 1833. Sent by Helene Potter, Col. Hall Chapter. Copied by Sarah Pepper McLaughlin, September 21, 1960. Witness: Helen McC.West.)

Marriages

Thomas Pepper and Rachel Lawless were married January 22, 1837.
Thomas B. Pepper and Mary E. White were married August 4, 1872.
Thomas B. Pepper and Martha Zimmerman were married February 21, 1906 at Carlisle, Pa. by Rev. A. N. Hagerty.

Births

Mary Elanor Pepper, daughter of Thomas Pepper and Rachel his wife, was born October 28, 1837.
George M. Pepper, son of Thomas Pepper and Rachel his wife, was born June 13, 1840.

Willard S. Warren, son of Rufus M. Warren and Mary Eleanor his wife, was born November 18, 1859.

Margaret Jane Pepper, daughter of George M. Pepper and Margaret his wife, was born September 10, 1863.
Thomas B. Pepper, son of Thomas B. Pepper and Mary E. his wife, was born June 12, 1873.

Deaths

Margaret Jane Pepper, daughter of George M. Pepper and Margaret his wife, died September 22, 1865, age 2 years and 12 days.
Rachel Pepper, wife of Thomas Pepper, died September 17, 1870, age 57 years, 8 months and 16 days.

Thomas B. Pepper died December 14, 1891, age 60 years, 11 months and 14 days.
Mary E. Warren, daughter of Thomas and Rachel his wife, died November 20, 1914, age 77 years and 22 days.
Margaret H., wife of George M. Pepper, died September 27, 1863.
Joshua Pepper, the first Pepper of all, died December 26, 1808, age 83 years.
Elizabeth Pepper, wife of Joshua, died September 21, 1811.

FRANKLIN PETERS - CHARLOTTE EDWARDS

(Published by A. J. Holmes & Co., 1222 Arch St., Philadelphia. 1881. Owned by Mrs. Leslie Bamberger, West Point, Ga. 1957.)

Marriages

John Franklin Peters and Charlotte M. Edwards were married April 6, 1881.
Leslie L. Bamberger of Wilmington, Delaware, and Alice M. Peters of Claymont, Delaware, were married May 20, 1919.

Births

Alice Maria Peters was born November 26, 1894 at Felton, Pa.
Alice Marie Bamberger was born December 18, 1920 at Claymont, Del.

Deaths

J. Franklin Peters died December 19, 1913.
Charlotte (Edwards) Peters died April 3, 1955.

John Franklin Peters was the son of John Peters and Jane W. Zebley, married in 1855.

Thomas B. Pepper died December 14, 1891, age
    60 years, 11 months and 14 days.
Mary E. Warren, daughter of Thomas and Rachel his
    wife, died November 20, 1914, age 77 years
    and 22 days.
Margaret H., wife of George M. Pepper, died
    September 27, 1863.
Joshua Pepper, the first Pepper of all, died
    December 26, 1808, age 83 years.
Elizabeth Pepper, wife of Joshua, died
    September 21, 1811.

FRANKLIN PETERS - CHARLOTTE EDWARDS

(Published by A. J. Holmes & Co., 1222 Arch St.,
Philadelphia. 1881. Owned by Mrs. Leslie
Bamberger, West Point, Ga. 1957.)

Marriages

John Franklin Peters and Charlotte M. Edwards were
    married April 6, 1881.
Leslie L. Bamberger of Wilmington, Delaware, and
    Alice M. Peters of Claymont, Delaware, were
    married May 20, 1919.

Births

Alice Maria Peters was born November 26, 1894 at
    Felton, Pa.
Alice Marie Bamberger was born December 18, 1920
    at Claymont, Del.

Deaths

J. Franklin Peters died December 19, 1913.
Charlotte (Edwards) Peters died April 3, 1955.

John Franklin Peters was the son of John Peters
    and Jane W. Zebley, married in 1855.

THOMAS PEPPER-RACHEL LAWLES BIBLE

(In possession of Thomas B. Pepper, September 7, 1960. H. E. Phinneys stereotype edition. The Holy Bible containing the Old and New Testament, together with the Apyocrypha. Translated out of the original tongue and with the formed translations diligently copied and revised. Cooperstown, N.Y. Printed and published by H. E. Phinney. 1833. Sent by Helene Potter, Col. Hall Chapter. Copied by Sarah Pepper McLaughlin, September 21, 1960. Witness: Helen McC.West.)

Marriages

Thomas Pepper and Rachel Lawless were married
    January 22, 1837.
Thomas B. Pepper and Mary E. White were married
    August 4, 1872.
Thomas B. Pepper and Martha Zimmerman were married
    February 21, 1906 at Carlisle, Pa. by Rev.
    A. N. Hagerty.

Births

Mary Elanor Pepper, daughter of Thomas Pepper and
    Rachel his wife, was born October 28, 1837.
George M. Pepper, son of Thomas Pepper and Rachel
    his wife, was born June 13, 1840.

Willard S. Warren, son of Rufus M. Warren and
    Mary Eleanor his wife, was born November 18,
    1859.

Margaret Jane Pepper, daughter of George M. Pepper
    and Margaret his wife, was born September 10,
    1863.
Thomas B. Pepper, son of Thomas B. Pepper and Mary
    E. his wife, was born June 12, 1873.

Deaths

Margaret Jane Pepper, daughter of George M. Pepper
    and Margaret his wife, died September 22,
    1865, age 2 years and 12 days.
Rachel Pepper, wife of Thomas Pepper, died
    September 17, 1870, age 57 years, 8 months
    and 16 days.

John F., second son of James and Mary Pennington, was born May 3, 1874.

J. Walker Pennington, eldest son of Laurence H. and Emma Walker his wife, was born June 22, 1896.
Helen Mae, eldest daughter of Laurence H. and Emma, was born April 26, 1901.
Sara Albina, second daughter, was born August 27, 1903.
Martin Beadenkopf, second son, was born May 16, 1908.

James Leslie Derickson, only son of Anna Pennington and Leslie Derickson, was born February 16, 1898.
Blanche Martha, only daughter of M. Anna Pennington and Leslie Derickson, was born July 13, 1899.

Mary Emilie, only daughter of Ella B. Pennington and Alfred G. Stroud, was born July 12, 1905.
William Bernard, only son of J. Walker and L. Rowena Pennington, was born October 2, 1929.
Emilie Ann, daughter of J. Walker and L. Rowena Pennington, was born December 24, 1936.

Lawrence H. II, eldest son of Martin B. and Louine H. Pennington, was born March 14, 1940.
Mary Ann, only daughter of Martin B. and Louine H. Pennington, was born March 1, 1942.
Martin Beadenkopf, youngest son of Martin and Louine Pennington, was born March 12, 1949.

Sallie Albina, daughter of Sara Pennington and G. Earle Evans, was born March 20, 1940.
Helen Brooks, second daughter of Sara Pennington and G. Earle Evans, was born February 4, 1943.

Eleanor Frances, eldest daughter of Blanche Derickson and Abner Woodward, was born December 30, 1927.
Margaret Ann, second daughter of Blanche Derickson and Abner Woodward, was born February 12, 1932.

James Leslie, Jr., eldest son of James L. and Mildred Dennison Derickson, was born December 23, 1935.

Mary Lou, daughter of James L. and Mildred E. Derickson, was born December 12, 1937.
Rodney Lynn Derickson, youngest son of James L. and Mildred Derickson, was born December 21, 1945.

Deborah Ann Schuyler, daughter of Emilie Ann Pennington and Oliver Schuyler, was born February 14, 1956.

Christina Kay Lilley, daughter of Eleanor Woodward and George Woodward, was born October 26, 1957.

Marriages

J. Walker Pennington, son of Laurence H. and Emma W. Pennington, and Leah Rowena Benard, were married September 17, 1927.
Martin Beadenkopf Pennington and Altie Louine Haines were married October 7, 1937.
Sara Albina Pennington and G. Earle Evans were married August 18, 1938.

Blanche Martha Derickson, daughter of Mary Ann Pennington and Leslie Derickson, and Abner C. Woodward were married October 23, 1926.
James Leslie Derickson and Mildred Dennison were married October 14, 1933.

Mary Emilie Stroud, only child of Ella B. Pennington and Alfred G. Stroud, and George Jackson were married October 20, 1924. She was married to Paul Skillman on July 1, 1949.

Eleanor Frances Woodward, daughter of Blanche Derickson and Abner Woodward, and George Lilley were married August 16, 1952.

Emilie Ann Pennington, only daughter of J. Walker and L. Rowena Pennington, and Oliver Schuyler were married July 9, 1955.

Ella Brooks Pennington, eldest daughter of James
   M. and Mary B. Pennington, and Alfred G.
   Stroud were married December 28, 1898.

Births

John Mercer was born June 14, 1778.
Rebecca was born September 19, 1810.
John was born April 16, 1813.
Nicholas was born June 19, 1816.

   The above three children were born of the
first wife of John Mercer, whose maiden name was
Mary Copes; born February 19, 1790.

   Ann Lambdin, the 2nd wife of John Mercer, was
born September 17, 1783.

Ann, their first child, was born December 31, 1820.
William was born June 10, 1822.
Sarah was born February 7, 1825.
Mary was born February 17, 1827.

John B. Pennington, son of Benedict Pennington and
   Sarah his wife, was born February 16, 1814.

James Mercer, eldest son of John B. Pennington and
   Ann his wife, was born July 13, 1839.
William Henry, second son of John B. Pennington
   and Ann his wife, was born February 13, 1842.
Benedict Chandler, third son of John B. Pennington,
   was born November 2, 1843.
John Wesley, fourth son of John B. Pennington and
   Ann his wife, was born November 4, 1845.
Sarah Ann, daughter of John B. Pennington and Ann
   his wife, was born June 3, 1848.
Thomas Franklin, third son of John B. Pennington
   and Ann his wife, was born September 11, 1850.
Delilah Jane, second daughter of John B. Pennington
   and Ann his wife, was born March 21, 1853.
Benjamin Sides, sixth son of John B. Pennington
   and Ann his wife, was born November 24, 1855.

Deaths

Mary, first wife of John Mercer, died June 23,
   1815.
Nicholas, their son, died July 8, 1816.
John, their son, died August 20, 1821.

John Mercer died August 24, (?), age 56 years.
Ann Mercer, wife of John Mercer, died October 22,
    1836, age 54 years.

John B. Pennington died June 9, 1860, age 47 years.
Ann Mercer, wife of John B. Pennington, died
    (no dates shown).

Benedict Chandler Pennington died (no dates shown).
William Henry Pennington died December 27, 1912.
Thomas Franklin Pennington died January 12, 1917.
Sarah Ann Pennington, wife of William Wilkins, died
    July 5, 1917.
Delilah Jane Pennington, wife of Martin Beadenkopf,
    died March 15, 1919.
Mary Brooks, wife of James Mercer Pennington, died
    April 24, 1918.
Emilie Evans, third daughter of James M. and
    Mary B. Pennington, died March 16, 1919.
James M. Pennington died June 3, 1920.
John W. Pennington, brother of James M. Pennington,
    died May 23, 1925.
Ella B. Stroud, eldest daughter of James and Mary
    B. Pennington, died December 1, 1941.
Anna M. Derickson, second daughter of James M. and
    Mary B. Pennington, died March 8, 1952.
Laurence Hipple Pennington died March 26, 1954.
John F. Pennington, youngest son of James M. and
    Mary B. Pennington, died July 1877 (not
    recorded in the Bible).

FAMILY RECORD

This record is not in the Bible.

Births

Laurence Hipple, eldest son of James Mercer and
    Mary L. Brooks Pennington, was born
    February 12, 1866.
Ella Brooks, eldest daughter of James and Mary B.
    Pennington, was born July 1, 1868.
Anna Mary, second daughter of James and Mary B.
    Pennington, was born May 22, 1871.
Emilie Evans, third daughter of James and Mary B.
    Pennington, was born September 10, 1872.

THE PETERSON FAMILY

Peter Jun. was married to Veronica Bermingham on March 8, 1735 by the Rev. John Pew of St. Georges in Newcastle County.
My father, Andrew Peterson, died 1740 suddenly without any sickness in the 57th year of his age.
My sister, Eliz. Garretson, died March 11, 1752 in the 47th year of her age and was interred on the 14 by Rt. Rev. Phillip Reading.
My beloved wife, Veronica, was born January 1, 1707 at Bohemia Landing.

Adam Peterson, son of Andrew Peterson Esq., was born November 25, 1709 at Middle Town.
Mr. Adam Peterson died January 27, 1763.
Veronica Peterson, wife of Adam Peterson, died July 29, 1785.
John McDonough and Veronica Harraway were married April 19, 1774. Married at Mrs. Veronica Peterson by Rev. Phillip Reading.

The age of the John McLean children:
Jacob McLean was born November 11, 1770.
Veronica McLean was born April 4, 1775 (or 11).
Richard B. M'Lean was born ? 1, 1775.

Note: Adam Peterson's will 11-26-1773, wife Rachel Peterson.
Ref.: New Castle Calendar of Wills, p. 73.
Veronica Peterson, St. Georges Hd. 7-15-1784-85;
Thomas & Letitia McKain, children of daughter Mary, decd., and her husband William McKain, decd., Jacob, Richard, John, Henry, Veronica McLean.
Children of granddaughter Nancy McLean: Granddaughter Mary O'Harra; pg. 107.

See Peterson Chart next page.

Peterson Chart

Andrew Peterson		2.		3.	
b. 1683		1. Elizabeth Peterson		1. Bridget Garretson	
d. 1740			b. 1705		m. Richard Colegat
			d. 3-11-1752		2. Richard
			m. Garretson		3. Mary
					m. --Cadogan
		2. Adam Peterson		4. Edmund Garetson	
			b. 11-25-1709		5. Cantwell
			d. 1-27-1763		6. Hallowell Garetson
			m. 3-8-1735 Veronica Bermingham		
			b. 1-1-1707		
			d. 7-29-1785		

Children of Bridget and Richard Colgate:
    John
    Richard
    Henry

Mary and her husband --Cadogan had a daughter:
    Elizabeth

Edmund Garretson had a son:
    Andrew

Above data was taken from the will of Elizabeth Garrestson, 1742.

WARREN J. & ELNOR ANN (JOHNSON) PHILLIPS

(Bible published by American Bible Society, New York. 1849. Owned by Miss Amanda Phillips, Wilmington, Delaware. 1956. Record given by Mrs. Charles Bird.)

Births

Samuel Phillips was born November 6, 1785.
Mary Phillips was born October 4, 1793.

Elender Ann Johnson, daughter of Robert M. Johnson
  and Hettie his wife, was born June 6, 1835.
Mary H. Phillips, born May 25, 1854.
Margaret Jane Phillips, born September 19, 1856.
Sarah Catherine Phillips, born November 27, 1858.
John Wingate Phillips, born November 19, 1861.
Isaiah Curtis Phillips, born April 18, 1865.
Robert W. Phillips, born May 10, 1868.
Theodore F. Phillips, born September 4, 1871.
Ida E. Phillips, born April 16, 1874.
Amanda Ellen Phillips, born November 30, 1875.
Hatie T. Phillips, born August 2, 1880.

Margaret Jane Phillips was married Oct. 4, 1873.

Nancy J. Phillips, born May 15, 1813.
Jacob E. Phillips, born March 23, 1816.
Comfort H. Phillips, born December 26, 1818.
Mary G. Phillips, born July 26, 1821.
Margaret H. Phillips, born September 8, 1823.
Priscilla S. Phillips, born January 6, 1826.
Warren J. Phillips, born October 10, 1828.
John S. Phillips, born October 14, 1830.
Sarah E. Phillips, born October 21, 1833.

    This is the names and ages of Daniel Phillips
children and Polly his wife.
                    December 30, 1848

Deaths

Margaret Phillips died July 25, 1861.
Jacob E. Phillips died February 1865.
Daniel Phillips died March 11, 1866.
Margaret Jane Willey died September 29, 1888.
Mary H. Willey died January 28, 1947.
Ida E. Phillips died November 10, 1874.
Sarah C. Hearn died April 24, 1885.
Hattie T. Phillips died October 26, 1890.
Warren J. Phillips died April 22, 1894.
Elnor Ann Phillips died February 16, 1906.
John Wingate Phillips died August 20, 1932.
Robert W. Phillips died July 14, 1947.
Theodore F. Phillips died June 22, 1953.

URIEL PIERCE & BRANDLING G. GRUBB
OF BRANDYWINE HUNDRED, DELAWARE

(Owned by Mrs. Clarence E. Potter, Wilmington, Delaware. 1957. Record copied by Mrs. Charles D. Bird.)

Marriages

Uriel Pierce and Brandling G. Grubb were married in Marcus Hook, Pa., April 8, 1841 by the Rev. J. Walker.

Births

Uriel Pierce, son of Joseph and Lena Pierce, was born July 19, 1808.
Brandling G. Grubb, daughter of Nicholas and Hannah Grubb, was born December 12, 1823.

Laetitia G. Pierce, daughter of Uriel and Brandling G. Pierce, was born March 6, 1842.
Lena A. Pierce, daughter of Uriel and Brandling G. Pierce, was born September 14, 1843.
Edward C. Pierce, son of Uriel and Brandling G. Pierce, was born June 4, 1846.
Uriel T. Pierce, son of Uriel and Brandling G. Pierce, was born August 31, 1848.
Robert C. Pierce, son of Uriel and Brandling G. Pierce, was born April 1, 1851.
Charles W. Pierce, son of Uriel and Brandling G. Pierce, was born September 11, 1853.
Amer Pierce, son of Uriel and Brandling G. Pierce, was born November 4, 1854.
Lewis C. Pierce, son of Uriel and Brandling G. Pierce, was born July 1, 1857.
Julia Ella, daughter of Uriel and Brandling G. Pierce, was born February 16, 1859.
Laura Amanda, daughter of Uriel and Brandling G. Pierce, was born March 12, 1863.
Clara G. Pierce, daughter of Uriel and Brandling G. Pierce, was born January 28, 1867.
George C. Pierce, son of Uriel and Brandling G. Pierce, was born April 28, 1870.

Deaths

Charles W. Pierce, son of Uriel and Brandling Pierce, died October 30, 1853, age 7 weeks.
Amer Pierce, son of Uriel and Brandling Pierce, died April 25, 1857, age 2 years, 5 months and 21 days.

Joseph Pierce Chart

1.
Joseph Pierce
b.
d.
m.
Lena

Nicholas
Grub
m.
Hannah

2.
Uriel Pierce
b. 7-19-1808
d.
m. 4-8-1841

Brandling
Grubb

3.
1. Laetitia
   b. 3-6-1842
2. Lena
   b. 9-14-1843
3. Edward
   b. 6-4-1846
4. Uriel
   b. 8-31-1848
5. Robert
   b. 4-1-1851
6. Charles
   b. 9-11-1853
   d. 1853
7. Amer
   b. 11-4-1854
   d. 4-25-1857
8. Lewis
   b. 7-1-1857
9. Julia
   b. 2-16-1859
10. Laura
    b. 3-12-1863
    m. 2-23-1881
    Charles Simon
    b. 2-28-1859
11. Clara
    b. 1-28-1867
12. George
    b. 4-28-1870

4.
See Below

Joseph Pierce Chart continued next page.

Joseph Pierce Chart Continued:

4.
1. Clara
   b. 1881
2. Charles
   b. 1883; d. 1940
3. Harry
   b. 1886; d. ?
4. Laura
   b. 1888; d. 1942
5. Oscar
   b. 1890; d. 1891
6. William
   b. 1892
7. Herbert
   b. 1894; d. 1943
8. Clarence
   b. 1897
9. Ernest
   b. 1900
10. Florence
    b. 1904

JAMES PONSELL - MAMIE C. RASH

(Bible published by Gately and Fitzgerald, 1025 Market Street, Philadelphia, Pa. Owned by Mrs. J. P. Ponsell, Sr., Wilmington, Delaware. 1956. Record given by Mrs. Charles Bird.)

Marriages

James P. Ponsell and Mamie C. Rash were married November 17, 1897, by Rev. John D. C. Hanna.
Ralph B. Chalfant and Edith E. Ponsell were married April 22, 1919, by Leonard White, Wilmington, Delaware.
Ira B. Stewart and Gladys R. Ponsell were married September 4, 1926 in Media, Pa.
James P. Ponsell, Jr. and Madaline G. Barnes were married June 4, 1927, by Vaughn Moore in Mt. Salem M.E. Church, Wilmington, Delaware.
Francis I. Ponsell and Mazie R. Campbell were married April 20, 1929, by Preston W. Spence, Jr., in Mt. Salem Church.

Gladys Stewart and William Maitland were married August 12, 1939, by Rev. Park Huntington, in St. Stephens Church.

Births

James Preston Ponsell, son of Michael and Sarah his wife, was born September 24, 1873, Ind.
Mamie Cooper Rash, daughter of John F. and Mariam E. Rash, was born December 5, 1878, Md.
Gladys Rash Ponsell, 1st daughter of James and Mamie his wife, was born November 20, 1898, Del.
Edith Elizabeth Ponsell, 2nd daughter of James and Mamie his wife, was born August 21, 1900. Del.
James P. Ponsell, 1st son of James P. and Mamie his wife, was born February 17, 1903.
Francis I. Ponsell, 2nd son of James P. and Mamie his wife, was born November 21, 1905. Del.

Deaths

James P. Ponsell died July 14, 1953 at Delaware Hospital, Wilmington.

1.
Jos. Rash, Sr.
b. 9-14-1757
d. 3-13-1836
m.
Hester

Jonathan
Finstwait
d. 6-6-1825
m.
Martha

2.
1. John H. Rash
b. 5-3-1798
d. 7-17-1870
m. 7-19-1821

Martha
Finstwait
b. 11-15-1794
d. 2-9-1866

2. Jos. Jr.
b.
d. 1827
m.
Martha

3.
1. Martha Ann
b. 5-11-1822
d. 9-6-1830
2. Miriam
b. 5-16-1825
d. 9-6-1831
3. Ann M.
b. 2-10-1828
4. Sarah J.
b. 3-12-1830
5. Jonathan
b. 4-4-1833
6. John F. Rash
b. 2-11-1836
d. 12-7-1915
m. 1-8-1861
Miriam Truax
b. 7-3-1843
d. 11-6-1907

Joseph Rash Chart continued next page.

                                    7. Mary P.
                                       b. 7-29-1838

Children of Jos. Jr.
    1. Jonathan
          b. 1818; d. 1882
    2. Eliza
          b. 1815; d. 1897

4.
1. Henry   b. 10-23-1862
2. Hannah   b. 1864
3. Herbert   b. 1866
4. John   b. 1868
5. Martha   b. 1870
6. Willie   b. 1873
7. Sarah   b. 1875
8. Walter   b. 1876
9. <u>Mary C.</u>   b. 12-5-1878;
    m. 11-17-1897
    <u>Jas. P. Ponsell</u>   (See 5. below)
10. Clara   b. 1882
11. Cora   b. 1884
12. Letitia   b. 1886
13. Irving   b. 1890

5.
<u>Mary C. Rash</u>
b. 12-5-1878   1. Gladys   b. 1898
m. 11-17-1897   2. Edith   b. 1900
<u>Jas. P. Ponsell</u>   3. James   b. 1903
b. 9-24-1873   4. Francis   b. 1905
d. 7-14-1953
Son of Michael and Sarah Ponsell.

<u>CLARENCE E. POTTER & LAURA L. SIMON</u>

(Bible published by A. J. Holman & Co., Phil.
Owned by Clarence E. Potter, Wilmington, Del. 1957.
Record given by Mrs. Charles D. Bird.)

<u>Marriages</u>

Laura L. Simon and Clarence E. Potter were married
    May 12, 1910.

- 284 -

Family Record

Clarence E. Potter, born Brandywine Hd., Delaware,
    March 14, 1886.
Laura L. Simon, born Brandywine Hd., Delaware,
    April 24, 1888.
Charles William Potter was born May 14, 1911, in
    Wilmington, Delaware.
Edith Winifred Potter was born March 2, 1913, in
    Wilmington, Delaware.

Charles Wm. Potter and Anna May Cloud were married
    February 17, 1939.
Edith Winifred Potter and Frank B. Moore were
    married July 10, 1937.

Children of Edith W. and Frank B. Moore:
    Frank Lee Moore was born September 17, 1938
        in Wilmington, Delaware.
    Richard Clarence Moore was born August 4,
        1940 in Wilmington, Delaware.
    Lela Jean was born (no dates shown) in
        Wilmington, Delaware.
    Robert Perry was born (no dates shown) in
        Wilmington, Delaware.
    Helen Edith was born (no dates shown) in
        Wilmington, Delaware.
    Eleanor Ethel was born (no dates shown) in
        Wilmington, Delaware.

Children of Charles and Anna May Potter:
    Daniel Eugene Potter was born June 26, 1940
        in Wilmington, Delaware.
    Ronald Arthur was born April 28, 1942;
        died April 2, 1943.
    Kenneth Vincent was born (no dates shown).
    Francis Carlisle was born (no dates shown).
    Carol Ann was born (no dates shown).
    Charles Simon was born (no dates shown).

WILLIAM NELSON POTTER & CLARA DAVIS HANBY
(Both of Brandywine Hundred
Wilmington, Delaware)

(Bible owned by Mrs. Helen Ferguson, Richardson Park, Delaware. 1957. Record given by Mrs. Charles D. Bird.)

Marriages

Marriage Certificate of William Nelson Potter and Clara Davis Hanby, were married at Wilmington, Delaware, second day of July, 1885 in the presence of Mary R. Adams. Signed: R. H. Adams, Pastor, St. Paul's Church.

Clarence E. to Laura L. Simon, May 12, 1910.
William N. Jr., to Rose McKnight, October 7, 1914.
George B. to Mabel B. Larsen, June 20, 1916.
Fred Potter to Ethel E. Gregg, April 6, 1918.
Helen E. to Alexander Ferguson, March 29, 1919.

Births

William Nelson Potter, Sr., born August 11, 1862.
Clara Davis Hanby Potter, born February 1, 1864.
Sarah Jane Bullock Hanby, born January 16, 1841.
Clarence Edward Potter, born March 14, 1886.
William Nelson Potter, Jr., born June 16, 1887.
Fred Potter, born February 16, 1889.
George Brinton Potter, born October 29, 1890.
Mabel Florence Potter, born August 9, 1892.
Helen Etta Potter, born January 14, 1894.
Josephine White Potter, born December 30, 1896.

Deaths

Josephine W. Potter, died March 16, 1897.
William N. Potter, died November 14, 1933.
Chara D. Potter, died December 5, 1938.
George B. Potter, died February 13, 1956.

PRINGLE - CLARK

(Bible published by New York American Bible Society. 1858. "To Robert Pringle from his affectionate Father, Alexander Pringle." January 1, 1862. Owned by Mrs. Marian A. Rowe, Wilmington, Delaware. 1956. Record given by Mrs. Charles Bird.)

Marriages

Robert Pringle and Anna C. Clark were married
    January 18, 1866.
Frank A. Razee and Margaret Anne Pringle were
    married August 3, 1911.

Births

Alexander Pringle was born March, 1793.
Elizabeth Pringle, wife of Alexander Pringle, was
    born June 16, 1797.

Robert Pringle was born February 28, 1838.
Anna C. Clark, wife of Robert Pringle, was born
    January 18, 1845.

Margaret Anna Pringle was born October 2, 1867.
Louise Stone Pringle was born October 4, 1871.
Mary Pringle was born January 28, ----.
Catharine H. Pringle was born October 2, ----.

Isabella E. Pringle was born December 2, 1832.
Margaret Pringle was born March 24, 1836.
Robert Pringle was born February 28, 1838.
Emma Pringle was born November 11, 1841.

Deaths

Robert Pringle died August 18, 1871, age 33 years.
Anna C. Pringle died October 5, 1871, age 26 years.
Louise Stone Pringle died December 30, 1871, age
    3 months.
Alexander Pringle died October 3, 1862, age 69
    years.
Elizabeth Pringle died February 27, 1863, age
    66 years.
Mary Pringle died August 10, 1895.

Catharine Pringle died January 25, 1908.
Isabelle E. Pringle died July 22, 1880.
Margaret Pringle died August 6, 1862.
Emma Pringle died July 3, 1885.

Alexander Pringle
b. 3-1793
d. 10-3-1862
m.
Elizabeth
b. 6-16-1797
d. 2-27-1863

Robert Pringle
b. 2-28-1838
d. 8-18-1871
m. 1-18-1866
Anna C. Clark
b. 1-18-1845
d. 10-5-1871

JOHN F. RASH & MARIAM TRUAX

(Bible published by Bradley, Garretson & Co., Philadelphia, Pa. 1872. Owned by Mrs. Jas. P. Ponsell, Sr., Wilmington, Delaware. 1956. Record given by Mrs. Charles Bird.)

Marriages

John F. Rash and Mariam E. Truax were married January 8, 1861.
Hannah T. Rash and Wm. S. Elben were married June 25, 1884.
H. Ernest Rash and Cora E. Hazzard were married October 23, 1884.
Matie Rash and David L. Short were married March 11, 1891.
Mattie R. Short and Isaac C. Conner were married April 1, 1896.
Walter Rash and Ida Williams were married June 3, 1896.
William B. Rash and Sallie E. Shinn were married March 31, 1904.
Mary C. Rash and Jas. P. Ponsellers were married November 17, 1897.
Letitia Rash and Elmer Fuller were married April 5, 1905.
Clara E. Rash and Herman Hopkins were married April 5, 1905.
Cora S. Rash and James K. Shinn were married March 1, 1906.

Births

John F. Rash, son of Jno. H. Rash and Martha his wife, was born February 11, 1836.
Mariam E. Rash, daughter of Jno. Truax and Hannah his wife, was born July 3, 1843.

1st.   Henry Ernest Rash, 1st son of Jno. F. Rash and Mariam his wife, was born October 23, 1862.
2nd.   Hannah Truax Rash, 1st daughter of Jno. F. Rash and Mariam his wife, was born October 6, 1864.
3rd.   Herbert Rash, 2nd son of Jno. F. Rash and Mariam E. his wife, was born November 15, 1866.
4th.   Jno. S. T. Rash, 3rd son of Jno. F. Rash and Mariam E. his wife, was born August 22, 1868.
5th.   Martha Rash, 2nd daughter of Jno. F. Rash and Mariam E. his wife, was born September 29, 1870.
6th.   Willie Rash, 4th son of Jno. F. Rash and Mariam his wife, was born September 16, 1873.
7th.   Sarah T. Rash, 3rd daughter of Jno. F. Rash and Marian his wife, was born October 11, 1875.
8th.   Walter Rash, 5th son of Jno. F. Rash and Mariam his wife, was born October 15, 1876.
9th.   Mary C. Rash, 4th daughter of Jno. F. Rash and Mariam his wife, was born December 5, 1878.
10th. Clara E. Rash, 5th daughter of Jno. F. Rash and Mariam his wife, was born December 11, 1882.
11th. Cora S. Rash, 6th daughter of Jno. F. Rash and Mariam his wife, was born June 15, 1884.
12th. Letitia P. Rash, 7th daughter of Jno. F. Rash and Mariam his wife, was born March 25, 1886.
13th. Irving Leroy Rash, 6th son of Jno. F. Rash and Miriam his wife, was born February 7, 1890.

Deaths

Herbert Rash, son of Jno. F. and Mariam Rash,
    died February 27, 1872, age 4 years,
    3 months and 12 days.
Jno. S. T. Rash, son of Jno. F. and Mariam Rash,
    died September 8, 1881, age 13 years and
    17 days.
Sarah T. Rash, daughter of Jno. F. and Mariam
    Rash, died September 18, 1893, age 17 years,
    11 months and 7 days.
Mariam E., wife of John F. Rash, died November 6,
    1907, age 64 years, 4 months and 3 days.
John F. Rash died December 7, 1915, age 79 years,
    9 months and 26 days.
Martha F. Rash died February 9, 1866, age 71
    years, 2 months and 24 days.
John H. Rash died July 17, 1870, age 74 years,
    2 months and 12 days.

JOHN H. RASH & MARTHA

(Bible published and sold by Kimber & Sharpless,
Philadelphia, Pa. 1824. Owned by Mrs. James P.
Ponsell, Wilmington, Delaware. 1956. Record
given by Mrs. Charles Bird.)

Marriages

John H. Rash and Martha his wife were married
    July 19, 1821.
Thomas Thomas and Mary his wife were married
    July 19, 1823.

Births

Martha Finstwait, daughter of Jonathan and Martha
    his wife, was born November 15, 1794.

Martha Ann Rash, daughter of John H. Rash and
    Martha his wife, was born May 11, 1822.
Mirium Rash, daughter of John H. Rash and Martha
    his wife, was born May 16, 1825.
Ann Mariah Rash, daughter of John H. Rash and
    Martha his wife, was born February 10, 1828.

Sarah Jane Rash, daughter of John and Martha his
    wife, was born March 12, 1830.

William Colgin, son of Rachel Colgin, was born
    November 1, 1818.

Martin Rash, son of Joseph and Martha his wife,
    was born June 28, 1812.
Elizabeth Rash, daughter of Joseph and Martha his
    wife, was born February 20, 1815.
Jonathan Rash, son of John H. and Martha his
    wife, was born April 4, 1833.
John F. Rash, son of John H. Rash and Martha his
    wife, was born February 11, 1836.
Mary P. Rash, daughter of John H. Rash and Martha
    his wife, was born July 29, 1838.

John H. Rash, son of Joseph and Hester his wife,
    was born May 3, 1798.

Joseph Rash, Sr., the elder, was born Sept. 14,
    1757; died March 13, 1836, age 79 years,
    5 months and 29 days.
Mariam Rash, daughter of Joseph Rash, was born
    December 11, 1779.
Martha Finstwait, daughter of Jonathan and Martha
    his wife, was born November 15, 1794.

Deaths

Jonathan Rash, son of Joseph Rash and Martha his
    wife, died January 25, 1882, age 64 years,
    6 months and 12 days.
Elizabeth (Eliza) Hoffecker, daughter of Joseph
    Rash and Martha his wife, died December 2,
    1897, age 82 years, 9 months and 12 days.
Joseph Rash, Jr. died March 11, 1827.
Jonathan Finstwait died June 6, 1825.
Obadiah Thompson died July 3, 1825.
Marthaann Rash, daughter of John H. Rash and
    Martha, died September 6, 1830.
Mirium Rash, daughter of John H. and Martha his
    wife, died September 6, 1831.
John, Jr., died June 6, 1835.
Martha Rash, wife of John H. Rash, died
    February 9, 1866, age 71 years, 2 months
    and 24 days.

Miriam Pamel died August 25, 1866, age 86 years, 8 months and 14 days.
John H. Rash died July 17, 1870, age 74 years, 2 months and 14 days.

REDISH BIBLE RECORD

(Owned by Mr. Harold W. T. Purnell, Georgetown, Delaware.)

Lewis A. Redish, husband, was born January 9, 1847.
Mary H. Redish, wife, was born December 31, 1852.
Granville A. Redish, son, was born October 20, 1870.
Ernest W. Redish, son, was born December 5, 1873.
Jackson L. Redish, son, was born April 2, 1876.
Katie M. Redish, daughter, was born August 11, 1879.
Larry A. Redish, son, was born September 13, 1887.
Mary J. Redish, daughter, was born October 24, 1885.
Earl D. Redish, son, was born April 12, 1898.
Lilliam M. Redish, daughter, was born October 28, 1899.

REES - McNEAL

John Rees or Rees John was born ca 1650 in Wales; died November 26, 1697/8 in Merion, Pa., Friends Meeting House (buried there). He was married in Wales, probably at "Dagelly Monthly Meeting" to Hannah ap Griffith ap Rhys, who was born 1656 in Wales. She died September 27, 1741 at Goshen, Pa. After the death of John Rees, his widow married Ellis Davis of Goshen, in 1702. After his death she married Thomas Evans in 1722.

The preposition "ap" means son of.

Children of John Rees and Hannah (Griffith):

1. Richard
2. Evan
3. Lowry, m. Hugh Evans, son of his mother's 3rd husband)
4. Jane, m. David Davies
5. John Rees
6. Sarah
7. Edward

John Rees, son of John Rees and Hannah (Griffith) was born in Wales. He married Hannah ----- by 1795. Their children:

1. Edward, born March 27, 1706.
2. Ellin, born August 7, 1708.
3. Rose, born January 4, 1710.
4. Hannah, Jr.)
5. Jane   ), born October 13, 1713.
6. John Rees, born September 12, 1718.

John Rees, son of John Rees and his wife Hannah, was born September 12, 1718; died December 1, 1807. He married Catherine Evans, September 11 or 28, 1746 at Plymouth Meeting, Pa. She was born July 7, 1724; died August 1805. Their children:

1. Sarah, born October 1, 1752.
2. John, born August 3, 1758.
3. Joseph Meredith, born February 14, 1761.
4. David, born 1764.
5. Daniel, born 1770.

Joseph Meredith Reese, son of John Rees and Catherine Evans, was born February 14, 1761, near Plymouth, Phil. Co., Pa. He married Mary Lee in 1785 in Harford County, Md. She was the daughter of William Lee and his wife Eleanor (Atkinson) Lee. She was born July 31, 1770. Their children:

1. John Lee, born August 1, 1788; died September 19, 1871.
2. Elenora, born 9-26-1786; died 9-15-1792.
3. Sarah; m. 1st George Jacobs; m. 2nd Richard Messeter.
4. William, born 4-14-1793; died 11-25-1870.

5. Ellenora; m. Edward Spedden.
6. Morris M., born 6-22-1800; died 1802.
7. Eliza; m. ---- Beard.
8. Aquilla, born 2-26-1798; died 10-19-1810.
9. **Daniel Meredith**, born December 10, 1805.
10. George J., born 1-15-1808; died 7-25-1882.

Daniel Meredith Reese, son of Joseph Meredith Reese and his wife Mary Lee Reese, was born December 10, 1805 in Baltimore, Md. He died on April 6, 1875 in Baltimore and was buried in Mt. Olivet Cemetery, Baltimore.

He married December 21, 1829 in Baltimore, Ann George, daughter of Stephen George and his wife Mary Simpers. She was born December 4, 1809 in Northeast, Cecil Co., Md.; died December 20, 1907 in Washington, D.C. and is buried in Mt. Olivet Cemetery, Baltimore, Md. Their children:

1. Mary Elizabeth, born January 20, 1831; died 1906; married Charles Gray.
2. Stephen - died young.
3. Ellen, born October 3, 1834; died 10-8-1917.
4. **Daniel Webster**, born December 7, 1835 (or 1836).
5. Ann Eliza, born July 27, 1839; died 5-30-1903.
6. Margaret, born March 3, 1842; died 11-23-1896; married Jacob Stoek.
7. Virginia, born May 2, 1844; died 1910.
8. Edward S., born August 1847; died 1907.
9. Sophia T., born March 4, 1849; married William C. Stewart.
10. Sarah R., born August 9, 1851 - single.
11. Fannie, born March 10, 1854; died 2-9-1933; married Will Stewart.

Daniel Webster Reese, son of Daniel M. Reese and Ann George Reese, was born in Baltimore, Md., December 7, 1835 or 1836. He died in Kensington, Md., May 19, 1891 and was buried in Mt. Olivet Cemetery, Baltimore, Md. He was a prisoner in Libby Prison during the Civil War.

Daniel W. Reese was married in Baltimore to Virginia Pattison on May 9, 1865. She was the daughter of William Pattison and Ann Jones. She was born 1844 and died March 23, 1888. Is also buried in Mt. Olivet Cemetery. Her full name was Maryland Virginia Pattison. Their children:

1. Annie Needham, born February 17, 1866;
    m. Charles Holton.
2. Charles Pattison, born July 17, 1867;
    m. Grace Blinn.
3. <u>Myrtie Virginia</u>, born February 14, 1869;
    m. H. W. McNeal.
4. Sallie P., born February 28, 1874;
    m. 1st Edgar Ferguson;
    m. 2nd W. C. Worley.
5. George
6. Bessie, born October 30, 1880 - died young.
7. Walter, born May 1, 1887.
8. Florence

NOTE: Information on children of Daniel M. Reese and Ann George is from the Family Bible and from living relatives.

(SEE McNeal Record for Children of Myrtie V. Reese and H. W. McNeal)

RICKARDS RECORD

(Published for the Methodist Episcopal Church at the Conference Office, 200 Mulberry St., N.Y. by S. Lane & C.B.T. Tippett. James Collard Printer. 1845. Owned by Mrs. Harry A. Ellis, Lewes, Delaware.)

On front fly leaves:

Family Record

<u>Marriages</u>

Eli Rickards and Hannah Rickards were married May 16, 1791.

Eli Rickards and Mary Eveans (Evans ?) were
    married November 12, 1793.
Eli Rickards and Rachel Derickson were married
    April 19, 1810.
James W. Rickards and Sarah T. West were married
    January 6, 1847.

Deaths

Eli Rickards died November 12, 1833, age 66
    years, 9 months and 23 days.
John M. Rickards died January 28, 1800.
Nathaniel Rickards died June 16, 1822.
Jobe M. Rickards died December 23, 1849.
William Rickards, son of Eli Rickards and Mary
    his wife, died January 5, 1836.
Mary Lynch, daughter of Eli Rickards and Rachel
    his wife, died January 4, 1845.
James W. Rickards died May 8, 1857, age 49
    years, 8 months and 10 days.
Hannah Daisy, daughter of Eli Rickards and Mary
    his wife, died February 18, (year blurred),
    age 75 years, 5 months and 27 days.

Births

Eli Rickards, son of Jones Rickards and Sidney
    his wife, was born February 19, 1767.
Mary Evans, daughter of John Evans and Catherine
    his wife, was born (no dates shown).
Hannah Rickards, daughter of Eli Rickards and
    Mary his wife, was born August 23, 1794.
Nathaniel Rickards, son of Eli Rickards and Mary
    his wife, was born May 19, 1797.
John Morris Rickards, son of Eli R. and Mary his
    wife, was born October 23, 1799.
William Rickards, son of Eli Rickards and Mary
    his wife, was born January 27, 1801.
Isaac Rickards, son of Eli Rickards and Rachel
    his wife, was born June 16, 1811.
Stephen Rickards, son of Eli and Rachel, was
    born February 24, 1814.
Kendal Rickards, son of Eli and Rachel his wife,
    was born August 8, 1816.
Mary Rickards, daughter of Eli R. and Rachel his
    wife, was born September 22, 1818.
Job Morris Rickards, son of Eli Rickards and
    Mary his wife, was born April 24, 1804.

James White Rickards, son of Eli Rickards and
    Mary his wife, was born August 28, 1807.

Marriages

James W. Rickards and Sarah T. West were married
    January 6, 1847.
James H. McLaughlin and Sarah T. Rickards were
    married March 26, 1862.
Benjamin D. Chamberlin and Laura A. Rickards
    were married December 11, 1867.
James P. Carey and Ida M. Chamberlin were
    married October 12, 1887.
William T. Moore and Sallie M. Rickards were
    married November 18, 1882.
Harry A. Ellis and Sophia L. Chamberlin were
    married June 18, 1903.
Elmer S. Murray and Ella F. Chamberlin were
    married December 20, 1905.
Benjamin C. Chamberlin and Amanda S. Pepper were
    married January 1, 1909.
William J. Faulkner and Sallie M. Chamberlin
    were married November 25, 1915.

Births

James White Rickards, son of Eli Rickards and
    Mary his wife, was born August 28, 1807.
Sarah Tunnell West, daughter of Isaac West and
    Nancy H. his wife, was born November 5, 1830.
Laura Ann Rickards, daughter of James W. Rickards
    and Sarah T. his wife, was born September 8,
    1849.
George Cornelius Rickards, son of James W.
    Rickards and Sarah his wife, was born
    May 20, 1851.
Sarah Mary West Rickards, daughter of James W.
    Rickards and Sarah his wife, was born
    September 7, 1853.

Clinton C. Chamberlin, son of Benjamin D. and
    Laura A. Chamberlin, was born July 23, 1868.
Infant son of Benj. D. Chamberlin and Laura his
    wife, was born November 9, 1869.
James West McLaughlin, son of James H. McLaughlin
    and Sarah T. his wife, was born January 2,
    1863.

Alfred Shelmerdine McLaughlin was born October 14, 1864.
Charles Kingsley McLaughlin was born September 21, 1866.

Ida M., daughter of Benjamin D. Chamberlin and Laura his wife, was born December 17, 1870.
Sallie M., daughter of Benjamin D. Chamberlin and Laura A. his wife, was born April 19, 1873.
James H. Chamberlin was born October 14, 1875.
Benjamin C. Chamberlin was born October 11, 1878.
Sophia L. Chamberlin was born April 13, 1882.
Ella Frances Chamberlin was born April 28, 1884.
Elmer C. Chamberlin was born November 5, 1887.

Baptisms

Sarah T. West was baptized by Rev. Porter (no dates shown).
Laura Ann Rickards was baptized March 17, 1850 by Rev. Daniel L. Pattison.
George Cornelius Rickards was baptized November 30, 1851 by Rev. David Daily.
Sarah Mary West Rickards was baptized December 25, 1854 by Rev. J. Pastorfield.
Ida May Chamberlin was baptized July 24, 1871 by Rev. P. Louis.
Sally Mary Chamberlin was baptized by Rev. W. R. Tubbs (no dates shown).
James Herbert Chamberlin was baptized by Rev. J. Arters (no dates shown).
Benjamin Clinton Chamberlin was baptized by Rev. J. Arters (no dates shown).

Births

Warren Thomas Moore, son of Wm. T. Moore and Sallie M. his wife, was born July 19, 1882.
Warren T. Moore was baptized November 25, 1882 by Rev. T. L. Tomkinson.
Sophia Laura Chamberlin was baptized by Rev. J. W. Dewhadaway (no dates shown).
Ella Frances Chamberlin was baptized February 17, 1895.
Elmer Curtis Chamberlin was baptized February 17, 1895 by Rev. C. P. Swain.

Deaths

George Cornelius Rickards died September 2, 1853, age 2 years, 3 months and 13 days.
James W. Rickards, died May 8, 1857, age 49 years, 8 months and 10 days.
Sarah T. McLaughlin died July 3, 1871, age 41 years, 9 months and 2 days.
Laura A. Chamberlin died May 4, 1890, age 40 years, 9 months and 26 days.
Ida M. Carey died August 8, 1891, age 20 years, 7 months and 21 days.
Laura A. Carey died August 15, 18??, age 11 months and 12 days.
Benjamin D. Chamberlin died August 7, 1899, age 57 years, 9 months and 22 days.
Elmer C. Chamberlin died February 11, 1916, age 28 years, 3 months and 6 days.
Sallie Faulkner died June 30, 1950.

On a blank page just after Family Record:

Births

George E. Cary, son of James P. and Ida M. Carey his wife, was born January 13, 1888.
Laura A. Cary, daughter of James P. and Ida M. Cary his wife, was born September 3, 1890.
Isaiah M. Ellis, son of Harry A. Ellis and Sophia his wife, was born July 14, 1907.
Clayton H. Ellis, son of Harry Ellis and Sophia his wife, was born February 4, 1909.
Lendley E. Murray, son of Elmer S. Murray and Ella his wife, was born March 13, 1907.
Ethia Murray, daughter of Elmer S. Murray and Ella his wife, was born April 14, 1911.

On back fly leaf of Bible:

Marriages

Isaac C. West and Nancy H. Derickson were married December 23, 1929.
Sarah T. West and James W. Rickards were married January 6, 1847.
George H. West and Eliza Ann Tunnell were married January 15, 1857.
Mary H. West and Ebe Townsend were married January 26, 1853.

Ezekiel L. West and Anna M. Rickards were married November 1, 1859.

Births

Isaac Collins West, son of Ezekiel West and Sarah his wife, was born May 29, 1805.
Nancy Hill Derickson, daughter of Handy Derickson and Sarah his wife, was born March 12, 1812.
Sarah Tunnell West, daughter of Isaac C. West and Nancy his wife, was born November 5, 1830.
George Handy West, son of Isaac C. West and Nancy his wife, was born February 22, 1832.
Ezekiel M. Lamden West, son of Isaac C. West and Nancy his wife, was born April 19, 1834.
Mary Hull (? Hill) West, daughter of Isaac C. West and Nancy his wife, was born June 12, 1836.
James Derickson West, son of Isaac C. West and Nancy his wife, was born November 10, 1838.
Isaac Collins West, son of (not legible).

JAMES ROBERTS BIBLE - SMYRNA, DELAWARE

(This Bible is in the possession of Mrs. Paul W. Taylor (granddaughter), b. 1-5-1879, 12 Silverside Rd., Wilmington, Delaware. Copied for Clara Wallace, Bird, Caesar Rodney Chapter. Published by Kimber & Sharpless, Philadelphia, Pa.)

Marriages

James Roberts and Arianna H. Green were married May 8, 1845 at Smyrna, Delaware.
James Roberts and Mary A. Voshell were married January 25, 1853 in Smyrna, Delaware.
Daniel Voshell and Elizabeth Crockett were married November 10, 1812.
James T. Farson and Sarah Voshell were married August 21, 1834.
William H. Blackiston and Mary E. Roberts were married December 4, 1877 in Smyrna, Kent Co., Delaware.
James Wesley Jones and Anna Spruance Roberts were married April 10, ----?

Paul W. Taylor and Elva Roberts Blackiston were
   married April 25, 1898.
Bayard Blackiston Taylor and Mabel Ellen Ford
   (Forb?) were married February 26, 1926.

Births

Anna Spruance Roberts, daughter of James Roberts
   and Arianna Green his wife, was born
   November 5, 1846 in Smyrna, Del.
Irene Levis Roberts, daughter of James Roberts
   and Arianna H. Green his wife, was born
   September 9, 1848.
Charles Clarence Roberts, son of James Roberts
   and Arianna H. his wife, was born
   December 4, 1850.
John Roberts, son of James Roberts and Mary A.
   his wife, was born April 30, 1854 in
   Smyrna, Del.
James V. Roberts, son of James Roberts and Mary
   A. Voshell his wife, was born June 22, 1856
   in Smyrna, Del. (V. is for Voshell)
Mary Elizabeth Roberts, daughter of James Roberts
   and Mary A. his wife, was born February 1,
   1858 in Smyrna, Del.

James Roberts, son of Samuel Roberts and Elizabeth
   his wife, was born April 10, 1818.
Mary A. Voshell was born November 12, 1816.

Children of Mary E. (Mary A.?) and Wm. H. Blackiston:
   Elva Roberts Blackiston, born January 5,
      1879.
   Bertha Watson Blackiston, born December 9,
      1880.
   Florence Voshell Blackiston, born
      November 7, 1882.
   William Edgar Blackiston, born February 3,
      1885.
   James Voshell Roberts Blackiston, born
      January 10, 1887.
   Helen Irene Blackiston, born April 25,
      1889.
   Mary Elizabeth Blackiston, born
      September 20, 1891.
   Herbert Keylor Blackiston, triplet
   O. Lee, triplet
   Anna Jones, triplet, were born December 8,
      1892.

John Wesley Blackiston, born July 23, 1894.
Gwendolyn Pyle, born November 18, 1894

Paul W. and Elva R. B. Taylor sons:
1. Bayard Blackiston Taylor, born
   September 4, 1900.
2. Joseph Pyle Taylor, born October 15,
   1905.
3. Daniel Voshell Taylor, twin
4. David Woolley Taylor, twin, born
   April 19, 1910.
5. Paul Woolley Taylor, born January 31,
   1915.
6. James Voshell Roberts Taylor, born
   August 12, 1917.
Paul W. Taylor, born December 21, 1876.

Deaths

Arianna Roberts, wife of James Roberts and
   daughter of Humphry and Hannah Green, died
   December 27, 1850 in Smyrna, Del.
Charles Clarence Roberts, son of James Roberts
   and Arianna H. his wife, died June 30,
   1851 in Smyrna, Del., age 6 months and
   22 days.
Elizabeth Crockett Voshell died June 24, 1833.

John Roberts, son of James Roberts and Mary A.
   his wife, died May 6, 1854 in Smyrna,
   Del., age 6 days.
James Roberts, son of Samuel and Elizabeth
   Roberts, died March 3, 1866, age 47 years,
   10 months and 23 days.
Mary A. Voshell, wife of James Roberts, died
   February 20, 1893 in Wilmington, Del.
Anna Spruance Roberts, wife of J. W. Jones, died
   November 7, 1911.
J. Wesley Jones died December 16, 1922.
Irene Levis Roberts died September 20 - 19?

Samuel Roberts, grandfather of Jas. V. Roberts,
   died February 15, 1827, age 39 years.
   Buried Old Drawyers near Odessa.

Elizabeth Price, his widow, married James Tapp,
   April 22, 1830. She is buried in Smyrna,
   Del. and James Tapp at Old Drawyers ?

NOTE: On the above James, I write here a record from a family Bible in the possession of Alfred Roberts:

"James Tapp and Elizabeth Roberts were married on the 22nd day of April in the year of our Lord One Thousand Eight Hundred and thirty two - 1832." Elva R. B. Taylor.

Also: She is buried at Smyrna, Del., Glenwood Cemetery in our Family lot. I have proof and explanations. Two husbands at Old Drawyers.

Isaac Hazel born January 8, 1801; died May 4, 1875, age 74 years, 3 months and 1 day. Grandfather of Emma Hazel and Maggie Hazel Harry.

James Voshell Roberts, son of James Roberts and Mary Ann Voshell Roberts his wife, died in Holly Oak, Del. on 10th month, 30th day, 1931. Cremated at Chelton Hill, Germantown, Pa. and ashes in bronze urn inscribed name and dates, placed with the key to same in a slate box in his mother's grave at Smyrna, Del., Glenwood Cemetery.

Webber children:
1. Virginia, 9 month 18th, 1917.
2. Arthur G., 3 month 1st, 1919.
3. Rebecca, 4 month 30, 1920.
4. Mary Winifred, 4 month 18, 1921.
5. Helen Irene, 5 month 10, 1922.
6. Elizabeth Browne, 11 month 3, 1923.
7. Joseph Roberts, 1 month 30, 1926.
8. James, twin
9. Elzie, twin (no dates shown).
   Written by James V. Roberts

Pasted in the Bible on page from another Bible in Benj. Ferris handwriting, he being the Benjamin Ferris who wrote the History of Wilmington, Del.

Exact copy: Benjamin Ferris to Mary Voshell, 3 month 2nd, 1838.

Daniel Voshell and Elizabeth Crockett were
    married November 10, 1812.
James T. Farson and Sarah Voshell were married
    August 21, 1834.
Mary Voshell was born November 12, 1816.
Sarah Voshell, daughter of Daniel and Elizabeth
    Voshell, was born June 24, 1814.
John C. Voshell, son of Daniel and Elizabeth
    Voshell, was born July 18, 1818.
Lewis Voshell, son of Daniel and Elizabeth
    Voshell, was born September 10, 1820.

Edward Farson, son of Jas. T. and Sarah V.
    Farson, was born October 20, 1830.
Edward Farson, son of James T. and Sarah V.
    Farson, was born January 14, 1838.

Mary Farson died 27 day of 5th month, 1838.
John Voshell died March 7, 1817.
Elizabeth Voshell, wife of Daniel Voshell, died
    June 24, 1833.

ROBESON BIBLE

(Printed by Alexander Kincaid. 1771. Now in the Delaware Historical Society, Wilmington, Del. Copied by Mrs. Alban Shaw.)

William Robeson and Elizabeth Miller were
    married April 1, 1773.

Alexander Robeson was born January 11, 1775.
Margaret Robeson was born October 16, 1776.

Alexander Miller died December 29, 1776.
Beata Miller, wife of Alexr. Miller, died
    October 1, 1778.
Elizabeth Robeson died August 4, 1779, age
    25 years and 10 months.

William Robeson and Ann Duff were married
    June 10, 1784.

Jane Robeson was born May 28, 1785.

Anne Robeson died June 29, 1785, age 15 years.

William Robeson and Elizabeth Wallace were married May 26, 1791.

Thomas Wallace Robeson was born September 12, 1792.

Aaron Paulson and Margaret Robeson were married September 4, 1800.
Alexander Robeson and Elizabeth Lenden (?) were married April 26, 1804.
Alen Thompson and Jane Robeson were married June 27, 1810.

Alexander Robeson died November 16, 1812; age 37 years, 10 months and 5 days.
William Robeson died April 23, 1815.
Margaret Paulson died November 4, 1823, age 47 years and 20 days.
Jane Thomson died February 6, 1824, age 38 years, 8 months and 29 days.
Elizabeth W. Robeson died September 12, 1828.

ROBESON BIBLE

(Bible printed by Alexander Kincaid. 1771. Record given by Mrs. Glenn S. Skinner, Newark, Delaware.)

In the front of Bible:

To the memory of William McKennan who departed this life May 5, 1809, age 90 years. He was born in Northern Ireland. He was the Pastor of White and Red Clay Creek Presbyterian Churches for 54 years, 34 of which was in connection with the First Church in Wilmington.

See chart next page.

Robeson Bible Cont'd.

From New Castle Calendar of Wills:

		Wm. Robeson	
		d. 4-25-1815	1. See
John		m. 4-1-1773	Below
Miller	Alexander		
m.	Miller		
Mary	d. 12-29-1776	Elizabeth Miller	
	m.	b.	
	Beata	d. 8-4-1779	
	d. 10-1-1778	age 25	

1. **Alexander**
    b. 1-11-1775
    d. 11-16-1812
    m. 4-26-1804
    Elizabeth Lawden

2. **Margaret**
    b. 10-16-1776
    d. 11-4-1823
    m. 9-4-1800
    Aaron Paulson

3. **Jane Robeson**
    b. 5-26-1785
    d. 2-6-1824
    m. 6-27-1810
    Alen Thompson

4. **Thomas W.**
    b. 9-21-1792

MARTIN & CHRISTINE ROSINBERGER

(Title page is missing - in German. Translated by Rev. Carl T. Smith. Original Bible is owned by the Genealogical Society of Pa.)

Births

Martin Rosinberger was born September 24, 1798.
Christina Rosinberger was born January 11, 1808.
Their children:
1. Hanna Rosinberger, born February 6, 1828.
2. Sophia Rosinberger, born February 3, 1831.
3. Jacob Rosinberger, born February 6, 1834.
4. Henrich Rosinberger, born March 5, 1840.
5. Christina Rosinberger, born April 24, 1842.
6. Daniel Rosinberger, born September 1, 1844.
7. Martin Rosinberger, born February 9, 1850.

Deaths

Henrich Rosinberger died July, 1841.
Martin Rosinberger died September 10, 1853.
Hannah Driesbach, daughter of Martin and Christina Rosinberger, died February 23, 1854.

Dear Father Martin Rosinberger died October 19, 1866.

RUDOLPH - GOLDER - WRIGHT

(From an old Bible at 7th & Market Sts., Phila., Pa.)

Marriages

William Rudolph and Hannah Golder were married February 27, 1812.
Christopher W. Rudolph and Hannah C. Mulford were married February 3, 1856.

Births

Salem B. Wright, son of William G. and Hannah G. Wright, was born August 15, 1865.
Lizzie Garrett Wright, daughter of William G. and Hannah G. Wright, was born July 15, 1867.
Helen B. M. Wright, daughter of William G. and Hannah G. Wright, was born August 1, 1869.
Ada S. Wright, daughter of William G. and Hannah G. Wright, was born July 25, 1871.

Deaths

Hannah Rudolph died December 30, 1856, age 72.
William Rudolph died April 7, 1860, age 72.
John C. Roberts, Jr., died October 24, 1861, age 1 year, 4 months and 24 days.
Christopher W. Rudolph died 1864, age 36 years.
Salem B. Wright died August 15, 1865.
Lizzie G. Wright died July 31, 1867, age 2 months and 4 days.
Ada S. Wright died July 30, 1872, age 1 year and 5 days.

Torn from an old Bible:
        William Wright - his Book 1795

William Wright was born October 17, 1760.
Ann Wright was born March 14, 1759.
Abraham Wright was born August 17, 1756.

SCALES - NICHOLS

Richard Scales was born 1834 in Norwich, Norfolk, England. He died in 1914. He married Sarah Nichols, who was born 1837 in Norwich, England. Their daughter:

Amelia Scales was born October 1876 in Norwich, England. She married George William Bacon. Their daughter:

Millie Frances Bacon was born Sept. 18, 1897 in Norwich, England. She married July 8, 1922 in Phil., Pa. James Hay, son of William S. Hay and his wife Mary E. (MacKenzie) Hay. Their daughter:

Edith MacKenzie Hay was born Feb. 9, 1924 in Phil., Pa. She married Daniel R. McNeal, Jr., son of Daniel R. NcNeal and Clara Louise (Berlin) McNeal. Their children:

1. Daniel R., III, born 9-11-1949; died 4-15-1951.
2. Debra Jeanne, born 11-24-1952.

(See McNeal, Berlin, etc.)

SHADINGER RECORD

(Bible published and for sale by Hogan & Thompson, 30 North Fourth Street. Published by Jesper Harding, 74 South Second Street. 1839. Bought at a sale in Greenwood, Delaware by Mrs. Ernestine Edwards, Lewes, Delaware. Record given by Mrs. D. A. Potter.)

Family Record

Marriages

Jonathan Shadinger and Susanna Geris (no dates)
Tobias Shadinger and Catherine Dilts were married September 30, 1837.
Joseph M. VanCleve and Esther A. Shadinger were married October 25, --62.
Lewis C. Paxson and Susanna Shadinger were married February 7, 1866.
William D. Shadinger and Margaret Ann Bird were married July 7, 1868.
Charles W. Bodine and Hannah R. Shadinger were married November (no dates shown).

Births

Jonathan Shadinger was born December 28, 1783.
Susanna Shadinger was born March 1, 1783.

Mary A. Shadinger was born August 4, 1804.
Nathan Shadinger was born July 27, 1809.
Joseph Shadinger was born April 5, 1812.
Tobias Shadinger was born March 28, 1815.
Catherine Dilts was born January 9, 1813.

Esther Ann Shadinger was born August 21, 1839.
Susanna Shadinger was born December 18, 1841.
Hannah Rebecca Shadinger was born October 18, 1844.
William Dilts Shadinger was born September 14, 1846.
Jonathan Shadinger was born January 13, 1850.

Births of William and Catharine Dilts and their children:
    William Dilts, born August 17, 1765.
    Catharine Dilts, born January 4, 1774.

    Esther Dilts, born July 12, 1794.
    John Dilts, born August 7, 1796.
    Holcomb Dilts, born May 12, 1798.
    Robert Dilts, born July 30, 1800.
    Mary Dilts, born February 14, 1803.
    Hannah Dilts, born June 28, 1805.
    Rebecca Dilts, born October 30, 1807.
    Susanne Dilts, born July 9, 1810.
    Catherine Dilts. born January 9, 1813.
    William Dilts, born May 21, 1815.
    Elizabeth Dilts, born January 8, 1821.

Deaths

Jonathan Shadinger died July 15, 1854, age 71 years, 6 months and 18 days.
Joseph Shadinger died July 22, 1854, age 42 years, 3 months and 17 days.
Elizabeth Shadinger died July 22, 1854, age 42 years.
Nathan Shadinger died April 2, 1855, age 45 years, 7 months and 28 days.
Tobias Shadinger died November 20, 1871, age 57 years.
Hannah R. Bodine died April 24, 1874, age 30 years.

Catharine Shadinger died April 26, 1893, age
   81 years.
Joseph M. VanCleve died July 27, 1896, age
   62 years.
Lewis C. Paxson died May 29, 1915, age 78
   years, 7 months and 4 days.
Jonathan Shadinger, Jr., died February 16, 1850.
William D. Shadinger died January 21, 1916,
   age 69 years.
Susanna S. Paxson died March 14, 1928, age
   86 years.
Margaret Bird Shadinger, wife of William D.,
   died October 3, 1923, age 73 years and
   8 months.

SHAKESPEAR FAMILY RECORD

(Bible published by Kimber & Sharpless, 93 Market Street, Philadelphia. 1827. Owned by Mrs. Marian A. (Shakespear) Rowe, Wilmington, Del. Record given by Mrs. Charles Bird.)

Marriages

John M. Shakespear and Mary E. McKinley were
   married April 21, 1804.
Jacob Hannah and Susanah Eliza Shakespear were
   married December 31, 1829 by Rev. Thos.
   Barton, and he departed this life
   December 11, 1830, and Jacob Hannah Jr. was
   born February 8, 1831.
Benja. W. Shakespear and Maria Stinson were
   married January 31, 1832.

Births

John Shakespear was born September 20, 1770.
Mary Shakespear was born November 13, 1784.

Benjamin W. Shakespear was born March 5, 1807.
Maryann Shakespear was born September 11, 1808.
Susannah Eliza Shakespear was born July 11, 1810.
Catherine L. Shakespear was born February 8, 1813.
John B. Shakespear was born October 15, 1815.
Thomas M. Shakespear was born May 21, (looks like
   1816)?

Elizabeth T. Shakespear was born May 11, 1818.
Rebeckah Jane Shakespear was born July 5, 1820.
Samuel C. Shakespear was born August 6, 1822.
Anamoriah Shakespear was born August 21, 1824.
James Strawbridge Shakespear was born July 24, 1826.
Faris Ives was born August 10, 1828.

John Shakespear became a member of the Baptist Church in August 1822.

The above are the ages of John and Mary Shakespear and children.

SHAKESPEAR RECORD

(Bible published by National Publishing Co., 724 Cherry St., Philadelphia, Pa. 1886. Owned by Mrs. Marian A. (Shakespear) Rowe, Wilmington, Del. Record given by Mrs. Charles Bird.)

Marriages

George W. Shakespear and Mary L. M. Clark were married March 16, 1886.
Mabel Margaret Shakespear and Thomas Garfield Duncan were married November 23, 1904.
Marian Ada Shakespear and William S. Rowe were married October 5, 1916.
Ella Mary Shakespear and William LeRoy Parker were married December 5, 1917.

Births

George Washington Shakespear was born March 15, 1848.
Mary Linda Minerva Shakespear was born November 30, 1855.

The children of George and Mary Shakespear:

    Mabel Margaret Shakespear, born July 26, 1887.
    Marian Ada Shakespear, born November 24, 1890.

Esther Garrett Shakespear, born July 10, 1894.
Ella Mary Shakespear, born October 8, 1898.

Deaths

George W. Shakespear died June 8, 1925.
Mary L. M. Shakespear died November 26, 1931.
Mabel M. Duncan died April 20, 1949.
Anna P. Razee died December 20, 1943.
William S. Rowe, husband of Marian A. Shakespear, died September 29, 1956.

JOHN A. SHELDON & REBECCA E. ERB

(Bible published by W. Henry Rice & Co., Philadelphia, Pa. Owned by Mrs. Elsie M. (Sheldon) Downing, Wilmington, Del. 1956. Record given by Mrs. Charles Bird.)

Marriages

This certifies that the Rite of Holy Matrimony was celebrated between Mr. John A. Sheldon of Lower Merion and Rebecca E. Erb of Philadelphia, on the Twelfth of November at Philadelphia by Rev. J. G. Walker.

Eli E. and Gertrude Howard, April 30, 1902.
Francis and Irene Benson, June 27, 1900.
Herbert H. and Bertha Grubb, October 12, 1904.
Elsie M. and Leslie F. Downing, October 14, 1914.

Births

Eli E. Sheldon, son of John A. and Rebecca E. Sheldon, was born June 21, 1877.
Francis Sheldon was born January 3, 1879.
John A. Sheldon was born April 21, 1881.
Herbert Sheldon was born December 28, 1882.
Rebecca E. Sheldon was born February 16, 1884.
Howard Sheldon was born August 3, 1885.
Elsie May Sheldon was born September 2, 1889.

Deaths

John A. Sheldon died September 29, 1881, age
    5 months.
Rebecca E. Sheldon died September 1884, age
    7 months.
Howard Sheldon died August 22, 1885, age
    3 weeks.
Francis Sheldon died September 2, 1940, age
    61 years.
Rebecca E., wife of John A. Sheldon, died
    September 30, 1933, age 75 years.
John A. Sheldon died November 12, 1942,
    age 85 years.

SHIPLEY BIBLE RECORD

(Bible was printed in London 1688, and was presented to the Delaware Historical Society, Wilmington, Delaware, by the Richardson Family. It was used in the home of Jane Richardson McKinley, wife of Dr. John McKinley, 1st President of Delaware State. Record was given by Mrs. Glenn S. Skinner, Newark, Delaware.)

This Bible belongeth to ye Church of Stoke in ye
    County of the City of Coventry and was
    bought at ye Parish Charge for that purpose.

Sarah Levis Shipley, daughter of William and
    Elizabeth Shipley, was born May 25, 1729.
William Shipley was born March 24, 1732. They
    were both born at Ridley.
Samuel Shipley was born June 2, 1736 at
    Willington (now called Wilmington, Del.).
Samuel Shipley died June 29, 1737 and was buried
    at Willington.
Samuel Shipley, son of William Shipley and Sarah
    his wife, was born in Willington on
    December 5, 1754.
Elizabeth Levis died in 1732, age about 75 or 76.
Samuel Levis died in 1739, age 86 years. Both
    are buried in Springfield graveyard.

William Shipley, ye elder, died 19 day of 12 month in year 1762, and was buried in Wilmington graveyard - aged seventy five - 1768.

Elizabeth Shipley died 16 day of 10 month 1777 - was buried in Marlborough graveyard in her 87th year.

Sarah Richardson died 29th of 6 month 1793 - was buried in Wilmington graveyard in her 65th year.

John Richardson arrived in Philadelphia on the ship "Endeavour" - Captain was George Thorp.

ELIAS & SARAH A. WARREN SHOCKLEY BIBLE

(Published by Hallowbush & Carey, Publishers and Booksellers, 215 Market Street, Philadelphia, Pa. Record given by Caroline Clark, Milford, Del. It is her grandfather's Bible.)

Marriages

Elias Shockley and Sarah A. Warren were married February 11, 1851.

Births

Elias Shockley, son of Wilson Shockley and Nancy his wife, was born March 17, 1820.
Sarah A. Warren, daughter of William Warren and Mary his wife, was born October 20, 1831.

George W. Shockley, son of the aforesaid, was born May 10, 1854.
Ann Eliza and Mary Catherine Shockley, daughters of the aforesaid, were born April 7, 1855.
John Henry Shockley, son of the aforesaid, was born July 4, 1856.

Willemina Shockley, daughter of Elias Shockley and Sarah his wife, was born July 24, 1852.
Ann Eliza Shockley, daughter of the aforesaid, was born October 25, 1857.
William B. Shockley, son of the aforesaid, was born April 12, 1859.

Elias Shockley, son of the aforesaid, was born
   June 30, 1860.
Elizabeth Shockley, daughter of the aforesaid,
   was born August 26, 1864.
Mark Shockley, son of the aforesaid, was born
   February 12, 1866.
Walker Shockley, son of the aforesaid, was born
   September 18, 1867.
Joseph Shockley, son of the aforesaid, was born
   April 23, 1869.
Lydia C. Shockley, daughter of the aforesaid,
   was born December 16, 1870.
David W. Shockley, son of the aforesaid, was
   born April 26, 1873.

Deaths

Ann Eliza Shockley, daughter of Elias Shockley
   and Sarah A. his wife, died August 26, 1856,
   age 1 year and 22 days. (This is the way
   it is written but it does not check with
   the birth).
John Henry Shockley, son of the aforesaid, died
   September 10, 1857, age 1 year, 2 months and
   6 days.
Mary Catherine Shockley, daughter of the aforesaid,
   died March 23, 1869, age 13 years, 11 months
   and 9 days.
Mrs. Sarah A. Shockley died February 7, 1890,
   age 58 years, 3 months and 18 days.
Elias Shockley of W. died December 5, 1896,
   age 76 years, 8 months and 22 days.

WILSON & NANCY SHOCKLEY BIBLE

(Published by William McCarthy, 27 North 5th St.
1842. Printed by I. Ashmead & Co. Record given
by Caroline Clark, Milford, Delaware.)

Marriages

William Shockley and Nancy B. Watson were married
   August 28, 1815.
William V. Shockley and Catherine Warren were
   married January 21, 1840 or 1841.

George W. Shockley and Louise Prettyman were
    married August 12, 1843.

Births

Wilson Shockley, son of Rhoades Shockley, was
    born November 14, 1788.
Nancy B. Shockley was born March 30, 1796.
William V., son of Wilson and Nancy B. Shockley,
    was born February 17, 1816.
George W. Shockley, son of Wilson and Nancy B.
    Shockley, was born March 31, 1818.
Elias Shockley, son of aforesaid, was born
    March 17, 1820.
    (This is my grandfather - who sent the
    record)

Deaths

Wilson Shockley, son of Rhoades Shockley, died
    May 25, 1856, age 67 years.
Nancy B. Shockley died January 24, 1868, age
    72 years.
William V. Shockley died August 25, 1881, age
    65 years, 6 months and 8 days.
George W. Shockley died April 25, 1880, age
    62 years and 25 days.

Births

Mary V. Shockley, daughter of the aforesaid, was
    born October 8, 1822.
Elizabeth B. Shockley, daughter of the aforesaid,
    was born February 11, 1825.
Wilson Shockley, son of the aforesaid, was born
    July 6, 1827.
David W. Shockley, son of the aforesaid, was born
    May 26, 1829.
Ann Eliza W. Shockley, daughter of the aforesaid,
    was born March 13, 1831.
Lydia Jane W. Shockley, daughter of the aforesaid,
    was born March 2, 1833.
Mavinda Shockley, daughter of the aforesaid, was
    born January 31, 1835.
John Wesley Fisher Shockley, son of the aforesaid,
    was born May 30, 1836.
Matilda Shockley, daughter of the aforesaid, was
    born July 9, 1838.

Mavinda Shockley, daughter of Wilson and Nancy B.
   Shockley, died January 31, 1835.
John W. Shockley died April 9, 1864.

SHORT - COOPER BIBLE

(Bible belongs to Mrs. Eugene C. Howard, R.F.D. 1,
Box 329, Rehoboth Beach, Delaware. Printed by
A. J. Holman & Co. Copyright 1891.)

Certificate

This certifies that the rite of marriage was
   celebrated between Fred Short of Georgetown
   and Nora Cooper of Georgetown, on April 23,
   1905 at Georgetown by Rev. Harry Taylor.
   Wit. Mrs. Harry Taylor.

Births

Fred Short was born June 23, 1880.
Nora Cooper was born December 29, 1883.

Mildred Short was born August 21, 1908.

Deaths

William J. Cooper died July 8, 1904.
Louisa Cooper died March 22, 1905.
Maggie Cooper Sharp died December 25, 1903.
George Cooper died in 1905.
Henriette Cooper Toomey died June 8, 1958.

- - - - - - - - - -

Copied from a Bible belonging to the above
mentioned Mrs. Howard.

On Fly-leaf "A Sacred token from your Mother,
   Nora Short to Mildred L. Howard,
   December 25, 1942."
National Bible Press, Philadelphia, Pa.

Family Register

This is to certify that Mildred L. Short, Georgetown, August 21, 1908 and Eugene C. Howard, Midway, October 10, 1910, were joined together in the bonds of Holy Matrimony at Lewes, Delaware, November 25, 1937 by Rev. Wm. Leishman.

Parents

Fred Short, born June 23, 1880; died May 13, 1942, Georgetown, Del.
Nora Short, born December 29, 1883; died December 30, 1958.

Children:

Margaret Frances Joseph, born June 13, 1928, Beebe Hospital, Lewes, Del.

NOTE: Mildred L. Short was married first to Clyde P. Joseph, April 24, 1926 in Snow Hill, Md. by Rev. Frank White. Cyde P. is the son of Leander & Viola (Pepper) Joseph. Information by Mrs. Mildred L. Howard.

Fred Short
                Margaret Frances Short
                m. 1st Clyde P. Joseph, 4-24-1926
Nora Cooper m. 2nd Eugene C. Howard

Copied from 2 pages of notepaper written in pencil and tucked between the pages of a Bible owned by Mrs. Eugene C. Howard, R.F.D. 1, Box 329, Rehoboth, Delaware.

Marriages

Thomas B. Short and Sarah E. Donovan were married February 9, 1875.
Fannie B. Short and Charles Collins were married March 1, 1899.

Births

Thomas B. Short was born October 20, 1855.
Sarah E. Donovan was born May 1, 1856.

Fannie B. Short was born July 25, 1877.
Fred Short was born June 23, 1880.
John E. Short was born March 21, 1883.
Ida M. Short was born June ?, 1886.
Luther B. Short was born February 14, 1890.
Bessie Short was born August 22, 1892.
Clara Short was born October 29, 1894.
Emery Short was born June 12, 1900.

Deaths

Thomas B. Short died August 6, 1928, age 73 years.
Sarah E. Short died April 19, 1935, age 78 years, 1 month and 18 days.
Bessie Short, daughter of Thomas B. and Sarah E. Short, died April 21, 1893.
Luther B. Short, son of Thomas B. and Sarah E. Short, died June 21, 1895.
Ida M. Short, daughter of Thomas B. and Sarah E. Short, died July 21, 1895.
Mary E. Short, wife of John Short, died November 6, 1891, age 65 years.
John Short died March 10, 1882, age 72 years.

THOMAS SILVER

(Record prepared and given by Mrs. Glenn S. Skinner, Newark, Delaware.)

John Silver, the emigrant ancestor of the Essex County, Mass., family was in New England before 1637, for on Feb. 5th in that year he was granted land in Ipswich, Mass. He soon removed to Newbury, Mass., where he was listed among the 91 Free holders who were the acknowledged Grantees of the town.

In the plan of the old town, a street was laid down extending from the east "gutter", so-called, along the bank of the river to the marsh land beyond, that was doubtless intended for a highway; but proving inconvenient, Thomas Silver, who owned ten acres of marshland, was induced to grant the inhabitants of the town liberty to pass and re-pass over his private property and in the Proprietors Records of Newbury is entered February 6th 1650, an extra grant of marsh as a recompense to him.

Thomas Silver's first wife, by whom he had a daughter Mary, is unknown. She died between 1645 and 1649. On Aug. 16, 1649 he married in Newbury, Katherine (whose last name was omitted from the record). She died in childbirth July ? 1665, 23rd. He died September 6, 1682.

Children born in Newbury. By first wife:
  i. Mary, born 1645; married Octo. 26, 1664 Robert Robinson.

By second wife:
  ii. Elizabeth, born Mar. 14, 1650-1; died before 1682.
  iii. Martha (her twin), born 3-14-1650-1; m. Dec. 20, 1669 Francis Willett.
  iv. Thomas, born Mar. 26, 1652-3; d. Mar. 3, 1655, age 3 years.
  v.   Hannah, born Oct. 18, 1655; m. Mar. 13, 1673-4 Henry Acres.
  vi. Sarah (her twin), born Oct. 18, 1655; m. Feb. 9, ---- Thomas Alley.
  vii. Thomas, born Mar. 26, 1658; m. Jan. 4, 1681-2 Mary Williams.
  viii. John, born Aug. 24, 1660; d. unmarried on the Expedition to Canada in 1690.

"John Silver of Rowley being called forth to go to Cannaday, made his will July 28, 1690; proved Apr. 22, 1691. He gave to his brother Thomas Silver; to brother Samuel Silver; to sister Willett; to sister Acres the residue to Jonathan Bayley of Rowley, if he lives to age of one and twenty - if not to Nathaniel Bayley; mentions wheat in my Master Bayley's hands."
Administration on the estate was granted to Thomas and Samuel Silver. (Essex Probate, 25331).

ix.   **Samuel**, born Feb. 16, 1662; m. and settled
          in Rowley.
    x.   Infant daughter born July 19, 1665; d.
          July 30, 1665.

   When Thomas Silver died, his son Thomas renounced his right to Administer, and the court granted the right to Henry Acres and Francis Willett, and ordered the division of the property as follows:
   To Thomas Silver, eldest son, a double portion and
   To the rest of the children, namely:
       John, Samuel, Mary Robinson, Martha
       Willett, Hannah Acres, Sarah Alley
       an equal portion with each other,
       September 26, 1682. The inventory
       amounted to L1o4 5s 6d.
           Essex Probate, 253339

Essex Co. Deeds, 25;109.

   Francis Willett and Henry Acres, as Administrators of Thomas Silver, late of Newbury, deceased, sell land in Newbury formerly belonging to their father-in-law, the said Thomas Silver, to Tristram Coffin, Oct. 26, 1682.
           Recorded 5-12-1711.

   Thomas Silver, Sen., of Newbury, sells to William Illsley of Newbury, land in Newbury that he bought of Henry Jacques.
           Recorded Oct. 1725.

   Samuel Silver(2) (Thomas(1)) born in Newbury, Mass. Feb. 16, 1662; died about 1739; married 1st, before 1689, Mary ---- who died in Rowley Jan. 4, 1700-1. He married 2nd, July 8, 1701 to Sarah Colby, daughter of Isaac and Martha (Parratt) Colby, born Jan. 28, 1674-5, living 1738. Her mother's father was Francis Parratt of Rowley, another daughter of whom married Deacon Ezekiel Hewett.

Children by 1st wife, born in Rowley, Mass.:
    i.   Mary, born Sept. 5, 1689; d. young.
    ii.   Mary, born July 24, 1692; Bapt. Oct. 16,
          1693.

- iii. Elizabeth, born Apr. 1, 1694; Bapt. May 6, 1694.
- iv. Mercy, born 1696; Bapt. Mar. 15, 1696; d. 3-30-1696.
- v. Ruth, born Mar. 4, 1697-8; Bapt. Mar. 6, 1697-8.
- vi. Infant born & died Jan. 4, 1698-9.
- vii. Samuel, born 1700; died young.

Children by 2nd wife, Sarah Colby, born in Amesbury:
- viii. Sara, born May 31, 1702; m. Nathaniel Davis.
- ix. Samuel, born Jan. 20, 1705-6; m. Martha Sargeant and Jemima Kimball.
- x. Mehetabel, born July 12, 1711; m. Nathan Currier.

    Samuel Silver removed to Amesbury about the time of his 2nd marriage. His wife joined the church there in 1714. In 1738 her son Samuel, mentions her in a deed, and does not call her deceased, and calls himself "Samuel Silver Junior", so presumably both his parents were alive in 1738. There is no record of their deaths in Amesbury and apparently no will or administration. About 1738 there are a number of deeds which may pertain to the settling of an estate, but proving nothing definite. He does not call himself Samuel Junior after 1738.

Essex County deeds:

    Samuel Silver (3) (Samuel 2, Thomas 1) born in Amesbury, Mass. Jan. 20, 1705-6; died between Jan. 4, 1770 and Nov. 5, 1776; married 1st in Amesbury, Nov. 9, 1727 to Martha Sargeant, who died between 1730-1734. He married 2nd in Amesbury, Feb. 14, 1733-4, Jemima Kimball, who was born 1709, daughter of Ebenezer and Ruth (Eaton) Kimball. Jemima was born Oct. 22, 1709; died after 1776 and before 1788.

    Her mother, Ruth (Eaton) Kimball was born 11-23-1684; died 4-6-1750.

    Her father, Ebenezer Kimball was born 6-20-1684 in Bradford, Mass.; died 1-13-1715; they were married 1708. (These are the ancestors of Mrs. Pauline K. Skinner).

Children born in Amesbury, Mass. by the 1st wife (Martha):
  i. John, born Aug. 9, 1729; died before 1749.
  ii. Samuel, born July 15, 1730-1; m. Nov. 6, 1750, Judith Colby.
Children by 2nd wife, Jemima:
  iii. Martha, born Jan. 24, 1734-5; m. John Knowlton.
  iv. Ruth, Bapt. Aug. 28, 1737; m. Samuel Morgeridge and Oliver Sawyer.
  v. Sarah, Bapt. June 1, 1740; m. William Page Jr., Oct. 20, 1761, Haverhill.
  vi. Eunice, born Mar. 15, 1743; m. Sept. 14, 1769, Samuel Hale.
  vii. Timothy, born July 20, 1746.
  viii. <u>John</u>, Bapt. Feb. 4, 1749-50; m. Sarah ---.

Samuel Silver lived his whole life in Amesbury but the marriage of only two of his children are of record there, one other is recorded in Haverhill. Samuel Silver, gentleman, of Amesbury, made his will Jan. 4, 1770 and it was proved Nov. 5, 1776. He left to his wife Jemima; to his son Samuel Silver; to his daughter Martha, wife of John Knowlton; Ruth, wife of Samuel Morgeridge; to Sarah, wife of William Page; to Eunice, wife of Samuel Hale; to son Timonthy Silver; to son John Silver, the residue and he to be executor.
                    Essex Co. Probate 253335.
                    Essex Co. Deeds 81:43.

Samuel Silver Jr. yeoman and Nathan Currier, yeoman and Mehetabel his wife, all of Amesbury, Essex Co., Mass., in consideration of certain rights in lands quitted to us by Nathaniel Davis, yeoman and Sarah his wife, of Amesbury, by deeds of even date with this, quit to them all right that we have or may have by virtue of the last Will of our grandfather, Isaac Colby, dec'd., set off to Mother, Sarah Silver, as her share in the estate of said Isaac Colby, March 29, 1738-9.
                    86:156.

Similar quit claim deed from Nathaniel Davis, yeoman and Sarah his wife and Nathan Currier, yeoman and Mehetabel his wife, to Samuel Silver, Jr., on same date.
                    86:157.

Richard Bartlett of Newbury, gentleman and Susanna, his wife, sell to Samuel Silver of Amesbury right in the estate of Amos Singletary, dec'd. of Haverhill, July 9, 1739. Similar deed from Stephen and Ruth Johnson of Haverhill and Peter and Martha Green of Haverhill and Sarah Page.
86:119; 87:2;3; 86:78

Samuel Silver of Amesbury sells to Enovh? Browne of Amesbury land in Amesbury bounded on Nathan Currier and on road leading to Kingston; Jemima Silver, wife of Samuel, releases her dower Sept. 3, 1739.
92:238

Samuel Silver of Amesbury, gentleman, sells to Abner Whittier, of Amesbury, part of farm in Amesbury originally granted to William Osgood, March 3, 1746. Jemima releases her dower March 3, 1746.
120:176

Samuel Silver, gentleman, of Amesbury gives to Samuel Silver, Jr. of Amesbury Gunsmith, the westerly corner of his homestead where the said Samuel, Jr. now lives, Apr. 8, 1760.
136:105

April 11, 1774, a committee chosen by Township of land in the County of Cumberland, adjacent to Androscoggin, Maine, sell the rights of various delinquent proprietors, amongst who was Samuel Silver.
62:152

Jemima Kimball of Haverhill, Spinster, for L1oo, quits to brother Abner Kimball, one half part of her right in the estate of her late father, Ebenezer Kimball, late of Haverhill, dec'd., Jan. 6, 1733-4.

Feb. 19, 1733-4, Jemima Kimball, now Jemima Silver, acknowledged the deed.
162:121

Thomas Clarke of Amesbury, gentleman sells to Richard Colby, of Haverhill, two thirds part of a meadow in Haverhill, bequeathed to heirs of

Jemima Silver, in will of Timothy Eaton, it being that part of the bequest that accrued to Timothy Silver, John Silver, Ruth Silver and Sarah Silver, Sept. 16, 1788. (The will of Timothy Eaton has not been examined, he was probably cousin or uncle of Jemima (Kimball) Silver).

John Silver 4) (Samuel 3), Samuel 2), Thomas 1), born in Amesbury, Mass., Baptized there Feb. 4, 1749-50; died in Sanbornton, N. H., July 30, 1831; married before 1776, Sarah ----, born about 1748; died May 3, 1806. The History of Sanbornton, N. H. gives death of a "widow" Silver, March 24, 1841, aged 87 and suggests she may be a second wife.

Children, born probably in Amesbury, but not recorded, taken from History of Sanbornton, N.H.:
   i. John, died young.
   ii. Moses, born Mar. 15, 1777.
   iii. <u>Sally</u>, born 1782; m. Jonathan Ward.
   iv. James, born 1783.
   v. John, born 1785.
   vi. Polly, born 1786.
   vii. Samuel, born 1788.
   viii. Timothy, born May 8, 1790.
   ix. Eunice, born 1795.
   x. Samuel, born 1798, "born after his mother was 50 years old."

It is evident that John Silver lived in Amesbury in 1790, as he appears in the Census of that year as a resident there, with one male above 16 (himself), four males below 16 (Moses, James, John and Samuel), and four females (his wife, Sally, Polly, and ?). It is probable that he always lived there before going to Sanbornton. His father left him the homestead and there is no deed of sale of record until 1797. So far the parentage of his wife is unknown. Neither he or his brother Timothy married in Amesbury, nor did his sisters. It is possible that he married in New Hampshire, as Amesbury is so near the line.
Stafford Co., Deeds 34:141, N.H.

Nathaniel Burleigh, Jr., of Sanbornton, N.H. cordwainer, sells to John Silver, of "Almsbury" Essex Co., Mass., parcel of land in Sanbornton, Nov. 9, 1797. Wit: Jno. Sanborn, Stuart Hoyt. Essex Co., Deeds 187:192. Mass.

John Silver of Amesbury, Essex Co., Mass., yeoman, sells to Nathan Currier, of Amesbury, land etc., in Amesbury, bounds Francis Chase and Pillsbury, reservation of right to flow land granted to Chase in 1751, Nov. 18, 1797, Sarah Silver, wife of John signed also. Wit: Christopher Sargeant, Polly Sargeant. (I found no deed to explain the ownership of this land which may have been originally Chase property, there are so many deeds that were never recorded that one can not be sure how ownership vests in certain individuals. It is possible that this deed may help to solve the problem of Sarah's people).

Sally Silver 5) (John 4), Samuel 3); Samuel 2); Thomas 1), born in Amesbury in 1782; died in Hardwick, Vt., July 2, 1876, age 94 years; married in Sanbornton, N.H., Feb. 1801, Jonathan Ward born in Sanborton, N. H., March 29, 1779; died in Greensboro (or Hardwick), June 10, 1837, age 57 years.

Thomas Silver 1) was not only the ancestor of Sally Silver, wife of Jonathan Ward and mother of Amasi Ward, but was also ancestor of Phebe Stephens, who married the said Amasi Ward for Martha, daughter of Thomas Silver, married Francis Willett, and they became, through their daughter, Elizabeth Willett, ancestors of John Gideon Bailey, who was ancestor of Phoebe Stephens.

Sarah Colby, wife of Samuel Silver, son of Thomas, had a sister, Dorothy, who married Samuel Hadley, and they were also ancestors of Phoebe Stephens.

Runnels, in his "History of Sanbornton" gives James instead of John as the first child of John Silver. Runnels states that Polly, daughter of John Silver, married Simeon Walton. Runnels also, in between Timothy and Eunice, gives Prudence, born Jan. 21, 1792, who married Samuel Davis. Prudence would account for the fourth female mentioned in connection with John and the Census of 1790.

Above record is the Ancestry of Herbert Ward's family and of Mrs. Pauline K. Skinner. Mr. Ward is President of the S. A. R. of Delaware 1957.

Silver Chart

1.
Thos. Silver
d. 9-6-1682
m. 1st
----
m. 2nd
m. 8-16-1649
Katherine
d. 7-23-1665

2.
1. Mary, b. 1645
   m. Robt. Robinson
2. Elizabeth), b. 3-14-1650
3. Martha   ), b. 3-14-1650
   m. Francis Willett
4. Thomas, b. 3-26-1652; d. 1655
5. Hannah, b. 10-18-1655
   m. 3-13-1673, Henry Acres
6. Sarah, b. 10-18-1655
   m. Thos. Alley
7. Thomas, b. 3-26-1658
   m. 1-4-1681, Mary Williams
8. John, b. 8-24-1660
9. Samuel   3.
   b. 2-16-1662   See 3. below
   d. 1793
   m. 1st 1689, Mary
   d. 1700

Isaac Colby
m. Martha
   Parratt
   daughter of
   Francis

m. 2nd 7-8-1701
Sarah Colby
b. 1-28-1674

Silver Chart continued next page.

- 328 -

3.
1. Mary, b. 1689
2. Mary, b. 1693
3. Elizabeth, b. 1694
4. Mercy, b. 1696
5. Ruth, b. 1697
6. Infant, b. 1698
7. Samuel, b. 1700
8. Sarah, b. 5-31-1702;
   m. Nathaniel Davis
9. Samuel
   b. 1-20-1705
   m. 1st 1727
   Martha Sargeant
   m. 2nd 2-14-1733

Ebenezer Kimball
b. 6-20-1684
d. 1-13-1715
m. 1708
Ruth Eaton
b. 11-23-1684; d. 4-6-1750

Jemima Kimball
b. 10-22-1709

10. Mehetabel, b. 1711
    m. Nathan Currier

4.
1. John, b. 1729
2. Samuel, b. 1730, m. 1750, Judith Colby
3. Martha, b. 1734
4. Ruth, b. 1737
5. Eunice, b. 1743
6. Sarah, b. 1740
7. Timothy, b. 1746
8. John b. 1749; m. Sarah

5.
Children of John Silver,
b. 2-4-1749; m. Sarah; b. 1748; d. 1806
1. John
2. Moses, b. 1777
3. Sally, b. 1782; d. 7-2-1876;
   m. 7-2-1801   Amasi Ward
   Jonathan Ward   m.
   b. 1779   Phebe Stephens
   d. 1837
4. James, b. 1783
5. John, b. 1785
6. Polly, b. 1786
7. Samuel, b. 1788
8. Timothy, b. 1790
9. Eunice, b. 1795
10. Samuel, b. 1798

JAMES SIMMONS - SARAH ANN DUBREE

(Copied from the Family Bible of Sarah Ann
(DuBree) Simmons. Gap, Lancaster County, Pa.
Owned by Mrs. Harry L. Morgan (Marion Simmons),
Wilmington, Del. 1957. Record given by Mrs.
Charles D. Bird, Wilmington. Both Mrs. Morgan and
Mrs. Bird are members of Caesar Rodney Chapter,
N. S. D. A. R., Wilmington.)

Marriages

James Simmons and Sarah Ann DuBree were married
   the 7th of the 3rd month 1832.
George H. Simmons and Mary Jane McMinn were
   married the 23rd of the 6th month 1855.
Wm. H. Beale and Hannah Ann Simmons were married
   the 16th of the 10th month 1856.
Thomas Mercer and Susan E. Simmons were married
   the 7th day of the 8th month 1860.
Robert J. Russell and Mary Emma Simmons were
   married the 13th day of the 8th month ----.
R. Barclay Simmons and Jennie --- were married
   (no dates shown).
Howard E. Simmons and Louise ---- were married
   (no dates shown).
Bernard J. Leckler and Sarah Ellen Simmons were
   married (no dates shown).
William H. Simmons and Clara M. Wallace were
   married the 21st day of the 12th month 1878.

Births

James Simmons was born at Simon's Town, Lancaster
   Co., Pa., the 28th day of the 1st month 1807.
Sarah Ann Simmons was born at Simon's Town,
   Lancaster Co., Pa., the 3rd day of the 5th
   month 1811.

Children of James and Sarah Ann Simmons, born at
Sadsbury, Pa.:
   Son born 20th day of 10th month 1832; died
      the next day.
   George H. Simmons, born 27th day of 7th
      month 1833.
   Susan E. Simmons, born 7th day of 8th month
      1835.

Hannah Ann Simmons, born 3rd day of 3rd
    month 1837.
Ruth Anna Simmons, born 12th day of 8th
    month 1839.
Lydia P. Simmons, born 20th day of 6th
    month 1841.
J. Channing Simmons, born 16th day of 7th
    month 1843.
Sarah Ellen Simmons, born 24th day of 3rd
    month 1846.
R. Barclay Simmons, born 6th day of 8th
    month 1848.
Mary Emma Simmons, born 18th day of 1st
    month 1851.
Wm. Henry Simmons, born 9th day of 2nd
    month 1853.
Howard Elwood Simmons, born 19th day of
    7th month 1855.

Deaths

Son of James and Sarah Ann Simmons died 21st of
    10th month 1832.
Lydia P. Simmons died 15th of 3rd month 1843,
    age 21 months.
J. Channing Simmons died 4th day of 6th month
    1868, age 24 years, 10 months and 19 days.
Father, James Simmons, died 30th day of 1st month
    1874, age 67 years and 2 days.
George H. Simmons died 25th day of 2nd month
    1875, age 41 years, 6 months and 28 days.
Susan E. Mercer died 9th day of December, 1876,
    age 41 years, 4 months and 2 days.
Mary Emma Russell died 5th day of July 1905,
    age 54 years, 5 months and 17 days.
R. Barclay Simmons died 16th day of 5th month
    1907, age 58 years, 9 months and 10 days.
Howard E. Simmons died 8th day of March 1920,
    age 64 years, 7 months and 17 days.
Ruth Anna Simmons died 12th day of April 1924,
    age 85 years and 8 months.
Sarah Ellen Leckler died 2nd June 1930, age
    84 years, 2 months and 8 days.
Wm. Henry Simmons died 2-19-38, age 85 years
    and 10 days.
Hannah Ann Beale died 1922, age 84 years.
Mother - Sarah Ann DuBree Simmons died 27th day
    of 10th month 1895, age 84 years.

John DuBree died January 25, 1834, age 77 years.
Lydia DuBree died June 2, 1839, age 79 years.

Family Record

Absalom DuBree was born November 14, 1780.
Rachel DuBree was born November 20, 1782.
Sarah DuBree was born March 12, 1785.
Elizabeth DuBree was born April 18, 1787.
Benjamin Lukens DuBree was born November 24, 1788.
-----? DuBree was born August 6, 1792.
Edith DuBree was born March 22, 1795.
Nathaniel DuBree) twin
Lydia DuBree) twin, were born October 26, 1799.
Letitia DuBree was born March 15, 1804.

Sarah Ann DuBree was born May 3, 1811.
Lydia DuBree was born November 3, 1814.
Hiram DuBree was born June 6, 1817.
Henry Small DuBree was born September 14, 1820.

Children of William H. and Clara (Wallace) Simmons:

1. C. Leroy Simmons, born 8-18-1879; died 10-17-1954 at Spartansburg, S.C. Married Helen Bowdle 7-27-1913 at Wilmington, Del. Helen died 10-28-1947 at Spartansburg, S.C. where they lived since 1926. They had the following children:

   1. Ruth Marion, born 4-3-1914; m. 6-12-1937 to Floyd William Vandiver at Spartansburg, S.C. Their children:
      1. Ruth Ann Vandiver, b. April 1, 1939.
      2. Floyd Wm. Vandiver, b. March 24, 1942.

   2. Virginia Wallace, born 11-9-1918; m. 3-18-1944 to George VonSeth at Spartansburg. Their children:
      1. Helen Anne VonSeth, b. 6-11-1948.

3. C. LeRoy, Jr., born 9-25-1920; m. 7-27-1946 to Emma J. Bowles of Kentucky.

2. Anna Wallace Simmons, born 2-23-1881; married 4-28-1909 to Stanley Steel and had:
   1. Stanley, Jr., born Wilmington, Del. 1-16-1911. He was killed in an auto accident 7-23-1931.
   2. Edward Newell, born Wilmington, Del. 8-31-1913; married 9-5-1937 to Patricia Gore of Los Angeles, Calif.

3. Marion E., born 4-13-1886; married Harry L. Morgan 6-27-1907. They had the following:
   1. Harry L. Jr., born Wilmington, Del. 2-23-1908; married 4-23-1937 to Frances Westervelt of Butler, N.J. born 6-25-1908. They had:
     1. Mary Ann Morgan, born Jan. 23, 1938.
     2. Robert Wm., 2nd, born July 17, 1943.
     3. Peter Westervelt Morgan, born 12-12-1954.
   2. Frederick E., born 11-19-1911; married 11-11-1939 to Ann Sherwood of Columbus, Ohio, who was born 10-29-1911. They had:
     1. Barbara Jeanne Morgan, born 1-12-1944.
   3. Robert W., born 4-4-1917; married 4-18-1942 to Helen A. Preston of Aberdeen, Md., who was born 12-8-1919. They had:
     1. Roberta Jane Morgan, born May 2, 1945.
     2. John Frederick Morgan, born Nov. 7, 1951.
     3. Amy Louise Morgan, born 1-13-1955.
   4. Marian Anne, born 8-7-1925; married 3-1-1947 to Raymond Shultz of Buffalo, N.Y. They had:

1. David Thomas Schultz,
   born Oct. 22, 1949.
2. William Morgan Schultz,
   born May 3, 1951.

CHARLES SIMON JUNIOR - LAURA A. PIERCE
OF BRANDYWINE HUNDRED, DELAWARE

(Bible published by A. J. Holman & Co., Phila. 1879. Owned by Mrs. Clarence E. Potter, Wilmington, Delaware. 1957. Record given by Mrs. Charles D. Bird.)

Marriage Certificate

Charles Simon Jun. of Brandywine Hd., Delaware and Laura A. Pierce of Brandywine Hd., Delaware, were married on 23 February 1881 at Booth's Corner by Rev. Samuel Hance, Minister of the Gospel. Witness: Mrs. Hance.

Births

Charles Simon Jun. was born February 28, 1859.
Laura A. Pierce Simon was born March 12, 1863.
Clara E. Simon was born December 31, 1881.
Charles H. Simon was born July 13, 1883.
Harry L. Simon was born May 19, 1886.
Laura L. Simon was born April 24, 1888.
Oscar Conly Simon was born April 13, 1890.
William Emmet Simon was born June 6, 1892.
Herbert Paul Simon was born December 1, 1894.
Clarence Elmer Simon was born April 3, 1897.
Ernest Allen Simon was born June 15, 1900.
Florence Ruth Simon was born December 22, 1904.

Deaths

Oscar Conly Simon died June 11, 1891.
Charles Simon died March 12, 1952, age 93 years.
Laura A. Pierce Simon died April 13, 1942.
Charles Harley Simon died February 3, 1940.
Herbert Paul Simon died October 1, 1943.

SIMPERS RECORD

The name is sometimes spelled "Sympers." Three brothers came early in the 18th Century to Cecil County, Maryland. They possibly came from Liverpool, England.

Thomas Simpers lived at "Wasps Nest" on the road leading from Northeast, Cecil Co., Md., across Elk Neck. He was buried by June 28, 1733/34; was married before August 7, 1719 to Amy Lewis, daughter of Richard Lewis, Sr., of Cecil Co., Md. Their children:

1. John Simpers, born 1722
2. Thomas
3. Richard
4. Nathaniel
5. Ann, born April 28, 1730
6. William, born March 12, 1732

John Simpers, son of Thomas Simpers and Amy Lewis, was born near Northeast, Maryland, 1722; died by February 24, 1806 near Northeast.

John Simpers was a Signer of the Oath of Allegiance, Cecil County, Md., March 2, 1778. His broher, Thomas, also signed.

John Simpers married Ann Nash, probably the daughter of Thomas Nash. Their children:
1. Jesse
2. William, born 1761; died 1842
3. John, born January 21, 1762
4. Rueben
5. Naomi
6. Ann
7. Mary
8. Rebecca
9. Joseph

John Simpers, son of John Simpers and his wife Ann Nash, lived in Northeast, Md. He was born January 21, 1762; died by January 20, 1842; married Margaret Crouch, who was born November 28, 1772; died by 1830. Their children:

1. Ann, born 9-30-1788
2. Mary, born 11-8-1790; m. Stephen George
3. Johnson, born 2-6-1793
4. John, born 3-26-1795
5. Isaac, born 3-31-1798
6. Naomi, born 5-19-1800
7. Sarah, born 3-29-1801
8. Jesse, born 5-14-1805
9. Elizabeth, born 3-21-1807
10. Margaret, born 3-18-1809
11. Sophia, born 1-10-1812
12. Martha, born 9-29-1818

Mary Simpers, daughter of John Simpers and his wife Margaret (Crouch), was born November 8, 1790. She married Stephen George, son of John George and his wife Frances Clark.

Stephen George was born January 18, 1787; died 8-24-1854. Mary Simpers George died September 13, 1854. Their children:
Ann George was born 1809; died 1907; married December 31, 1829, Daniel Reese, who was born December 10, 1805.

(See George line for rest of children)

Their son, Daniel W. Reese, was born December 7, 1835; died May 19, 1891; married May 9, 1865 Maryland Virginia Pattison, daughter of William Pattison. She was born 1844; died March 23, 1888.

Their daughter, Myrtie Virginia Reese, was born February 14, 1869; married November 4, 1891, H. W. McNeal.

(See McNeal, Reese Records for children of Myrtie V. Reese and H. W. McNeal)

JOHN & ELIZABETH (HENTON) SITES

(Bible printed and published by M. Carey & Son, 121 Chestnut St., Philadelphia. 1817. Present owner Mrs. Eugene Hackendorn, Jr., Claymont, Del. Copied by Clara Wallace Bird, Feb. 22, 1960.)

Marriages

John Sites and Elizabeth Henton were married on
    May 2, 1816.

Births

John Sites was born June 15, 1794.
Elizabeth Henton Sites was born March 3, 1794.

George Sites was born March 1, 1817.
Benjamin Henton Sites was born December 13, 1818.
Amanda Jane Sites was born October 15, 1820.
Elizabeth Sarah Sites was born March 7, 1823.
Mary Katherine Sites was born May 22, 1825.
Martha Louise Sites was born May 15, 1829.
John Alpheus Sites was born December 19, 1831.
William Price Sites was born June 12, 1834.
Frances Cornelia Coken ? Sites was born
    April 21, 1837.

Deaths

John Alpheus Sites died May 21, 1904, age 72
    years, 5 months and 2 days.
Amanda Jane Earman died June 11, 1855.
Martha Louise Miller (nee Sites) died May 23, 1909.
George Sites died September 15, 1818, age 1 year,
    6 months and 15 days.
Benjamin Henton Sites died May 27, 1823, age 4
    years, 5 months and 15 days.
Mary Katherine Duke (nee Sites) died September
    1899, age 74 years and 4 months.
Elizabeth Sarah Sites died May 8, 1901, age 78
    years, 2 months and 1 day.
John Sites died August 18, 1861, age 67 years,
    two months and 3 days.
Elizabeth Sites died June 26, 1864, age 70
    years, 3 months and 23 days.

Frances Cornelia Sites died February 25, 1894, age 56 years, 10 months and 4 days.
William Price Sites died February 27, 1897, age 62 years, 8 months and 15 days.

SMITH - HITCHENS RECORD

Births

Nathanial, son of Levin Smith and Mary Hitchens, was born July 3, 1822.
Sarah Elizabeth, daughter of William and Lurana Bryan, was born February 7, 1828.
Wm. G. Hitchens, son of Miles B. and Lavenia C. Hitchens, was born November 15, 1873.
Roland Nathaniel Hitchens, son of Miles and Lavenia C. Hitchens, was born October 23, 1875.
Victor C. Hitchens, son of Miles and Lavenia C. Hitchens, was born November 20, 1878.
William Smith, son of Nathaniel and Sarah E. Hitchens, was born January 15, 1846.
Miles Burton, son of Nathaniel and Sarah E. Hitchens, was born May 19, 1850.
Nathaniel Peoples, son of Nathaniel and Sarah E. Hitchens, was born February 15, 1855.
Sheppard Jackson, son of Nathaniel and Sarah E. Hitchens, was born April 19, 1863.

SAMUEL SMYTH AND JANE

(Bible published by Mathew Carey, 122 Market St., Philadelphia, Pa. 1803. Owned by Mrs. Margaret (Orr) Bradbury, Wilmington. Record given by Mrs. Charles Bird.)

FAMILY RECORD

Marriages

Samuel and Jane Smyth were married March 4, 1781.
Do to Rachel Mercer November 7, 1815?
Margaret McClintock married February 20, 1806.

1808 Violet McClintock married April 22nd.
John Smyth, November 9, 1809, to Jane Miller.

Births

Margaret Smyth, born June 11, 1782.
John Smyth, born December 9, 1787.
Violet Smyth, born March 23, 1784.
William Smyth, born September 4, 1792.
Elizabeth Smyth, born November 15, 1795.
Alexander Smyth, born October 2, 1799.
S. James Smyth, born October 20, 1802.
Robert Smyth, born March 15, 1791.

Samuel Smyth, born December 5, 1761.
Jane Smyth, born September 10, 1762.

Samuel Smyth died April 20, age sixth (sixty?)
    nine years
This Book became My property May twenty fourth 24
    Rachel Smyth
May this Book be my Protection May God grant
    and to his name be Praesed.

Deaths

Robert Smyth died September 6, 1791.
Jane Smyth died September 5, 1812.
Violet McClintock died December 25, 1814,
    age 29 years.
William Smyth died June 26, 1818.
Margaret McClintock died January 19, 1817,
    age 37 years.
John Smyth died January 29, 1818, age 32 years.
James Smyth died March 11, 1827.

JEREMIAH SPRINGER

(This record was given by Mrs. Courtland Springer, Upper Darby, Pa.)

Jeremiah Springer (1755-1842) was a son of Charles Springer (1722-1796) and Mary Ball (-1799) his wife and a grandson of Christopher Springer (1696-1755) and Catherina Hendrckson (-   ) his wife. Christopher Springer was a son of Charles Springer, Sr. (1658-1738) and therefore Jeremiah was a great-grandson (not a grandson of the first Charles Springer "from Sweden" as the Bible record states.

Jeremiah Springer was married on March 12, 1788 by the Rev. Charles Wharton (See records of Immanuel Church, New Castle, Delaware) to Mary Reese (1765-1831), daughter of John and Jane Reese.

Their first child, Catherine, married 1st Calvin Philip and 2nd married Justa Justis.

One of their younger daughters, Sabilla Ann (christened Isabella Ann, according to the records of Immanuel Church) was born May 4, 1804 and died April 23, 1873 near Zanesville, Ohio, although her body was returned to Delaware for burial in St. James Churchyard near Stanton.

Sabilla Ann Springer was married 1st on February 19, 1833 by Rev. Stephen Freeman to Joseph Springer (1795-1842), a son of John Springer (1766-1837) and Rebecca Stidham (1769-1861) his wife, and a grandson of Joseph Springer, who was a son of Christopher and Lydia Anderson his wife.

At the time Joseph Springer, Sabilla Ann's husband, was born December 23, 1795, his parents John and Rebecca, were living in Frederick County, Maryland, but they continued to move westward and found a permanent home in Muskingum County, Ohio. Both John and Rebecca were buried in Woodlawn Cemetery, Zanesville, Ohio. Joseph's grave, however, will be found in St. James Churchyard, Stanton, Delaware. There seems to be some variation in dates given for his death, but we believe the one on his tombstone is correct, June 9, 1842. Letters of Administration were granted June 13, 1842.

Sabilla Ann married 2nd, July 18, 1846 in Zanesville, Ohio, to Thomas Cleveland (1822-1852) a lawyer. The ceremony was performed by the Rev. Mr. Smallwood, an Episcopal minister. Thomas Cleveland born in Belmont County, Ohio was a son of Timothy and Sarah (Pierce) Cleveland, who came to Ohio from Emden, Maine.

JOSEPH SPRINGER BIBLE RECORD

(This record was found in a box in the Delaware Historical Society, Wilmington, Delaware. Copied by Mrs. Glenn S. Skinner, Newark, Delaware.)

Joseph Springer was born 1796.
Sabilla Ann Springer was born May 8, 1804.

Jeremiah C. Springer, son of Joseph and Sabilla Springer, was born December 31, 1833.
Catheriness Justa Springer, son of Joseph and Sabilla Ann Springer, was born May 16, 1836.
Sarah Emma Springer, daughter of Joseph and Sabilla Ann Springer, was born September 9, 1838.
Rebecca Ann Springer, daughter of Joseph and Sabilla Ann Springer, was born February 14, 1841.

Deaths

Joseph Springer died June 16, 1842 near Stanton, Delaware of Dropsy, was interred at St. James Cemetery, Delaware.
Rebecca Ann Springer died December 13, 1857.
Cathariness J. Springer, son of Joseph and Sabilla Springer, died at Annapolis, Md. by heart disease while a paroled soldier of Co. E. 19th-- on February 2, 1863.
Sabilla A. Cleveland died April 23, 1873 of piermoid; was buried at St. James Church, Stanton, Delaware.

Mary Springer, daughter of Jeremiah and Mary Springer, died August 8, 1795.
Mary, wife of Jeremiah Springer, died February 27, 1831.
Lewis Springer, M.D., son of Jeremiah and Mary Springer, died at Pennington, N. J. by spasmodic Cholera, August 27, 1832.
Sarah R. Springer, daughter of Jeremiah and Mary Springer, died March --, 1838 of consumption.
Maria Springer, daughter of Jeremiah and Mary Springer, wife of David Justis, died August 28, 1840 of congestion fever.
Lavenah Springer, wife of Nehemiah Delaplain, died October 1840, of congestion fever.

Jeremiah Springer died April 1842 of old age. He
was the third descendant of Charles the first
from Sweden.
David Justis died June 1843.
Justa Justis died October 1836.
Catherine Justis died May 16, 1856.

Jeremiah Springer Chart

```
   1.                2.
Charles           Christopher        3.
Springer          b. 1696            Charles
b. 1658           d. 1755            b. 1722
d. 5-26-1738      m.                 d. 1796
m. 12-27-1685     Catherine          m. 1748
Maria             Hendrickson        Mary Ball
Hendrickson                          d. 1799
d. 3-15-1727
                                     John
                                     Reese
                                     m.          Mary
                                     Jane        Reese
                                                 b. 2-27-1831

Christopher
Springer          Joseph
b. 1696           Springer
d. 1755                              John
m.                m.                 Springer
Catherine                            b. 1766
Hendrickson                          d. 1837      Joseph
                  Lydia              m.           Springer
                  Anderson           Rebecca      b. 12-23-1795
                                     Stidham      d. 6-9-1842 ?
                                     b. 1769      m. 2nd
                                     d. 1861      Thomas Cleveland
   5.
Sabilla Ann
b. 5-4-1804
d. 4-23-1873
m. 1st
2-19-1833
```

Springer Chart continued next page.

Springer Chart continued:

6.
Jeremiah C. Springer
b. 12-31-1833

Catherness Springe
b. 5-16-1836
d. 2-2-1863

Sarah E. Springer
b. 9-9-1838

Rebecca A. Springer
b. 2-14-1841
d. 12-13-1857

Above are the children of Sabilla and Joseph Springer.

STEVENSON – BAILEY

(Bible was published by Edward W. Miller, Phil. 1848. Owned by Mrs. John M. Collins, Laurel, Del.)

Marriages

Hugh S. Stevenson and Jennie C. Bailey were
    married March 8, 1864.
Benjamin T. Wooley and Alice Belle Stevenson were
    married December 9, 1885.
Llewllyn Keiss and Ida Virginia Stevenson were
    married December 9, 1888.
Orlondo V. Wootten and Anna May Stevenson were
    married November 27, 1907, Laurel, Del.
Charles Hugh Stevenson and Elizabeth Nelson were
    married April 21, 1909.
John M. Collins and Elizabeth Stevenson were
    married September 7, 1904 at home Snow Hill.
Chas. H. Savage, M.D. and Helen Stevenson Wooley
    were married August 18, 1919, Washington, D.C.
Harold G. Connelly and Jennie Maude Wooley were
    married October 18, 1920, Washington, D.C.

Charles Hugh Stevenson and Mary Hazle Miller were
    married January 30, 1925 (1925 is crossed
    out and changed to 1935 - Detroit, Mich.)
Richard Helson Stevenson and Barbara Holmes were
    married September 15, 1940, Detroit.
Mary Elizabeth Stevenson and Francis James
    McDonald were married February 3, 1940.

Births

Hugh Sanders Stevenson was born February 25, 1823.
Jennie C. Bailey, wife of H. S. Stevenson, was
    born March 6, 1844.
Alice Belle Stevenson was born February 1, 1865.
Ida Virginia Stevenson was born November 1, 1866.
Anna May Stevenson was born March 25, 1868.
Charles Hugh Stevenson was born December 6, 1869.
Rosalie Stevenson was born October 23, 1871.
Two infants, a boy and a girl, were born and died
    on the same day August 5, 1872.
Maggie Snow Stevenson was born January 29, 1874.
Elvira B. Stevenson was born September 3, 1875.
Mary Stevenson was born September 28, 1879;
    died May 28, 1860 (Note: These dates are
    either reversed or are incorrect).

Helen Stevenson Wooley, first born of Benjamin T.
    and Alice Stevenson Wooley, was born March 2,
    1888.
Jennie Maud Wooley, second child of Benjamin T.
    and Alice Stevenson Wooley, was born July 7,
    1890.
Stevenson Luck Wooley, third child of Benjamin T.
    and Alice Stevenson Wooley, was born
    August 3, 1901, Centerville, Ala.

Marriages

Llewellyn Keiss, born October 27, 1858, married
    December 9, 1888 Ida Virginia Stevenson,
    born November 1, 1866.

Births

Jane Stevenson, born December 1, 1869.
Edith Marie, born September 12, 1892.
Hugh Llewellyn, born October 14, 1895.
Leonard Stevenson, born March 7, ----.
Mildred Margaret, born May 14, 1900.

Walter Bailey, born August 14, 1902.
William Alfred, born May 12, 1907.
Elizabeth Collins, born September 7, 1904.

Deaths

Edith Marie died October 30, 1905.
Llewellyn Keiss died June 14, 1936.

Births

Orlando Valentine Wooten, son of Orlando V.
    Wooten and Anna May Stevenson, was born
    October 22, ----.
Charles Hugh Stevenson, son of Charles Hugh
    Stevenson and Elizabeth Helson, was born
    June 9, 1911.
Richard Helson Stevenson, son of Charles
    Stevenson and Elizabeth Helson, was born
    May 1, 1914.
Mary Elizabeth Stevenson, daughter of Charles H.
    Stevenson and Elizabeth Helson, was born
    July 21, 1920.
John Stevenson Collins, son of John M. Collins
    and Elizabeth Stevenson, was born May 26,
    190-?
William Turpin Collins, son of John M. Collins
    and Elizabeth Stevenson, was born June 13,
    1909.

On the Family Record page:

Littleton R. Bailey died Sepember 10, 1876.
Elizabeth Bailey, wife of Littleton R. Bailey,
    died August 14, 1867.
William Henry Stevenson died July 18, 1879.
Jennie C. Stevenson, wife of H. S. Stevenson,
    died September 15, 1882.

Hugh Mills Stevenson died March 25, 1884, age
    89 years.
Hugh Saunders Stevenson died February 4, 1909,
    Laurel, Del.
Alice Stevenson Wooley died September 28, 1935,
    New Bedford, Mass.
Anna May Wooten died August 17, 1940, Lewes, Del.
Charles Hugh Stevenson died August 30, 1943,
    Detroit, Mich.

Littleton R. Bailey	Jennie C. Bailey		
d. 9-10-1876	d. 9-15-1882	Charles H.	
m.	m.	m.	1. Charles
Elizabeth	Hugh	Elizabeth	2. Richard
d. 8-14-1867	Stevenson	Helson	3. Mary E.
	d. 2-4-1909		m.
			Francis J. McDonald

STEWART FAMILY RECORD

(Bible published by M'Carty & Davis, 171 Market St., Philadelphia. 1834. Owned by Mrs. Hallie (Hendrick) Evans, Concord Pike, Wilmington, Del. Record given by Mrs. Charles Bird.)

Marriages

Elizabeth Stewart, February 14, 1877.
Martin Hendrick,, October 3, 1901.
Hallie Hendrick, March 22, 1911.

Births

Charles Stewart, born January 4, 1834.
Mary Jain Stewart, born April 13, 1835.
Mathew Stewart, born October 24, 1836.
Rebecca Stewart, born September 22, 1838.
John Stewart, born February 28, 1840.
Margaret Stewart, born May 10, 1842.
Elizabeth Stewart, born January 10, 1845.
Elmer Hendrick, born December 14, 1877.
Martin Hendrick, born March 26, 1879.
Hallie Hendrick, born April 18, 1881.
Willard S. Hendrick, born September 26, 1882.
Florence Hendrick, born June 23, 1884.

Deaths

John Stewart died January 20, 1887; born
    May 6, 1811.
Charles Stewart died April 2, 1891.
Martin Hendrick died August 1, 1890.
Elmer Hendrick died April 14, 1895.
Florence Hendrick died April 13, 1903.

Willard S. Hendrick died in Brandywine Hundred
    August 23, 1914.
Elizabeth Hendrick died March 16, 1937, age 92.

Births

Elwood Brinton Evans was born February 1, 1912.
Stewart Evans was born July 19, 1913.
Elizabeth Evans was born August 19, 1914.
Helen Evans was born August 29, 1918.
Clifford Lewis Evans was born February 6, 1920.
Harold Mousley Evans was born November 15, 1921.

(Louise White) and Elwood Evans
    Elwood B. Evans, Jr., born April 14, 1939.
    Arlene Mae Evans, born February 22, 1940.

(Miriam Metten) Stewart Evans were married
    August 29, 1943.
    Ann Evans born May 14, 1956.

(Albert Forwood) Elizabeth Evans married
    December 11, 1937
    Martha Lea Forwood born June 23, 1941
    Betty Mae Forwwod born February 15, 1944
    W. Albert Forwood born February 14, 1947
    Wayne Robert Forwood born July 10, 1949

(Roy Schenerman) Helen Evans married
    July 15, 1942
    Helen Lee Schenerman born October 13, 1950
    John Henry Schenerman born June 3, 1953

(Madelyn Major) Clifford Evans married
    January 12, 1946
    Clifford Evans, Jr., May 18, 1948
    Deborah Lynn Evans born September 17, 1951

(Elinor Taylor) Harold Evans married
    November 26, 1947
    Faye Evans born December 7, 1948 (twin)
    Ellen Evans, born December 7, 1948 (twin)

ISAAC STIDHAM BIBLE

(From Photostat copy, Delaware Historical Society. Isaac Stidham's Book 1705 & Mary Stidham. Printed by T. Wright and W. Gill, Printers to the University and sold by R. Baldwin and S. Crowder, in Paternoster Row, London by W. Jackson in Oxford. 1770. cum Privilegio.)

Isaac Stidham, son of Jonas Stidham and Mary Stidham his wife, whose maiden was was Colesberry, was born July 18, 1762.

Anna Mary Stidham, wife of Isaac Stidham, was born January 10, 1763; died June 18, 1792, maiden name Bird?

Mary Stidham, second wife of Isaac Stidham, whose maiden name was Britton, was born April 5, 1767.

Sarah Stidham, daughter of Isaac and Anna Mary, was born March 13, 1783/4.
Mary Stidham, daughter of Isaac and Anna, was born January 4, 1785.
Susan, daughter of Isaac and Anna, was born October 24, 1786.
Eliza, daughter of Isaac and Anna, was born September 24, 1788.
Rachel Stidham, 5th daughter, was born October 2, 1790.

Catherine Stidham, daughter of Isaac and Mary Stidham, was born October 9, 1795.
Isaac, son of Isaac and Mary, was born February 6, 1797.
Jonas, son of Isaac and Mary Stidham, was born March 29, 1799.
Anna Stidham, daughter of Mary, born March 8, 1800.
Richard Britton Stidham was born November 8, 1801.
Lemna Stidham was born December 19, 1806.

JOHN STONE & GRACE MILLER

(Copy of Bible bought at 47 N. 11th St., Phil.,
Pa. By James M. Holm, March 1945.)

John Stone and Grace Miller were married
   May 16, 1816 ? 1806?

John Stone was born March 27, 1782.
John Stone died August 27, 1847.

Grace Stone was born July 27, 1787.

Euphanie Stone was born May 5, 1807.
Joel Stone was born April 3, 1809.
Samuel M. Stone was born May 10, 1811.
Thomas P. Stone was born November 25, 1815.
Daniel C. Stone was born September 18, 1817.
Mary T. Stone was born November 6, 1818.
Rebecca P. Stone was born February 29, 1820.
Oliver P. Stone was born January 18, 1822.

THE LEMUEL STURGES BIBLE

(This Bible was Stereotyped by Jesper Harding &
Son, 37 South Third Street, Philadelphia, Pa.
1859. The original owner was Lemuel Sturges of
Whitford and West Chester, Pa. Now owned by Alban
P. Shaw, Wilmington, Delaware.)

Marriages

Lemuel Sturges and Elizabeth Bruce were married
   December 26, 1834.
Thomas Bengless and Hannah Sturges were married
   February 26, 1856.
Alfred Sturges and Elizabeth Arnt were married
   February 1861.
Johnson C. Baldwin and Elizabeth Sturges were
   married October 24, 1863.
Joseph Taylor and Rebecca Sturges were married
   (no dates shown).

Births

Lemuel Sturges, son of Jonathan and Hannah, was
   born November 5, 1809, died in his 93rd year.
Eliza Bruce, daughter of Isaac and Elizabeth
   Bruce, was born December 29, 1812; died
   5-9-1868.
Their children:
   1.   Hannah Sturges born September 7, 1835
   2.   Matilda Sturges born March 2, 1836
   3.   Alfred Sturges born January 10, 1837
   4.   Wilmer Sturges born April 7, 1838
   5.   Elizabeth Sturges born February 2, 1841
   6.   Isaac Sturges born December 26, 1842
   7.   Rebecca Sturges born October 22, 1844
   8.   Catharine Sturges born September 24,
           1846
   9.   Wm. Henry Sturges born August 26, 1848
   10. Lida Jane Sturges born September 8, 1849

Deaths

1. Matilda Sturges died July 2, 1836
2. Wilmer Sturges died July 7, 1838
3. Wm. Henry Sturges died December 20, 1848
4. Lida Jane Sturges died October 9, 1849
5. Isaac Sturges died March 8, 1863
6. Eliza Sturges died May 9, 1868
7. Hannah Sturges *Bengles died June 21,
       1908 *(Beugless)
8. Thomas Hyde *Bengles died December 18,
       1865
*9. Kate (Bengles) Shaw died October 5, 1918
10. William Guillan Shaw died January 22, 1932
11. William G. Shaw died December 20, 1909
12. James Bagshaw Shaw died March 9, 1893

*Name should be "Beugless"
See letter back of Book
Page 188 in Volume 2.

Births

Isaac Bruce, son of Isaac and Elizabeth Bruce,
   was born January 10, 1768. He married
   Elizabeth Bruce, daughter of Isaac Melon,
   was born July 15, 1777. Their children:

1. Joel Bruce born February 4, 1794
2. Gideon Bruce born March 5, 1796
3. Tanzend Bruce born April 14, 1797
4. Lydia Bruce born January 14, 1800
5. Richard Bruce born October 14, 1801
6. Phebe Bruce born May 20, 1804
7. C. Bruce born January 10, 1806
8. Isaac Bruce born September 7, 1808
9. William Bruce born NOvember 17, 1810
10. Eliza Bruce born December 29, 1812
11. Elijah Bruce born March 1, 1815
12. Rebecca Bruce born December 30, 1817) twin
13. Rachel Bruce born December 30, 1817)twin
14. Melon Bruce born April 2, 1819
15. ---- Bruce born September 2, 1821

Charles L. Bengless *Beugless, son of Thomas and Hannah (Sturges), was born November 30, 1856.
Frank *Bengless, son of Thos. and Hannah, was born August 23, 1858.
Kate *Bengless, daughter of Thos. and Hannah, was born November 15, 1862.
Fred J. Baldwin, son of Johnson and Elizabeth Baldwin, was born July 22, 1865.
George D. Baldwin, son of Johnson and Elizabeth Baldwin, was born October 20, 1867.
William W. Courtney, son of James and Catherine Courtney, was born November 19, 1864.
Harry W. Taylor (no dates shown)
Eddy Taylor (no dates shown)
Warren Baldwin (no dates shown)
William Shaw and Katie *Bengless were married February 13, 1883.
William G. Shaw Jr., was born December 16, 1883.
Alban P. Shaw was born September 23, 1886.
James Bagshaw Shaw was born October 14, 1890; died March 9, 1893.
Thomas Hyde *Bengles was born 10-11-1834; died 12-18-1865, West Chester, Pa.
Thomas H. *Bengles served with Brandywine Guards of Chester Co., in the Civil War; was wounded, buried in Goshen Hickite Friends Burial Grounds at Goshenville, Pa.

*"Name should be Beugless" per letter back of Book. For proof of change in spelling see Vol. 2, page 188.

Hannah Sturges, wife of Thomas *Bengless, married first Thomas Hyde *Bengless; married 2nd Benjamin Helderman; married 3rd Willian Conyers. She died June 21, 1908, buried in Shaw plot in Riverview Cemetery, Wilmington, Del.

*"Name should be Beugless" per letter back of Book. For proof of change in spelling see Vol. 2, page 188.

— — — — — — — — —

SHAW

William Guillian Shaw was born 2-13-1860, Wilmington, Del.; died 1-22-1932 in Wilmington, Del. He married Catherine (Kate) *Bengless, daughter of Thomas and Hannah 2-15-1883 at Phil., Pa.. by Rev. Alfred Harris, a Baptist minister at Messiah Baptist Church. Catherine Shaw was born 11-15-1862; died 10-5-1918. Children of William G. and Catherine Shaw:
1. William Gavin Shaw born 12-16-1883, Wilmington, Del.; married Elizabeth Morton - no children; died 12-20-1909.
2. Alban Peoples Shaw born 9-23-1886, Wilmington, Del.; married 10-14-1914 at Liftwood Cliffs, Del., Harriett Anne Wallace, daughter of William Hayes Wallace and Hannah Perkins Goodley Wallace by Rev. William J. Rowan, Presbyterian minister at Delaware College, Newark.

Harriett Ann Wallace was born July 4, 1888 at Christiana, Lancaster County, Pa.

3. James Bagshaw Shaw was born 10-14-1891; died 3-9-1893.

Children of Alban P. and Harriett W. Shaw:
1. Alban Peoples Shaw, Jr., born 11-28-1915; died 12-4-1915 at Atlantic City, N.J.

2. William Gullian Shaw, III, born 4-30-1918, Wilmington, Del.; married in 1st Methodist Church, 6-18-1942 at Las Vegas, Nev. to Anita Louise Hygate, daughter of Anita Callaway and Harry B. Hygate of Wilmington, Del.
3. Alban Peoples Shaw, III, born 10-12-1921, Wilmington, married Mildred May Grimes 9-25-1943 in Wilmington by Rev. Earl Shockley. She is the daughter of Mabel Broadbent and Horace Grimes.

Their children:
1. Sally Anne Shaw, born 7-6-1944, Wilmington.
2. David Bruce Shaw born 6-1-1947, Wilmington.

TALLEY - MILLER

(Bible was published by A. J. Holman & Co., 930 Arch St., Phila. 1875. Owned by Mrs. Jennie G. Talley, Faulk Road, Wilmington, Del.)

Marriages

This certifies that the Rite of Holy Matrimony was celebrated between Lewis F. Talley of New Castle County and Mary E. Miller of New Castle County on February 15, 1870 at George L. Miller's by the Rev. Valentine Gray. Witness: George W. Miller, Susan R. Watson.

Births

Lewis F. Talley was born March 26, 1844.
Mary E. Miller was born October 24, 1844.

*"Name should be Beugless" per letter back of Book. For proof of change in spelling see Vol. 2, page 188.

Leonard C. Talley was born December 24, 1871.
Lewis M. Talley was born November 19, 1873.
Clyde E. Talley was born February 1, 1876.
Jane Elizabeth Talley was born April 12, 1878.
Howard Talley was born October 4, 1880.
Watson Talley was born January 9, 1883.
Harold Watson Talley was born November 12, 1922;
    son of Watson and Jeannie Galbreath Talley.

Deaths

Clyde E. Talley died March 22, 1876.
Howard Talley died May 19, 1881.
Lewis F. Talley died November 24, 1930.
Mary (Miller) Talley, wife of Lewis F. Talley,
    died February 26, 1935.
Lewis Talley, son of Lewis F., died
    September 13, 1955.
Watson Talley, son of Lewis F., died December 25,
    1955.

Watson Talley married Jennie C. Galbreath on
    December 5, 1914. Their son, Harold W.
Talley, married Jean A. VanPelt on
    October 11, 1943. Their children:
        Cheryl Jean born December 24, 1946
        Ronald Harold born January 30, 1950.

(Above record given by Mrs. Charles D. Bird,
Caesar Rodney Chapter.)

TALLEY - MILLER

Mrs. Jennie Talley, owner of the Bible added the following:

Lewis M. Talley (always known as Lewis Prince
    Talley) married twice:
        1st: Cassandra Cloud, daughter of George
              Cloud and had a daughter:
              Jennie, who married Harry Ramsey.
        2nd: Ella M. Galbreath, daughter of Willard
              and Eva Galbreath, December 8, 1917.
              They had no children.

Leonard C. Talley married Annie Clark and had two
sons and 2 daughters:
1. Norman, who married Margaret Ford
2. Albert
3. Dorothy
4. Elsie, who married William M. Clay,
son of Florence Anna Malin and
William Clay.

Jane Elizabeth Talley married Henry Weldin on
November 24, 1904?

Funeral Notices in the Bible

1. Lewis Talley buried from the residence of his son, Lewis F. Talley, in Brandywine Hundred on Sunday, October the 12th, 1890. Leave the house at 10 o'clock to proceed to Bethel M. E. Cemetery - services at the Church.

2. Elizabeth Talley, aged 88 years, to be buried from the residence of her son Lewis F. Talley on Thursday, November 14, 1901. Leave the house at 10 o'clock for serves at Bethel M. E. Church. Interment at Bethel Cemetery.

3. Beloved wife, Clara V. Weldin, aged 38 years, buried from the residence of her husband, J. Atwood Weldin in Brandywine Hundred, Delaware on Tuesday afternoon, August 6, 1895 at 2 o'clock. Services at the house. Interment at Lombardy Cemetery.

The above Clara V. Weldin was a daughter of Lewis and Elizabeth Talley and a sister of Lewis F. Talley.

Talley Chart next page.

Talley Chart:

Adam Talley
b. 1770
d. 7-28-1844
m.
Rebecca
b. 1774
d. 4-8-1838

2.
Lewis Talley
b. 11-4-1810
d. 10-9-1890
m.

Elizabeth
b. 2-12-1814
d. 11-14-1901

3.
1. Thomas
   b. 12-27-1834
2. William
   b. 4-2-1836
   m. Emily Forwood
3. Robert
   b. 8-29-1837
   m. Emily Beeson
4. Mary
   b. 7-23-1839
   m. Charles
      Poole
5. Lewis F. Talley
   b. 3-26-1843/4
   d. 11-24-1930
   m. 2-15-1870
   Mary Miller
   b. 10-24-1844
   d. 2-26-1935
6. Hannah
   b. 3-12-1841
   m. John Prince
7. Elizabeth
   b. 1847
   m. H. C. Bird
8. Beulah Z.
   b. 11-9-1849
   b. 11-9-1849
   m. C. W. Baldwin
9. Albert
   b. 2-22-1852
   d. 1852
10. Clara
    b. 2-12-1858
    m. Atwood Weldin
    d. 8-6-1895

Tally Chart continued next page.

Talley Chart Continued:

Children of
Lewis F. Talley
b. 1843
d. 1930
m. 1870
Mary Miller

1. Leonard
   b. 12-24-1871
2. Lewis M.
   b. 11-19-1873
   d. 1955
3. Clyde
   b. 2-1-1876
   d. 1876
4. Jane E.
   b. 4-12-1878
5. Howard
   b. 10-4-1880
   d. 1881
6. Watson

   See below:

6. Watson
   b. 1-9-1883
   d. 12-25-1955
   m.
   Jennie Galbreath

   Harold Talley
   b. 11-12-1922   Cheryl
   m. 10-11-1843   Ronald
   Jean VanPelt

LEWIS TALLEY AND WIFE ELIZABETH

(Bible was published by J. W. Bradley, Phila. Owned by Mrs. Lewis P. Talley, Naaman's Road, Wilmington.)

Marriages

Lewis and Elizabeth Talley were married
    February 27, 1834.
Hannah Talley was married to John Prince
    October 9, 1862.
Mary Talley was married to Charles W. Poole
    December 9, 1863
Beulah Talley was married to Clark W. Baldwin
    December 23, 1869.
Lizzie Talley was married to Henry C. Bird
    January 7, 1875.

Clara Talley was married to Atwood Weldin
    January 23, 1879
William Talley was married to Emily Forwood
    February 22, 1866.
Robert Talley was married to Emily Beeson
    March 8, 1866.
Lewis F. Talley was married to Mary Miller
    February 15, 1870.

Births

Lewis Talley was born November 4, 1810.
Elizabeth Talley was born February 12, 1814.

Thomas M. Talley was born December 27, 1834.
William A. Talley was born April 2, 1836.
Robert Talley was born August 29, 1837.
Mary Talley was born July 23, 1839.
Hannah Talley was born March 12, 1841.
Lewis F. Talley was born March 26, 1843.
Elizabeth J. Talley was born April 9, 1847.
Beulah Z. Talley was born November 9, 1849.
Albert Talley was born February 22, 1852.
Clara V. Talley was born February 12, 1858.

Deaths

Rebecca Talley, wife of Adam Talley, died
    April 8, 1838, age 64 years and 13 days.
Adam Talley died July 28, 1844, age 74 years
    and 21 days.
Albert, son of Lewis and Elizabeth Talley, died
    September 2, 1852.
Lewis Talley died October 9, 1890, age 80 years.

(Record given by Mrs. Charles Bird.)

CHARLES TALLEY AND MARY ZEBLEY

(Bible published by Davies and Kent, New York City. 1869. Owned by Thomas Z. Talley, Claymont, Delaware. 1956.)

Marriages

Charles Talley and Mary Zebley were married
    March 18, 1858.

Births

Wilmer Talley was born November 20, 1858; died 9-20-1939.
Penrose R. Talley was born July 25, 1861; died 12-15-1947.
Sarah Anna Talley was born February 21, 1865; died 1885.
Mary Ellen Talley was born June 28, 1868.
Charles Talley was born July 22, 1872; died young.
Thomas J. Talley was born December 12, 1874.

Marriages

Wilmer Talley and Mary E. Barlow were married April 11, 1882. (Wife died Jan. 8, 1903).
Penrose R. Talley and Hannah L. Foulk were married April 2, 1890.
Wilmer Talley and Rose Robeleu (?) were married June 8, 1905.

Deaths

Charles Talley (son) died in infancy.
Mary E. (Barlow) Talley died January 8, 1903.
Charles Talley, Sr. died October 1, 1898.
Mary Zebley Talley died May 24, 1897.
Sarah Anna Talley died May 4, 1885.
Wilmer Talley died September 20, 1939.
Penrose R. Talley died December 15, 1947.
Hannah L. (Foulk) Talley died November 26, 1936.

(Record given by Mrs. Charles Bird.)

Talley Chart:

1.
Wm. Talley
m. abt. 1690
Elinor Jensen

2.
Thomas
m.

3.
Wm. Talley
m. abt. 1735
Hannah Grubb

4.
Thomas Talley
m. 11-4-1766
Hannah Grubb

Talley Chart continued next page.

5.
Richard
Talley   6.
m.   Penrose R.   7.
Sarah   Talley   1. Ezra
Cartnell   b. 5-19-1805   b. 11-6-1832
             d.   2. Thomas
             m. 12-8-1831   b. 11-13-1833
                                 m. Sarah Hanby
Thomas   Edith G.   3. Charles
Smith   Smith   (See 8 below)
m.   b. 11-27-1809   4. Louisa
Margary   b. 2-26-1837
                             5. Brinton
                                 b. 6-29-1839
                                 m. Rebecca Weldin
                             6. Sarah
                                 b. 6-14-1841
                                 m. Lewis Hickman
                             7. Eliza
                                 b. 10-20-1842
                                 m. George Weldin
                             8. Edith
                                 b. 4-24-1845
                                 m. Jeremiah Harvey
                             9. Penrose
                                 b. 8-16-1847
                            10. Abner
                                 b. 10-1-1849
                                 m. Hannah Eldridge

7.
Charles Talley
b. 3-4-1835   8.
m. 3-18-1858   1. Wilmer
Mary Zebley   2. Penrose
daughter of   3. Sarah
Thomas Zebley   4. Mary
                          5. Charles M.
                          6. Thomas

TAYLOR BIBLE

(The Psalms of David in Metre. Allowed by the
Authority of the Gen. Assembly of the Kirk of
Scotland, and appointed to be sung in
Congregations and families. Edinburgh. Printed
by Mark and Charles Kerr, His Majesty's Printers.
1793 - loose pages from this Bible - Delaware
Historical Society.)

Matthew Kines was born March 18, 1804.

Eliza Server was born March 17, 1808.
John Server was born May 5, 1810.
Juleann Server was born January 13, 1812.
Mahlon Server was born February 8, 1820.
Allun T. Server was born May 2, 1823.

Isabel Taylor was born January 3, 178?.
William Taylor was born May 19, 1780.
Eliza Taylor was born December 10, 1878.
Samuel Taylor was born August, 1789.
John Taylor was born December 2, 1794.
Sarah Taylor was born July 25, 1797.
Benjamin Taylor was born September 3, 1799.
Joseph Taylor was born August 30, 1801.

THE TAYLOR BIBLE
KENT COUNTY, DELAWARE

(Published in Philadelphia by A. J. Helman & Co.,
930 Arch Street. 1876. Copy made by Elva R. B.
Taylor (Mrs. Paul W. Taylor), 12 Silverside Rd.,
Wilmington, Delaware for Clara Wallace Eyre,
Caesar Rodney Chapter.)

Marriages

Thomas W. Taylor and Mary Woolley were married
    February 8, 1847.
Samuel W. Taylor and Laurette Miller were
    married May 20, 1876.

Paul W. Taylor and Elva R. Blackiston were
   married April 25, 1898.
Howard Taylor and Bertha Able were married
   June 13, 1903.
Warren A. Taylor and Henrietta Puhl were
   married October 11, 1905.
Walter J. Taylor and Lillian Ott were married
   May 18, 1912.

Births

Thomas W. Taylor was born February 22, 1808.
Mary Woolley was born September 8, 1812.

Samuel W. Taylor, son of Thomas W. and Mary W.,
   was born June 23, 1848.
Laurette J. Miller, wife of Samuel W., was
   born June 11, 1856. They had 4 sons:
   Paul Woolley Taylor, born December 21, 1876.
   Howard Taylor, born January 9, 1879.
   Warren A. Taylor, born January 23, 1884.
   Walter J. Taylor, born January 21, 1889.
Elva Roberts Blackiston was born January 5, 1879.
The 6 sons of Paul and Elva:
   Bayard Blackiston Taylor, born Sept. 4, 1900
   Joseph Pyle Taylor, born Oct. 15, 1905
   Daniel Voshell Taylor, born April 19, 1910
   David Woolley Taylor, born April 19, 1910
   Paul Woolley Taylor, Jr., born Jan 31,
      1915 (born with a veil)
   James Voshell Roberts Taylor, born
      Aug. 12, 1917.

- - - - - - - - - -

Bayard Blackiston Taylor, born Sept. 4, 1900 and
   Mabel Ford, born Feb. 13, 1898, were married
   February 26, 1920.
Joseph Pyle Taylor, born Oct. 15, 1905 married
   1st. Elizabeth Ralph
   2nd. Alice Mackey
Daniel Voshell Taylor, born April 19, 1910, and
   Magaret Mink, born June 10, 1918, were
   married May 25, 1940.
Paul Woolley Taylor, Jr., born Jan. 31, 1915, and
   Emily M. Bent, born April 17, 1924, were
   married September 21, 1938.

James Voshell Roberts Taylor, born Aug. 12, 1917
and Beatrice Clayton King, born Dec. 30,
1919, were married August 9, 1941. Beatrice
was the daughter of Alexander and Jennie
Neville King.

Children of Bayard B. and Mabel F. Taylor:

Bayard Joseph Taylor, born Dec. 17, 1921; m.
Eloise Carriger 12-20-1943. Eloise,
10-1-1921. She was the daughter of Leonard
Carriger (Tenn.) and Mary Katherine
Fitzsimmons.
Mildred E. Taylor, born (no dates shown).
Robert Samuel Taylor, born (no dates shown).

Kent Co. Wills:

1.	2.	3.
<u>John Taylor Sr.</u>	John Taylor Jr.	Halburt Taylor
prov. 11-2-1752		Thos. Taylor
	? William Taylor -	dau. Rachel

John Taylor Sr., Farmer, will made 1-21-1796;
prob. 2-14-1799.
Ch: Peter   Lida
    William   Chana
    John   Sarah
    Robert   Stace
    Major   Eliz
    George   Mary Ann Kirk

Voshell, Obediah Sr. Will made 6-25-1778;
prob. 9-16-1778.
Wife, Elizabeth   p. 508. Obadiah Voshell
                         will prob. 5-1796
                         Wife - Hannah
                         sons - Titus, Owen, James
                         dau. - Nancy & Daniel
p. 319   Sons - John, Joseph, Obediah
          Dau. - Elizabeth Jackson, Mary Thomson
George Blackiston, will made 8-9-1778;
prob. 10-1-1778.
Wife - Martha; m. James Berry
p. 319 sons: - Ebenezar, John
daus. - Frances, Sarah, Prisilah

(For Rev. Service look up the Taylors)

Mildred E. Taylor's 1st marriage to Joseph Bernard
    Regan, Jr., April 26, 1945. He was lost at
    sea (Atlantic) during the war on the USS
    Frederick. Her 2nd marriage to Edward F.
    Fabryka, born 5-11-1924, on Aug. 18, 1951.
    She was born November 12, 1923.
Robert Samuel Taylor married Doris (no last name
    or dates shown).

Children of Joseph P. Taylor and Elizabeth Ralph
Taylor, 1st wife:
    Stephen Ralph Taylor, born (no dates shown);
        m. Buteau Logan.
Joseph Pyler (?) Taylor, Jr., unm. lives in France.
Patsy Ann Taylor, born June 11 (no year shown),
    daughter of Joseph Pyle Taylor and Alice
    Mackey (2nd wife).

Children of Daniel V. Taylor and Margaret Mink
Taylor:
    Nancy Jane, born November 6, 1943.
    Peggy, born July 31, 1945.
    Daniel V. Taylor, Jr., born July 1, 1950.

Children of Paul W. Taylor Jr., and Emily Bent
Taylor:
    Emlee Marie Taylor, born December 5, 1941.
    Paul Woolley Taylor, III, born Jan. 3, 1944.
    Rodney Scott Taylor, born August 8, 1945.

Children of James V. R. Taylor and Beatrice C.
King:
    Marion Elizabeth, born July 16, 1946.
    Christine, born November 20, 1948.
    Susan Beatrice, born October 14, 1953.
    Carol Ann, born December 8, 1958.

Children of Bayard Joseph Taylor and Eloise
Carriger:
    Ann Celeste Taylor, born October 17,
        (no year shown).
    Wayne Charles Taylor, born April 14,
        (no year shown).

Children of Mildred E. Taylor Falryka & Edward F.:
    Eugene F., born March 13, 1952.
    June Taylor, born December 26, 1953.
    Kevin Victor, born November 15, 1958.

Children of Robert Steven Taylor and Doris:
  David Robert, born July 28 (no year shown).
  Diane Su?, born December 31 (no year shown).
  Dale, born September 28 (no year shown).

Children of Joseph P. Taylor ??

Stephen Ralph Taylor and Buleau Logan Taylor:
  Barbara Taylor, born (no dates shown).
  Stephen Ralph Taylor, born (no dates shown).

WILLIAM TOWNSEND'S RECORD OF GOVEY TOWNSEND

(The Holy Bible containing the Old and New Testaments. Translated out of the original tongue. Stereotyped by James Conner for the American Bible Society. 1828. Bible is owned by Mrs. William Rickards, Lewes, Delaware. Record given by Mrs. Robert Kennedy, Lewes, Delaware.)

Note: Written on the fly leaf:
      WILLIAM J. TOWNSEND.

Govey Townsend and Nancy Sharpley were married
    September 22, 1790.
Rebecca Townsend, daughter of the above parents,
    was born August 22, 1791.
The above mentioned mother died February 17, 1804.
The above mentioned Govey Townsend was married to
    Rebecca Read, August 8, 1804.
Nancey Townsend, daughter of the above mentioned
    parents, was born December 11, 1805.
Betsey Townsend, 2nd daughter of the above
    mentioned parents, was born February 7,
    1808; died October 1810.
John Townsend, first son and 3rd child, was born
    March 27, 1810.
Elizabeth Townsend, 3rd daughter and 4th child of
    above, was born March 3, 1814.
James Townsend, 5th child and 2nd son of above,
    was born May 10, 1817.
Stephen Townsend, 6th child and 3rd son, was
    born September 9, 1820, died October 1823.

- 365 -

Elizabeth Blades, daughter of Nancy the above mentioned, was born May 4, 1821.
Elizabeth Townsend, first daughter of Anna Townsend, was born December 30, 1833.
Nansey Townsend, second daughter of Anna Townsend, was born August 30, 1838.

Note: In the back of the book, Rebecca Townsend her book.
"Stell not this book my onist friends for fear the gallows will be your end."

Govey Townsend died June 4, 1864, age 73 years.
Rebecca Townsend died June 4, 1853, age 72 years.

ELIZAH TYSON & ARABELLA ROSS

(Bible published by Henry F. Cook, 76 W. Baltimore Street, Baltimore. Owned by Mrs. Paul Watkin, 1308 Veale Rd., Wilmington, Del. 1956. Copied by Mrs. Charles Bird, Caesar Rodney Chapter, Wilmington.)

Marriage Certificate

"This is to certify that Mr. Elizah Tyson and Miss Arabella Ross was solemnly United by me in Holy Matrimony at Hopewell, Md., on the Tenth day of November in the year of our Lord One Thousand Eight Hundred and Fifty Six conformably to the Ordinance of God and the Laws of the State. In the presence of Ruban Harlan and Mr. Gallion."

Family Record - Births

Elizah Tyson was born August 27, 1833.
Arabella Ross Tyson was born August 29, 1835.
Hall R. Tyson was born December 20, 1858.
Henerette Tyson was born March 1, 1863.
David E. Tyson was born March 1, 1863.
Mary Bell Tyson was born January 9, 1865.
Sarah T. Tyson was born November 20, 1867.
George Henry Tyson was born January 21, 1869.
William A. Tyson was born September 2, 1871.
Alice R. Tyson was born June 17, 1876.

Helen E. Gamble was born January 26, 1896)
William M. Gamble, Jr. was born Sept. 22, 1900)
    Children of Alice R. Tyson and Wm. M. Gamble.

Deaths

Mary Bell Tyson died April 13, 1882.
Heneretta Keen died October 19, 1898.
Elizah Tyson died April 23, 1904.
Arabella Ross Tyson died March 29, 1919.
Sarah T. Whitson died July 9, 1922.
Hall R. Tyson died 1924.
William E. Tyson died April 28, 1925.
George Henry Tyson died July 23, 1926.
Alice Richardson Tyson Gamble died July 27, 1939.

VANDEVER FAMILY

(Chart by Pauline K. Skinner from data collected from Del. Hist. Magazine, v. 5, 6. 7, and other sources.)

   Capt. Jacob Vandever arrived on the Brandywine 1637/8 on what is known as Vandever Island. He was the first navigator to ever ascend the Brandywine in a vessel of European construction. He made friends with Mattehoven the Indian Chief. He came from Middleburg on the Island of Zeeland, Holland and came as an adventurer, not as a colonist. He died on the Island at the advanced age of 100 years. His will which was probated March 31, 1699 and written in Swedish by the Rev. Ericus Biork, first pastor of Old Swedes Church is dated, written upon the Island North from Christiana the 3 of April 15, 1698 as witness - Ericus Biork, Peist Locs and Asmund Stiddhem. Signed Jacop Ver D'Ver. Wife - Katherine. Children:

Vandever continued next page.

1. John Vandever

2. Cornelius
    Vandever
    Will p. 16 N.C.
    Cal. 1712
    * Margaretta
    Peter Stalcop
    Catherine

    1. John
        Vandever
        d. bef. 5-3-1720
        Sweden   Catharina
        m.
        Maria Stalcop
        d. 11-19-1750
        m. Hans Geo
        Smith   p. 196

*   m. John H. Lerchen-
    Zeiler 4-19-1720

    D.H. v. 5, p. 279

    2. William

    3. Henry

    4. Jacob
        Vandever   1. Jacob
        bur.   See 4. Below

Dr. T. Stiddam
Adam Stidham

    d. 11-16-1739
    Maria Stidham

    D.H. v.5, p. 194
         v.6, p. 53

4. Jacob
    Vandever
    1. Jacob, Bapt. 1714
    2. Magolena, Bapt. 1718
        m. 1735 O.S.
        John Stille, b. 4-22-1727
        son of Jacob & Rebecca Springer
        and son of Andrew ? and
        and Annettje. Rebecca dau. of
        Charles & Maria Hendrickson
    3. Catharine, Bapt. 1721
    4. Elizabeth, Bapt. 1724
    5. Tobias, Bapt. 1728; m. Jane
    6. Peter, Bapt. 1732; Ferry
    7. John
    8. Cornelius
    9. Susan, Bapt. 1730
    10. Adam, d. 1737

Vandever Chart continued:

```
              5. Philip Vandever  (4 wives)
                 d. 8-1750        1. Cornelius
                 m. 1                b. 12-12-1718
                 Elizabeth           O.S. p. 252
                 bur. 2-5-1728    2. Andreas
                 D.H. v.5 p 189      b. 11-25-1719
                 m. 2             3. Elizabeth
                 Brita               m. Peter Smith
                 bur. 11-1-1730      son of Hans G.
                 D.H. v 5 p 191      and Maria Stalcop
                 m. 3             4. Susanna
                 Kirstin             b. 12-25-1726
                 D.H. v 6 p 332   5. Tobias
                 m. 4                b. 10-6-1722
 N.C. Cal        Beata Hopman     6. Maria
 Wills           wid. of John        b. 1-20-1717
 p. 47           Vanneman         7. John
 D.H. p 5                         8. Peter
 v. 7 p 66                        9. Rachel
                                 10. Rebecca


   possibly  6. Elizabeth

             7. Margaretta

             8. Katherine

3.  William Vandever - Inkeeper
    bur. 10-11-1718
    m. Alice Smith, dau. of Francis Smith -
    will 4-26-1712
    will 1731
    m. Samuel Kirk 1-8-1720
    will - all to Alice.  No children.

4.  Jacob
    Vandever  1. John Vandever  1. Judith m.
                 d. 1713            Jonas Stalcop
    Katherine                   2. Ann m. Samuel
                                   Fowdrie
                                3. Catherine m.
              2. Jacob             John Scroffin
                 Vandever      4. Mary m. Henry
                                   Van Nynam
                 Margaret
                 Mansson
```

VANDEVER RECORD

(The Holy Bible published by M. Carey & Son, Philadelphia. 1819. Bible by Peter B. Vandever and Catherine McCullough Vandever. Now owned by Delaware Historical Society, Wilmington. 1957. Record given by Mrs. Alban P. Shaw, Wilmington. 1957.)

Marriages

Married on Tuesday the nineteenth of December eighteen hundred and forty-three (1843) by the Rev'd. Doctor Freeman, Pastor of Immanuel Church at New Castle in the State of Delaware, Peter B. Vandever and Catherina McCullough, both of the said town of New Castle.

Births

Peter B. Vandever was born February 19, 1816.
Catharina McCullough was born November 29, 1822.

Charles M. Vandever, son of Peter B. and Catharina Vandever, was born October 26, 1844.
Henry H. Vandever, son of Peter B. and Catharina Vandever, was born July 26, 1846.
Walter Vandever, son of Peter B. and Catharina Vandever, was born November 28, 1853.
Carrie Vandever, daughter of Peter B. and Catharina Vandever, was born January 28, 1856.
Mary Vandever, daughter of Peter B. and Catharina Vandever, was born December 20, 1857.
Emma Hooton Vandever, daughter of Peter B. and Catharina Vandever, was born December 25, 1861.

Deaths

Henry H. Vandever, son of Peter B. and Catharina Vandever, died January 25, 1854.
Carrie Vandever, daughter of Peter B. and Catharina Vandever, died August 6, 1862.

VANSANT FAMILY BIBLE

(The Illustrated Polyglot Bible, published by J. W. Goodspeed & Co., 87 Park Row, New York. Bible is now owned by the Delaware Historical Society, Wilmington, Del. Copied by Mrs. Alban Shaw.)

Family Bible of:
Mary C. Whaley & Francis VanZant, married February 8,, 1859 from Mrs. Mary V. Donaldson of Palo Alto, Calif.

Marriages

Mary C. Whaley and Francis VanZant were married February 8, 1859.

Births

1. Francis A. Vansant, born December 26, 1859.
2. Harrison J. Vansant, born April 12, 1861.
3. Sadie Vansant, born July 20, 1862. (corrected to 1865)
4. Mariella Vansant, born November 9, 1864.
5. Marian Vansant, born June 1, 1866.
6. William Wirt Vansant, born July 9, 1869.
7. Blanchard Arthur Vansant, born November 20, 1873.
8. Marietta Vansant, born November 9, 1864 (is this the same as Mariella)?
9. Nellie Marie Vansant, born May 7, 1878.

Deaths

Marietta Vansant died July 9, 1865, age 8 months.
Francis A. Vansant died January 29, 1879, age 54 years and 4 months.
Harrison J. Vansant died October 3, 1883, age 22 years and 6 months.

Francis A. Vansant, Jr., died February 7, 1905.
Marion H. Vansant died January 10, 1939.
David K. Donaldson, husband of Nellie May Vansant, died February 1, 1920.
Mary Catherine, wife of Francis A. Sr., died January 22, 1926.
Jennie Green, wife of Wm. W. Vansant, died February 2, 1931.
Sadie L. Vansant died April 2, 1938.

Robert Whaley came from England.
Sarah Harding came from England.

Births:
William Whaley, son of Robert Whaley and Ann his wife, was born February 5, 1820.
Sarah Ann Whaley, daughter of Robert and Sarah his wife, was born Dec. 28, 1827
Thomas Henry Whaley, son of Robert and Sarah Whaley his wife, was born March 27, 1831.
John Whaley, son of Robert and Sarah his wife, was born February 12, 1834.
May Cathern Whaley, daughter of Robert and Sarah his wife, was born August 25, 1838.

Marriages

Robert Whaley and Ann Edingfield were married April 14, 1819.
Robert Whaley and Sarah Hardin were married January 19, 1824.
Grandfather VanZant married Mary Ann Benson January 20, 1820.

This Bible belonged to his son, Francis Asbury Vansant and the children of his wife Mary Catherine Whaley.

Her mother's name was Ann Hardin (? Sarah).
Father's name was Robert Whaley; married January 19, 1824.
Grandfather, Joshua Vanzant, enlisted in War of 1812, came home unhurt.

Vansant continued next page.

Robert
Whaley   William Whaley
b. 2-5-1820

m. 1st 1819
Ann Edingfield

m. 2nd 1824
Sarah
Hardin   Sarah Ann, b. 12-28-1827
Thomas H., b. 3-27-1831
John,   b. 2-12-1834

          Mary C. Whaley
          b. 8-25-1838   Frances,   b. 1859
          d. 1-22-1926   Harrison, b. 1861
Joshua   m. 2-8-1859   Marietta, b. 1864
Vansant   Sadie,   b. 1865
m. 1-20-1820   Marion,   b. 1866
Mary Ann   Francis A.   William,   b. 1869
Benson   Vansant   Blanchard b. 1873
                         Nellie   b. 1878

CORNELIUS VANZANT BIBLE

(Bible was presented to the Delaware Historical Society by Mrs. Mary V. Donaldson, Palo Alto, Calif. Record copied by Mrs. Glenn S. Skinner, Newark, Delaware.)

Cornelis Vanzant was born September 5, 1776. He married Jane Price, who was born February 21, 1781. Their children:

    1.   Elizabeth Vanzant, born August 28, 1804; died November 7, 1805.
    2.   William Vanzant, born October 3, 1806; died September 8, 1809.
    3.   Deborah Vanzant, born December 27, 1808; died January 22, 1809.

         - - - - - - - - -

William Faulkner married first Mary ----. Their son ? Robert Faulkner died August 2, 1836. He married 2nd to Elizabeth ----. Their children:

1. Mary Jane Faulkner, born May 17, 1835; died September 7, 1855.
2. William Robert Cornelius Faulkner, born (no dates shown); died March 28, 1836.

VANZANT BIBLE RECORD

(This record was taken from a Bible presented to the Delaware Historical Society, Wilmington, Delaware. Presented by Mrs. Mary V. Donaldson, Palo Alto, Calif. Copied by Mrs. Glenn S. Skinner, Newark, Delaware.)

Joshua Vanzandt died August 10, 1874 in his 79th year. He married January 20, 1820 Mary Ann Benson, who died May 28, 1862, age 65 years, 9 months and 3 days.
Their children were:
Daniel Nowland Vansant, born October 25, 182-; died December 12, 1821, age 1 year. 1 month and 18 days.
John Hyland Vansant, born April 7, 1822; died May 3, 1822, age 26 days.
Peregrine Ward Vansant, born July 6, 1823; died October 24, 1823, age 3 months and 18 days.
Francis Asbury Vansant, born September 3, 1824; died January 29, 1879, age 54 years and 4 months.
Walter Benson Vansant, born September 14, 1826; died August 12, 1870, age 43 years, 10 months and 29 days.
George Reed Vansant, born January 4, 1829; died February 3, 1888; married 1st Catherine, who died March 19, 1843; married 2nd Anne E. Nowland on December 24, 1873.
Joshua Vansant, born February 1, 1831; died January 15, 1853, age 21 years, 11 months and 17 days.

May Rebecca (twin) born February 1, 1831; died
    February 19, 1831, age 19 days.
Daniel Nowland Vanzandt, born January 23, 1834;
    died June 7, 1834, age 1 year, 4 months
    and 15 days.
Hamilton Marion Vansant, born August 14, 1834?
    1835; died February 11, 1863, age 28
    years, 5 months and 28 days. He married
    Anne E. Nowland on April 16, 1857.
Henrietta Ann Vansant, born March 18, 1836;
    died October 15, 1897, age 61 years.
Mary Louisa Vansant, born January 3, 1838; died
    September 20, 1849, age 11 years, 8 months
    and 17 days.

Children of George Reed Vansant:
    1. Daniel V. Vansant; died March 11, 1843.
    2. Anetta Vansant, born September 30,
        1874; baptized by Rev. E. P.
        Aldred, Pastor of Cecilton, St.
        Paul's Church, John Town 1879.

Children of Hamilton Marion Vansant:
    1. Arrie Rebecca, born September 6, 1858;
        died February 23, 1884; married
        Robert C. Lambert, March 23, 1882.
        They had:

        Arrie J. Lambert, born and died
            1889, age 5 months.
        Mary Louisa, born September 27,
            1891?

SAMUEL WALKER

(Bible printed by Mathew Carey, 122 Market St.,
Philadelphia. MDCCCVIII. Owned by Mrs.
Margaret (Orr) Bradbury, Wilmington, Del. 1957.
Record given by Mrs. Charles Bird.)

Samuel Walker his Bible, Price $5.00 Bot.
    January 6, 1809.
Margaret Walker her Book took the Praisement
    September 24, 1828. Price Two Dollars.

Marriages

Samuel and Jane Walker were married June 2, 1784.
Samuel Walker and Margaret Orr were married June 15, 1820.

Births

Samuel Walker was born 1755.
Jean Walker was born April 6, 1763.

Landed in Wilmington in the year 1788.

Deaths

Jean Walker died July 15, 1817, age 54 years.
Samuel Walker died September 21, 1828.

WALTER FAMILY RECORD

(This record is a copy of a paper in the Bible belonging to William Stidham Goodley. Record was given by Mrs. Charles Bird, Wilmington, Delaware.)

First Generation - Godwin Walter

Godwin Walter arrived at Philadelphia on the ship "Unicorn" December 16, 1685 from Bristol, England. On November 27, 1686 he purchased one hundred acres of land of George Strode for 12 pounds 10 shillings. He married Elizabeth Langhurst, November 2, 1696 by Concord Meeting (Pa.). They had 10 children to wit:

John	Ann	Joseph	James
Mary	William	Elizabeth	
Sarah	Rachel	Lydia	

Second Generation

Of these, William Walter,, born June 8, 1707; died September 20, 1781; married Rachel Newlin, April 25, 1734, daughter of

- 376 -

Nathaniel and Jane Newlin. She died June 9, 1802. He became the owner of the original tract of land and had nine children:

Elizabeth	Thomas	Lydia
John	Hannah	Isaac
William Jr.	Nathaniel	Ruth

Note: For Newlin Record see Vol. VIII, p. 120-21.

Third Generation

Of these, Nathaniel Walter, born March 13, 1745; died December 13, 1805; married Mary Mancil 1766, daughter of William and Elizabeth Mancil, born March 31, 1746; died December 13, 1797. They had 12 children.

Fourth Generation

Of these, their oldest child, Thomas Walter, born May 2, 1767; died January 1832; married Marshall (first name not mentioned).

Fifth Generation

| Thomas, Jr. | Mary | Cidney |

This stone is erected to mark the lot wherein were interred:
Thomas Marshall (son of John Marshall, who emigrated from Elton in Derbyshire, England to Chester Co., Pa.)
Born 12-10-1684 - 1740, age 56.
His son, Thomas Marshall, born 7-26-1727.
His son Thomas Marshall, born 12-8-1756; died 8-13-1844.
His son, Samuel Marshall, born 3-26-1789; died 8-27-1852.

AN ACCOUNT OF REBECCA WARDELL'S FAMILY

(A copy of a hand written paper found in Alfred Bird's Bible. North Burton, Yorkshire, Old England. Scarborough, 1860. Account by Craven Wardell. Recopied by Neice, Ellen E. Lawson, maiden name. Mrs. Ellen Elizabeth Bird, present name.)

Charles Wardell was born April 23, 1790.
Mary Wardell was born July 13, 1791.
John Wardell was born August 16, 1793.
Craven Wardell was born March 12, 1795.
Edward Wardell was born February 25, 1797.

Deaths

Charles died August 20, 1800, age 10 years.
Aunt Mary Craven died February 26, 1824,
    age 79 years.
Aunt Elizabeth Wardell died June 30, ----,
    age 80 years.
Frances Wardell died October 30, 1830,
    age 86 years.
Rebecca Wardell died December 31, ----,
    age 93 years.

- - - - - - - - -

An account of the births of the sons and
    daughters of William and Mary Lawson by
    Ellen E. Bird.
Copy of a handwritten paper found in the Bible
    of A. Bird. He married Ellen Lawson
    December 11, 1850 at Philadelphia.

Jane Lawson, July 25, 1808.
Francis Lawson, born January 21, 1811.
William Lawson, born December 20, 1812.
Charlotte Lawson, born November 18, 1816.
Rebecca Lawson, born November 14, 1819.
John Lawson, born July 20, 1823.
Craven Lawson, born June 18, 1827.
Ellen E. Lawson, born November 5, 1829.
Mary Ann Lawson, born April 29, 1833.

WATERS - KILLINGSWORTH RECORD

(John C. Waters Book. In front is Mr. William Weston Waters name. Bible published by Charles Gatlord, 1832. Now owned by Mrs. Sterling Brinkman.)

Marriages

John C. Waters and Rebecca W. Onion were married November 12, 1812.
Oliver P. Killingsworth and Elizabeth Ann Waters were married September 30, 1838.

Births

Elizabeth Ann Waters, daughter of John C. and Rebecca W. Waters, was born April 28, 1820.
William Weston Waters, son of John C. and Rebecca W. Waters, was born October 12, 1828.
Edwin Colgate Waters, son of John C. and Rebecca W. Waters, was born May 1, 1831.

Deaths

Edwin Colgate Waters, son of John C. and Rebecca W. Waters, died September 9, 1832, age 1 year, 4 months and 8 days.
Departed this life the 16th day of September 1849, our Dearly beloved grandson, William B. Killingsworth, age 2 years, 7 months and 14 days.
Oh My God, may I be as fortunate as to follow those two dear Angels to Heaven where parting will be no more. J.C.W. Sunday night Sept. 16, 1849?

John C. Waters died November 5, 1850, age 62 years.

CLARK WEBSTER & ELIZABETH ABBITT

(Bible published by C. Ewer, T. Bedlington & J.H.A. Frost, Boston. 1828. Owned by Viola (Webster) Derickson, Chads Ford, Pa. 1956.

(Note: Mrs. Derickson said that all of the Websters were born in Delaware). Record given by Mrs. Charles D. Bird.)

FAMILY RECORD

Marriages

Clark Webster and Elizabeth Abbitt were married in Salem County, State of New Jersey, March 23, 1809 by Rev. Nathaniel Chew.
William M. Webster and Lottie W. Edwards were married in Camden, New Jersey on July 22, 1886 by Rev. T. Dobbins.
William Derickson and Mary E. Powell were married in Elam, Pa., August 28, 1947 by Rev. Francis Charlton. Mary 22 and William 24 years.
Clark Webster and Mary Derickson were married August 9, 1911 by Rev. George Wolf.
Viola Webster and Joseph S. Derickson were married January 5, 1921 at Wilmington by Rev. Chas. Bohner.
Arthur E. Webster and Lillian Talley were married March 1920.
Vesta Webster and Lewis Clark were married January 28, 1927.

Births

Clark Webster, son of Thomas and Margaret Webster, was born August 18, 1786.
Elizabeth Abbitt, daughter of John and Rebecca Abbitt, was born September 8, 1790.

Margaret Webster, daughter of Elizabeth and Clark Webster, was born April 3, 1810.
Thomas Webster, son of Clark and Elizabeth Webster, was born June 19, 1812.
Rebecca Webster, daughter of Clark and Elizabeth Webster, was born September 18, 1814.
Mary Webster, daughter of Clark and Elizabeth Webster, was born March 19, 1817.
John Webster, son of Clark and Elizabeth Webster, was born August 6, 1819.
Isaac Webster, son of Clark and Elizabeth Webster, was born October 29, 1821.
Sarah Webster, daughter of Clark and Elizabeth Webster, was born March 5, 1825.

Martha Webster, daughter of Clark and Elizabeth
    Webster, was born June 14, 1827.
Elizabeth Webster, daughter of Clark and
    Elizabeth Webster, was born June 14, 1827.
Jane Ann, daughter of Clark and Elizabeth Webster,
    was born May 4, 1830.
Clark Webster, son of Clark and Elizabeth
    Webster, was born November 16, 1834.

William M. Webster was born December 23, 1863.
Lottie M. Webster was born December 9, 1868.

Children of William and Lottie Webster:
    Clark W. Webster, born October 26, 1887.
    Viola A. Webster, born June 15, 1893.
    William A. Webster, born September 25, 1895.
    Arthur E. Webster, born January 28, 1898.
    Vesta Webster, born October 11, 1903.

Joseph S. Derickson, born June 15, 1883.
Viola W. Derickson, born June 15, 1893.

Children of Joseph and Viola Derickson:
    William J. Derickson, born Oct. 6, 1923.
    Vesta Charlotte Derickson, born May 31,
        1930.
    Willard Derickson, born May 27; died
        May 27, 1934.
    William J. Derickson, born Oct. 6, 1923,
        son of Joseph and Viola Derickson.
    Mary Derickson, born January 27, 1925.

Children of William and Mary Derickson:
    Nancy Derickson, born August 4, 1949.
    Joseph W. Derickson, born March 11, 1956.

Deaths

Thomas Webster, son of Clark and Elizabeth
    Webster, died November 14, 1825, age
    13 years, 3 months and 12 days.
Rebecca Webster, daughter of Clark and Elizabeth
    Webster, died February 2, 1837, age 22
    years, 4 months and 14 days.
Elizabeth, wife of Clark Webster, died April 23,
    1850, age 59 years, 7 months and 15 days.
Jane Ann Perkins, daughter of Clark and
    Elizabeth Webster, died March 1856, age 25
    years, 10 months and 15 days.

Mary Amanda Perkins, daughter of Jane A. Perkins,
    died March 22, ----, age 1 year, 10 months
    and 28 days.
Margaret Lodge, daughter of Clark and Elizabeth
    Webster, died January 10, 1864, age 53
    years, 9 months and 7 days.
Clark Webster, son of Thomas and Mary Webster,
    died February 16, 1874, age 87 years,
    5 months and 29 days.
Mary Webster, daughter of Clark and Elizabeth
    Webster, died August 18, 1884, age
    67 years and 5 months.
John Webster, son of Clark and Elizabeth
    Webster, died June 5, 1896, age 77 years.
Isaac Webster, son of Clark and Elizabeth
    Webster, died January 19, 1897, age
    75 years, 2 months and 23 days.
Elizabeth Bird, daughter of Clark and Elizabeth
    Webster, died May 28, 1895, age 70 (or 71)?
    years.
Clark Webster, son of Clark and Elizabeth
    Webster, died May 17, 1901, age 67 years
    and 6 months.
Martha Webster, daughter of Clark and Elizabeth
    Webster, died February 10, 1908, age
    81 years and 8 months.
Sarah Baldwin, daughter of Clark and Elizabeth
    Webster, died December 29, 1908, age
    83 years, 1 month and 24 days.

Herman Webster, son of Edward and Sarah Webster,
    died October 6, 1918, age -- years,
    4 months and 8 days.
Rebecca A. Webster, wife of Clark Sr., died
    February 27, 1914, age 75 years.
Clark Webster, son of Clark and Rebecca Webster,
    died March 30, 1912, age 38 years.
Edward Webster, son of Clark and Rebecca
    Webster, died June 2, 1913, age 44 years.
Sarah Webster, wife of Edward Webster, died
    July 15, 1911, age 41 years.
Clark W. Webster, son of William and Lottie
    Webster, died April 27, 1926, age 38 years.
William M. Webster, son of Clark and Rebecca
    Webster, died November 15, 1941, age 77
    years and 11 months.
Clark Webster, son of Clark and Mary Webster,
    died March 29, 1937, age 22 years.

Arthur E. Webster, son of William and Lottie
     Webster, died December 16, 1947, age
     49 years and 11 months.
Lottie E. Webster, daughter of James and Mary
     Edwards, died May 1, 1942, age 73 years.
Joseph H. Derickson, son of Jacob and Mary
     Derickson, died December 10, 1942, age
     59 years and 6 months.

ISAAC WEBSTER AND SARAH E. WILSON

(Bible published by Whilt and Yost, Philadelphia,
Pa. 1858. Owned by John C. Webster, Jr.,
Wilmington, Delaware. 1956. Record given by
Mrs. Charles Bird.)

Marriages

Isaac Webster and Sarah Elizabeth Wilson were
     married February 14, 1856.
Cassius C. Webster and Anna Todd were married
     (no dates shown).
Anna Webster and Wm. E. Wamock were married
     (no dates shown).
John C. Webster and Mary P. Connell were
     married (no dates shown).
Lillian C. Webster and Ledru O. Guthrie, Jr.
     were married (no dates shown).
John C. Webster and Rachel Louise Rotthouse
     were married (no dates shown).

Births

Isaac Webster was born October 26, 1821.
Sarah Elizabeth Wilson was born May 17, 1829.
Clark I. Webster was born January 22, 1857.
Cassius Webster was born November 15, 1858.
John C. Webster was born January 20, 1861.
Sarah Elizabeth Webster was born February 20,
     1863.
Isaac Webster, Jr. was born September 1, 1864.
Rachel Anne Webster was born May 6, 1870.
Lillian Connell Webster was born November 10,
     1898.
John Coleman Webster, Jr., was born July 20,
     1901.

Rachel Barbara Webster was born October 11, 1927.
Elaine Bradford Webster was born March 22, 1929.
Joan Louise Webster was born March 17, 1930.
Elizabeth Webster was born January 15, 1936.
Martha Penelope Webster was born July 2, 1942.
Rachel L. Rotthouse was born June 11, 1908.
Marie P. Guthrie was born October 25, 1923.

Deaths

Isaac Webster, son of Isaac and Sarah E. Webster,
    died September 12, 1865.
Isaac Webster Sr., died January 19, 1897.
Clark J. Webster, son of Isaac Webster, Sr.,
    died July 3, 1901.
Sarah Elizabeth Webster, wife of Isaac Webster,
    died July 14, 1901.
John C. Webster died June 21, 1931, age 70
    years and 6 months.

Isaac Webster
b. 10-26-1821   Clark Webster
d. 1-19-1897   b. 1-27-1857
m. 2-14-1856   d. 7-3-1901
Sarah E.   Cassius
Wilson   b. 11-15-1858
b. 5-17-1829   m. Anna Todd
d. 7-14-1901   John C.
                 b. 1-20-1861 John C. Webster Jr.
                 d. 6-21-1931 b. 7-20-1901
                 m.   m.
                 Mary Connell Rachel Rotthouse
                                  b. 6-11-1908
                 Sarah E.
                 b. 2-20-1863
                 Isaac Jr.
                 b. 9-1-1864
                 d. 9-12-1865
                 Rachel A.
                 b. 5-6-1870

ISAAC WELDIN'S BIBLE

Bible was printed by the Executor of David Hay, Assignee of the late Boulter Grierson, Printer to the King's Most Excellent Majesty. 1782.

This Bible belonged to Isaac Weldin who died 1788. It was bequeathed to L. Emma Weldin by her Grandmother, Beulah Weldin. 1879.

It is now owned by Miss Emma Weldin, Weldin Road, Wilmington, Delaware, November 7, 1956.

At the top of the next page is written:
 "Written by Amos Wickersham, Register of Wills of New Castle County."

But the page is entirely blank and the handwriting on the next page is not the same.

George Weldin, son of Jacob & Mary Weldin, was
 born January 10, 1796.
Beulah Ann Pettit, daughter of Peter and Mary
 Pettit, was born October 16, 1804.

George Weldin and Beulah Ann Pettit were married
 July 1, 1824.

Mary Weldin, daughter of George and Beulah Ann
 Weldin, was born March 4, 1825.
Charles Pettit Weldin, son of George and Beulah
 Ann Weldin, was born August 11, 1827.
Sarah Campbell Weldin, daughter of George and
 Beulah Ann Weldin, was born Sepember 25, 1829.
Beulah Weldin, daughter of George and Beulah Ann
 Weldin, was born November 7, 1831.
Eliza and Hannah Weldin, daughters of George and
 Beulah Ann Weldin, were born November 11,
 1833.
Lydia Ann Weldin, daughter of George and Beulah
 Ann Weldin, was born October 2, 1835.
Rebecca Weldin, daughter of George and Beulah Ann
 Weldin, was born March 17, 1838.
George Washington, son of George and Beulah Ann
 Weldin, was born November 7, 1840.

Children of Isaac Weldin.

Elizabeth Weldin was born June 27, 1752.
George Weldin was born December 29, 1753.
Mabel Weldin was born July 13, 1755.
Eli Weldin was born April 1, 1757.
Margaret Weldin was born January 29, 1759;
    died 1843.
Jacob Weldin was born December 14, 1760.
Sarah Weldin was born November 22, 1762.
Mary Weldin was born November 6, 1764.

Elizabeth Weldin died June 26, 1775.

Isaac Weldin Chart.

```
1.
Isaac Weldin      2.
b.                1.  Elizabeth
d. 1788               b. 6-27-1752
m.                    d. 6-26-1775
_____       2.  George
                      b. 12-29-1753
                      d.
                  3.  Mabel
                      b. 7-13-1755
                      d.
                  4.  Eli
                      b. 3-1-1757
                      d.
                  5.  Margaret
                      b. 1-29-1759
                      d.
                  6.  Jacob Weldin       3.
                      b. 12-14-1760      1. Isaac Weldin
                      d. 11-26-1844         b. 10-17-1790
                      m.                    d. 5-2-1836
                      Mary               2. John A.
                      b.                    Weldin
                      d. 3-31-1839          b. 9-27-1792
                  7.  Sarah                 d. 10-13-1833
                      b. 11-22-1762     *3. George
                      d.                    Weldin
                  8.  Mary
                      b. 11-6-1764          See 4. below
```

Isaac Weldin chart continued next page.

*3. George Weldin
   b. 1-10-1796
   d. 11-5-1850
   m. 7-1-1824
   Beulah A. Pettit
   b. 10-16-1804
   dau. of Peter &
   Mary Pettit

4.
1. Mary Weldin
   b. 3-4-1825
2. Charles
   b. 8-11-1827
3. Sarah
   b. 9-25-1829
4. Beulah
   b. 11-7-1831
5. Eliza
   b. 11-11-1833
6. Lydia
   b. 10-2-1835
7. Rebecca
   b. 3-17-1838
8. George
   b. 11-7-1840

Children of George W. Weldin and Eliza J.

Harry Manship Weldin was born November 4, 1866; married Janice E. Talley; born April 12, 1878 - no issue.
Estelle Jane (Weldin) Robinson, born Ocober 18, 1867; married William F. Robinson, born December 8, 1867.
Beulah May (Weldin) Missimer, born May 8, 1869; married Warren Pyle Missimer, born December 11, 1867.
Lillian Emma Weldin, born February 28, 1871.
Lewis Weldin, born May 21, 187?; died 11-25-1875.
Sallie Harriett Weldin, born October 21, 1873; died November 25, 1875.
Charles Pettit Weldin, born April 11, 1875.
George Harriott Weldin, born February 18, 1877.
Winifred Weldin, born February 5, 1879.
Bertha Weldin, born July 26, 1881; died June 15, 1909.
Florence Hammersly (Weldin) Fennimore, born July 31, 1884; married George Harlan Fennimore, born August 18, 1881.

Above recorded by Albert Watson Pettit, November 8, 1932.

Deaths

George Weldin, son of Jacob and Mary Weldin, died
    November 5, 1850, age 54 years and 10 months.
Charles P. Weldin, son of George and Beulah A.
    Weldin, died August 6, 1828, age 1 year.
Beulah Weldin, daughter of George and Beulah A.
    Weldin, died July 1, 1844, age 13 years and
    6 months.
Eliza and Hannah Weldin, daughters of George and
    Beulah A. Weldin, died 1834. Aged 7 and
    9 months.
Maria Ellma Weldin, daughter of George and Beulah
    A. Weldin, died March 3, 1844, age 11 months.

Isaac Weldin, son of Jacob and Mary Weldin, was
    born October 17, 1790.
John A. Weldin, second son of Jacob and Mary
    Weldin, was born September 27, 1792.
George Weldin, son of Jacob and Mary Weldin, was
    born January 10, 1796.

John A. Weldin, son of Jacob and Mary Weldin, died
    October 13, 1833, age 41 years and 17 days.
Isaac Weldin, son of Jacob and Mary Weldin, died
    May 2, 1836, age 45 years, 6 months and
    15 days.

Sacred to the Memory of Mary Weldin, wife of
    Jacob Weldin, who departed this life
    March 31, 1839.

In Memory of Jacob Weldin who departed this life
    November 26, 1844, age 83 years, 11 months
    and 12 days.

(Record given by Mrs. Charles Bird.)

EXACT COPY OF WILL OF REBECCA WESTON - 1812

In the name of God. Amen. I, Rebecca Weston of
Harford Co. in the state of Maryland, do make and
declare this my last will and testament, hereby
revoking all wills by me heretofore made.

Item. I give and devise to my daughter Elizabeth Onion the sum of two thousand four hundred dollars, to be paid to her in cash immediately after my decease.

I give and devise to my granddaughter Rebecca Weston Onion the sum of thirteen hundred and thirty-three dollars to be paid to her at my decease. I give her this sum of money in lieu of a tract of land in Baltimore County which I had intended to have given her and which is now otherwise disposed of by me.

I give and bequeath to my grandson John Weston Onion the sum of four hundred dollars in cash. I give and bequeath to my grandson Lloyd Day Onion the sum of four hundred dollars in cash.

I give and bequeath to my granddaughter Hannah Juliet Onion the sum of four hundred dollars in cash.

Item. I give and bequeath to my grandson Beals Onion the sum of four hundred dollars in cash.

Item. I give and bequeath to my other granddaughter Rebecca Young Day the sum of one hundred dollars in cash and a small silver can and one dozen china plates to her and her heirs forever.

Item. I give and devise to my grandson Edward Augustus Day one tract of land lying on the waters of the Gunpowder and Bird River in Baltimore County nearly opposite Joppa, called Long Point containing forty-nine acres more or less, to him and his heirs forever.

Item. I give and devise to my grandson William Young Day the sum of one hundred dollars in cash. I also give and devise to my grandson John Young Day the sum of one hundred dollars in cash.

Item. I give and bequeath to my son Lloyd Day one piece of gold called a Joe of the value of sixteen dollars. I give him this as a small token of my love and affection for him that he may remember me, as I know he is not in a situation to want any property I can give him being already well provided for, I give him this and no more of my estate.

Item. I now give and bequeath all the remainder of my estate not already devised to my daughter Elizabeth Onion and all her children to be equally divided amongst them after my decease.

In witness where of I have herewith set my hand and seal this twenty-ninth day of May in the year of Our Lord Eighteen hundred and twelve.

      Signed, Rebecca Weston

Witnesses

Isaac Hollingsworh
John Mason
Benjamin Devall

Probated
Third December 1812

GEORGE W. & MARY E. WILSON

(Bible published by Whilt & Yost, Philadelphia. Owned by Frank L. Wilson, New Castle, Delaware. He is the father of Jessie (Wilson) Lunt (Mrs. Buford) of New Castle. Record given by Mrs. Charles D. Bird, Wilmington, Delaware.)

Marriages

George W. Wilson and Mary E. Simons were married July 27, 1869 by Rev. S. E. Smith in the presence of numerous witnesses. (Mr. Wilson has the original certificate framed.)

Births

George W. Wilson, born December 24, 1839.
Mary E. Simons, born February 18, 1842.
Samuel Simons Wilson, born February 18, 1870.
George W. Wilson Jr., born September 10, 1871.
Albert Hoopes Wilson, born November 23, 1872.
Thomas Paul Wilson, born September 17, 1874.

Sarah Matsinger Wilson, born July 7, 1876.
Frank Leshem Wilson, born August 30, 1878.
Margaret Wey---? Wilson, born August 3, 1880.
Ella Worth Wilson, born April 9, 1882.

Deaths

George W. Wilson Jr., died December 28, 1877,
    age 6 years, ? months and 18 days.
George W. Wilson Esq., died July 16, 1883, age
    43 years, 7 months and 13 days.
Mary E. Wilson, died May 19, 1893, age 51 years,
    ? months and 1 day.
Samuel S. Wilson, died December 7, 1943, age
    73 years and 11 months.

1.
Geo. W.
Wilson
b. 12-3-1839
d. 7-16-1883
m. 7-27-1869
Mary E. Simons
b. 2-18-1842
d. 5-19-1893

2.
1. Samuel
   b. 2-18-1870
2. George Jr.
   b. 9-10-1871
   d. 1877
3. Albert H.
   b. 11-23-1872
4. Thomas P.
   b. 9-17-1874
5. Sarah
   b. 7-7-1876
6. Frank Wilson
   b. 8-30-1878
   m.
   _____
7. Margaret
   b. 8-3-1880
8. Ella
   b. 4-9-1882

3.
Jessie
Wilson
m.
Buford
Lunt
b.
4-9-1901

4.
Ira C. Lunt
b. 11-30-1937
m.
Ruth

CHARLES I. WILLIAMS & ELIZA EDWARDS

(Hitchcock's New and Complete Analysis of the Holy Bible. Published by A. J. Johnson, 276 Mulberry St., New York. MDCCCLXXI. Owned by Edward B. Grubb, Holly Oak, Del. 1956. Record given by Mrs. Charles Bird.)

Mrs. Eliza Williams, Claymont, Delaware.

Marriages

Charles I. Williams and Eliza Edwards were
    married June 22, 1854.
Annie E. Williams and Edward Grubb were married
    April 15, 1874.
John L. Bird and Georgiana Williams were
    married July 13, 1882.
Chas. H. Williams and Mary A. Morris were
    married May 28, 1900.

Births

Charles I. Williams, born April 9, 1830.
Eliza Edwards, born December 14, 1831.

Ann Eliza Williams, born December 2, 1856.
Amanda Mary Williams, born March 12, 1857.
Grace Elizabeth Williams, born October 25, 1858.
Emma Lodge Williams, born April 7, 1860.
Georgiana Williams, born February 24, 1862.
Theophilus Williams, born June 26, 1864.
Rachel Jane Williams, born September 26, 1867.
Charles Henry Williams, born May 26, 1870.

Edward Bunn Grubb, born January 28, 1875.
Charles Henry Grubb, born February 7, 1877.
Mary Sheperson Grubb, born September 17, 1879.
Ellen Sloan Grubb, born November 17, 1880.

Mattie Arnold Williams, born February 20, 1887.
Elsie Bird, born April 19, 1890.
Lillian Bird, born April 5, 1892.

Deaths

Charles I. Williams died March 19, 1871.
Amanda Mary Williams died October 11, 1866.
Grace Elizabeth died September 7, 1882.
Eliza Williams died June 12, 1887.
Chas. H. Williams died May 21, 1901.

Note: Elsie and Lillian Bird are daughters of William Bird and Rachel Jane Williams. Two brothers married sisters.

WINSOR-BULLOCK BIBLE

(This Bible is owned by Miss A. Louise Matthews of Rodney Court Apts., 1100 Penn. Ave., Wilmington, Delaware. Published, 126 Chestnut St., Philadelphia. Printed by M. Carey & Son. 1818.)

Marriages

Nicholas Winsor and Mary Bullock were married
    September 2, 1789.
Nathan C. Lewis and Louise Winsor were married
    May 25, 1818.

Children:

Mary Bullock and Ezra Baker in Seekonk,
    June 18, 1843.
Nathan Child and Nancy Waria Rice.
Silvanus G. Martin and Mary Jane Seagrave in
    Province, R.I., September 18, 1854.

Maria Louise and Benjamin W. Parsons,
    November 17, 1856.
Eliza Bullock and Jesse W. Denison in Providence,
    R.I., August 3, 1859.
John Child and Patience Andrews Palmer in
    Providence, R.I., November 23, 1859.

Births

Nicholas Winsor, born March 4, 1867 ? (1767?)
    (The date 1867 has been changed in ink to
    1767).
Mary Bullock, born November 13, 1768.

Their first child, Mary, was born September 8,
    1790.
Second child, Obil Anson, was born March 12, 1792.
Third child, William Bullock, was born
    December 24, 1793.
Fourth child, Louise, was born March 21, 1796.

- - - - - - - - - -

Nathan Child Lewis was born December 18, 1790.
Louisa Winsor was born March 21, 1796.

Their first child, Mary Bullock, was born
    February 27, 1819.
Second child, William, was born March 10, 1821.
Third child, Nicholas Winsor, was born
    May 7, 1823.
Fourth child, Nathan Child, was born August 23,
    1824.
Fifth child, Silvanus G. Martin, was born
    January 11, 1827.
Sixth child, John Child, was born April 15, 1829.
Seventh child, Maria Louisa, was born
    October 5, 1831.
Eighth child, Eliza Bullock, was born
    October 24, 1834.
Ninth child, William Wins, was born
    November 10, 1839.

Deaths

Nicholas Winsor died July 24, 1822, age 11 weeks.
William Lewis died February 7, 1833.
William Winsor Lewis died November 3, 1854.
Nathan Child Lewis, died September 13, 1868.
Mary Bullock Baker, wife of Ezra, died
    February 28, 1878.
Nathan Child Lewis Jr., died in Boston,
    May 1, 1885.
Nancy Maria Rice Lewis died in South Woodstock,
    Conn., February 14, 1887.

Nathan Lewis Baker, son of Ezra and Mary B. Baker,
    died in East Province, August 9, 1870.
Mary B. Baker, wife of Ezra Baker, died
    February 28, 1876.
Nicholas Winsor, son of Ezra and Mary B. Baker,
    died in East Providence, January 10, 1885.
Ezra Baker died in East Providence, March 30,
    1886.
Jesse W. Denison died in Denison, Iowa,
    October 2, 1881.
Louisa W. Lewis, daughter of N. C. Lewis Jr.,
    died in Medford, Mass., December 18, 1926.

Nicholas Winsor died August 20, 1797, age 30 years.
Mary, wife of Nicholas Winsor, died
    February 4, 1816.
Nathan Child Lewis died September 13, 1868.
Louisa Winsor Lewis died March 5, 1887.
Patience Andrews Lewis died (no dates shown).
Sylvanus G. Martine Lewis died (no dates shown).
Mary Jane Lewis died (no dates shown).
Maria Louisa Persons died January 12, 1906.
John Child Lewis died (no dates shown).
Benjamin W. Persons died February 1914.

1.
Nicholas Winsor
b. 3-4-1767
d. 8-20-1797?
m. 9-2-1789
Mary Bullock
b. 11-13-1768
d. 2-4-1816

2.
1. Mary
2. Obil Anson
3. William
4. Louisa Winsor   See 3.
   b. 3-21-1796   Below
   d. 3-5-1887
   m. 5-25-1818
   Nathan C. Lewis
   b. 12-18-1790
   d. 9-13-1868?

3.
1. Mary Bullock; m. Ezra Baker
2. William
3. Nicholas
4. Nathan C.; m. Nancy Maria Rice
5. Silvanus G. Martin; m. Mary Hane Seagrave
6. John Child
7. Maria Louisa; m. Benjamin W. Persons
8. Eliza Bullock
9. William Winsor

Chart continued next page.

Thomas Denison
4.
J. W. Denison
b. 4-9-1818
Bern, Albany, N.Y.
m. 1st
Mary W. Briggs
b. 1-1-1822
d. 1855
m. 2nd
8-3-1859

Nathan

Eliza B. Lewis
b. 10-24-1834

5.
1. Mary Louise Denison
   b. 12-5-1848
   m. Thomas Hooker
2. Julia Porter Denison
   b. 12-5-1848
   m. Rev. Albert W. Duboc
   m.
   Wm. Chipman Matthews
   b. 5-31-1861
   d. 9-30-1928
   m.
3. Maria Louisa
   b. 8-17-1866
   d. 3-15-1945

4. Jesse Lewis
   b. 5-13-1876

5. Percy Nightingale
   b. 1-19-1881
   m. Isobelle Stimmel

6.
1. Adaline Louise
   b. 4-7-1886
2. Margaret
3. Paul Denison Matthews
   b. 1-21-1896, Denver Colo.
   m.
   Mildred McCardell, Wilmington

7.
Paul Denison Matthews, Jr.
b. 12-17-1918, Wilmington
m.
Cecilia Riley, Wilmington

Ch: 1. David Cameron Matthews
       b. 10-4-1939
    2. Claire Louise
       b. 8-31-1940
    3. Elaine Matthews
       b. 8-1-1943

WOLFE FAMILY RECORD

(Data taken from three large old sheets of paper in the possession of Fred C. Wolfe, Jr., Lewes, Delaware. Record given by Mrs. D. A. Potter.)

William S. Wolfe, son of Reece Wolfe, was married to Mary J. Virden, daughter of Mitchel Virden, January 29, 1846.
William Smith Wolfe, son of Reece Wolfe and Maretta Wolfe, was born October 14, 1822.
Mary Jane Wolfe, daughter of Mitchel and Ellen Virden. This wife was born December 19, 1822.
Benjamin C. Wolfe, son of William S. and Mary J. Wolfe, was born October 3, 1847; died July 28, 1904. (This death notice is in different type of pencil but handwriting is the same.)
Samuel Cornelius Wolfe, son of William S. and Mary J. Wolfe, was born January 19, 1850.
William Cornelius Wolfe, son of William S. and Mary J. Wolfe, was born October 19, 1852; died December 23, 1923.
John White Wolfe, son of William S. and Mary J. Wolfe, was born September 5, 1854.
Clifford Paynter Wolfe was born February 3, 1857.
Frank Henry Wolfe was born August 31, 1858.

(This next entry was inserted later)
Mary Cornelia Wolfe was born June 4, 1850 (?); died 5-23-1926.

Lizzie E. Wharton, daughter of John Wharton and Elizabeth his wife, was born January 22, 1840; married William S. Wolfe, December 1, 1867.
Mary Wolfe, daughter of William S. and Lizzie E. Wolfe his wife, was born September 10, 1868.
John Wolfe, son of William S. and Lizzie E. Wolfe his wife, was born August 9, 1870.
Reece B. Wolfe, son of William S. and Lizzie his wife, was born January 16, 1873; died February 11, age 1 month and 5 days.
Lizzie Wolfe, daughter of William S. Wolfe and Lizzie his wife, was born April 3, 1874.

Charles F. Wolfe, son of William S. Wolfe and
    Lizzie his wife, was born December 1, 1877.

Louis ? Wolfe, son of William C. and Louise Wolfe
    his wife, was born February 9, 1884.
Louis H. Wolfe, son of William C. Wolfe, married
    Effie L. Murphy, daughter of Orlando and
    Ella Murphy, February 26, 1903.
Ella Louise Wolfe, daughter of Louis H. and Effie
    L. Wolfe, was born April 4, 1910; died
    September 22, 1916.
Louis H. Wolfe Jr., son of Louis H. and Effie L.
    Wolfe, was born January 1, 1912; died at
    birth.

THOMAS WOLVERTON - REBECCA CRAWFORD

(Bible was printed and published by William W. Woodward, 2nd & Chestnut Streets, Philadelphia, Pa. 1814. Owned by Mrs. Gerald L. Montague (nee Edith Neal), Claymont. Record given by Mrs. Charles D. Bird. Both are members of Caesar Rodney Chapter, N.S.D.A.R., Wilmington, Del.)

Marriages

Thomas Wolverton and Rebecca Crawford were married
    March 1, 1827.
John R. McMiller (McC.Miller) and Mary Wolverton
    were married November 2, 1848; daughter of
    Thomas and Rebecca Woolverton.
George W. Aydelott and Ann Woolverton were married
    October 24, 1850.
Henry C. Jerome and Isabella Jane Woolverton were
    married November 2, 1855.
Joseph M. Neal and Elizabeth Woolverton were
    married November 6, 1873. Joseph M. Neal
    was born in Gallis County, Ohio.

Births

Mary Woolverton was born July 25, 1772.
Thomas Woolverton was born February 23, 1794,
    in Pennsylvania near Uniontown.
Rebecca Crawford Woolverton was born December 6,
    1810 in Hamilton, Ohio.

Mary Woolverton was born February 5, 1828 in
    Parke County, Indiana.
Ann Woolverton was born February 19, 1830 in
    Parke County, Indiana.
John Woolverton was born July 2, 1832 in
    Parke County, Indiana.
Isabella Jane Woolverton was born October 28,
    1834 in Parke County, Indiana.
Sarah Woolverton was born December 11, 1836
    in Parke County, Indiana.
Eleanor Woolverton was born February 3, 1838
    in Parke County, Indiana.
William Woolverton was born August 2, 1840
    in Parke County, Indiana.
James Woolverton was born October 1, 1842
    in Parke County, Indiana.
Thomas J. Woolverton was born January 20, 1845
    in Parke County, Indiana.
Elizabeth Woolverton was born January 24, 1848
    in Parke County, Indiana.

Deaths

Mary Woolverton Sen. died March 18, 1850.
Thomas Woolverton died July 20, 1849.
Sarah Woolverton died March 20, 1837.
Isabella Jane Jerome died August 15, 1857.
Henry C. Jerome died April 5, 1856.
William Woolverton died June 20, 1862.
Thomas Woolverton died November 15, 1862.
John Woolverton died October 11, 1872.
Rebecca Woolverton died June 13, 1893.
Eleanor Woolverton died December 1, 1893.
Elizabeth Neal died February 12, 1904.
James Woolverton died May 11, 1922.

George Duncan Neal, son of Joseph M. Neal and
    Elizabeth Woolverton, was born November 27,
    1879 in Parke Co., Indiana; died
    February 20, 1949 in Chestter, Pa.

George Duncan Neal and Carrie Amelia Swain were
    married December 27, 1905.

Carrie Amelia Swain was born February 8, 1881 in
    Bellmore, Indiana.

Children of George Duncan Neal and Carrie Amelia
Swain:
    Joseph Duncan Neal, born September 27,
        1906, Parke County, Indiana.
    John Edwin Neal, born February 12, 1914,
        Parke County, Indiana.
    Edith Neal, born January 29, 1922,
        Parke County, Indiana.

Joseph Duncan Neal and Louise McCarns were married
January 21, 1925. Their two sons:
    Joseph Duncan Neal, born June 7, 1925;
        died November 3, 1929.
    George Duncan Neal, born June 17, 1928;
        married Ruth Weichardt, Jan. 27, 1951.

    Children:
        Deborah Lynn Neal, born Nov. 10, 1951
        Donna Lynn Neal, born NOv. 16, 1954

John Edwin Neal and Della Lois Hopkins were
    married September 21, 1935. Children:
        Nancy Carrie Neal, born Feb. 13, 1946
        David John Neal, born Jan. 3, 1950
        Susan May Neal, born May 26, 1952;
            died June 26, 1954.

Edith Neal and Gerald Lawrence Montague were
    married 6-15-1946. Children:
        Patricia Neal Montague, born
            April 10, 1951.
        (Is a member of Blue Hen's Chicken
        Chapter of C. A. R.)

CHRISTOPHER & HANNAH YOEST

Christopher and Hannah Yoest were married July 12, 1781.

Mary Yoest was born May 31, 1782.
Rachel Yoest was born June 26, 1784; died June 30, 1784.

Hannah Yoest died July 2, 1784.

Christopher and Rebekah Yoest were married February 7, 1786.

Doratha Yoest was born December 31, 1786; died January 9, 1787.
Charles Yoest was born January 21, 1788.
John Yoest was born April 21, 1790.
George Himes Yoest was born September 7, 1792.

Rebekah yoest died October 20, 1793.
George Himes Yoest died October 29, 1793.

INDEX

ABBITT
   Elizabeth 379; John 380; Rebecca 380.

ABLE
   Bertha 362

ACRES
   Hannah 322; Henry 321, 322, 328.

ADAMS
   Charlotty 1; Corelay (ius) 1; Donald W. 202;
   Elizabeth 1; Henry 1; Hester Ann 1; James 1;
   Jane 33, 34; John Henry 1; Margaret 34;
   Martha 34; Mary 34; Mary R. 285; Peter 1;
   R. H. 285; Stansberry 1.

AIKENS
   Anna Susan 27.

ALBITE
   Vesta 132.

ALDERSON
   G. T., Rev. 257.

ALDRED
   Alice 2; Betty 2; Ellen 2, 3; E.P., Rev. 375;
   Hannah 2; John 2,3; Lydia 3; Margaret 2;
   Mary 2, 3; Richard 3; Sarah 2, 3; Thomas
   Jefferson 3; William 2, 3.

ALEXANDER
   Marvey T., Mrs. 246.

ALLEN
   Benjamin 120; Ella 137; Ellen A. 136;
   Ellie 120; Emery 119; G. S., Rev. 184;
   Hannah 120; Jane 119; John 119, 120;
   Joseph 120; Matthew 198; Sarah 119, 120,
   199; William 119, 120, 197.

ALLERDICE
    Abram (Abrahm) (Abraham) 3,4,5; Alphonso 5;
    Anna T. 3, 4; Eliza 4, 5; Gilbert, Rev. Dr. 4;
    James 4, 5; James Henry 4; Jane 5; Jane E. 4;
    Jane Eliza 4, 5; John 4; John A. 4, 5;
    John Alphonso 4, 5; Joseph 3, 4, 5; Joseph
    Emmor 4; Mary C. 5; Mary Caroline 4; Ruth 4,
    5; Sarah 5; William 5; William Hilary 4.

ALLEY
    Sara 322; Thomas 321, 328.

ALLMOND (ALLMON - ALLEMOND)
    Amer Bayard 8; Anna Maria 8; Barbara 6;
    Benjamin 6; Beulah 63; Beulah Ann 7; Beulah
    Caroline 8; Elizabeth 7; Elizabeth Jane 7;
    Henrietta Matilda 8; John 6, 7, 63, 64;
    John Bary 7; John Grubb, Jr. 7; Joseph 6, 7;
    Lydia 7; Margarette 6; Mary 6, 7; Solomon 6;
    Thomas 6; William 6.

ANDERSON
    Ann 11, 12; Ann Elizabeth 10; Catherine 11;
    Cathron 9, 10; Christopher 340; Eliza 11;
    Elizabeth 11; Emily 10; George Washington 10;
    Jacob 11; James 10; James C. 9, 10; John 9,
    10, 11, 12; John Soulsbury 10; Joseph B. 10;
    Lavania (Levenia) 10; Lizey 10; Lydia 340,
    342; Margarett 10; Mary 11; Mary Ann 10;
    Martha 241; Melinda 54; Rebecca 11, 12;
    Sally Ann 10; Sarah 9, 10, 11; Susannah 11,
    12; William Henry 10; William Smith 11.

ANDRE (ANDREW)
    James Ridgeway, Dr. 242.

ANDREWS
    Mabel 202.

ARNT
    Elizabeth 349.

ARTERS
    Rev. J. 298.

ARTHINGTON
    Mary 147.

ARTHUR
    John 211.

ASH
    Allen 15; Amanda 14, 15; Charles G. 15;
    Charles Granville 15; Cornelia 14, 15;
    Emma Louise 15; George 14, 15; George C. 14,
    15; John 14, 15; John P. 15; Laura C. 15;
    Louise 14; Mathew 145; Matilda 14; Robert 15;
    Ruth Ann 14, 15; Susan 14, 15; Thomas 15.

ASHBRIDGE
    George 16; Jane 16; Lydia 16; Mary 16; Phoebe
    16; Rebecca 16; Susanna 16, 144; William 16.

ASHCRAFT
    Rhoda 204.

ATKINS
    Allen R. 18; Arcada (Arcadia) 17, 18, 19;
    Arcada E. L. 18, 19; David 17; George W. 17,
    19; Henry W. 18, 19; Isaac 17, 19; John S.
    17, 18, 19; Joseph C. 17, 18, 19; Leah 17,
    18, 19; Lydia 17, 18, 19; Peter Edward Page
    18, 19; Sarah 17, 18, 19; Thomas C. 17, 18,
    19; Thomas J. 17, 18, 19.

ATKINSON
    Annie 241.

ATWOOD
    Anthony, REv. 93.

AYDELOTT
    George W. 398.

BABB
    Ann 20, 21; Bethsheba 19; Caleb 21; Emma F.
    20, 21; Hannah 20, 21; Jacob 21; John 19, 20,
    21; John W. 19, 20; Lydia 19, 20, 21; Lydia
    Clark 20, 21; Mary P. 20, 21; Matilda 64;
    Peter 19; Phebe H. 19, 20; Rebecca S. 20, 21;
    Samson 19, 20, 21; Sarah E. 20; Thomas 20,
    21, 64, 177; Thomas C. 20; Thomas Sr. 19;
    Wm. H. 20, 21.

BACON
    Amelia 22; Amelia (Scales) 163; Cecil
    Williams 22; George W. 163; George Williams
    22, 309; Herbert 22; Millie Frances 22, 163,
    221, 248, 308.

BAILEY (BAILY)
    Ann Elizabeth 23, 24; Brandt 24; Brandt
    VanBlarcom 23; Edith Pritchett 22, 23, 24;
    Edward 24; Edward T. 23; Elizabeth 23, 24,
    345, 346; George William 23, 24; James 24;
    James Edward 23; Jane 23, 24; Jennie C. 343,
    344, 346; John Gideon 327; Joseph 23, 24;
    Joseph Hatton 23, 24; Joseph T. 22, 23,
    24; Joseph T. Jr.23; Littleton R. 345, 346;
    Priscilla 22, 23, 24; Sidney 24; Sidney Ann
    23; Susan 123, 125; Tatnall 23, 24; William
    P. 24; William Pritchett 23.

BAKER
    Ezra 393, 395; Lewis, Rev. 206; Mary 395;
    Mary Bullock 394, 395; Nathan Lewis 395;
    Nicholas Winsor 395.

BALDWIN
    Catherine 233; C. W. 356; Clark W. 357;
    Elizabeth 351; Fred J. 351; George D. 351;
    John, Col. 233, 237; Johnson 351; Johnson C.
    349; Sarah 382; Warren 351.

BALL
    Mary 339, 342.

BALLANCE
    John 194.

BALYS (BALYE)
    Elenor 189, 190.

BAMBERGER
    Alice Marie 276; Leslie L. 276; Mrs. 123.

BANCROFT
    Elizabeth H. 234; R. H. 234; Rachel 70;
    Rebecca 70; Robert 70, 235; William 70;
    William Woodcock 70.

BARBER
    Emma 232; John 232.

BARCUS
Anna 28; Anna Bell 27, 28; Anna Susan 27; Daisy May 27; Edna 25; Edna P. 26; Edna R. 27; Edward 28; Gilbert Laben 25; James Herman 27; John E. 25, 26; John Edgar 26, 27, 28; Laura Etta 27, 28; Martha Ellen 27, 28; Mary Elizabeth 27, 28; P.L. 28; Peter L. 26, 27, 28; Peter L. Sr., 28; Peter L. Jr. 27; Peter Laban 26, 27; Rebecca L. 25, 26; Rebecca Louise 25; Richia Ann 27; Sarah A. 25, 26, 28; Sarah Ann 26, 27, 28; Sarah Emily 27, 28; Viola L. 26; W. E. E. 25, 27; William Elmer Ellsworth 27, 28, 29; William Herman 25, 26.

BARLOW
Anna E. 31; Ann Eliza 30, 31; Annie 231; Annie E. 226; Clara 31; Clara Bell C. 29; D. Elizabeth 33; Eliza 31; Eliza Ella 29; Eliza F. 30, 31; Eliza L. 29; Ella G. 33; Emma L. 30, 31; Emmor L. 30, 31; Esher Anna 32; Esther 32; Esther A. 33; Estella 30, 31; George 31; George Taylor 29; Hannah 31; Hannah R. 30, 31; Harry M. 33; Henry 32; Henry M. 29, 30, 31; Henry Myers 32; James W. 32, 33; James Wilson 33; Levenia H. L. 32, 33; Lydia 31; Lydia Ann 30, 31, 240; Maggie W. 29; Malachi 29, 30, 31; Margaret 31; Margaretta 30, 31; Margaretta Wilson 29; Mary E. 29, 31, 33, 359; Mary Emma 29; Mary J. 31; Mary Jane 30; Phebe E. 31; Phebe Ella 30, 31; Raymond 32; Raymond H. 33; Raymond Hanby 32; Rebecca 33; Sara E. 30, 31; Susanna 31; Susanna T. 30; William G. 32, 33; William Gilbert 33; William L. 31, 32, 33, 160; William Lewis 29.

BARNES
Madaline G. 282.

BARNITZ
Alexander Hamilton 165; Ann Grier 166; Anna Marie 165; Charles 164, 167; Charles A. 164, 165, 167; Charles Jacob 166; David Grier 166; Geroeg Washington 165; Jacob 164,165; Jane Grier 166, 167; Margaret 167; Mary 165;

BARNITZ Cont'd.
Mary McClean 166, 168; McPherson 166; Rebecca 165; Samuel McClean 165; Sarah Rebecca 164, 166; William 165.

BARR
Elizabeth 33, 34; Eugene 33, 34; Eugene W. 33, 34; Franklin 33, 34; Jane 33, 34; John Adams 33; Joseph M. 33, 34; Marion 33, 34; Martin 33, 34; Mary 34; Mary Adams 34; Mary Chambers 33, 34; Robert L. 169; Virginia 33, 34; William 34; William H. 33.

BARRETT (BARRATT)
Alice C. 239; Anna 239; Joseph P. 239; L. E., Rev. 162; Maud N. 239.

BARTLETT
Richard 325; Susanna 325.

BARTON
Thos., Rev. 311.

BASSETT
Hannah 174, 200; Joseph 35; William 35.

BATCHELDER
Rev. Stephen 176; Theodate 176.

BAUMGARDNER
Paul W. 140.

BAYLEY
Jonathan 321; Nathaniel 321.

BAYLIS
Samuel 189, 190.

BEALE
Hannah Ann 331; Wm. H. 330.

BEARSADALE
Cora A. M. 233; John S. T. 231, 233; Mary E. 231, 233; Samuel F. 232; S. L. 232.

BEDELL
G. T. Rev. 41.

BEALE
	J. Hervey 261.

BEECHER
	Susannah 169.

BEESON
	Addie 7; Addie L. 7; Addie Lucinda 8; Alice 35; Alice Isabella 8; Amanda 37; Amanda McCullough 38; Ann 7, 36; Anna Marie 38; Edward 38; Eliza 38, 39; Elizabeth 7, 35, 36, 37; Elizabeth Ann 37; Elizabeth Mansel 36; Emily 356, 358; Emma 7; Esther 35, 36; Edward 38; Hannah 35, 36; Hannah P. 37; Harry 7, 8; Harry Allmond 7, Harry Snyder 8; Harry Snyder II 8; Henry 38; Jethron 37; John 35, 36, 37, 38; John Franklin 37; John M. 37; John Smith 7; Joseph 7; Lydia 36, Lydia Ann 38; Martha 35; Mary 35, 36; Mary B. 37; Mary Jane 38; Mary Simmons 35; Philena 37; Sallie Ann 37; Sarah 7, 36; Sarah Ann 37; Susan H. 37; Susannah 36; Susannah Mansel 36, 37; William 7, 36, 37, 38; William Mansel 37, William Mansil Sr. 37.

BEHLES
	Catherine 140; George 140; Rosa May 140.

BELL
	Ann 40; Edward 40; John G. 40; Mary Elizabeth 40; Richa 28; Richia 40; Richie Bell 40; Rosinal 153; Sarah A. 26, 27; Sarah Ann 40; William 40; William H. 40; Wm. P. 40; William P. 28, 40; William P. Jr. 40.

BELLVILLE
	Ann K. 15; Catherine 15; Elizabeth 15; Ely 15; Dr. Frank 15; Jacob 15; John 15; John P. 15; Margaret 15; Mary 15; Rev. R. B. 15; Robert C. 15; Sarah 15; Thomas 15.

BENARD
	Leah Rowena 274.

BENGE
	Ellen 232; Rachel 232.

BENGLESS (BENGLES) (BEUGLESS)
    Catherine (Kate) 352; Charles L. 351; Frank 351; Hannah 352; Hannah Sturges 350, 351; Kate 351; Katie 351; Thomas 349, 351, 352, Thomas H. 351; Thomas Hyde 350, 351, 352.

BENJAMIN
    Almond 153.

BENNETT
    Mariam 254; Mary E. 27; Pernal 254; Susanna 131.

BENSON
    Alexander 41, 42; Alexander Jr. 41; Alexander Sr. 41; Edwin North 41; Edythe Louise 117; Emily North 41; Charles 117; Harriet(t) Smith 41; Herman Roach 117; Irene 313; Janet 117; Mary Ann 372, 373, 374; Mary Louisa 41; Richard 41, 42; Rosalie 41; Ruth Adella 117; Sarah 41; Theodore 41; Washington 41.

BENT
    Emily M. 362.

BERLIN
    Clara Louise 47, 58, 59, 245, 247, 248; George w. 47, 59, 245; George Washington 59, 247; Jacob 58; Joseph 47, 58, 245; Susannah (Brinker) 58.

BERMINGHAM
    Veronica 277, 278.

BERRY
    Ebenezer 363; Frances 363; James 363; John 363; Prisilah 363; Sarah 9, 363.

BETHERTON
    Anna 125.

BEUGLESS
    See: Bengless

BIEDERT
    Marjorie 202.

BIGGER
    George S. 257.

BIORK
    Ericus, Rev. 367.

BIRD
    A. 378; A.D. 42, 43; Alfred 44, 45, 97;
    Alfred D. 42, 43, 44, 45, 46, 97; Alfred
    D. Jr. 97; Alfred Dupont 42, 44, 45, 212;
    Anna Mary 44, 45, 348; Charles Cheyney 44,
    45; Charles D. 43, 46, 97; Charles D. Sr.
    43; Charles Deacon 42, 44; Charlotte 46;
    Clara Wallace 212; E.E. 42; Edward Grubb 44,
    45; Edward Mississippi 42, 44, 45; Elizabeth
    104, 382; Ellen E. 42, 43, 44, 45, 46;
    Ellen Elizabeth 42, 43, 44, 45; Ellen
    Wardell 43, 44; Elsie 392, 393; Emma
    Rebecca 42, 43, 44, 45; Eunice 103, 104;
    H.C. 356; Henry C. 357; Horace Greeley 43,
    44; John 43, 44, 45; John L. 392; John
    Lawson 42, 44, 45; Joseph 104; Julia Grubb
    43, 44, 45, 268; Julianna 43, 44, 45; Laura
    Craven 43, 44, 45; Laura E. 43, 46; Lillian
    392, 393; Margaret Ann 309; Mary 44, 104;
    Mary Ann 44, 45; Matilda 103, 104; Nellie A.
    43; Rebecca 104; Thomas 44, 45; Thomas Babb
    44, 45; William 393; William Suddards 42,
    44, 46.

BIRTWELL
    Daniel, Rev. 108.

BISHOP
    Sarah 174, 202.

BLACK
    Clara A. 247; Clara Amanda 47, 59, 244, 245;
    Hanna 210; Hanna E. 207; Ida Jane 47, 244;
    John 46; John Wesley 47, 244; Kate Young 47,
    244; Margaret 46; Margaret E. 46; Mary 46;
    Minnie 47; Minnie M. 244; Robert 46; Sarah
    47; Sarah Jane 46, 47, 245; Thomas 46;
    Thomas Howard 47, 244; Thomas J. 46, 47, 244;
    Thomas R. 46.

BLACKISTON
    Albert 50; Albert Watson 49; Anna Jones 48, 49, 301; Anna 50; Bertha Watson 48, 49, 50, 301; Elva R. 362; Elva Roberts 48, 50, 300, 301, 362; Florence 50; Florence Voshell 48, 301; George 363; Gwendolyn 50; Gwendolyn Pyle 49, 302; Helen 50; Helen Irene 48, 49, 301; Herbert 50; Herbert Keyler 49, 301; James V. 50; James Voshell Roberts 48, 49, 301; John W. 50; John Wesley 49, 302; Martha 363; Mary 48; Mary A. 301; Mary E. 48, 49, 301; Mary Eliz 50; Mary Elizabeth 49, 301; O. Lee 49, 50; William 48; Wm. E. 50; William Edgar 48, 301; William H. 48, 49, 50, 300; Wm. H. 48, 49, 301; William Watson 49.

BLINN
    Grace 295.

BLITTERDORF
    Viola Roberta 25.

BLIZZARD
    Sarah E. 140.

BLOYKE
    Mary Ann 204.

BODINE
    Charles W. 309; Hannah R. 310.

BOHNER
    Chas., Rev. 380.

BONSALL
    Edward 144.

BOOTH
    Elizabeth 189, 191.

BORON
    rebecca Ann 117.

BOSTICK
    James 11.

BOUGHMAN
    Elizabeth R. 52; Emanuel G. 52; Fanny G. 51,
    53; Florence 53; Florence I. 52; Hannah 51,
    53; Henry 51, 53; Henry R. 51, 52, 53; Ida
    B. 52; I. Lukens 52; Jacob 51, 53; John 51,
    53; John G. 52; Joseph 51, 53, 53; Joseph
    Jr. 51, 53; Lewis T. 51, 52, 53; Lydia A.
    52; Lydia Ann 51, 53; Manuel 53; Manuel G.
    51; Mary 53; Mary A. 51; Mary Ann 51; Mary
    Jane 51; Sarah 52, 53; Sarah A. 51, 52;
    S. Lukens 51, 53; Susan 51, 53; William 53;
    William H. 52; William Hanson 51; William B.
    Harrison 51, 52; William W. 52.

BOWDLE
    Helen 332.

BOWERS
    George S. 54; Henrietta H. 54; John Draper
    54; Mary Ann 54; Melinda A. 54; Walter
    Quigley 54.

BOWLES
    Benjamin 55; David 55, 56; Davis 56;
    Elizabeth 55; Elizabeth Thomas 56; Emma J.
    333; Hanna 56; Hughes 56; Jesse 55, 56;
    John 55; John II 55; Nancy 55; Nelson 55;
    Pariot 55; Robert 56; Sarah 55, 56;
    Stephen 56; Thomas 55; Winney Rice 55.

BOWMAN
    Joshua R. 88; Mary 180.

BOYCE
    Dawson Noah 56; Gertha Martin 56; Iou(?) May
    56; J. S. 56; John S. 56; Mina Ruth 56;
    Minnie 56; William Minous 56.

BOYCXE
    John 105.

BOYER
    Clarence 98; Else May 98; George F. 97, 98.

BOYS
    Almon I. 232; Alvina 231, 232; Charlotte 232;
    Mary E. 231, 232; Mary Eliza 232.

BRACKIN (BRACKEN)
    Elizabeth R. 57; Jane 57; John F. 57; John
    G. 57; Mary 57; Sarah A. 57; Sarah Ann 57;
    Watson 57; William H. 57.

BRACKLIN
    Sarah A. 51, 53.

BRAD
    Wm. Ives 258.

BRADBURY
    Wm. Ives 257.

BRADEN
    Anna M. 58; David 58; Edward 58, Elizabeth
    58; Elizabeth Jane 58; George L. 58; James
    58; Jane 58; John L. 58; Margaret 58;
    Maria 58; William 58.

BRADLEY
    Sarah E. 20, 21.

BRENNESSER
    Benjamin 169.

BRERENTON
    Henry 154, 155; Sarah 154.

BRIGGS
    A. Briggs, Prof. 106; F. F., Rev. 179; Mary
    W. 106, 396; M. W. 106.

BRINSMADE
    Lois 152.

BRISBAND
    Wm. H., Rev. 178.

BRITTON
    Mary 348.

BROADBENT
    Mabel 353.

BROADWAY
    Catharine 100, 102; Mary 102; Robert 101;
    Sarah Russum 101.

BROGAN
    Mary Louise 26.

BROOKS
    Mary L. 270, 272.

BROWN
    Allerdice 4; Charlotte 59, 60, 61; Elizabeth
    60, 61; Isabella 4; Newton C. 60; William
    59, 60.

BROWNE
    Enovh? 325.

BRUCE
    Alexander 112, 115, 116; C. Bruce 351;
    Eleanor (Eleanore) 112, 115; Elijah 351;
    Eliza 350, 351; Elizabeth 349, 350; Ester
    (Esther) 112, 115, 116; Gideon 351; Isaac
    350, 351; Joel 351; Lydia 351; Melon 351;
    Phebe 351; Rachel 351; Rebecca 351; Richard
    351; Tanzend 351; William 351.

BRYAN (BRIAN) (BRION)
    Andrew 263, 264; George A. 263, 264; George
    Andrew 263; J. E., Rev. 257, 261; Lurana
    338; Mary 263; Mary A. 263; Mary C. 263;
    Mary E. 264; Sallie A. 263, 264; Sarah 264;
    Sarah Brine (Bryan) 263; Sarah Elizabeth
    338; Wm. 264; William 263, 338.

BUCHANAN
    Laura Ella 165.

BUCHER
    J. S., Rev. 169.

BUCKELLEW (BUCKELEW)
    Abraham 61; Ann 61; Ann Elizabeth 62;
    Catherine 61; Eliza 61; Fannie 62;
    Franklin Thompson 62; Frederick 61;
    Garett 61; Garrett 61; George Washington
    61; Jane 61; Jeremiah 61; Jesse 61;
    John 61; John Alexander 62; Howard 61;
    Lydia Belle 62; Margaret 61; Margaret
    Ellen 62; Mary Emma 62; Phobe Jane 62;
    Rachel Eva 62; Samuel 61; Sarah 61; Sarah
    Jane 62; Theodore Howard 62; Thompson

BUCKELLEW (Cont'd).
   McCarrell 61; Warren Thomas 52; William 61.

BUCKINGHAM
   James 194.

BUCKLEY
   Adam 156; Ann 63; Anne 7, 62; Beulah 63;
   Hanna 37; Hepzibah 63; John 62, 63, 64;
   Mary ? 63.

BULL
   Rachel 71, 72.

BULLOCK
   Eliza 393, 395; Kirk 104; Mary 393, 394,
   395.

BUNKER
   George 176; Jane 176; Martha 176.

BUNTING
   Maxwell H. 201.

BURLEIGH
   Nathaniel Jr. 327.

BURK
   Rev. J. 141.

BURKE
   Sarah 47.

BURNETT
   Wm. 121, 122.

BURNS
   George 95; Mary E. 268.

BURRITT
   C. D., Rev. 232.

BURTON
   Annie E. 65, 67; Cecilia K. 67; Clara W. 65,
   66, 67; Clara Wilimina 66; Clifton 66, 67;
   Cornelius T. 65, 66, 67; Elizabeth 65, 67;
   Eunice 263; Fred 65, 67; H. Mae 66; Hannah
   Mae 66; Hannah W. 65, 67; Helen M. 65;

BURTON (Cont'd.)
Helen Mae 66; Henry P. 263; Jane Ennis 66; John C. 65, 66, 67; John Clifton 66; Kate R. 67; Lida Erneison 66; Lidie E. 65; Mary 65; Mary H. 67; Virginia 65, 66, 67; Virginia E. 65; William E. 66; William V. Jr. 66; Wm. H. V. 65; William Virden 66; Willie E. 67.

BUSH
Charles 93, 95; David Potter 93; Elizabeth McCain 93; Ellen 93; Samuel 93.

BYERLY
Eleanor 243, 244; John 244; Mary 243, 244.

BYRNES
Anna 70; Caleb 68, 69, 70, 71; Charles 68, 69, 72; Daniel 68, 69, 70, 71, 72; Dinah 69, 70, 72; Eleanor 68, 71, 72; Elizabeth 69, 70, 72; Esher Fussell 68, 69; Esther 69, 71, 72; Hannah 69, 70; Jacob F. 69, 71, 72; Jacob Fussell 69; James Fitch 69; Jonathan 68, 69, 71, 72; Joseph 70, 72; Joshua 69, 70, 72; Lydia 70; Martha 68, 71, 72; Mary 68, 69, 71, 72; Rachel 68, 69, 70, 71, 72; Rebecca 70, 72; Ruth 69, 70, 72; Samuel 69, 70; Sarah 70, 72; Sarah Palmer 69; Susanna 68, 71, 72; Tacy 68, 71, 72; Thomas 70; Williams 70, 72; Woodnut 70.

CABELL
Samuel Jordan, Capt. 55.

CADOGAN
Elizabeth 278; Mary 278.

CALDWELL
Wm. P. 14.

CALE
Elizabeth 121, 122.

CALLAHAN
    Ann 101, 102; Anna M. 104; Author 105;
    Edward, Rev. 101; Francis Frederick 104;
    Freddie Wm. 104; Gean 105; George LeClarice
    104; Haddie May 104; Sam 105.

CAMPBELL
    Mazie R. 282.

CANBY
    Mary 145.

CANN
    Susannah 157.

CANTWELL
    Andrew 74; Edmund 73, 74; Edmund, Capt. 73;
    Eleanor 74; Elizabeth 74; Johanna 74; Lydia
    74; Mary 73, 74; Richard 73, 74.

CAREY (CARY)
    George E. 299; Ida M. 299; James P. 299;
    Laura A. 299.

CARL
    Elias 70.

CARPENTER
    Annie Eliza 256; Catherine 256; Catherine F.
    256; F. F., Rev. 257; Louis Marshall 256;
    Mary M. 256; Thomas 256; Thomas H. 256;
    Ursula Berleda 131.

CARRIGER
    Eloise 363, 364; Leonard 363.

CARROLL
    Anastasia 237; Mrs. Dominick 237; Mrs.
    Charles 235; Hon. Charles 235; Sophia 234;
    Thomas 202.

CARTER
    Emma 172; Charlotte 59; Edward 101; Mary
    101; Mary Broadway 102; Nellie 131;
    Orlando F. 171.

CARTMELL
    George 75, 76; George T. 75. 76; John 75,

CARTMELL (Cont'd.)
    76; John B. 75, 76; Joseph 75, 76;
    Margaret 75, 76; Margaret Ellen 75; Margret
    75, 76; Margary 360; Mary 75, 76;
    Rachel 75, 76; Rachel H. 75, 76; Rebecca
    76; Rebecca Ann 75; Sarah 76, 360; Sarah
    Ann 75; Thomas 75, 76; Thomas B. 75, 76;
    Thomas C. 75.

CASEY
    Adelaide Roberta 77; Amy Estelle 77; Ann
    Archer 77; Catherine 77; Catherine W. 77;
    Catherine Walker 77; Cora Rebecca 77; Ethel
    May 77; George 76; George M. 77; George
    Merritt 77; Helen Marie 77; James Elliot 77;
    John M. 77, 78; John Miller 77, 78; Katherine
    W. 77; Katherine Winifred 77; Lena Eva 77;
    Lena Virginia 77; Mary Ellen 77; Martha
    Marian 77; Mildred Frances 78; Mildred Jane
    77; Robert 77; Virginia 77, 78.

CAULK
    Levin 102.

CHALFANT
    Ralph B. 282.

CHAMBERLIN
    Benjamin C. 297, 298; Benjamin Clinton 298;
    Benjamin D. 297, 298, 299; Clinton C. 297;
    Ella F. 297; Ella Frances 298; Elmer C. 298,
    299; Elmer Curtis 298; Ida M. 298; Ida May
    298; James H. 298; James Herbert 298; Laura
    297, 298; Laura A. 297, 299; Sallie M. 298;
    Sallie May 298; Sophia L. 298; Sophia Laura
    298.

CHAMBERS
    Joseph 196.

CHAMPNEY(S)
    Mary 204.

CHANDLER
    D. Webster 20, 21; Emma B. 20.

CHANEY
    Cecil 203; Hannah 131.

CHARLTON
    Francis, Rev. 380.

CHASE
    Emily B. 78; Ezra 153; George 78; James T. 78; Mary B. 78; Mary E. 78; Peter Dailey 78; Phebe 78.

CHERRY
    Rebecca 121, 122.

CHEW
    Chief Justice 235; Harriett 235; Nathanial, Rev. 380.

CHILD
    John 393, 395; Nathan 393, 394, 395; Nathan Jr. 394; Nathan C. 395.

CHILDRY
    J. M. T. 38.

CHISHOLM
    Mary Jane 131.

CHRISTIE
    James 233.

CHURCH
    Helen 148.

CHURCHMAN
    Phebe 264.

CLADDEN
    Eliz 145.

CLARK (CLARKE)
    Abishai 145; Anna C. 287, 288; Annie 355; Edith 88; Frances 143; Hanna 20, 21; Helen 202; John 79; Isaac 15; James 20, 21; Jas. 20; John 143; John S. 78, 79; Lewis 380; Lydia 15, 21; Mary L. M. 312; Nathaniel 89; Tabitha 143; Thomas 325.

CLARKSON
    Jennie E. 65; Lewes F. 65; Samuel 145.

CLAY
    Florence Malin 222, William 355; William M. 355.

CLEMSON
    Hannah 62; John 64.

CLEVELAND
    Sabilla A. 341; Sarah (Pierce) 340; Thomas 340, 342; Timothy 340.

CLIFTON
    Hannah W. 65, 253; John 253; Mary 253.

CLOUD
    Abner 80; Ann 80, 81; Ann Mary 80; Anna May 285; Cassandra 354; Charity 80, 81; Elmira 80; George 354; George Lodge 80; Jane 120; Joel 80, 81; Lot 80; Maria 80; Maria Elizabeth 80; Rebecca 80; William 80, 81; William L. 123; Wm. 80, 125.

CLUNGIS
    Mary 94.

COARD (COMBS?)
    Richard V. 170

COATES
    Clifton 2.

COCREN
    James 94.

CODINGTON
    Phebe 232.

COFFIN
    Tristram 322.

COLBY
    Dorothy 327; Isaac 322, 324, 328; Judith 324, 329; Martha (Parrott) 322; Richard 325; Sarah 322, 323, 327, 328.

COLEGAT
    Richard 278.

COLES
Cooper 203; Edwin 203; Edwin C. 203; Frances Vera 203; Frances Willard 203; Jacob Kirby 203; Margaret 203; Marjorie 203; Mary Elizabeth 203; Merton 203; Oliver Hammond 204; William 203; William M. 203.

COLESBERRY
Mary 348.

COLESS
----? 200.

COLGATE
Henry 278; John 278; Richard 278.

COLGIN
Rachel 291; William 291.

COLLINGS
John 81; William 81.

COLLINS
Charles 319; John 84; John M. 343, 345; John Stevenson 345; Samuel 177; William 84; William Turpin 345.

COLLISON
Samuel F. 2.

COLSON
Sara 203.

COMSTOCK
Abigail 152.

CONCKLIN
Edith B. 23, 24; George W. 22, 23, 24.

CONDE
Annettet Norman 204; Joseph 204.

CONNAWAY
Minos T. 170.

CONNELL
Mary 384; Mary P. 383.

CONNELLY (CONELLY)
Carrie A. 86; David 82, 85; Edna 81, 82, 84; Edna N. 82; Eliza 81, 82, 85; Eliza Jane 82; Elizabeth 81, 82, 84, 85; Gray 81, 82, 84; Harold G. 343; Harrison 82, 84; James 81, 82, 84; James H. 82; James Harvey 81; Jesse 81, 82, 84; Lucinda 82, 85; Mary 84, 85; Mary J. 82, 84, 85; Mary T. 81; Mary Thatcher 82; Nancy 85; Nancy D. 81, 82, 83; Polly 82; Polly Mary 81; Rhoda 81, 84; Sarah 84; Sarah Ann 81, 82; Susan 84; Susan Frances 82.

CONNER
Isaac C. 288.

CONWELL
Anne C. 88; Asbury 79; Edward W. 79; John 79; Martha C. 79; Martha S. 79; Sarah 79; Sarah E. 78; Sarah S. 79; Susan R. 78, 79.

CONYERS
William 352.

COOLETT
Mary 130.

COOPER
Catherine 175; George 318; John 212; Louisa 318; Maggie 318; Maria 101; Nora 318, 319; Thereon 232; William J. 318.

COPES
Mary 270, 271.

CORD
Isair 87; Jane 87, 88; Joseph 87; Mary 87; Miers 87; Samuel 87; William 87.

COULTER
Edith 88, 89; George 88, 89; Ingebar Bryon 88; Mary 88; William 88, 89.

COURTNEY
Catherine 351; James 351; William W. 351.

COUSTON
Elizabeth 78.

COVERDALE
    George 110; Jim 110.

COVINGTON
    Algey 92; Algey T. 90; Algey Thomas 90;
    Charlott 92; Charlott M. 91; Charlott Matilda
    90; Elizabeth 90; Francis A. 90, 91; George
    W. 92; George Washington 90; Henry 92; Henry
    M. 90, 91; Hester Ann 90, 92; Jacob H. 91;
    Jacob Hargis 90; James 90, 91; James R. 92;
    James Rider 90, 91; John 91; John James 90;
    Kitty 92; Margaret 90, 92; Martha Jane
    Hargis 90, 91; Mary 90, 91, 92; Mary Anna
    90; Nancy 89, 90, 91; Nancy Wilson 91;
    Royston 89, 90, 91; Sallie 92; Sallie E. 90;
    Sarah Elizabeth 91; Southey Taylor 90;
    Virginia 90; William 92; William R. 90;
    William Royston 90; William Wilson 90, 91.

COX
    Samuel Kiner 229.

COXE
    Albert 95; Albert Fisher 93, 94; Alfred 148;
    Ann 95; Ann Patterson 94; Caroline 148;
    Catherine 95; Charlott 93; Eliza 93, 94;
    Elizabeth 93, 94, 95; Elizabeth McKain 94;
    Ellen 93, 95; Esau 93, 94, 95; Esau Lyon 93,
    94; James 93, 94, 95; James M. 94; James
    McK. 94; Laurette deT. 148; Louis 95;
    Louis H. 93; Louis Henry 93, 94; Margaret
    95; Martha 95; Martha Ann 93; Mary 93, 95;
    Rebecca 93, 94, 95; Sarah 93, 95; Thomas 93,
    94, 95.

CRAIGHEAD
    Jennie D. 151.

CRAMPTON
    Naomi 152.

CRANE
    Annie 96; Annie E. 96; Clara M. 96; David
    95; George O. T. 96; George T. 96; John C.
    96; Jonathan 96; Josephine 95, 96;
    Josephine T. 96; Margaret 95; Mary 95;
    Mary E. 96; Mary L. 96; Mary P. 96;

CRANE (Cont'd.)
   Stephen M. 95, 96; Stephen M. Jr. 96;
   Stephen P. 96; Stephen R. 96; Stephen W. 96;
   Thomas H. 96; William H. 95, 96; William K.
   96.

CRANOR
   Elizabeth 1, Joshua 1; Margaret D. 1.

CRAWFORD
   Leon Wilde 48; Rebecca 398.

CREWE
   Elizabeth 192.

CROCKETT
   Eliz 50; Elizabeth 300, 304; Kendall B.
   169, 170.

CROSSAN
   Anna 39; Clara E. 39; Clara Mae 38; George
   A. 39, Lydia 39; Reuben 39.

CROUCH
   C. J., Rev. 259, 260; Margaret 335, 336.

CROWNINSHIELD
   Eliz 204, 205.

CUBBAGE
   Ida 117, Samuel 117.

CULLIGAN
   Josie 232.

CURRIER
   Mary (George) 142; Nathan 323, 324, 325,
   327, 329; Sarah 142; William 142.

DACIS
   Martha H. 188.

DAILEY (DAILY)
   David, Rev. 298; Edistina M. 97; Elenora 97;
   Joseph 78; Joseph L. 97; Laura E. 78, 97;
   Peter C. 96, 97; Rebecca 96; Rebecca E. 96,
   97; Samuel J. 97.

DANIEL
    Andrew 145; Hannah 145; Wm. 145.

DANIELS
    Charles Hugh 229; Charles Joseph 229; Hugh Miller 229.

DARBY
    A, B. 97, 98; Alex 98; Alex B. 98; Alex Burtin 97; Alexander Burton 98; Amandus B. 97, 98; Burtin 98; Clarence A. 98; Eliza 97, 98; Eliza J. 98; Eliza May 98; Emily F. 97; Evva G. 97, 98; Harry A. 98; Nancy M. 98; Rachel Lizzie 98; William 98.

DARLINGTON
    Nee 265.

DAUGHADY
    Norman 8.

DAVID
    Elisha 241; Margaret 241; Martha 242; Mary 241; Rebecca 241.

DAVIDSON
    Elizabeth 99, 100; Emma 133, 135; Esther 99, 100; Francis Jr. 99, 100; Francis Sr. 99, 100; Grizelda 99; Isaac 99, 100; James 99, 100; Jane 99, 100; John 99; June 99; Lizzie 135; Mary 99, 100; Rachel 99; Ratchel 99; Robert 99, 100; William 99, 100.

DAVIES
    David 293.

DAVIS
    Ann 118; Dr. Davis 141; Ellis 292; Hannah 245, 246, 292; H. W. 47; Kastron 151; Margaret E. 90, 92; Mary, 37, 69, 71, 72; Nathaniel 323, 324, 329; Samuel 328.

DAWSON
    Ann 101; Anna 100, 102 Catharine 100, 102; Edward 100, 102; Elisha 100, 101, 102; Eliza 100; Elizabeth 100, 102; Elizah 102;

DAWSON (Cont'd.)
    Frederick 101, 102; Ida Frances 250;
    Isabella 100, 102; John 100, 102; Jonas 100,
    102; Joseph 101, 102; Lydia 101, 102;
    Margaret 100, 102; Maria 101; Mary 101, 102;
    Mary B. 101; Robert 101; Sarah 101; Shadrack
    101, 102; William 100, 101, 102, 250;
    William Percifer 250.

DAY
    Addie May 104; Alfred 103; Anna Margaret
    104; Benjamin 103; Benjamin H(?) 103;
    Edward Augustus 389; Elica 105; Eliza M.
    103; Elmer W. 104; Elmer Watson 104; Elsie
    M. 105; Francis 103; George Bayard 104;
    George W. 103; Hannah Mary 104; Harriett
    105; Harry C. 103; Harry John 104; Harry
    Lore 104; John 103, 105; John B. 103;
    John Young 389; Lewis B. 103; Lewis F. 103;
    Lloyd 389; Maggie E. 103; Mary 103, 105;
    Mary Ida 103; Matilda 103; Priscilla 103;
    Rebecca Young 389; Sarah 105; Sarah E. 103;
    William Cleveland 104; William S. 103;
    Wm. S. 104; William Young 389.

DEACON
    Ann 106; Ann D. 106; Benjamin 105, 106;
    Benjamin D. 106; Benjamin F. 106; Charles
    T. 106; George H. 106; Hannah 105, 106;
    Hannah H. 106; Hannah Heulings 105; John
    105; John E. 105; Joseph H. 105; Mary M.
    106; Sarah H. 105, 106.

DEBELL
    Isabell 205.

DEHASS
    Mary 73.

DELAPLAIN
    Nehemiah 341.

DEMARIS
    Eleanor 203.

DENNISON (DENISON)
    Eliza B. 107, 108; Isabelle 107; J. W. 106,
    107, 396; Jesse Lewis 107, 108, 396; Jesse
    W. 393, 395; Jesse Wood 108; Julia P. 107;

DENNISON (DENISON) Cont'd.
Julia Porter 107, 396; Maria Louisa 107, 396; Mary 107; Mary Louise 107; Mary W. 108; Mildred 274; Nathan 396; Percy Nightingale 107; Percy W. 107, 108; Theo. 106; Thomas 396; William C. 108; William S. 108; William Sprague 107.

DERBOROUGH
Rev. John 270.

DERICKSON
Anna M. 272; Anna Pennington 273; Bessie A. 109, 110; Blanche 274; Blanche Martha 273, 274; Handy 300; Hannah 109; Isabella A. 109, 110; Jacob 108, 109, 383; James L. 273, 274; James Leslie 273, 274; James Leslie Jr. 273; Jane 109, 110; John H. 109; John S. 381; Joseph 381; Joseph H. 109, 110, 383; Joseph S. 380; Leslie 270, 273, 274; Mary 110, 380, 381, 383; Mary E. 108, 109, 110; Mary Emilie 273; Mary Lou 274; Mildred Dennison 273; Mildred E. 274; Nancy 110, 381; Nancy H. 299; Nancy Hill 300; Rachel 296; Rodney Lynn 274; Sarah 300; Vesta C. 110, Vesta Charlotte 381; Viola 381; Viola W. 381; Willard 110, 381; William 380, 381; William C. 109, 110; William J. 109, 110, 381.

DEVALINGER
Emma 46; Emma Rebecca 43, 45; Harry 46.

DEVALL
Benjamin 390.

DEWHADAWAY
Rev. J. W. 298.

DICKERSON
Mrs. J. 147; Thomas Lee 263.

DICKINSON
Caroline 201; Caroline H. 201; Christina 185.

DICKS
Lydia 145.

DIEHL
    Mary 146.

DILTS
    Catherine 309, 310; Elizabeth 310; Esther
    310; Hannah 310; Holcomb 310; John 310;
    Mamry 310; Rebecca 310; Robert 310;
    Susanne 310; William 310.

DILWORTH
    ary 147.

DIRICKSON
    Elizabeth 128, 129; J. B. 129, 130; John B.
    128, 129; Nathaniel M. 128, 129; Peter M.
    129; Sally 128, 129; Stephen E. 128, 129.

DIXON
    Mary B. Beeson 37.

DOBBINS
    Rev. T. 380.

DODD
    Absalom 110, 111; Amy 112, 115; Anna B. 116;
    Annie 111; Carrie Lee 111; Comfort Bruce
    112, 115; Effie 111; Eleanor 112, 115, 116;
    Eleanor Bruce 115; Elener 112; Elenor 112;
    Eliza 111, 115; Eliza J. 111; Eliza Jane
    111; Eliza T. 112; Eliza Turner 112,
    Elizabeth 112, 115, 116; Frank Wiltbank 111;
    Hannah 111, 112, 115, 116; Hannah Maria 115;
    Hannah Marshall 111; James Ralph Coverdale
    111; John 111; John Paynter 111; Joseph 112;
    Joseph H. 116; Joseph Hazlett 112, 115;
    Maria 112, 115; P. Norman 111; Pernel Norman
    111; William 112, 115, 116; William A. 114,
    115, 116; William Alexander 112, 155;
    William Bruce 115, William G. 116; Wm. 112,
    115, 116.

DOLE
    Albert Galatin, Rev. 165; Florence Eugenia
    165; Maria (Jefferis) 165.

DONALDSON
    David K. 372; Mrs. Mary V. 371.

DONOHO
    A. 138; A. E. 138; A. Elizabeth 138; Ann
    Elizabeth 138; Anna R. 138, 139; Attalus
    138, 139; Carrie A. 139; George Smith 138,
    139; Harriet 138; Harriet George 138, 139;
    James 138, James E. 138; J. Pemberton 138;
    John Pemberton 138, 139; Joseph 138, 139;
    Joseph F. 138; Joseph Franklin 138, 139;
    M. Edgar 138; Mathew Edgar 138; Mathew E.
    139; William Randall 138, 139.

DONOVAN
    Sarah E. 319, 320.

DOOLEY
    Rev. Alvah 81, 85.

DOW
    Henry 176.

DOWDY
    Estella 127; N. Estella 126; Nannie Estella
    126.

DOWNING
    Elijah J. 136, 137; Emma V. (Farra) 136,
    137; Ethel B. 136, 137; George A. 16;
    Herbert 137; Herbert E. 136; Jane 16;
    John M. 136; John R. 136, 137; Leslie 137;
    Leslie F. 136, 313; Mildred 137; Mildred L.
    136, 137; Rebecca 136, 137; Samuel 16; T. W.
    136.

DRAGOO
    Alice 117; Elmer Elsworth 117; Emma G. 117;
    Henryetta 117; Ida Romilda (Millie) 117;
    James Ezekiel 117; John Adelbert 117; John
    C. 117; M. H. 117; Martha A. 117, Martha
    Adella 117; Sarah E. 117.

DRIESBACH
    Hannah 307.

DUBAC
    Rev. Albert M. (W.?) 107, 396.

DUBREE
Absalom 332; Benjamin Lukens 332; Edith 332; Elizabeth 332; Henry Small 332; Hiram 332; John 332; Letitia 332; Lydia 332; Nathaniel 332; Rachel 332; Sarah 332; Sarah Ann 330, 331, 332.

DUDDINGTON
O. G. 178.

DUDLEY
O. Dudley 254.

DUEL
Chalkey 173.

DUFF
Ann 118, 304; Edward, Dr. 118; Henry 118; Henry, Capt. 119; Jane 119; John 119; Richard 118; Thomas 119; Thomas, Col. 118.

DUKE
Mary Katherine (Setes) 337.

DUNBAR
Mary C. 246; Morris 246.

DUNCAN
Mary M. 313; Thomas Garfield 312.

DUNLAP
Jane 219.

DYE
Elizabeth 152, 153.

DYER
Mary 73, 74; William 74.

EASTBURN
Doris Ann 239; Joseph Buford 239; Patricia Jane 239; Rozanne Lee 239.

EASTWICK
    Eliza 121, 122; Emeline 121, 122; Hannah
    121, 122; John 120, 121, 122, 123; Letitia
    121, 122; Mary 121, 122; Matilda 121, 122;
    Rachel 121, 122; Sarah 121, 123; Stephen
    121, 122; Thomas 121, 122, 123; William S.
    122; Wm. Smith 121.

EATON
    Ruth 329; Timothy 326.

EBERT
    Adam 164; Eliza 164; Sally 167.

EBRIGHT
    Mary 32, 33.

EDGELL
    Sallie 1.

EDGEN
    Carnelia 2; Charlotty A. 1, Erma 2, George
    R. 2; Horace G. 2; Ida E. 2; James 1; Jessey
    G. 2; Martha Frances 1; Mary 1; Mary E. 1;
    Mary Effie 2; Roland C. 2; Sallie 2; Wm. 1;
    William H. 1.

EDGIN
    Jesse 1.

EDINGFIELD
    Ann 372; 373.

EDWARDS
    Abner 9; Albert L. 123, 125; Alice 125;
    Alice L. 124; Andrew 9; Charlotte 125;
    Charlotte M. 123, 276; Dorothy 203;
    Edna 174, 203; Eliza 392; Emily Ruth 203;
    Isabella 125; Isabella R. 123, 124; James
    109, 383; John Jacob 203; Lavania 9; Lorena
    125; Lorena W. 123, 124; Lottie 109, 308;
    Marian 203; Mary 109, 125, 383; Mary A. 124;
    Mary Ann 9; Mary E. 123, 124; Richard 123,
    125; Richard W. 124; Sara 202; Sherman 174,
    203; Sherman Jr. 203; William S. 65.

ELBEN
    Wm. S. 288.

ELDER
   Alma Royall 127; Charles Oliver 126; Emma
   126; Ephriam 126; Estella 127; George
   Washington 126; John Wesley 125; Josephine
   127; Llewellyn (Llewllyn) 125, 126, 127;
   Louise Estella 127; Lucy Elnora 126; Lula
   126; Martha 126; Martha Ann 127; Martha
   Ann Foster 125, 126, 127; Martha Jones 125;
   Mary Elizabeth 127; Nannie Witt 126;
   Oliver 125, 126, 127; Robert Lee 126;
   Rosa Holmes 126; Roxana 126; Russell Burns
   127; Samuel Bunyan 126; Sylvester 126, 127;
   Virginia Gillem 127; William Henry 126;
   William Lee 127.

ELDRIDGE
   Hannah 360.

ELLINGSWORTH
   Ann Eliza 208; Caroline 208; Henry Smith
   208; James Wise 208; John Henry 208; Johnson
   208.

ELLIS
   Clayton H. 299; Elizabeth 128, 129; Harry
   299; Harry A. 297, 299; Hetty P. 127, 128;
   Isaiah 127, 128, 129, 130; Isaiah M. 128,
   299; John 129; John S. 1127, 128; John T.
   128, 129; Levin 128, 129, 130; Lovey 128,
   130; Martha 128, 130; Martha E. 128;
   Martin L. 127; Mary 128, 129; Mary H. 128;
   Nathaniel 128, 129; Sally 128, 130;
   Sophia 299; Stephen 128, 129, 130; Thomas
   70; William 70, 128, 129; Wm. 129.

ELLISON
   Curtis B. 15.

ENCK
   Ruben 169.

ENTRIKIN
   Albert 131; Ann Amanda 131; Caleb 131;
   Caleb Barton 131; Edwin 131; Emmer 131;
   Emmor Elwood 131; Ellwood 132; Ferdinand
   131; Franklin Wayne 131; Grace Anna 132;

ENTRIKIN (cont'd.)
    James Bennett 131; Laura Edna 131; Malvern
    Edwin 132; Mary Ruby 132; Richard Dean 132;
    Zela Alberta 131.

ERB
    Rebecca E. 313.

ERVIN
    Edward 232.

ESTELL
    Anna 134; Anna B. 133, 134; Anna May 133,
    134; Annie 134; Annie M. 133, 134; Beatrice
    133, 134; Elizebert (Elizabert) Anna 133,
    134, 135; Frank Stephens 133, 134; Harry
    133, 134; Harry H. 135; Harry Howard 133;
    John B. 133, 134; John Black 132, 133, 134,
    135; John Vedder 133; Morris Leslie 133,
    134; Robert Clark 133, 134; Thomas 133, 134;
    Westley Orcutt 133, 134; William 134;
    William Raymond 133, 134.

EVANS
    Ann 347; Arlene Mae 347; Catherine 293, 296;
    Clifford 347; Clifford Jr. 347; Clifford
    Lewis 347; Deborah Lynn 347; Ellen 347;
    Elwood 347; Elwood B. Jr. 347; Elwood
    Brinton 347; Faye 347; G. Earle 273, 274;
    Harold 347; Harold Mousley 347; Helen 347;
    Helen Brooks 273; J., Rev. 293; John 296;
    Martha 129; Mary (Eveans) 296; N. W. 130;
    Sallie Albina 273; Stewart 347; Thomas 292.

EYRE
    Manuel 264.

FABRYKA (FALRYKA)
    Edward F. 364; Eugene F. 364; June Taylor
    364; Kevin Victor 364; Mildred E. Taylor
    364.

FAILOR
    Elizabeth J. 169.

FARMER
    Hannah 242.

FARRA
    Emma V. 135, 136, 137; Esther 135, 136, 137;
    George D. 135, 136, 137; H.M. 136; Hannah
    137; Hannah M. 135; John 135; John M. 135,
    136, 137; John W. 135, 137; J. Worthington
    136; Louisa A. 135, 136, 137; Maggie 135,
    137; Mary J. 135; Mary T. 137; Sarah 137;
    Sarah E. 135; Wilmer R. 135, 137.

FARSON
    Edward 304; James T. 300, 304; Jas. T. 304;
    Mary 304; Sarah V. 304.

FAULKNER
    Elizabeth 374; Mary 374; Mary Jane 374;
    Robert 374; Sallie 299; William 374; William
    J. 297; William Robert Cornelius 374.

FENEMORE
    A. Elizabeth 137, 139; James L. 138; James
    Lord 137, 139; John 137, 138, 139; John F.
    139; John Ford 138; Keria E. 139; Keria
    Ellen 137, 138; Mary R. 139; Mary Rebecca
    138; Sarah 137, 138; Sarah J. 137, 139.

FENNIMORE
    Florence Hammersly (Weldin) 387; George
    Harlan 387.

FERGUSON
    Alexander 286; Edgar 295.

FERRIS
    Benjamin 145, 303; Charles E. 251; Zeba 70.

FEYHL
    Charles 203.

FIELDS (FIELD)
    Bessie J. 140; George E. 140; George W. 139,
    140; Ira T. 140; Ira Thomason 140; Joseph H.
    140; Mary 140; Mary Pennington 15; Rosa M.
    140; T. Fields 140; Verna 140.

FINLEY
    Margaretta 241.

FINSTWAIT
  Jonathan 283, 290, 291; Martha 283, 290, 291.

FISHER
  James 13, 14; Martha 14; Marthy F. 12; Marthy J. 13; Mary 195; Mary Bracken 57; Sarah 13, 14.

FITCHCRAFT
  Hannah 200.

FITZSIMMONS
  Mary Katherine 363.

FITZRANDOLPH
  Jane 192.

FLAGG (FLAG)
  Thankful L. 216, 218, 219.

FLEETWOOD
  John 215.

FLICKWIR
  Rebecca W. 141.

FLOWER
  Ann 118.

FLOWERS
  Elizabeth Ann 163; William N. 163.

FOOKS
  Benjamin 172; Eleanor 172.

FOOT
  Jane 57.

FORD
  Chester K. 142; Edward 27; Ernest C. 142; J. Ralph 33; John W. 142; Mabel 362; Mabel Ellen 301; Maggie T. 141; Margaret 355; Margaret E. 142; Muriel J. 142; Ralph 32; Rebecca 32, 33; William J. 141.

FORWOOD
  Albert 347, Amer Grubb 64; Betty Mae 347; Elizabeth 189, 190; Emily 356, 357; Hary

FORWOOD (Cont'd.)
    Garland 65; I. Howard 172; Martha Lea 347;
    Mary E. 65; Robert 64; W. Albert 347; Wayne
    Robert 347.

FOSTER
    Benjamin F. 232; Emily F. 97.

FOULKE (FOULK)
    Elizabeth 194; Hannah 359.

FOWDRIE
    Samuel 369.

FRAIM
    Charles 230; Charles F. 227; Edward T., Rev.
    229; Eliza Jane 227; Eugene 230; Eugene F.
    227; Ida 230; Ida Jane 227; Laura 227, 230;
    Martha 230; Martha Ann 227; Martin 230;
    Martin F. 227; Robert 230; Robert C. 226,
    227; Robert Franklin 227; Theodore 230;
    Theodore O. 227.

FRANCIS
    Lula 126; Marien 131.

FRAZIER
    Harriett 216, 220.

FREEMAN
    Rev. Doctor 370; Rev. Stephen 340.

FRENCH
    Joseph Henry 241.

FRICK
    John 169.

FRIEDEL
    Frederick 188; John Jacob 188; Mary Ellen
    188, 189; Rachel Adel 188, 189; Reuben 189;
    Reuben Franklin 188; Rosana Heyd 188.

FRIEZE
    Rev. H. 225.

FRITZ
    Etta 149.

FULLER
    Elmer 288.

FUSSELBACK
    Anna 51, 53.

FUSSELL
    Esther 69, 71, 72; Jacob 72.

GALBRAITH
    Amy A. 211; Elizabeth 211; Elizabeth Ann 211; John 211.

GALBREATH
    Eliza Eva 240; Ella M. 354; Eva 354; Jennie 352; Jennie C. 354; Willard 354; Willard Talley 240; William I. 240.

GALLION
    Mr. 366.

GAMBLE
    Helen E. 367; William M. 367; William M. Jr. 367.

GAMPTON
    Thomas 196.

GARRETSON (GARETSON)
    Andrew 278; Bridget 73, 278; Cantwell 278; Edmund 278; Elizabeth 73, 277, 278; Hallowell 278; Henry 73, 74; Mary 73, 278; Richard 278.

GARRETT
    Lydia 145; Margaret 145.

GARRIGUES
    Frank 201; Ruth Alta 201.

GASSNER
    George Sears, Rev. 263.

GATES
    Thomas Sr. 55.

GAYNER
    Ann 144.

GEBHART
    Josephine 228.

GEORGE
    Abby 143; Alfred 143; Ann 142, 143, 294,
    336; Charles W. 143; Eliza Jane 143;
    Elizabeth 142; Frances 143, 336; Jacob 143;
    James 143; John 142, 143, 336; John Jr. 143;
    John B. 142; John S. 143; Joseph 143;
    Margaret 143; Martha 143; Mary 142, 143,
    294; Mary Simpers 336; Millicent 143;
    Nicholas 142; Rachel 142; Rebecca 142;
    Sampson 142, 143; Sarah (Currier) 143;
    Sarah F. 143; Sophia 143; Stephen 143, 294,
    336; Thomas 143; Weston 143; William 143;
    William S. 143.

GERIS
    Susanna 309.

GIBBONS
    Abraham 145; Alice 145; Ann 145, 146;
    Daniel 145; Eleanor (Peters) 146; Eliz 145;
    Elizabeth 146; Geo. W. 145; Hannah 145, 146;
    Jacob 145, 146; Jame 145; James 144, 145;
    Jane 144, 146; John 144; John III 144;
    John H. 144; Joseph 144, 145, 146; Lydia
    145; Margery 144; Marshall 145; Mary 144,
    145, 146; Rachel 146; Rebecca 145; Samuel
    145; Sarah 145; Thomas 144, 145; Wm. 144,
    145.

GIBSON
    Anna 146; Mary 94; Mary Seely 93.

GILBERT
    Armour M. 131.

GILPIN
    A. 148; Alfred Cox 148; Arthington 148;
    B--- Georgianna 148; B--- Watmough 148;
    C. C. 148; E. C. 148; Edmund Watmough 148;
    Elizabeth 147; Henry Dilworth 147; Henry
    Edmund 148; Jane 147; Louisa 264; Margaret
    Ann 246; Maria Julianna 148; Mary 147;

GILPIN (Cont'd.)
Mary L. 147; R. A. 148; Richard Arthington 147; Richard Church 148; Richard William 148; Sarah Elizabeth 148; Sarah Lydia 147; Thomas William 147; William 147; William Bernard 148; William H. 246.

GLADFELTER
Lizzie 246

GODFREY
Jos. C. 215.

GOFF
Richard S. 153.

GOLDEN
Albert 180.

GOLDER
Hannah C. 308.

GOODLEY
Bertha 149; Bertha Claire 150; Charles P. 149, 150; Charles Pusey 149, 150; Edward Calmer 150; Egbert S. 149; Etta L. 150; George M. W. 149; George M. Walter 149; George W. 150; George Walter 150; Harold E. 149; Horace 149, 150; Horace Greely 149; Laura 149, 150; Laurence Elbert 150; Lillian 150; Lillian May 150; Lydia May 150; Marion Esther 150; Matilda 149, 150; Matilda B. 149, 150; Matilda W. 150; Samuel 149; Samuel Jr. 149; Samuel Alvin 150; Sarah W. 150; William S. 149, 150.

GOODWIN
Sarah 74.

GORDON
Henery 154, 155; Hetty 154, 155; James 151; Jerusha 151; John 151; Jonathan 154, 155; Kastron 151; Lydia 151; Lydia (Pratt) 151; Nathaniel 154, 155; Orson W. G. 151; Polly 154, 155; Ralph P. 154, 155; Rutha 154, 155; Sally 154, 155; Samuel 151; Sarah 154; Sophia 151; Thomas 151, 154, 155; Thomas L. 151; Tarbell 151; William 151; Wilson 151.

GORE
    Patricia 333.
GRAHAM
    Robert, Rev. 243.
GRAVES
    Addie C. 12; Ann 239; David 12; Hayes 239;
    Isaac 12; James 12; Jean 239; John A. 12;
    Jonathan 239; Marshall 12; Mary Ann 12;
    Rebecca (Kellam) 12; Robert 239; Samuel 239;
    Sarah J. 12; Susannah A. 12.
GRAY
    Charles 294; Ebe 214, 215; Emma 117; George
    214; Levi Lewis 117; Valentine 353; Wm. 146.
GREEN
    Arianna 300, 301; Arranna 50; Hannah 302;
    Humphrey 50, 302; Jennie 372; Gen. Jesse
    170; Martha 325; Peter 325.
GREENLEA
    Richie 40.
GREGG
    Ethel E. 286.
GRIER
    David 164, 168; Jane 167, 168; Jannet 168;
    John 167; Margaret 164; Mary 168; Nancy
    Agnes 168.
GRIERSON
    Boulter 385.
GRIFFIN
    Anne 8; Frederick H. 8; George 8; John
    Allmond 8; Helen 8.
GRIFFITH
    Edward K. 195; Hannah 194, 195, 292, 293;
    James A. 9; Jane 195; John G. 194, 195;
    Joseph W. 9; Margaretta 195; Mary 153; Mary
    Catherine 9; Rhody Ann 9; Sarah 9.
GRIFFITHS
    Martha 144.

GRIMES
　　Horace 353; Mabel Broadbent 353; Mildred
　　May 353.

GRIMSHAW
　　Arthur H., Dr. 23, 24.

GRING
　　Anna E. 168, 169; Catherine 155; Daniel 155;
　　David Martain 155; Eliza Ann 155; Fanny 155;
　　Israel 155; John 155; Rebecca 155; Suphyah
　　155.

GROFF
　　Abram 138, 139; Carrie A. 138, 139;
　　S. E. 138, 139.

GRUBB
　　Amer 7, 8, 44, 62, 63, 64; Ann 44, 63, 64;
　　Bertha 313; Beulah 7, 63, 64; B. R. 156;
　　Brandling G. 280, 281; Buckley 63, 65;
　　Charles Henry 392; Charlotte 63, 64; Deborah
　　156; Edward 44, 392; Edward Bunn 392;
　　Ellen Sloan 392; Hannah 53, 63, 65, 280,
　　281, 359; Harriett Amelia 63; Heneretta 64,
　　65; Ignatius C. 8; Isaac 156; Joseph 63, 64;
　　Juli Ann 63; Julia Ann 44; Julianna 43;
　　Julianne 63; Louise O. 8; Lydia 156; Lydia
　　Ann 53; Margaret 156; Mary Sheperson 392;
　　Matilda 63, 64; Nicholas 121, 122, 280, 281;
　　Peter 53; Rachel 63, 156; Rebekah 156;
　　Samuel 156; Wellington 8; William 156.

GRUWELL
　　Caroline 102; Elizabeth 101; Elizabeth A.
　　102; Eliza Ann 102; Henry 102; Isaac 101;
　　John 101, 102; Joseph 102; Joseph D. 102;
　　Joseph Edward 102; Mary 101; Mary Emily 102;
　　Rachel 101; Walter 102; Watson 102, William
　　102.

GUANT
　　Samuel 173.

GUEST
　　Albert Reuben 38; Alice Rebecca 39; Anna J.
　　238; C. Edgar 239; Charles Edgar 38, 39;
　　Charles Robert 38; Clara Mae 38; Clara R.
　　239; Edith Barton 38, 39; Elizabeth 239;

GUEST (Cont'd.)
    Everett 238; Fred Harrison 39; George Willie
    238; Harry Beeson 38, 39; Irvine W. 238;
    Lewis B. 239; Lydia 239; Lydia Amanday 238;
    Mary Lizzie 238; Mary R. 239; Nathan 239;
    Palmer 238, 239; William P. 239.

GUTHRIE
    Ledru O. Jr. 383; Marie P. 384.

HABBART
    W. E., Rev. 258.

HADLEY
    Dale Hale 258; Margaret Elizabeth 258;
    Samuel 3278; Virginia Orr 258; Wm. F.
    258; Wm. Frederick 257; Wm. Frederick Jr.
    258.

HAGERTY
    A. N., Rev. 275.

HAINES
    Altie Louine 274; Ann 199; Elenor 199;
    Hannah 199; Phoebe 199.

HALDEMAN
    J. M., Rev. 179.

HALE
    Samuel 324.

HALLEMAN
    Martha E. 268.

HALLOWELL
    Bedford 73; Bridget 73; Cantwell Garretson
    73; Edmund 73; Elizabeth 73; Henry Garretson
    73; Jasper 73; Mary 73; Priscilla 73;
    Richard 73; Thomas 73; Yeota Jr. 73; Wm. 73.

HAMILTON
    Alexander 158, 159; Ann 157, 158, 159; Anna
    158, 159; Ann Elizabeth 158; Archbald
    (Archibald) 157, 158; Charles 157, 158, 159;
    David 157, 158; Eliza 158; Isaac 159; James

HAMILTON (Cont'd.)
157, 158; James Henry 158; John 157, 158;
Maria Louisa 158; Mary 159; Martha 157;
Mary 157; Richard 157; Robert 157, 158, 159;
Sarah 159; Susan 159; Susannah 157, 159;
William Penn 158.

HAMMOND
Dollie Barden 258.

HANBY
Anna E. 228; Ann Eliza 160; Arthur 160;
Arthur S. 190; B. Frank 190; Benjamin F. 189,
191; Charles 190, 228; Charlottte 228;
Charlotte Prince 160; Clara 190; Clara
Davis 285; Edward Larkin 160; Emma 228;
Emma A. 228; Emma Amanda 227; Esther 159,
160; Esther Ann Larkin 160; George 227, 228;
Geo. M. 231; George W. 226, 228; Georgie N.
228; Harry Sharpley 160; Ida 231; Ida Jane
227; Jacob Benjamin 160; Jacob K. 159, 160;
Jacob Klough 160; James 190; Jesse H. 190;
L. Martin Miller 228; Lewis M. 228;
Levenia 31; Levenia H. L. 32; Levenia
Humphrey Larkin 160; Lotie D. 190; Mabel
190; Mabel R. 190; Mary 231; Mary Emma 190;
Mary M. 229; Samuel Larkin 159, 160; Sarah
360; Sarah Jane Bullock 286; Ulyses 231;
Ulyses M. 228; Viletta P. 171; Willard
Saulisbury 160; William Saulisbury 159.

HANCE
Mrs. 334; Samuel, Rev. 334.

HAND
Alety 111; Hannah 111; Nehemiah 111.

HANNA
J. D. C., Rev. 258; John D. C. 282.

HANNAH
Jacob 311; Jacob Jr. 311.

HANNUM
Abagail H. 161; Annie T. 161; Elizabeth 161;
Elizabeth Y. 161; Esau P. 161; Hannah 264;
Henry W. 161; John 144; Jos. 146; Maggie G.
161; Margaret G. 161; Mary 144, 146; Norris
161; Norris M. 160, 161; Susanna Y. 161.

HARDING (HARDIN)
    Ann 372; Sarah 372; 373.

HARE
    Mary Esher 165.

HARGIS
    Comfort Waples 90; Jacob 90, 91; Martha Jane 90, 91.

HARKER
    Charlotte 64; Joseph 173.

HARLAN
    Enoch 145; Ruban 366.

HARPER
    Mary 20.

HARRIS
    Alfanza Kate 163; Alfred, Rev. 352; Anna 100, 101, 102; Anna Catherine 162; Annie E. 162; Benjamin C. 162; Elizabeth 162; Ellen 202; George W. 162; James 161, 162, 163; John 162; John B. 162; John R. 162; Josephine 163; Joshua 162; Lily M. 163; Lydia 101, 102; Martha 162, 163; Martha E. 162; Martha Evalin 163; Mary 162; Mary Emma 162; Sallie C. 162; Sarah Cole 162; Temperance 162; William 100, 101.

HARROWAY
    Veronica 277.

HARRY
    Maggie Hazel 303.

HARVEY
    Jeremiah 360.

HARWOOD
    Dorothy 130.

HATFIELD
    James B. 117; Lanah E. 117; Martha Adella 117.

HATTON
    Joseph 23; Priscilla 22, 23, 24.

HAY
Albert 163; Alexander 163; Andrew S. 163, 221; Ann (Dollie) 163; Annie C. (Stuart) 221; Bessie Barnitz 167; Charles 165; Charles A. 164, 165, 166; Charles Augustus 166, 167; Charles Barnitz 166; Charles E. 167; Charles Ebert 165, 166; Charles Livingston 167; David 385; Edith MacKenzie 22, 59, 163, 164, 245, 248, 308; Edward 166; Edward Buchanan 166; Edward Grier 165, 166; Eliza 165, 166, 167; Elizabeth 163; Ella 166; F. E. 167; Florence Eugenia 165; Frances Elizabeth 165, 166; George Washington 166, 167; Henry 165; Jacob 164, 165; James 25, 59, 163, 164, 221, 245, 308; Jean 163; John 164, 165, 166, 167; John Andrew 167; John DeYoe 167, 168; John W. 167; John William, M.D. 164, 166; Laura Ella 165; Lillian Jeffries 167; Margaret Rebecca 166, 167; Martin Luther 167; Mary 163, 167; Mary Ann 165; Mary E. (MacKenzie) 22, 308; Mary Jane 164, 166; Mary Jean 163; Michael 165; Millie Frances (Bacon) 59, 164, 245; Nellie McKnight 167; Rebecca Jane 167, 168; Ruth Stevenson 167, 168; Sallie J. 167; Sarah 165; Sarah H. 166; Sarah Rebecca 167; William 163; William E. 167; William Ebert 166; William S. 22, 163, 309; William Stuart 163, 221; William Welty 167, 168.

HAYES
Hannah 20, 21.

HAYNES
Annie H. 162; Arrabell 162; Eva M. 162; Herbert 162; Jennie M. 162; Lulu H. 162; Mary Emma 162; Martha E. 162; Sallie C. 162.

HAZEL
Emma 303; Isaac 303; Maggie 303.

HAZZARD
Agnes 207, 209; Barbara L. 210; Barbara Lacey 209; Cora E. 288; Franklin W. 207, 210; Franklin William 207, 209; John B. 207, 209, 210; John Benjamin 207; John F. 210; John Franklin 209; Nancy J. 210; Nancy Johnson 209; Thelma Townsend 209.

HEARN
    Sarah C. 279.

HEAVELOW
    Dan--- 87.

HEFELBOWER
    Beth 165.

HEFFLEBOWER
    Alice Kate 168; Samuel 168, 169; Samuel
    Gring 168.

HEISLER
    Rev. M. L. 165.

HELDERMAN
    Benjamin 352.

HELSON
    Elizabeth 343, 345, 346.

HENCH
    Alice Caroline 206; Edward Warren 206;
    John B. 206, John Benjamin 205, 206;
    Mary Ann 206; William Channing 206.

HENDERSON
    Anna Mary 132; Annie M. 135.

HENDRICK
    Elizabeth 347; Elmer 346; Florence 346;
    Hallie 346; Martin 346; Willard S. 346,
    347.

HENDRICKS
    James, Lt. Col. 55.

HENDRCKSON (HENDRICKSON)
    Catherina 339, 342; Charles 368; Maria 342,
    368.

HENRY
    Anna M. 246; Viletta P. 171; W. F. J. 246.

HENTON
    Elizabeth 337.

HERMAN
    Ann Marie 237; Augustine 237; Ephraim 6.

HERSEY
    Martha 241.

HEULING
    Hannah 105; Joseph 105; Keturah 105.

HEWETT
    Ezekiel 322.

HEYD
    Rosannna 188.

HEYSHAM
    Mary 144.

HEYSINGER
    J. L., Rev. 39.

HIBBARD
    Isaac 146; Mary 194, 195.

HICKEN
    Dinah 69, 70, 72.

HICKMAN
    Annie E. 96; Lewis 360.

HICKS
    Frank, Rev. 25; Mary E. 95.

HICKSON
    Margaret 264; Sarah Ann 264.

HIGGENS
    Annemary 117; Merit Elmer 117; Sarah E. 117.

HILL
    Anna 146; David 169, 170; Deborah 146; Elezey 170; Hannah 146; Humphrey 146; John 146; Joseph 146; Lydia 146; Mary 146; Nancy 170; Nancy Ann H. 170; Norris 146; Rachel 146; Sidney 146; Tacy 146; Wm. 146.

HILLIARD
    DeWitt 132; Wm. C. 132.

HIMES
Edwin Hay 166, 167; John A. 166; John Andrew 164; Margaret Rebecca 165, 166; Mary Hay 166; Mary J. 166; Mary Jane 167.

HINKSON
Ella C. 171, 172; Harry C. 171, 172; Harry M. 171, 172; Henry C. 171; Lewis W. 171, 172; L. Jennie 171, 172; Mary 231; Mary Elizabeth 228; Mattie R. 171, 172; Sallie E. 171, 172; Thomas L. 171, 172; V. Emma 171, 172; Viletta P. 171, 172.

HINSLEY
Elizabeth (Ellen) 242.

HITCH
Benjamin Franklin 173; Ellen Fooks 173; George Washington 173; Levin 172; Samuel Benjamin 172.

HITCHENS
Lavenia C. 338; Mary 338; Miles B. 338; Miles Benton 338; Nathaniel 338; Nathaniel Peoples 338; Roland Nathaniel 338; Sarah E. 338; Sheppard Jackson 338; Victor C. 338; Wm. G. 338; William Smith 338.

HOFFECKER
Elizabeth (Eliza) 291.

HOKE
Gloria 164.

HOLLAND
Albert Bruce 113; Ann Robbins 113; Annie E. 113; Comfort B. 116; Ebenezer 112, 113; Eleanor Bruce 116; Eliza 112, 113; Eliza T. 113, 116; Elizabeth 113; Hannah Newbold 113; Hetty Elenor 113; John 113; John P. 113, 114; John Paynter 113; Joseph 112, 113; Maggie 113, 114; Maria 113; Mary B. 114; Mary H. 114; Tabitha 113, 114; William Dodd 113.

HOLLINGSWORTH
Isaac 390; J. Walter 268.

HOLLIS
John A. 1; Mary E. 1.

HOLLOWAY
    Martin E. 65.

HOLMES
    Barbara 344.

HOLSTON
    Ruth Edna 263.

HOLT
    Jacob 169.

HOLTON
    Charles 295.

HOOKER
    Thomas 107, 396.

HOOPES
    Charles 266; Davis H. 264; Deborah 145; Mary H. 264.

HOPKINS
    Della Lois 83, 86, 400; Herman 288.

HOPMAN
    Beata 369.

HORNER
    Alice 173; Caroline 173; Cora 203; Elijah 173; Eliza 173; Elizabeth Coles 173; Elma 173; Erna 202; George 173; Gladys 202; Jacob 202; Joan 203; Kirby 203; Martha 173; Mary 203; Mary Ann 173, 201; Thomas 173; Thomas Coles 173.

HORTON
    James 187; Thomas 187.

HOUGH
    Margaret 203.

HOUSTON
    Curtis 210; Curtis S. 210; Hester A. P. Lacey 207.

HOWARD
    Alice 146; Mrs. Eugene C. 319; Eugene C.
    319; Gertrude 313; Mildred L. 318, 319;
    Sarah 144; Sarah Jane 62.

HOWELL
    Ebenezer K. 153.

HOWES (HOWSE)
    Catherine 219; Eliza J. 219; Gersham 219;
    Henry 219; Jane 219; Lorenzo 219; Mary J.
    219; Rebecca 219; Rebecca A. 217, 218;
    Susan 219.

HOWLAND
    Abigail 198.

HOYT
    Stuart 327.

HUDSON
    Caroline 208; Comfort 225; Daniel 207, 208,
    210; Edna M. 177; Frances 204; Harlie W.
    177; John P. 225; Louvenia (Levenia) 210;
    Orbourne W. 177; Peter 215; Preston J. 177;
    Priscilla S. 210; Priscilla Shepherd 207;
    Ruth 177.

HUGHES
    Amy 175; Amy Catherine 175; Amy E. 175;
    Carl 175; Edward 175; James H. 175;
    James H. Jr. 175; Nellie Esher 175;
    Paul Bryan 175; Rebecca 175; S. Carl 175;
    Samuel C. 174, 175; Samuel Carl 175.

HUNT
    Abraham 144; Hannah 144; Henry 202; John
    146; Mary 144.

HUNTER
    Charlie 126.

HUNTINGTON
    Park, Rev. 283.

HURSH
    Lydia B. 169.

HUSBANDS
    Harry 7; Mary E. 108, 109.

HUSSEY
    Ann 177; Bethsheba 19, 177; Christopher
    176, 177; Eliakin 177; Hope 177; Hulda 176,
    177; John 175, 176; Joseph (Joshua) 176;
    Judith 177; Mary 176, 177; Rebecca 177;
    Sarah 177; Stephen 176; Susannah 177;
    Theodate 176, 177.

HUTCHINSON
    Ann Elizabeth 158, 159; Mahlon 158, 159;
    Mary Eliza 158.

HUTSON
    Arla Thomas 177; Charles James 177; Edgar L.
    177; Edna Belle 177; George B. 177; Harry
    Carl 177; Martha J. 177; Roy 177; Reuben
    Jester 177.

HUTTON
    Lillian 149.

HYATT
    Ben. Merritt 179; Charles Edward 179;
    Mary Jane 178, 179; Peter, Capt. 179;
    Samuel 179.

HYGATE
    Anita Calloway 353; Anita Louise 353;
    Harry B. 353.

ILIFF
    Elizabeth 194; Ella 195; Carrie 194; George
    Washington 194; John K. 194; John Wesley
    194; Joseph 194, 195; Josephine 194; Lydia
    194; Margaret 194; Mary 194; Minnie 195;
    Tillie 195.

ILLSLEY
    William 322.

INGRAM
    Mary 172.

IREDELL
----? 200.

JACKSON
   Elizabeth Virtue 268, 269; George 274;
   Laetitia V. 268; Williamina 241.

JACOBS
   Ester 112; George 293.

JACQUES
   Henry 322.

JAMES
   Howell 192.

JAMISON
   Agnes 180, 181, 251; Albert 181; Albert
   Vandergrift 180, 181, 182; Anna 181; Charles
   Henry 181, 182; Clarence 180, 181, 182, 251;
   Clarence Lee 181, 182; Edgar 181; Florence
   Vane 181; Laura 180, 181, 251; Margaret 181;
   Margaret McWhorter 182; Mary 181; Mary Ann
   181; Oliver 181, 182; Raymond Leslie 181, 182;
   Thomas 180, 181.

JANVIER
   Sarah 181; William G. 251.

JARDEN
   Alexander 182, 183; Charles 182; Christianna
   182, 183; Margaret 182, 183; Mary 182, 183;
   Robert 182, 183; Samuel 182, 183; William 182.

JATTA (LATTA)
   John 88.

JAUSS
   Frances Louise 25.

JEFFERSON
   Ann 170; James K. P. 170, 171; Jennie 170,
   171; Lydia O. 170; Thomas P. 170; Virginia
   F. 170; William Bagwell 170.

JENKINS
   James 170; John, Rev. 4.

JENKS
    Edwin L. 25, 26.

JENNINGS
    Francis A. 248.

JENSEN
    Elinor 359.

JEROME
    Henry C. 398, 399; Isabella Jane 399.

JEWEL
    Rev. I. 174.

JOHN
    Rees 292.

JOHNS
    Anne 183, 184; Fidelia 183, 184; Henry Vandyke 183, 184; John 183; Kensey 183, 184; Susan 184; Susanna 183; Vandyke 183.

JOHNSON
    Abraham 13, 14; Abraham (Abram) W. 12, 13; Abrum W. 13, Andrew M. 184; Andrew Manship 185; Anna Mary 185; Annie Mary 184; Benjamin Y. 13, 14; Benton H. 170; Charles E. 13, 14; Clifford Edward 184, 185; Clifford Edward Jr. 185; Conealy A. 13, 14; Ebe Tunnell 184, 185; Elender Ann 279; Elizabeth 81, 84; George P. 13, 14; Hannah E. 13, 14; Hettie 279; James A. 13, 14; Lydia 170; Maggie Emma 185; Maggie Susan 184; Margaret 185; Martha 13; Martha J. 13; Marthy W. 13, 14; Mary Elizabeth 185; Mary J. 170, 171; Mary L. 13, 14; Nathaniel W. 13, 14; Phebe C. 78; Phyllis Lillian 185; Prudie 13; Rasmus D. 13, 14; Rhoda Ann 13, 14; Robert M. 279; Rolley 13; Rosa 13, 14; Ruth 325; Sarah 13; Stephen 325; Thomas J. 48; Tilleta E. 184; Tilleta Emily 184; William Perry 184, 185.

JOHNSTON
    Caroline White 185, 186; Eliza 147; James Gardner 185, 186; John 185, 186; John Jr. 185, 186; Margaretta 185, 186; Mary Ann Elizabeth 185; Thomas 185, 186.

JONES
    Adeline Beeson 7; Alexander 242; Ann 267, 295; Elizabeth 7, 228; Ezekiel 267; Hannah 146; Hazel 203; Henry Laban 7; J. Wesley 302; J. W. 50, 302; James Wesley 300; John 74; Joseph 146; Kitty 90; Lewellyn 126; Lydia 70; Marshall 146; Martha 126; Norris 146; Rachel 146; Sarah 234; Sarah Cantwell 234; Walter B. 231; Walter Beeson 7; Walter S. 228.

JOSEPH
    Clyde P. 319; Leander 319; Margaret Frances 319; Viola (Pepper) 319.

JOYCE
    Anney R. 187; Betsy R. 187; Garret 187; Liddy R. 187; Nancy R. 187; Nelly R. 187; Patty R. 187; Phillip R. 187; Rebecky R. 187; Samuel R. 187; Thomas R. 187.

JUN.
    Peter 277.

JUSTIS
    Catherine 342; David 341, 342; Justa 340, 342.

JUSTISON
    Ann 226, 230; Elizaann 228; John 226, 230; Rebecca 226, 230.

KAVANAGH
    Ann Elizabeth 229; Elizabeth 228; Janet Louise 228; Joan Miller 228, 229; Joseph C. 228; Joseph Charles 228.

KEEN
    Heneretta 367.

KEISS
    Llewllyn 343, 344, 345.

KELLAM
    Ann 190; David 190; Elizabeth 190; Eveline 190; John H. 12; Joseph 12; Margaret 190; Mary 189, 190, Priscilla 103; Rebecca 190; Richard 190; Sarah 190.

KELLY
    Elizabeth Jane 58.

KELSO
    Annie 188; Elizabeth 187; Etruria McKay
    188; Frederick 188; Hugh Klair, Rev. 188;
    Jane 188; Jane Fipps 187; John 187, 188;
    John Friedel 188; John M. 187, 188; John
    Mason, Rev. 188; John Mitchell 187; Margaret
    Jane 188; Rose Mary 188; Sofia 187; Susan
    188; Susan J. 187; William T. H. 187.

KENDALL
    Elizabeth 189; Henry 189; Henry R. 189, 191;
    James 189, 190; Jesse 189, 190; John 145;
    Lydia 189, 191; Margaret 191; Margaret L.
    189; Martha 189; Martha C. 189, 191; Mary
    189; Mary E. 189; Mary Emma 189, 191;
    Rebecca 189, 190; Sarah H. 189, 190; Susan
    189, 190.

KENNARD
    Joseph H. 42; Rev. 44.

KERBIN
    Enols B. 65; Virginia 66.

KILLINGSWORTH
    Oliver P. 379; William B. 379.

KIMBALL
    Abner 325; Ebenezer 323, 325, 329; Jemima
    323, 325, 326, 329; Ruth (Eaton) 323.

KINES
    Matthew 361.

KING
    Alexander 363; Anna M. 131; Beatrice C. 364;
    Beatrice Clayton 363; Eli T. 131; Jennie
    Neville 36; John 131.

KINGSLEY
    William 219.

KINKARD
    John, Mrs. 14.

KINSEY
    Abigail 194, 195; Anna 194, 195; David 191, 192, 193, 194; Edmund 192, 193, 194; Elizabeth (Crewe) 193, 194; John 192, 193, 194; John Jr. 194; John Edmund 193; Magdalen 192; Margaret 194; Margaret (Kitchen) 194; Martha 194; Mary 194; Nathaniel 194; Rachel 194; Samuel 192, 193, 194; Sarah 193.

KIRBY
    Abigail 197; Abraham 199; Alice 205; Alice Richman 201; America 202; Amos B. 203; Ann 205, 206; Ann Warren 206; Anne 199, 200; Arlene Louise 202; Asa M. 200; Bassett 174, 201, 204; Beatrice 203; Benjamin 199; Belleville 206; Chalkey 174, 201, 202; Charles 200; Christian 200; Clayton J. 200; David 200; Deborah 200, 201; Ebenezer 200; Edward 200; Edward Warren 204, 206; Edwin 174; Edwin C. 201; Eleonora 174, 203; Eliza B. 203; Elizabeth 174, 199, 200, 201, 202, 205; Elizabeth Ann 200; Elizabeth Crowninshield 205; Elizabeth Drake 206; Elizabeth Horner 202; Elsie 202; Emily 174, 201; Emily R. 201; Emily Ruth 203; Enoch 200; Frances B. 201; Frank 174, 200; George 174, 200, 203; George H. 201; George Horner 202; Grace 203; Granville 202, Granville Jr. 202; Hannah 200, 201, 203; Hannah Horner 206; Hannah T. 205; Horace 203; Ida 174, 201, 203; Increase 197; Isaac 199; Isabel 206; Jacob 173, 174, 204, 205; Jean 202; Jennie Doone 202; Jane 197, 198, 201; Jo 198; Job 200; John 174, 198, 199, 200, 201, 204, 205; John Smith 205; Jonathan 199; Joseph 198, 199; Maggie P. 200; Malisa 201; Maria 204; Mark M. 205; Martha 200; Mary 199, 200, 202, 204, 205; Mary Ann 205; Mary Ann Horner 202, 204; Mercy 200; Patience Gilford 198; Rachel 200, 201; Rebecca 198, 199, 204; Recompence 196, 197, 198, 199; Reginald W. 204, 206; Reginald Warren 206; Richamath 197; Richard 198, 199, 200, 204, 205, 206; Richard Jr. 197; Richard Sr. 197, 205, 206; Richard III 199; Robert 204, 205; Ruth 201; Samuel S. 199; Sarah 198, 200;

KIRBY (Cont'd.)
    Theophilis 203; Thomas 202; Verna Black 201;
    Viola Matilda 201; Wilhelmina 206; William
    199, 200, 202; William Shreve Warren 206;
    Wilson 204; Winifred 205.

KIRK
    Alice 369; Samuel 369.

KIRKBRIDE
    Robert 173.

KIRUSO (?)
    Amelia 162.

KITCHEN
    Margaret 183; Thomas 193.

KNAPP
    Mary Esther 166; Rebecca Jane 166; Thomas
    166; Thomas Dheridan 165.

KNIGHT
    Sarah 55.

KNOWLES
    Elizabeth 170; Isaac 170; Nancy 169;
    Phillip W. 170; Thomas 169.

KNOWLTON
    John 324.

KOLLOCKS
    Adeline 223; Hannah 223; Hetty 223; John 223;
    John 2nd 223; Mary Fields 223; Mira 223;
    Nancy 223; Penelope Rodney 223; Phillip
    223; Polly 223; Polly Scott 223; Sarah S.
    223.

KROMER
    Margaret 258.

KUHNS
    Jacob 47.

LACEY
Agnes 207, 209, 210; Charles F. 209. 210;
Chas. Franklin 207, 208, 209; Dorothy 209,
210; Ella 180; Elizzabeth (Elizabeth) 207,
209, 210; George R. 210; George Robert 209;
Hannah Eliza 209; Hester 209; Hester A. P.
207, 209, 210; James E. 210; James Emery
208, 209; John F. 210; John Fletcher 207,
209, 210; Katherine Morse 209; Mary B. 210;
Mary Boone 207, 208; Priscilla 207, 208,
209; Priscilla S. 209; Robert 209;
Robert L. 207, 208, 209, 210; Robert Louis
207; Spencer 207, 209, 210; William H. 210;
William Henry 208, 209.

LAHUE
Gordon 229; Virginia 229.

LAMB
Raeburn 132.

LAMBDIN
Ann 270, 271.

LAMBERT
Arrie J. 375; Mary Louisa 375; Robert C.
375.

LAMBERTON
Samuel, Mrs. 15.

LAMBORN
Louis 203; Patricia 174; R. Louis 174;
Rebecca 174.

LANE
Annie 211; Amy A. 211; Amy Augusta 211;
Charles B. 211; Florence G. 211; James 211;
John Galbraith 211; Marion 211; Martha S.
211; William Brasher 211; William Steel 211.

LANGHURST
Elizabeth 376.

LANK
Ella S. 115; Hannah 113; Hannah N. 112, 113;
James 115, 116; John C. 113; Maria 115, 116.

LANNING
    Thomas 81, 85.

LARKIN
    Rhea W. 178, 180.

LARSON
    Mabel B. 286.

LATIMER
    Jane 260; Joseph 260; Margaret 259, 260.

LATOMIS
    John S. 162.

LATTA (JATTA)
    John 88.

LAW
    Edward E. 212.

LAWLESS
    Rachel 275.

LAWSON
    Charlotte 124, 212, 378; Craven 124, 125, 212, 378; Ellen 125; 378; Ellen E. 124, 212, 378; Ellen Elizabeth 42, 44, 212; George 124; Francis 124, 212, 378; Jane 124, 212, 378; John 124, 125, 212, 378; Luke 124; Mary 124, 378; Mary A. 123; Mary Ann 124, 125, 212, 378; Rebecca 124, 212, 378; Robert 124; Robert C. 124; William 124, 212, 378; William Jr. 124.

LEAKIN
    George P., Rev. 96.

LEAR
    Ralph W. 231.

LEARY
    Jeanette Y. 178, 180.

LECKLER
    Bernard J. 330; Sarah Ellen 331.

LEE
    Eleanor (Atkinson) 293; Mary 293; William 293.
LEISHMAN
    Rev. Wm. 319.
LENDEN ? (LAWDEN)
    Elizabeth 305, 306.
LENHOFF
    Leo G. 67.
LERCHENZEILER
    John H. 368.
LEVERIDGE
    Rev. 197.
LEVIS?
    Elizabeth 314; Mary 130; Samuel 314.
LEVY
    Martha 234; Martha M. 237; Martha Mary Anne 234; Mary 236; Moses 237.
LEWIS
    Amy 335; Caroline 102; Eliza B. 106, 107, 396; Eliza Bullock 394; Elizabeth A. 102; Jane (Barnitz) 168; John 102; John Child 394, 395; Louisa 394; Louisa W. 395; Louise 106, 394, 395; Maria Louisa 394; Mary Bullock 394; Mary Jane 395; Nathan C. 106, 393, 394; N. C. Jr. 395; Nicholas Winsor 394; Patience Andrews 395; Richard Sr. 335; Susan Cooper 102; William 394; William Winsor 394.
LILLEY
    Christina Kay 274; George 274.
LIND
    Carl Jr. 248; Carl Richard 248; Warner 248.
LINDSEY
    Harriett G. 51; James S. 51; Joseph E. 51; Mary A. 51, 52.

LLOYD
    General Lloyd 236; Hannah 146; Isaac 145,
    146; James 146; Joseph 146; Mary 146;
    Richard 146; Robert 93, 95.

LOCKMAN
    Rev. 164.

LOCKTON
    Elizabeth 212; James 213; John 212, 213;
    Martha Jaquet 213; Mary 212, 213; Robert
    213; Thomas 213.

LOCKWOOD
    Arena 215; Katherine 215; Louise 215;
    Lucinda 215; Maria Long 215; Mary 215;
    Noah 215; Sarah Pauline 215.

LOCS
    Peist 367.

LODGE
    Alfred J. 213; Anna Maria 213; Charles L.
    214; Elizabeth Ann 213; Hiram H. 213;
    John S. 213; Jospeh P. 213; Margaret 382;
    Samuel 213; Samuel Sr. 213; Samuel W. 213.

LOFLAND
    Eliza 98; Eliza Jain 97.

LOGAN
    Anne J. 246, 247; Anne Jane 246, 247, 249;
    Buteau 364; Indiana T. 246; Indiana Townsend
    249; Sarah Reed 246; Samuel 246, 249.

LOMAN
    George 142.

LONG
    Col. Armwell 214, 215; David 215; Elam 214;
    Elizabeth 214, 215; Elizabeth Robinson 214;
    Handy M. 255; Hester 214; Isaiah 214; James
    214; Jeremiah 214; John 214; Leurander C.
    214; Lydia 214, 215; Martha 214; William 214.

LONGFELLOW
    Amy E. 174, 175; James P. 175.

LONGLAND
    Sarah Elizabeth 52.

LONGSTAFF
    Edith 53; Edith D. 52; James 53; James
    Howard 52; Mary Jane 52; Samel 51, 53;
    Samuel James 52; William 53; William
    Henry 52.

LORD
    Sarah 137, 139.

LOTZ
    Don 132; Mary Elizabeth 132; Paul Eugene
    132; Teresa Joan 132.

LOUIS
    Rev. P. 298.

LOWE
    Bridget 74; Cantwell 74; Edmund 74; Henry
    74; Hollowell 74; Mary 74; Richard
    Garrestson 74.

LOWERY
    Isaac 146.

LOWNS
    Edwin 70; Hannah 70.

LUCAS
    Margaret R. 95.

LUNT
    Abigail 216, 219; Abraham 216, 220; Buford
    216, 220, 391; Buford Thomas 218; Charles
    (Charlie) C. 216, 217, 220; Emily F. 217;
    Elmira 216, 220; Eva M. 217; Fannie 220;
    Fannie M. 217; Flora 220; Flora A. 217;
    Francis 216, 220; Grace 216, 220; Hannah
    216, 220; Hannah A. Bee 217; Ira 216, 218,
    219; Ira C. 391; Ira Charlie 218, 220; Isaac
    217, 218, 220; Isaac L. 218; Jerusha M. 218;
    Jesse Wilson 218; John 216, 219; Joshua 216,
    219; Joshua Jr. 216, 217, 219; Joshua M. 217;
    Julia 220, Julia F. 217; Lucy A. 217, 218,
    219; Margaret 216, 220; Mary 216, 219;

LUNT (Cont'd.)
    Melinda B. 217, 218; Norma M. 217, 219;
    Olive 216, 220; Ozra S. 217; Phebe Jane
    217, 218; Phoebe 220; Ruth 220, 391;
    Ruth Christine 218; Susan 216, 220;
    William 216, 220.

LYBRAND
    Geo. W. 232; Kate C. 232.

LYON
    Eliza 94; John 94; Rebecca 94; Sarah 131.

MABEE
    Charles W. 232.

MACDONOUGH
    Commodore 190.

MACKENZIE
    Alexander 163, 221; Edith 221; Elizabeth
    (Stone) 163; Mary Elizabeth 163, 221.

MACKEY
    Alice 362, 364.

MACMILLIAN
    Barbara 6.

MACNAMEE
    Georg W. 27.

MAGANY
    John B., Rev. 270.

MAINLY
    William 142.

MAITLAND
    William 283.

MAJOR
    Madelyn 347.

MALCOLM
    Robert Monckton 144.

MALIN
    Adda Emma 222; Alice Matilda 222; Anna Mary
    222; Ella Bertha 222; Elmer 221; Florence
    Anna 222, 355; Horace L. 250; Lydia 16;
    Rachel (Haines) 221; Thomas E. 222; Thos
    Elmer 221.

MANCILL (MANCIL)
    Elizabeth 377; Mary 202, 377; William 377.

MANSEL (MANSIL)
    George P. 37; James 37; Susannah Jr. 37.

MANSSON
    Margaret 369.

MARKWOOD
    Ellen Nora 169.

MARSH
    Donald Shankland 66; Ralph C., Dr. 146;
    Roland S. 66.

MARSHALL
    Catherine Franklin 256; David 256, 257;
    David J. 255, 256; Edwin Connor 255;
    Eliza 255, 257; Eliza Ann 256, 257;
    Emily Annie 256; Emma A. 255; Essie 255;
    Hannah 144; John 377; John M. 256, 257;
    Kitty 256; Samuel 377; Sarah Rowland 256;
    Thomas 377; Thomas C. 255; Thomas Connor
    257; Thomas Griswold Connor 256; William
    256; William M. 256, 257.

MARTIN
    Ellis G. 132; Eliza 269; John J. 189, 191;
    Lillie C. 190, 191; Silvanus G. 393, 395.

MASON
    John 390; Kate 121, 123; Susan Jane 187;
    Thomas 126.

MASSEY
    Mary 145.

MATTEHOVEN
    Indian Chief 367.

MATTHEWS
    Cecilia 108, Claire Louise 108, 396; David
    Cameron 108, 396; Elaine 108, 396; Margaret
    107; Maria Louise 107; Martha Patsy 126;
    Mildred 108; Paul Denison 108, 396; Paul
    Denison Jr. 108, 396; William C. 107;
    William Chapman (Chipman) 396.

MAULL
    Betsey 256; E. Edward 67; Eliza Ann 256,
    257; Harry Edward 66; Harry Messick 66;
    Helen M. 253; Henry Edward 67; J. Burton 66;
    John 256, 257; John Burton 66; Lewes
    Delaware 66; Mary Jane 256; Sarah 256, 257.

MAURICE
    Albert Henry 232, 233; Alvina 233; Cora A.
    231, 232; Cora Amelia 233; Edgar L. 233;
    Edgar Lucas 232; Eugene B. 232, 233;
    Frances Ella 232, 233; Jennie F. 231;
    John F. 233; John Franklin 233; Mary E. 233.

MAURY
    Alfred Blake 147; Fountain 147; James
    Fontain 147; Mary H. 147.

MAXWELL
    Benjamin 104; John 104, 105; Mary 104; Mary
    Jane 268; Sarah 104, 262; Sarah A. 257;
    Sarah Annie 261.

MELON
    Isaac 350.

MELVIN
    Brummel 10, Sarah 10.

MENDENHALL (MENDINHALL)
    Alice 130; Esther 146; Lydia 239; Mary L.
    131; Wm. 130.

MERCER
    Ann 270, 271, 272; James 272; John 270, 271,
    272; Laurence Hipple 272; Mary 271; Nicholas
    271; Rachel 338; Rebecca 271; Sarah 271;
    Susan E. 331; Thomas 330; William 271.

MEREDITH
    Peter, Rev. 27; Sarah 27; ----? 102.

MERION
    Bertha G. 150; John 150; John C. 149, 150;
    John C. Jr. 150; William Goodley 150.

MESSETER
    Richard 293.

MESSICK
    Betsey Miller 224, 226; Comfort 222, 223,
    224, 225; Eleanor (Elenor) A. 225; Eliza
    Jane 111; Elizabeth 223; Ellener 223;
    Ellonder 224, 225; George 222, 224, 225;
    George Sr. 224, 225; George Michel 225;
    George Miller 222, 224, 225; George Mitchell
    224; Geo. Roland 223; Jane 222, 225; Jane
    Sandres 224; John Hall 222, 224, 225; John
    William 224, 225; Lina (Swain) 223; Mary E.
    225; Minos (Minas) 222, 224, 225; Nelly 224, 225;
    Roland 223; Sallie 223; Sally Thoroughgood
    224, 226; Sarah (Kollock) 223, 224, 225;
    William 223, 224, 225, 226.

METTEN
    Miriam 347.

MIERS
    Jane 87, 88; John 88.

MILHOUS
    Sarah 144.

MILLER
    Albert 231; Albert LeRoy 229; Albert M. 227,
    229; Alexander 304, 306; Angeline 227, 228,
    230; Ann 228; Anna 226, 227, 228; Anna
    Barbara 164; Anna M. 230; Anna Mary 77, 226,
    227; Anna P. 227; Annie E. 227, 228; Beata
    304, 306; Carolyn Mae 229; Catherine 76, 77;
    Catherine Walker 77; Charles 226, 227, 230;
    Charlotte 227; David 114, 115; Eliza J. 230;
    Eliza Jane 226; Elizabeth 304, 306; Emma
    23; Emma A. 226; Emma Amanda 227; Ester
    (Esther) 114, 115; Frank 231; Frank C. 228;
    George 223, 226, 228, 230; George Hiram 227,
    228; George L. 353; George W. 353; Georgie
    N. 231; Georgianna (Georgine) 47, 228;

MILLER (Cont'd.)
  Grace 349; Hannah 230; Hannah Ann 226, 228;
  Helen G. 228; Jane 339; John 306; J. S. 77;
  Laurette 361; Laurette J. 362; Lewis 227,
  231; Lewis M. 226, 227, 228; Martin 226,
  227, 228, 230; Mary 306, 356, 357, 358;
  Mary E. 353; Mary Ellen 229; Mary Hazle 344;
  Sarah 226, 228, 230; Sarah Elva 227.

MILLIGAN
  Catherine 233, 234; Elisa 234; George 233;
  George B. 234; George Baldwin 234; John
  Jones 234; Lydia 234; Margaret 235;
  Martha Elizabeth 235; Mary 233; Mary L.
  235; Peggy 235; Robert 233, 234, 235.

MINER
  Absalom, Rev. 153.

MINK
  Margaret 362.

MISSIMER
  Beulah May (Weldin) 387; Delilah 54;
  Warren Pyle 387.

MITCHELL
  Joseph 266; Hannah 266; Sarah N. 266.

MOFFETT
  Mary L. 96.

MONROE
  Charlie 126; Edna 126.

MONTAGUE
  Gerald Laurence 84, 86, 400; Patricia Neal
  84, 400.

MONTAIGUE
  Gerald Jr. 229; Gerald III 229; Jospeh
  Fenwick 229.

MONTGOMERY
  Ann 238; Anna 238; Anna J. 239; Anna Mary
  238; George 238; George C. 238; George
  F. C. 238; George Franklin 238; James 238;
  Jeane 238; Jennie Herdman 238; John 238;

MONTGOMERY (Cont'd.)
    John H. 238; John Herman 238; John Herdman
    238; Mart. T. 238; Martha 238; Mary E. 238;
    Mary J. 238; Rachele 238; Robert 238; Sarah
    238; Thadeus 195; Thomas 238; Thomas Lynch
    148; William 238.

MOOR (MORE)
    Phebe 192.

MOORE
    Ann 118, 195; Caroline 202; Carlton E. 202;
    Dallas C. 188; David W. 202; Edith W. 285;
    Eleanor Ethel 285; Ella 32; Elizabeth 202;
    Emma 195; Florence H. 202; Frank B. 285;
    Frank Lee 285; Helen Edith 285; Jacob 196;
    Legrand W. 202; Lela Jean 285; Martha 118;
    Martha E. 202; Martha (Patsy) Elder 127;
    Martha --? Rachel 118; Mary Elizabeth 196;
    Mathew 118; Rachel 196; Richard Clarence
    285; Robert Perry 285; Sallie 196; Sallie M.
    298; Samuel 202; Samuel M. 202; Susanna 196;
    Vaughn 282; Warren T. 298; Warren Thomas
    298; Wilbert Jacob 202; William T. 297, 298.

MORGAN
    Amy Louise 333; Anderson J. 242; Anderson
    Jackson 241; Barbara Jean 333; Charlotte
    Jane 241, 242; David 241, 242; Elisha D.
    241, 242; Elishua 241, 242; Emly Sophiah
    241, 242; Evan F. 241, 242; Frederick E.
    333; Harry L. 333; Harry L. Jr. 333;
    John Frederick 333; Margaret 241, 242;
    Marian Anne 333; Mary A. 242; Mary Ann
    241, 333; Peter Westervelt 333; Robert W.
    333; Robert Wm. 333; Roberta Jane 333.

MORGERIDGE
    Samuel 324.

MORLEY
    George E. 171; Sara E. 172.

MORRICK
    Helena Ennis 66.

MORRIS
    E. P. 225; Edward P. 225; Eleanor A. 225; Hester 90, 91, 92; Hester A. 91; Mary A. 392; Samuel Hollie 90, 91, 92.

MORROW
    Eliza Eva 240; Hannah Ella 240; Ida Lizzie 240; Lydia A. 240; Mary Emma 240; Robert I. 240; R. J. 240; William 240; William Henry 240.

MORSE
    Katherine 207.

MORTON
    Elizabeth 352.

MOTTES
    Theodore 143.

MOUL
    John 164.

MOUSLEY
    Ruben 121, 123; William 105; William R. 104.

MULFORD
    Hannah C. 308.

MURPHY
    Effie L. 398; Ella 398; Joseph E. 241; Orlando 398.

MURRAY
    Ella 299; Elmer S. 297, 299; Ethia 299; J. A. 169; Lendley E. 299; Mary M. 65.

MYERS
    Mildred 8.

McARDLE
    Martha E. 141.

McCALL
    Abigail 152; Ansel 153; Benajah 152, 153; Catherine J. 153; Catherine Janette 153;

McCALL (Cont'd.)
 Corvie Ellsworth 152; Della 154; Della Maria 152; Eliza Ann 152, 153; Ella Sophia 152; Elizabeth (Dye) 153; Emila 152, 153; Ethel Della 152; Frank 154; Frank Erwin 152; Genieve J. 152; Gordon A. 152; Ira Newell 151, 152, 153, 154; Jacob 153; James 152, 153, 154; James Clark 153; James Wilson 152; Jerusha 154; John Erwin 152; Lydia Washburn 153; Mariah 152, 153, 154; Mary Jane 153; Mathilda 152, 153; Milton 152, 153, 154; Naomi 153; Nelson 152, 153; Orson Gordon 152, 154; Seneca 152, 153, 154; Sophia 152, 153; William Wallace 152, 154.

McCALLA
 Margaret 121, 122.

McCARDELL
 Mildred 108, 396.

McCARNS
 Louise 83, 86, 400.

McCLEAN
 Mary 164.

McCLINTOCK
 Jane 7; Margaret 338, 339; Violet 339.

McCLOSKEY
 Anne 233; Beverly Jane 233; Carolyn Ann 233; Harold F. 233; Harold Fowler 233; Henry 233; Henry Maurice 232, 233; John Ralph 232, 233; Mary Ann 233; Ralph A. 231; Vaughn Arthur 232, 233; William 232.

McCLUNE
 Cora M. 231, 233; J. Otis 231, 233; Jennie F. 233.

McCLURE
 Frances 132.

McCOY
 Mary Ann 15; Robert 15.

McCRACKEN
  Sarah S. 59; Sarah Jane 46, 47, 244; Thomas J. 59.

McCREA
  Sarah E. 261, 262.

McCRANE
  Ann Jane 242, 251; George P. 242; Hannah Mary 242; James Jr. 242; John Hannibal 242; John Sr. 242; John III 242; Margaret 242; Sarah 242; Wm. Brooks 242.

McCULLOCK
  Elizabeth 213.

McCULLOUGH
  Catherina 89, 370; Charles 89, 243, 244; Eleanor 243, 244; Eliza 243, 244; George 244; George W. 243, 244; Hannah 243, 244; John 89, 243, 244; John B. 243, 244; Margaret 244; Margaret Carey 243; Mary 89, 243; Mary Ellen 243, 244; Matilda 243, 244; Sarah Ann 89; Thomas 243, 244; William 243, 244.

McCURDY
  Rev. T. S. 178.

McDADE
  Elizabeth 47, 244; James 47, 244; John 244; Sarah Jane 46, 47, 244; William 244.

McDONALD
  Anna R. 206; Francis J. 346; Francis James 344.

McDONOUGH
  John 277.

McFADDEN
  Alice Alta 201; Charles 201; Charles III 201; Frank G. 201.

McGARRY
  Carol Lynne 229; Frank 229; Michael 229.

McGARVEN
  Martha 131.

McGINNES
    Mary Anne 232.

McGLAUGHLIN
    Bessie 122, 123; Esther A. (Weer) 122;
    George 122.

McILVAIN
    Handy 114; Harriet 114; Richard 11.

McINTYRE
    Francis 15.

McJUNKEN
    Lloyd 202.

McKAIN
    Ann 94; Eliza 93, 94, 95; Henry 277; Jacob
    277; James 94, 95; John 277; Letitia 277;
    Mary 277; Richard 277; Thomas 277;
    Veronica 277; William 277.

McKAY
    James 111.

McKENNAN
    William 305.

McKINLEY
    Mary E. 311.

McKNIGHT
    Rose 286.

McLANE
    Louis Hon. 234.

McLAUGHLIN
    Alfred Shelmerdine 298; Charles Kingsley
    298; James H. 297; James West 297; Sarah T.
    297, 299.

McLEAN
    Jacob 277; John 277; Nancy 277; Richard B.
    277; Veronica 277.

McMICHAEL
    W. W. 171.

McMILLER
    John R. (McC.Miller) 398.

McMINN
    Mary Jane 330.

McNEAL
    Amos E. 246; Anne Jane Logan 247; Anne Logan
    246; Annie 246; Bertha Brown 247; Clara
    Louise (Berlin) 22, 164, 221, 248, 309;
    Daniel R. 22, 47, 164, 221, 309; Daniel R.
    Jr. 22, 59, 221, 245, 247, 309; Daniel
    Raymond 59, 245, 247, 248; Daniel Raymond
    Jr. 248; Daniel Raymond III 59, 164, 221,
    248, 309; Debra Jeanne 22, 59, 164, 221,
    245, 248, 309; Dorothy Warner 247; Eliza S.
    247; Elizabeth Reese 247, 248; George V.
    247; George W. 246; George Washington 246,
    249; H. Warner 248; H. W. 22, 47, 59, 221,
    245, 267, 336; Hannah 245, 246; Helen Louise
    247; Henry W. 247; Henry Warner 247; Hiram
    Rudolph 247; Joan Pattison 248; John T.
    246; Joseph 246; Joseph H. 246; Joseph Henry
    246, 247, 249; LeRoy Cooling 247; Lydia 246;
    Mary C "Pink" 246; Mary H. 247; May Belle
    247; Mildred Stock 247, 248; Minnie T. 247;
    Myrie (Myrtie) W. (Reese) 22, 221, 245, 247,
    248; Samuel Jr. 249; Sarah M. 247; Susan J.
    246; Thomas 245, 146.

McNEILL
    Charlotte 46.

McPHERSON
    Janett 164; William G. 167, 168.

McSORLEY
    Anna Maria 249, 250; Clarence Stewart 249,
    250; Ellis Alvin 249, 250; Everett Newton
    249; Francis 250; Francis L. 249; Frank
    Leland 249, 250; Ida 249; Ida Alice 249,
    250; Ralph Leonard 249; Samuel Lodge 249,
    250; Wilfred Earl 249, 250.

McWHORTER
    Agnes Irene 180; Agnes Jamison 182; Ann
    Jane 251, 252; Caroline H. 152; Caroline
    (Carrie) Hurlock 252; Charles Henry 180,

McWHORTER (Cont'd.)
    251, 252; Ella Olivia 251, 252; Emerson H.
    251, 252; Emerson Hopkins 252; Emma Frances
    251, 253; Jennie Craighead 252; John Thomas
    180, 251; Laura Jamison 182; Leontine 242,
    251, 252; Leontine James 251; Leontine N.
    251, 252; Margaret 180, 251; (Maggie)
    Margaret NcCrone 251; Mary E. 251; Mary
    Elizabeth 251, 252; Mary Emeretta 252;
    Rachel P. 251; Rachel Packard 252; Theresse
    252; Thomas 251, 252.

NAGLE
    Chas. Rev. 206.

NASH
    Ann 335; Thomas 335.

NEAL
    David 86; David John 83, 400; Deborah 86;
    Deborah Lynn 83, 400; Della 86; Donna 86;
    Donna L. 83; Donna Lynn 400; Edith 84, 86,
    400; Elizabeth 399; George 86; George D.
    85, 86; George Duncan 83, 399, 400; John
    86; John Edwin 83, 400; Joseph 86; Joseph
    Duncan 83, 400; Joseph M. 398, 399; Joseph
    Wm. 83; Louise 86; Nancy 86; Nancy Carrie
    83, 400; Patricia 86; Ruth 86; Susan 86;
    Susan May 83, 400.

NEEDLES
    Allie B. 9; Anna 9; Catherine 9, 10; Cora 9;
    Edith 9; James 9; James C. 9, 10; Sally
    Berry 10; Samuel 9, 10; Wilbur 9.

NEILD
    Jane 144; John 144.

NELL
    Sarah Ann 26.

NELSON
    Elizabeth 343.

NEWBOLD
    Hannah 116, James 116.

NEWLAND
    John 197.

NEWLIN
    Jane 377; Nathaniel 377; Rachel 376.

NEWTON
    Rev. Richard 211.

NIGHTINGALE
    Percy 296.

NORMAN
    Anner 254; Annes (?) 254; Benjamin White
    253; Cecilia B. 253; Cecilia Bennett 253;
    Eliza 254; Emily Anne 257; Emma A. 255, 256;
    Fanny Helen 253; Geo. Francis 253; John 254;
    John B. 254; John White 253; Joshua L. 254;
    Lenora L. 255; M. B. 255; Mariam 254, 255;
    Mariane 253; Martha 253; Mary 253, 254;
    Mary H. 253, 255; Mills R. 254; P. B. 253,
    255; Patience 254; Purnal 254; Purnal B.
    253; Purnal B. Jr. 253; Purnal P. 253;
    Thomas 253, 254, 255; Judge Thomas L. 255;
    W. J. 255, 256; Wilbur T. 255, 256; William
    James DeWolfe 253; Wrexham 253.

NORTH
    Caleb 41, 42; Lydia 41, 42; Sarah 41, 42.

NOWLAND
    Anne E. 374, 375.

NUTGRASS
    James 82, Poly 84, Poly Mary 81, 82, 84.

OAKFORD
    Isaac 146.

OBIER
    Henson 1; Thomas F. 1.

OFFNER
    Elizabeth 58.

OGBORN
    Jane Fitzrandolph 193; Sarah 192, 193.

O'HARA
    Mary 277.

OLIVER
    Canby 145; Mary 145.

ONION
    Beals 389; Elizabeh 389, 390; Hannah Juliet 389; John Weston 389; Lloyd Day 389; Rebecca W. 379; Rebecca Weston 389.

ORAM
    Rev. 241.

ORNSEN
    Katie Claudia 25.

ORR
    Alice 262; Alice Barbara 261, 262; Amor P. 259; Barbara 258; Beula Ruby 132; Clarence 132; Dollie H. 258; Edwin Clarence 132; Eliza Ann 259; Elizabeth 259, 260; Elizabeth Ann 260; Helen Elizabeth 261, 262; J. C. 261; Jacob 258, 261, 262; Jacob Z. 257, 258, 261, 262; Jacob Zebley 258, 261; Jane 259, 260, 262; Joseph 259, 260; Joseph C. 261, 262; Joseph Carr 258, 262; Lillie 257, 258, 261, 262; Margaret 257, 258, 259, 260, 261, 262, 376; Marjorie Jean 258; Mary Elizabeth 132; Richard Maxwell 259; Robert 258, 259, 260; 261, 262; Robert Winfield 259, 261; Roger Cooper 259; Samuel 259, 260; Sarah 257, 262; Sarah A. 261; Sarah Annie 258; Sarah E. 258, 259, 261, 262; Sarah Elizabeth 257, 258, 261; Sarah Ellen 261, 262; Viola Ursula 132; Willard Jacob 258; William 260, 262; William S. 259, 260, 261, 262; William Smith 248; William Smyth 262; Winfield 262; Winfield Scott 258.

ORRIS
    Levan H. 169

ORTON
    George 255; Hannah 255; William 255.

OSBOURN
    Elizabeth 59, 60.

OSGOOD
    William 325.

OTIS
    Richard 177.

OTT
    LIllian 362.

OUTTEN (OUTEN)
    Elizabeth 263, 264; Joseph F. 263; Joseph
    Frank, Captain 263, 264; Mary Elizabeth 263;
    Seth 264; Seth L. 263.

OWENS
    Belle 200; Rev. J. C. 169.

PAGE
    Christian I. 229; Thomas 176; William 324.

PAINTER
    Charles 264, 265; Cidney 265; Darwin 264,
    265; Edward 264, 265; Eliza 264, 265;
    Elizabeth 265; Hannah 265; Jane 265; John
    264, 265, 266; Margaret 265; Margaret C.
    264; Mary W. 264, 265; Milton 264, 265;
    Phebe 265; Samuel 264, 265; Sarah 265;
    Sarah D. 265; William 264, 265.

PALMER
    Eliza C. 158; John 104; Martha Jane 104;
    Patience Andrews 393; Rebecca 104; Sarah 69;
    Susan 104.

PAMEL
    Miriam 292.

PANCOAST
    Sarah 70.

PARKER
    William LeRoy 312.

PARKS
    J. 265; Sarah 265.

PARRATT
    Francis 322, 328; Martha 328.

PARSONS (PERSONS)
    Benjamin W. 393, 395; Maria Louise 393, 395.

PASSMORE
    Carleton 266; Edward B. 266, 267; Hannah
    Mitchell 266; Harry C. 266; Helen 267; Lydia
    267; Mary 266; Mary Bertolet 266; Orphia
    266, 267; Pusey 266; Samuel S. 267; Sarah
    267; Sarah N. 266; Thomas H. 266, 267;
    Thomas Hoopes 266; William 266; William P.
    266, 267; Wills 266, 267.

PAST
    Molly 196.

PASTORFIELD
    Rev. J. 298.

PATTERSON
    Alice R. 39; Ann 94, 95.

PATTISON
    Ann 295; Daniel L., Rev. 298; George 267;
    Joan 248; Maryland V. 247; Maryland Virginia
    267, 295, 336; Sallie Ann Elizabeth 267;
    Virginia 295; William 267, 295, 336.

PATTON
    A. 268; Alex. N. 269; Alexander 268, 269;
    A. N. 268; Alexander N. 268; Alexander Nesbit
    268, 269; Alexander Sr. 269; Edmund 269;
    Edmund R. 268; Edmund Richardson 268;
    Elizabeth J. 270; Hannah 269; Harvey Burns
    269; J. R. 268; Jas. 268; James 269; James
    R. 268; James Rice 268; Janey 268; J. Frank
    269; Joseph 268; Joseph D. 268, 270;
    Joseph David 268; Jos. Franklin 268;
    Joseph Leslie 269, 270; Julia G. 45; L. 268;
    Leslie 268; Leslie H. 268; Leslie Hallam
    269; Letitia L. 268; Letitia V. 269;
    Lettie 269; Lettie S. 268; Lizzie J. 268;
    Lizzie Jackson 269; Lottie V. 269; M. E. P.
    268; M. J. P. 268; Martha 268; Martha E.
    268, 269; Martha Hallam 269; Mary 269;
    Mary E. 268, 269; Mary Elizabeth 268, 269;

PATTON (Cont'd.)
Mary G. 269; Mary Jane 269; Thomas Nesbit 268, 269; William Alexander 268, 269; William Jackson 268, 269.

PAULDING
Florence 203.

PAULSON
Aaron 305, 306; Margaret 305.

PAXSON
Lewis C. 309, 311; Susanna S. 311.

PAYNE
John 55.

PEARCE
Ann 144; Col. Benj. 237; George 144; Henry W. 237; Henry Ward 236; Mary 237.

PEARSON
George 20, James Ahab 27, Phebe H. (Babb) 19, 21,; Samuel 196.

PENNELL
Dell 146; Robert 145.

PENNINGTON
Ann 143, 271; Ann Mary 270, 272; Ann Mercer 270, 272; Anna M. 272; Benedict 271; Benedict Chandler 271, 272; Benjamin Sides 271; Delilah Jane 271, 272; Ella B. 274; Ella Brooks 271, 272, 273; Emilie Ann 274; Emilie Evans 272; Emma 273; Emma Walker 273, 274; Helen Mae 273; James 272, 273; James B. 272; James M. 270, 271, 272; James Mercer 270, 271; John B. 270, 271, 272; John F. 272, 273; J. Walker 273, 274; John W. 272; John Wesley 271; Laurence H. 273, 274; Lawrence Hipple 270, 272; Martin Beadenkopf 273, 274; Mary 272, 273; Mary Ann 274; Mary B. 270, 271, 272; Mary Brooks 272; Sallie Albina 273; Sarah 271, 273; Sarah Albina 273, 274; Sarah Ann 271, 272; Thomas Franklin 271, 272; William Henry 271, 272.

PENNOCK (PENNICK)
Ann 130; Christopher 130; Elizabeth 130; Hannah 130; John 130; Joseph 130; Phoebe 130; Sarah 130; William 130.

PEPPER
Amanda S. 297; Bessie 13, 14; Elizabeth 276; George M. 275, 276; Joshua 276; Margaret 275; Margaret H. 276; Margaret Jane 275; Mary E. 275; Mary Elanor 275; Nellie 13, 14; Rachel 275, 276; Ralston 13, 14; Raymond 13, 14; Susan 78, 79; Thomas 275, 276; Thomas B. 275, 276; Truitt 13, 14.

PERKINS
Hannah 55, 63; Isaac 176; Jane A. 382; Jane Ann 381; Mary Amanda 382; Rebecca 176.

PERRY
Mr. Perry 100, 102.

PERSHING
Anna M. 58.

PETERS
Alice M. 276; Alice Maria 276; Charlotte (Edwards) 276; Frank J. 123, 125; J. Franklin 124, 276; John 276; John Franklin 123, 276; Mary 203.

PETERSON
Adam 277, 278; Andrew 277, 278; Eleanor 74; Elizabeth 278; Rachel 277; Veronica 277, 278.

PETTIT
Albert Watson 387; Beulah A. 387; Beulah Ann 385; Elizabeth 204; Elmer 204; Emily Ruth 204; Frank 204; Marian 204; Mary 385, 387; Peter 385, 387.

PETTYJOHN
Maggie E. 184; William A. 185.

PEW
John, Rev. 277.

PHILIP
Calvin 340.

PHILLIPS
Albanas 259; Amanda Ellen 279; Comfort H.
279; Daniel 279; Elnor Ann (Johnson) 278,
279; (Hattie) Hatie T. 279; Helen 165;
Ida E. 279; Isaac T. 18; Isaiah Curtis 279;
John Wingate 279; Jacob E. 279; John S. 279;
Margaret 279; Margaret H. 279; Margaret Jane
279; Mary 278; Mary G. 279;1 Mary H. 279;
Nancy J. 279; Polly 279; Priscilla S. 279;
Robert W. 279; Samuel 278; Sarah Catherine
279; Sarah E. 279; Theodore F. 279; Warren J.
278, 279; William Joseph 27.

PICKLES
Ann 118; John 118; John Sr. 118; Richard
118; Sarah 118.

PIERCE
Amer 280, 281; Brandling 281; Brandling G.
280; Charles 281; Charles W. 280, 281;
Clara 281, 282; Clara G. 280; Edward C. 280;
George 281; George C. 280; Joseph 280, 281;
Julia 281; Julia Ella 280; Laetita 281;
Laetitia G. 280; Laura 281; Laura A. 334;
Laura Amanda 280; Lena 280, 281; Lena A.
280, 281; Lewis 281; Lewis C. 280; Nellie V.
159; Robert 281; Robert C. 280; Sarah B.
264; Uriel 280, 281; Uriel T. 280.

PIERSON
John W. 20; Phebe 20.

PIGOTT
Edna R. 25, 27; Linda King 25; William 26.

PIM (PIMM)
Wm. 144, 201.

PONSELL
Edith 284; Edith E. 282; Edith Elizabeth
283; Francis 284; Francis I. 282, 283;
Gladys 284; Gladys R. 282, 283; Gladys
Rash 283; James 283, 284; James P. 282, 283;
James P. Jr. 282; James Preston 283; Jas. P.
284; Michael 283, 284; Momie 283; Sarah 283,
284.

PONSELLERS
Jas. P. 288.

POOL
    Burrues E. 126.
POOLE
    Charles 356; Charles W. 357.
POPLOS
    Charles M. 48.
PORTER
    Edward Hyatt 180; Eva E. 179; Mabel H. 179;
    Mabel Hyatt 178; Rev. 298; W. Frank 179;
    William Frank 178, 180.
POSEY
    Albert W. 181.
POTTER
    Anna May 285; Carol Ann 285; Charles 285;
    Charles Simon 285; Charles William 285;
    Clara Davis 286; Clarence E. 284, 285, 286;
    Clarence Edward 286; Daniel Eugene 285;
    Edith Winifred 285; Francis Carlisle 285;
    Fred 286; George B. 286; George Brinton 286;
    Helen E. 286; Helen Etta 286; Josephine
    White 286; Kenneth Vincent 285; Mabel
    Florence 286; Ronald Arthur 285; William N.
    286; William Nelson 286; William Nelson Jr.
    286.
POULTNEY
    Ann 70; Daniel 70; John 70; Lydia 70;
    Sarah 70.
POWELL
    Mary E. 380.
PRACKETT
    Abby 195; Gertrude 195; Maggie 195.
PRATT
    Mary Ann 1.
PRESTON
    Helen A. 333.

PRETTYMAN
    A. P. 32; George E. L. 114; Jannette
    (Janette) 114, 115; Joshua 114, 115; Louise
    317; Rodney K. 114; Sarah J. 114; Sarah T.
    115.

PRICE
    Eliz 50; Elizabeth 302; Jane 373.

PRINCE
    John 356, 357.

PRINGLE
    Alexander 287, 288; Anna C. 287; Catharine H.
    287, 288; Elizabeth 287, 288; Emma 287, 288;
    Isabella E. 287, 288; Louise Stone 287;
    Margaret 287, 288; Margaret Ann 287; Mary
    287; Robert 287, 288.

PUHL
    Henrietta 362.

PUSEY
    Betsy 222, 224, 225; David 266; George 223;
    Naomi 266; Nellie (Nelly) 222, 223, 224,
    225; Orphia 266; Pusey (?) 14; Wm. 224, 225;
    William 222, 224.

PYLE
    Beulah 63, 64, 156; Buckley 63; John 63, 64;
    Martha Hallam 270; Nicholas 63; William 264.

QUILLEN
    Annie B. 65, 66; Edward 65; Emma 66; Libbie
    67.

RAISIN
    Joseph C. 162.

RALPH
    Elizabeth 362.

RAMSEY
    Harry 354.

RAPPLEYE
   James 153; Sarah 153.

RASH
   Anna M. 283; Ann Mariah 290; Clara 284;
   Clara E. 288, 289; Cora 284; Cora S. 288,
   289; Eliza 284, 291; Elizabeth 291;
   H. Ernest 288; Hannah 284; Hannah T. 288;
   Hannah Truax 289; Henry 283; Henry Ernest
   289; Herbert 284, 289, 290; Hester 283,
   291; Irving 284; Irving Leroy 289; Jno. H.
   289; Jno. F. 289, 290; Jno S. T. 289, 290;
   James 283; John 284; John Sr. 283; John Jr.
   283, 284, 291; John F. 283, 288, 289, 290,
   291; John H. 283, 290, 291; Jonathan 283,
   284, 291; Joseph 291; Joseph Sr. 291;
   Letitia 284, 288; Letitia P. 289; Mamie 283;
   Mamie C. 282; Mamie Cooper 283; Mariam
   (Mirium) 283, 289, 290, 291; Mariam E. 283,
   289, 290; Martha 283, 284, 289, 290, 291;
   Martha Ann 283, 290, 291; Martha F. 290;
   Martin 291; Mary C. 284, 288, 289; Mary P.
   291, Matie 288; Sarah 284; Sarah J. 283;
   Sarah Jane 291; Sarah T. 289, 290; Walter
   284, 288, 289; William B. 288; Willie 284, 289.

RAUGHLEY
   Belle 2.

RAZEE
   Anna P. 313; Frank A. 287.

READ
   Rebecca 365.

READING
   Phillip, Rt. Rev. 277.

REDISH
   Earl D. 292; Ernest W. 292; Granville A.
   292; Jackson L. 292; Katie M. 292; Larry A.
   292; Lewis A. 292; Lilliam M. 292; Mary H.
   292; Mary J. 292.

REED
   Anna 37; Annie F. 17; Elias 6; Sarah 246,
   249.

REES (REESE)
  Ann George 294, 295; Anna Eliza 294; Annie
  Needham 295; Aquilla 294; Bessie 295; Charles
  Pattison 295; Daniel 293, 336; Daniel M.
  143, 294, 295; Daniel Meredith 294; Daniel W.
  295, 336; Daniel Webster 247, 267, 294;
  David 293; Edward 293; Edward S. 294; Elenora
  293; Ellen 294; Ellenora 294; Eliza 294;
  Ellin 293; Evan 293; Fannie 294; Florence
  295; George 295; George J. 294; Hannah 292,
  293; Hannah Jr. 293; Jane 293, 340, 342;
  John 292, 293, 340, 342; John Lee 293;
  Joseph Meredith 293, 294; Lowry 293;
  Margaret 294; Mary 340, 342; Mary Elizabeth
  294; Maryland V. (Pattison) 247; Mary Lee
  294; Morris M. 294; Myrtie Virginia 247,
  248, 267, 295, 336; Richard 293; Rose 293;
  Sallie P. 295; Sarah 293; Sarah R. 294;
  Sophia T. 294; Stephen 294; Virginia 294;
  Walter 295; William 293.

REGAN
  Joseph Bernard Jr. 364.

REYNOLDS
  Martha A. 161.

RYHS
  Hannah Griffith 292.

RICE
  Nancy Waria 393, 394; Winney 55.

RICKARDS
  Anna M. 300; Eli 295, 296, 297; George
  Cornelius 297, 298, 299; Hannah 295, 296;
  Hannah Daisy 296; Ida M. 297; Isaac 296;
  James W. 296, 297, 299; James White 297;
  Jobe M. 296; Job Morris 296; John 315;
  John M. 296; John Morris 296; Jones 296;
  Kendall 296; Kaura A. 297; Lauran Ann
  297, 298; Mary 296, 297; Mary Lynch 296;
  Nathaniel 296; Rachel 296; Sallie M. 297;
  Sarah Mary West 297; Sarah 315; Sarah T.
  297; Sidney 296; Sophia L. 297; Stephen 296;
  William 296.

RIGDON
  Charles H. 62.

RILEY
   Cecilia 108, 396.

RITTENHOUSE
   D. 71.

ROBBINS
   Ann C. 88, Elizabeth 87,

ROBELEU (?)
   Rose 359.

ROBERTS
   Alfred 303; Anna Spruance 50, 300, 301, 302; Arianna 302; Arianna H. 301, 302; Charles C. 50; Charles Clarence 301, 302; Elizabeth 301, 302, 303; Irene 50; Irene Levis 301, 302; James 50, 300, 301, 302, 303; James V. 301, 303; James Voshell 303; Jas. V. 302; John 50, 301, 302; John C. 308; Mary A. 301, 302; Mary Ann Voshell 303; Mary E. 48, 300; Mary Elizabeth 50, 301; Samuel 50, 301, 302; Wm., Rev. 25.

ROBESON
   Alexander 304, 305, 306; Anne 305; Elizabeth 304; Elizabeth W. 305; Jane 304, 305, 306; Margaret 304, 305, 306; Thomas W. 306; Thomas Wallace 305; William 304, 305; Wm. 306.

ROBINS
   Ann 88.

ROBINSON
   Catherine 3; Elizabeth 214, 215; Estelle Jane (Weldin) 387; Henry 94; John 94; Mary 156, 322; Priscilla 73; Robert 321, 328; Sara L. 206; William F. 387.

RODERICK
   Reubena 39; Theodore 39.

RODNEY
   Leah 18; Mary 18; William 18.

ROGERS
   Rev. 208.

ROOT
    Brener 148; Gilpin Church 148.

ROSINBERGER
    Christina 307; Daniel 307; Hanna 307;
    Henrick 307; Jacob 307; Martin 307;
    Sohpia 307.

ROSS
    Arabella 366.

ROTTHOUSE
    Rachel 384; Rachel L. 384; Rachel Louise 383.

ROWAN
    Henry 15; Henry, Capt. 14; Lackey 14; Mary
    15; William J., Rev. 352.

ROWE
    William S. 312, 313.

RUDGWAY
    ? 200.

RUDISILL
    Mary 164.

RUDOLPH
    Christopher W. 308; Hannah 308; William 308.

RUMFORD
    Catherine 94; Samuel 94, 95; Thomas 95.

RUMSEY
    Charles 175.

RUNNELS
    ? 327.

RUSH
    Rhoda 81, 84.

RUSSELL
    Judge 168; Mary 240; Mary Emma 331;
    Robert J. 330.

RUST
    Amy 116; James 17; Leah R. 17; Maria 116.

RYECRAFT
 Elizabeth 152.

SAMIS
 Frankie 117; Ida May 117; Julia 117;
 Mr. Samis 117.

SANDBORN
 Elder, Rev. A. R. 54; Jno. 327.

SANDUSKY
 Betsy 56; Isaac 56; Mourning 56; Sally 56.

SARGEANT
 Christopher 327; Martha 323, 329; Polly 327.

SAULSBURY
 John 9, Lavania 9; Temperance 9.

SAUNDERS
 Theodore 198.

SAVAGE
 Chas. H. 343; John 77.

SAWYER
 Oliver 324.

SCALES
 Amelia 22, 309.

SCHALL
 Absolom 58; Andrew 58; Andrew J. 58; Jane Braden 47, 58, 245.

SCHENERMAN
 Helen Lee 347; John Henry 347; Roy 347.

SCHOLTY
 Alice C. 8.

SCROFFIN
 John 369.

SHULTZ
 David Thomas 334; Raymond 333; William Morgan 334.

SCHUYLER
   Deborah Ann 274; Oliver 274.

SCROGGIS
   William C. 163.

SEAGRAVE
   Mary Jane 393, 395.

SEARL
   David 153; Lucy R. 153.

SEEBACH
   Arthur 167; Beth 167; Esther 166; Helen 166;
   Helen Fleming 166; Joan Phillips 166;
   J. Arthur 165; John Arthur 166, 167; Julius
   166; Julius F. 165; Julius Frederick 165;
   Julius Frederick Jr. 166; Julius Frederick
   III 165, 166; Margaret 166; Mary Esther 165,
   166.

SERRILL
   John L. 20, 21.

SERVER
   Allun T. 361; Eliza 361; John 361; Juliann
   361; Mahlon 361.

SEWALL
   Mary 237.

SHADINGER
   Catharine 311; Elizabeth 310; Esther A. 309;
   Esther Ann 310; Hannah R. 309; Hannah
   Rebecca 310; Jonathan 309, 310; Jonathan Jr.
   311; Joseph 310; Margaret Bird 311; Mary A.
   310; Nathan 310; Susanna 309, 310; Tobias
   309, 310; William D. 309, 311; William Dilts
   310.

SHAFFER
   Elenora 174; Elenora M. 203; George M. 174,
   203; George M. Jr. 203.

SHAHAN
   Daisy May 27.

SHAKESPEAR
    Anamoriah 312; Benja W. 311; Catherine L. 311; Elizabeth T. 312; Ella Mary 312, 313; Esther Garrett 313; Fares Ives 312; George 312; George W. 312, 313; George Washington 312; James Strawbridge 312; John 311, 312; John B. 311; John M. 311; Mabel Margaret 312; Marian Ada 312; Mary 311, 312; Maryann 311; Mary L. M. 313; Mary Linda Minerva 312; Rebeckah Jane 312; Samuel C. 312; Susanah Eliza 311; Thomas M. 311.

SHANKLAND
    Donald 67.

SHARP
    Maggie Cooper 318.

SHARPLESS
    Amos 146; Annie T. 161; Benjamin 161; Emma 267; Nathan 146.

SHARPLEY
    Nancy 365.

SHAW
    Alban P. 351, 352; Alban Peoples 352; Alban Peoples Jr. 352; Alban Peoples III 353; Catherine 352; David Bruce 353; James Bagshaw 350, 351, 352; Harriett W. 352; Kate (Bengles/Beugless) 350; Sally Anne 353; William 352; William G. 350, 352; William G. Jr. 351; William Gavin 352; William Guillan 350, 352; William Guillan III 353.

SHELDON
    Eli E. 313; Elsie 137; Elsie M. 136, 313; Elsie May 313; Francis 313, 314; Herbert 313; Herbert H. 313; Howard 313, 314; John A. 313, 314; Rebecca E. 313, 314.

SHELLEY
    Parson 88.

SHELLHORN
    Andrew H. 222.

SHEPPARD
    Mae 202.

SHERWOOD
    Ann 333.

SHEWARD
    Jane 144.

SHINN
    George R. 202; James K. 288; Mary 202;
    Sallie E. 288; Verna Florence 202; Wilbert
    Rollen 202.

SHIPLEY
    Anna 70; Charles 143; Eliz 145; Elizabeth
    314, 315; Elizabeth Levis 314; Samuel 314;
    Sarah Levis 314; Thomas 70; William 314,
    315.

SHOCKLEY
    Anna Eliza 315, 316, 317; Catherine 315;
    David W. 315, 317; Earl, Rev. 353; Elias
    315, 316, 317; Elizabeth 316; Elizabeth B.
    317; George W. 315, 317; John Henry 315,
    316; John W. 318; John Wesley Fisher 317;
    Joseph 316; Lydia C. 316; Lydia Jane W. 317;
    Mark 316; Mary Catherine 316; Mary V. 317;
    Matilda 317; Mavinda 317, 318; Nancy 315;
    Nancy B. 317, 318; Rhoades 317; Sarah 315,
    316; Sarah A. 316; Walker 316; Willemina
    315; William 316; William B. 315; William V.
    316, 317; Wilson 315, 317, 318.

SHORT
    Bessie 320; Clara 320; David L. 288; Emery
    320; Fannie B. 319, 320; Fred 318, 319, 320;
    Ida M. 320; John 320; John E. 320; Luther B.
    320; Margaret Frances 319; Mary E. 320;
    Mattie R. 288; Mildred 318; Mildred L. 319;
    Nora 318, 319; Sarah E. 320; Thomas B. 319,
    320.

SHUFF
    Barbary 4, 5; Eliza 4, 5; Elizabeth 3; John
    4, 5.

SILVER
    Elizabeth 321, 323, 328, 329; Eunice 324,
    326, 327, 329; Hannah 321, 328; James 326,
    327, 329; Jemima 324, 325, 326; John 320,
    321, 322, 324, 326, 327, 328, 329;

SILVER (Cont'd.)
Katherine 321, 328; Martha 321, 324, 327, 328, 329; Mary 321, 322, 328, 329; Mehetabel 323, 324, 329; Mercy 323, 329; Moses 326, 329; Polly 326, 327, 329; Prudence 328; Ruth 323, 324, 326, 329; Sally 326, 327, 329; Samuel 321, 322, 323, 324, 325, 326, 327, 328, 329; Samuel Jr. 323, 324, 325; Sarah 321, 324, 326, 327, 328, 329; Thomas 320, 321, 322, 323, 326, 327, 328; Thomas Sr. 322; Timothy 324, 326, 327, 329.

SIMMONS
Anna Wallace 333; Clara (Wallace) 332; C. Leroy 332; C. LeRoy Jr. 333; George H. 330, 331; Hannah Ann 330, 331; Howard E. 330, 331; Howard Elwood 331; J. Channing 331; James 330, 331; Jennie 330; Louise 330; Lydia P. 331; Marion E. 333; Mary 35; Mary Emma 330, 331; R. Barclay 330, 331; Ruth Anna 331; Ruth Marion 332; Sarah Ann 330, 331; Sarah Ellen 330, 331; Susan E. 330; William H. 330, 332; Wm. Henry 331.

SIMON
Charles 281, 282, 334; Charles H. 334; Charles Harley 334; Charles Jr. 334; Clara 282; Clara E. 334; Clarence 282; Clarence Elmer 334; D. Elizabeth 33; Elizabeth 32; Ernest 282; Ernest Allen 334; Florence 282; Florence Ruth 334; Harry 282; Harry L. 334; Herbert 282; Herbert Paul 334; Ida E. 105 Laura 282; Laura A. 334; Laura L. 284, 285, 286, 334; Maggie E. 105; Oscar 282; Oscar Conly 334; William 282; William Emmet 334; William I. 105.

SIMONS
Mary E. 390, 391.

SIMPERS (SYMPERS)
Ann 335, 336; Elizabeth 336; Isaac 336; Jesse 335, 336; John 143, 335, 336; Johnson 336; Joseph 335; Margaret 336;

SIMPERS (Cont'd.)
Margaret (Crouch) 143, 335, 336; Martha 336; Mary 143, 294, 335, 336; Naomi 335, 336; Nathaniel 335; Rebecca 335; Reuben 335; Richard 335; Sarah 336; Sohpia 336; Thomas 335; William 335.

SIMPKINS
William 241.

SIMPLER
Arcadia 17, 18; Hester 207; Hester A. 210; Hester A. P. 207; Hester Ann Parker 207; Leah 17, 18; Louvenia 207, 210; Peter R. 207, 210; Phillip 18; Suzannah 18; Thomas 17, 18.

SIMPSON
Martha 157; Ruth 2202.

SIMS
Joseph Jr. 234.

SINGLETARY
Amos 325.

SITES
Amanda Jane 337; Benjamin Henton 337; Elizabeth 337; Elizabeth Henton 337; Elizabeth Sarah 337; Frances Cornelia 338; Frances Cornelia Cohen 337; George 337; John 337; John Alpheus 337; Martha Louise 337; Mary Katherine 337; William Price 337, 338.

SKEAN (or HEAN)
Delilah 55; Sarah Lovering 55; Theodor 55.

SKILLMAN
Paul 274.

SKINNER
Pauline K. Mrs. 323, 328.

SLACK
William 245.

SLICER
Therese Ralston 151.

SLOAN
    Allerdice 4; David 4, 5;

SLOOP
    Judith 177.

SLUSHER
    Annie Lizenia 232.

SMALLEY
    Elizabeth 56; Hannah 56; F. M. 56; Frances 56; Jacob 56; Joshua 56; Mary L. 56; Matilda 56; Nancy 56; Oliver F. 56; Richard T. D. 56; Stephen 56; Wm. 56.

SMALLWOOD
    Rev. 340.

SMITH
    Alice 369; Edith 360; Ella 77; Frances 369; Hans Geo. 368; John 176; Joseph 10; Jos. H. Jr. 205; Levin 338; Nathaniel 338; Peter 369; Rebecca 11, 12; Sarah 121, 122; S. E., Rev. 390; Susan Nellie 175.

SMITHERS
    Ruth Ann 14.

SMYTH
    Alexander 339; Elizabeth 259, 339; James 339; Jane 338, 339; John 339; Margaret 339; Rachel 339; Robert 339; S. James 339; Samuel 338, 339; Violet 339; William 339.

SNYDER
    Caroline 185; Isabella 7.

SOMERS
    George 55; Martha 200; Richard 201; Talitha 213.

SPAHR
    William A. 169.

SPARKS
    Sarah 93, 95.

SPEDDEN
    Edward 294.

SPENCE
    Preston W. 282.

SPERRY
    Ann 94.

SPRINGER
    Catherine 340; Catheriness Justa 341, 343;
    Charles 339, 340, 342; Charles Sr. 340;
    Christopher 339, 340, 342; Fannie Boughman
    52; Jacob 368; Jeremiah 339, 340, 341;
    Jeremiah C. 341, 342, 343; John 340, 342,
    368; Joseph 340, 341, 342, 343; Lavenah 341;
    Lewis 341; Maria 342; Mary 341; Mary Ball
    339; Rebecca 340, 368; Rebecca A. 343;
    Rebecca Ann 341; Sabilla Ann 340, 341, 342,
    343; Sarah E. 343; Sarah Emma 341; Sarah R.
    341.

SPRUANCE
    Anna 50.

STALCOP
    Catherine 368; Hans G. 369; Jonas 369;
    Maria 368, 369; Peter 368, 369.

STAMBAUGH
    Jean 67.

STARK
    James 81, 85.

STEEL
    Edward Newell 333; Stanley 333; Stanley Jr.
    333; Thomas 146.

STEELE
    Effie, Mrs. 111; Lida May 185.

STEPHENS
    Nannie 126; Phebe (Phoebe) 327.

STERNEGAN
    James 177.

STEVENS
    Harry F. 162; J. T. 232; Phebe 329.

STEVENSON
Alice 344, 345; Alice Belle 343, 344; Anna May 343, 344, 345; Charles H. 345, 346; Charles Hugh 343, 344, 345; Edith Marie 344, 345; Elizabeth 343, 345; Elizabeth Collins 345; Elvira B. 344; H. S. 344; Helen 343; Hugh 346; Hugh Llewellyn 344; Hugh Mills 345; Hugh S. 343, 345; Hugh Sanders 344, 345; Ida Virginia 343, 344; Jane 344; Jennie C. 345; Leonard 344; Maggie Snow 344; Mary 344; Mary Elizabeth 344, 345, 346; Mildred Margaret 344; Richard 346; Richard Helson 344, 345; Rosalie 344; Walter Bailey 345; William Alfred 345; William Henry 345.

STEWART
Charles 346; David, Doctor 184; Elizabeth 346; Gladys 283; Ira B. 282; John 346; Jospeh 114; Lydia 114; Margaret 346; Mary Jain 346; Mathew 346; Rebecca 346; Samuel 114; Will 294; William C. 294.

STIDDHEM
Asmund 367.

STIDHAM
Adam 368; Anna 348; Anna Mary 348; Catherine 348; Eliza 348; Isaac 348; Jonas 348; Lemna 348; Maria 368; Mary 348; Rachel 348; Rebecca 340, 342; Richard Britton 348; Sarah 348; Susan 348; Dr. T. 368.

STILES
A. R. 94.

STILLE
John 368.

STIMMEL
Florence 396; Isabelle 107.

STINSON
Maria 311.

STOCKTON
Major Thomas 184.

STOEK
    Jacob 294.

STONE
    Daniel C. 349; Elizabeth 221; Euphane 349;
    Grace 349; Joel 349; John 349; Mary T. 349;
    Oliver P. 349; Rebecca P. 349; Samuel M.
    349; Thomas P. 349.

STOUFFER
    Herbert 250; Herbert Earl 250; Herbert
    William 250; Shirley 250; Shirley Dawson
    250.

STOUT
    Mary J. 84; Mary Jane 81.

STRADLING
    Charlotte Melinda 54; Henrietta H. 54; John
    Draper Bowers 54; Mary Elizabeth 54.

STRATTON
    (?) 173.

STRICKLER
    Jacob 58.

SRODE
    George 376.

STROUD
    Alfred G. 271, 273, 274; Elizabeth 68;
    Ella B. 272; Joshua 68; Martha 68; Mary
    Emilie 274.

STUART
    Anne C. 163.

STUBBS
    Enech (Enoch), Pastor (H.) 48.

STURDIVANT
    Edward Walker 66; Ethel Mae 66, 67; Helen
    66; Jeanne (?) C. Lenhosse 67.

STURGES
    Alfred 349, 350; Catharine 350; Eliza 350;
    Elizabeth 349, 350; Hannah 349, 350, 352;
    Isaac 350; Jonathan 350; Lemuel 349, 350;

STURGES (Cont'd.)
    Lida Jane 350; Matilda 350; Rebecca 349,
    350; Wilmer 350; Wm. Henry 350.

SUDDITH
    Inman 126.

SULLIVAN
    Mary E. 268.

SUTTON
    John 121, 122.

SWAIM
    Addie 85; Addie Ellen 83; Alice 85; Alice
    Edna 83; Carrie 85; Carrie Amelia 83, 84;
    David 85; David Howard 83; Fred 85; Fred
    Harrison 83; George D. 83; George Duncan 84;
    Col. John E. 83, 85; Lottie 85; Lottie Ann
    83; Mary 85; Mary Emily 83; William P. 81,
    82, 83, 85.

SWAIN
    C. P., Rev. 298; Carrie Amelia 399, 400;
    Lottie Ann 149.

SWAYNE
    Jonathan 194.

SWEET
    Benjamin 177; Moses 177.

TAGGART (TAGGERT)
    Beulah Jane Allmond 8; John 8.

TALLEY
    Abner 360; Adam 356, 358; Albert 355, 356,
    358; Anna 356; Anna M. 227; Beulah 357;
    Beulah Z. 356, 358; Brinton 360; Charles
    230, 358, 359, 360; Charles M. 360; Cheryl
    357; Cheryl Jean 354; Clara 358; Clara V.
    358; Clyde 357; Clyde E. 354; Curtis M. 226,
    227; Dorothy 355; Edith 360; Eliza 360;
    Elizabeth 355, 356, 357, 358; Elizabeth J.
    358; Elsie 355; Ezra 360; Hannah 356, 357,
    358; Hannah L. (Foulk) 359; Harold 357;
    Harold W. 354; Harold Watson 354; Howard
    354, 357; Howard D. 171; Jane E. 357;

TALLEY (Cont'd.)
Jane Elizabeth 354, 355; Janice E. 387;
Jeanne Galbreath 354; Laura 230; Laura V.
227; Leah (?) 104; Leonard 357; Leonard C.
354, 355; Lewis 354, 355, 356, 357, 358;
Lewis F. 353, 354, 355, 356, 358; Lewis M.
354, 357; Lewis Prince 354; Lillian 380;
Linda 227, 230; Lizzie 357; Louisa 360;
Mary 227, 230, 356, 357, 358, 360; Mary E.
359; Mary Ellen 359; Mary (Miller) 354;
Mary Zebley 359; Norman 355; Penrose 360;
Penrose R. 359, 360; Rebecca 356, 358;
Richard 360; Robert 356, 358; Ronald 357;
Ronald Harold 354; Sarah 360; Sarah Anna
359; Susie A. 159; Thomas 104, 356, 359,
360; Thomas J. 359; Thomas M. 358;
Watson 354, 357; William 356, 358, 359;
William A. 358; Wilmer 29, 31, 359, 360.

TAPP
James 302, 303.

TARBELL
Jerusha 151.

TAWES
Roy L., Rev. 25.

TAYLOR
Allerdice 4; Ann Celeste 364; Arena 215;
Barbara 365; Bayard 50; Bayard B. 363;
Bayard Blackiston 301, 302, 362; Bayard
Joseph 363, 364; Benjamin 361; Buleau Logan
365; Carol Ann 364; Chana 363; Christine
364; Dale 365; Daniel 50; Daniel V. 364;
Daniel V. Jr. 364; Daniel Voshell 302,
362; David Robert 365; David W. 50; David
Woolley 302, 362; Diane S? 365; Doris 364,
365; Eddy 351; Elenor 347; Eliza 361, 363;
Eliza F. 30, 31; Elizabeth Ralph 364;
Emily Bent 364; Emlee Marie 364; Elva R. B.
50, 302, 303; George 363; Harry, Rev. 318;
Harry W. 351; Harry, Mrs. 318; Howard 362;
Isabel 361; James V. 50; James V. R. 364;
James Voshell Roberts 302, 362, 363; John
361, 363; Joseph 349, 361; Joseph B. 215;
Joseph P. 364, 365; Joseph Pyle 50, 302,
362, 364; Katherine 215; Laurette J. Miller
48; Levy 4; Lida 363; Louise 215; Lucinda 215

TAYLOR (Cont'd.)
    Mabel E. 364; Mabel F. 363; Margaret Mink
    364; Marion Elizabeth 364; Major 363; Mary
    129; Mary Ann Kirk 363; Mary W. 362; Mildred
    E. 363, 364; Nancy Jane 364; Patsy Ann 364;
    Paul W. 301, 302, 362; Paul W. Jr. 50, 364;
    Paul Woolley 48, 50, 302, 362; Paul Woolley
    III 364; Peggy 364; Peter 363; Robert 363;
    Robert Samuel 363, 364; Robert Steven 365;
    Rodney Scott 364; Samuel 361; Samuel W. 48,
    361, 362; Sarah 215, 361, 363; Sarah
    Elizabeth Covington 91; Souhey 92; Stace
    363; Stephen Ralph 364, 365; Susan Beatrice
    364; Thomas W. 361, 362; Walter J. 362;
    Warren A. 362; Wayne Charles 364; William
    361, 363; Wm. 129; Wm R. 215.

TAYNTOR
    Charles Laurence 77; Mary E. 77; Mary
    Estelle 77.

TEMPLE
    Edward E. 146.

THATCHER
    Mary E. 179.

THOCKMORTON
    B. Pearson 19, 21; Jos. F. 20, 21; Mary P.
    20.

THOMAS
    Edwin 118; Mary 290; S. W., Rev. 241; Thomas
    290.

THOMPSON
    Alen 305, 306; Obadiah 291.

THOMSON
    Jane 305.

TITUS
    Frances 229; Rev. T.T. 169.

TODD
    Anna 383, 384.

TOMKINSON
    Rev. T. L. 298.

TOOMEY
    Henrietta Cooper 318.

TOWSEND (TOWNSEND)
    Anna 366; Betsey 365; Ebe 299; Elizabeth 365; Elizabeth Blades 366; Govey 365, 366; Hetty 127; Hetty P. 127, 130; James 365; John 127, 365; Nancey 365; Nancy 365, 366; Nansey 366; Rebecca 365, 366; Sarah 70; Stephen 365; Thelma 207, 209, 210; William J. 365.

TRAYNER
    William 196.

TRENCHARD
    Jospehine 95.

TROTTER
    Daniel 158; Maria Louisa 158; William Hamilton 158.

TRUAX
    Hannah 289; Jno. 289; Miriam 283; Miriam E. 288.

TRUITT
    Levina 222.

TUBBS
    W. R., Rev. 298.

TULL
    Charles W. 90; Charlotte 39, 60; Elizabeth 59, 60; Elizabeth Osbourn 59, 60; Francina 60; Frisby 59, 60; Harriette 61; Hariette Parker 60; John 59, 60; John F. 60; John Frisby 59; Lizzie O. 60; Mary 60; Mary Ann 59; Robert F. 61; Robert Frisby 60; Sarah 59, 60; Thomas 60; Thomas Peregrine 59.

TULLINGS
    Rev. Henry 211.

TUMBELTY
    Betty Ann 201; Francis G. 201; Franklin 201; Rhoda Ashcroft 201.

TUNNELL
    Eliza Ann 299; Sarah 300.

TURNER
    Irene Jeanette 67; Rev. 178.

TURPIN
    Sarah A. 56.

TWIFORD
    Alan 1, Charles 1, Charlot 1, Charlottea 1.

TWIGG
    Howard T. 140.

TYSON
    Alice R. 366, 367; Alice Richardson 367;
    Arabella Ross 366, 367; Benjamin 146;
    David E. 366; Elizah 366, 367; George Henry
    366, 367; Hall R. 366, 367; Henerette 366;
    Henry 121, 123; Mary Bell 366, 367; Sarah T.
    366; William A. 366; William E. 367.

UPSALL (UPSAILL)
    Nicholas 197.

URGUHARD
    Mary 234.

VALENTINE
    Jessie P. 171; Phoebe 16.

VALUE
    Jesse R. 23, 24.

VANBIBBER
    Geo. 132; Julietta 132; Stella 132.

VANBLARCOM
    Jane 23, 24.

VANCLEVE
    Joseph M. 309, 311.

VANDERGRIFT
    Abraham 180, 181, 182; Mary Ann 180, 181;
    Mary B. 181; Mary Bowman 181.

VANDEVER (VER D'VER)
    Adam 368; Andreas 369; Ann 369; Brita 369;
    Carrie 370; Catharina 368, 369, 370;
    Charles M. 370; Charles McCullough 89;
    Cornelius 368, 369; Elizabeth 368, 369;
    Emma Hooton 370; Henry 368; Henry H. 370;
    Henry Harvey 89; Jacob 368, 369; Jacob
    (Jacop), Capt. 367; John 368, 369; Judith
    369; Katherine 367, 369; Kirstin 369;
    Magolena 368; Margaretta 368, 369; Maria
    369; Mary 369, 370; Peter 368, 369;
    Peter B. 89, 370; Phillip 369; Rachel 369;
    Rebecca 369; Susan 368; Susanna 369;
    Tobias 368, 369; Walter 370; William 368,
    369.

VANDIVER
    Floyd William 332; Ruth Ann 332.

VANNEMAN
    John 369.

VANNYNAM
    Henry 369.

VANPELT
    Jean 357; Jean A. 354.

VANSANT (VANZANT)
    Anetta 375; Arrie Rebecca 375; Blanchard
    373; Blanchard Arthur 371; Catherine 374;
    Cornelis 373; Daniel Nowland 374, 375;
    Daniel V. 375; Deborah 373; Elizabeth 373;
    Francis 371, 373; Francis A. 371, 372, 373;
    Francis A. Jr. 372; Francis Asbury 372, 374;
    George Reed 374, 375; Grandfather 372;
    Hamilton Marion 375; Harrison 373; Harrison
    J. 371; Henrietta Ann 375; John Hyland 374;
    Joshua 373, 374; Marian (Marion) 371, 372,
    373; Mariella 371; Marietta 371, 373; Mary
    Catherine 372; Mary Louisa 375; Mary Rebecca
    375; Nellie 373; Nellie Marie 371; Nellie
    May 372; Peregrine Ward 374; Sadie 371, 372,
    373; Walter Benson 364; William 373; William
    W. 372; William Wirt 371.

VARNON
    May 200.

VEALE
    John F., Jr. 123, 125.

VERNON
    Thomas 144.

VICKERS
    Abram 121, 122.

VIRDEN
    Ellen 397; Mary J. 397; Mitchel 397.

VONSETH
    George 332; Helen Anne 332.

VOSHEL (VOSHELL)
    Daniel 50, 300, 304, 363; Elizabeth 304, 363; Elizabeth Crockett 302; Hannah 363; James 363; John 304; John C. 304; Lewis 304; Mary 303, 304; Mary A. 50, 300, 301, 302; Nancy 363; Obediah Jr. 50, 363; Obediah Sr. 50, 363; Owen 363; Sarah 300, 304; Titus 363.

WALKER
    Emma 270, 273; J. Rev. 280, 313; Jane 376; Jean 376; Margaret 375, 376; Pauline 151; Samuel 259, 375, 376; Thomas, Rev. 17.

WALLACE
    Clara M. 330; Elizabeth 305; Hannah Perkins Goodley 352; Harriett Anne 352; Virginia 332; William Hayes 352.

WALLS
    Matilda 140; Sarah E. 139, 140.

WALTER
    Abagail H. 161; Ann 376; Cidney 377; Elizabeth 376, 377; Godwin 376; Hannah 377; Isaac 377; James 376; John 161, 376, 377; Joseph 376; Lydia 376, 377; Mary 376, 377; Matilda 149; Nathaniel 377; Rachel 376; Ruth 377; Sarah 376; Susanna 161; Susanna Y. 160, 161; Thomas 377; Thomas Jr. 377; William 376; William Jr. 377.

WALTON
    Jane 92; Max 92; Peggy 92; Roy T. 90, 91,
    92; Simeon 327.

WAMOCK
    Wm. E. 383.

WAPLES
    Ann 114; Comfort 91; James 114.

WARD
    Amasi 327, 329; Ann (Herman) 237; Henry 237;
    Herbert 328; Jonathan 326, 327, 329;
    Margaret 237.

WARDELL
    Charles 378; Craven 378; Edward 378;
    Elizabeth 378; Frances 378; John 378;
    Mary 378; Rebecca 378.

WARE
    Nathaniel 177.

WARLOW
    Charlott 93, 95.

WARMICK
    E. 122; Elizabeth 121.

WARNER
    Henry 247.

WARREN
    Ann 186; Caroline 186; Caroline W. 185;
    Caroline Williamson 186; Catherine 316;
    Charles Henry Bell 185, 186; Charles S. 186;
    Elizabeth 186; Eunice 186; George S. 185;
    Isaac 186; Jacob 186, 205; John 186; Mary
    186, 315; Nancy Eleanor 275, 276; Priscilla
    186; Rebecca 186, 205; Rufus M. 275; Sarah
    186; Sarah A. 315; Shreve 185, 186; Willard
    S. 275; William 186, 315.

WARRINGTON
    Walter L. 184.

WASHBURN
    Lydia, Mrs. 153.

WASHINGTON
    Clara M. 96.

WATERS
    Edwin Colgate 379; Elizabeth Ann 379;
    Elizabeth Jane 52; John C. 379; Rebecca W.
    379; William Weston 379.

WATMOUGH
    Mary E. C. 147.

WATSON
    John A. 111; Nancy B. 316; Susan R. 353.

WATTS
    Anna 126.

WAY
    Anna 230; Annie 131; Charlotte 226, 230;
    Jacob 130; L. Martin 230; Sarah 230.

WEABER
    Anna E. 262; Anna Edna 261.

WEBBER
    Arthur G. 303; Arthur Green 48; Elizabeth
    Browne 303; Elzie 303; Helen Irene 303;
    James 303; Joseph Roberts 303; Mary Winifred
    303; Rebecca 303; Virginia 303.

WEBESTER
    Alfred 203; Alice 203; Audrey 203; Bassett
    203; Edith 203; Edna 203; John 203; Melvin
    203; Ruth 203.

WEBSTER
    Anna 383; Arthur E. 380, 381, 383; Cassius C.
    383, 384; Clark 379, 380, 381, 382, 384;
    Clark I. 383; Clark J. 384; Clark W. 381,
    382; Edward 382; Elaine Bradford 384;
    Elizabeth 380, 381, 382, 384; Ella 221;
    Elsie May 48; Henry 48, 221; Herman 382;
    Isaac 380, 382, 383, 384; Isaac Jr. 383,
    384; Jane Ann 381; Joan Louise 384; John
    380, 382; John C. 383, 384; John Coleman Jr.
    383, 384; Lillian Connell 383; Lillian C.
    383; Lottie 381, 382, 383; Margaret 380;
    Martha 380, 382; Martha Penelope 384;
    Mary 380, 382; Priscilla 221; Rachel A. 384;

WEBSTER (Cont'd.)
Rachel Anne 383; Rachel Barbara 384; Rebecca 380, 381; Rebecca A. 382; Sarah 380, 382; Sarah E. 384; Sarah Elizabeth 383, 384; Temperance Alston 48; Thomas 380, 381, 382; Vesta 380, 381; Viola 109, 380; Viola A. 381; William 381, 382, 383; William A. 381; William M. 109, 380, 381, 382.

WEER
Esther 122; Isaac 121, 122; Mary (Eastwick) 122.

WEICHARDT
Ruth 83, 86, 400.

WELDIN
Atwood 356; 358; Bertha 387; Beulah 385, 387, 388; Beulah A. 388; Beulah Ann 385; Charles 387; Charles P. 388; Charles Pettit 385, 387; Clara V. 355; Eli 386; Eliza 385, 387, 388; Eliza J. 387; Elizabeth 386; Emme 385; George 7, 360, 385, 386, 387, 388; George Harriett 387; George W. 387; George Washington 385; Hannah 385, 388; Harry Manship 387; Henry 355; Isaac 385, 386, 388; Jacob 7, 385, 386, 387, 388; J. Atwood 355; John A. 386, 388; L. Emma 385; Lillian Emma 387; Lydia 387; Lydia Ann 385; Mabel 386; Margaret 386; Maria Ellma 388; Mary 385, 386, 387, 388; Rebecca 360, 385, 387; Sallie Harriett 387; Sarah 386, 387; Sarah Campbell 385; Winifred 387.

WELLS
Richard B. 188.

WELTY
Jane 164; Sarah Jane 164; Solomon 164.

WESSELLS
Elizabeth Anne 232.

WEST
Ezekiel L. 300; Ezekiel M. Lamden 300; George H. 299; George Handy 300; Isaac 297; Isaac C. 299, 300; Isaac Collins 300; James

WEST (Cont'd.)
   Derickson 300; Mary H. 299; Mary Hull (Hill)
   300; Nancy 300; Nancy H. 297; Sarah 300;
   Sarah Mary 297, 298; Sarah T. 296, 297, 298,
   299; Sarah Tunnell 297, 300.

WESTERFIELD
   H. A. G., Rev. 258.

WESTERVELT
   Frances 333.

WESTLER
   Nancy A. 169.

WESTON
   Rebecca 388, 390.

WHALEY
   Ann 372; John 372, 373; Mary C. 371, 373;
   May Cathern (Catherine) 372; Robert 372,
   373; Sarah 372; Sarah Ann 372, 373; Thomas
   H. 373; Thomas Henry 372; William 372, 373.

WHARTENBY
   Alfred 249, 250; Edith 250; Edith Lodge 250;
   Edna 250; Edna Ellis 249, 250; Elizabeth
   250; Marion 250; Marion Leiter Curzon 249;
   Robert J. 250.

WHARTNABY
   Anna 133, 135; Anna B. 133; Ellen F. 133,
   134, 135; Joseph (Joesph) 133, 134, 135.

WHARTON
   Charles, Rev. 340; Elizabeth 397; John 397;
   Lizzie E. 397.

WHITCRAFT
   Eliza 31; Eliza L. 29; Jacob 29; Marg 29.

WHITE
   Albert Hyatt 178, 179, 180; Benjamin 253;
   Benjamin B. 113; Clara C. 113; Eva E. 178,
   179; Eva Estella 178, 180; Florence 179;
   Florence H. 178; Frank, Rev. 319; Hannah 53,
   253; Homer M. 178, 179, 180; John R. 113;
   Katie C. 113; Leonard 282; Louise 347;
   Louizzie May 113; Mabel 178, 179; Maggie 114;

WHITE (Cont'd.)
Mary E. 225, 226, 275; Mary H. 253; Mary Jane 178, 179; Mary Thatcher 178, 179; Morrison D. 178, 179; Moses 194; Tabitha 113, 114; Wallace W. 113, 114; William M. 178, 179; William Morris 178.

WHITEMAN
Amos 196; Andrew Jackson 196; Anna 195; Arthur 196; B. 196; Belle 195; Bertha 196; Bessie 195; Clara 195; Emma 195; Enos 196; Florence 195; George 196; George Washington 195; Gilbert 195; Henry 194, 195; Irma 196; Jefferson 195; Jesse 196; John Kinsey 195; Kicel 195; Laura 195; Lemuel 196; Levenia 195; Louis 195; Louise 196; Margaret 195; Margaret Jane 196; Molly 196; Sarah 195; Sarah Ann 196; William 196.

WHITSON
Sarah T. 367.

WHITTIER
Abner 325.

WHITTINGTON
Mary S. 143.

WIBLE
John 121, 122.

WICKERSHAM
Amos 385.

WILEY
David W. 202; Elizabeth m. 202; Horace 202.

WILKINS
Ella Marie 117.

WILKINSON
Laura 149.

WILLETT
Elizabeth 327; Francis 321, 322, 327, 328; Martha 322.

WILLEY
    Margaret Jane 279; Mary C. 263, 264;
    Mary H. 279.

WILLIAM-NEERING
    Andrew 74; Lydia 74.

WILLIAMS
    Amanda Mary 392, 393; Ann Eliza 392; Annie E.
    392; C. H. 261; Campbell 66; Charles H. 392,
    393; Charles Henry 392; Charles I. 392, 393;
    Eliza 392, 393; Emma Lodge 382; Georgiana
    392; Grace Elizabeth 392, 393; Ida 288;
    Jessie, Rev. 204; Mary 321, 328; Mattie
    Arnold 392; Rachel Jane 392, 393; Rebecca
    124; Sarah 118; Theophilus 392; William 124;
    William, Rev. 270.

WILLS
    George A. 240.

WILSON
    Albert H. 391; Albert Hoopes 390; B. Wilson
    69; Benjamin 70; Elizabeth 70; Emma 72; Ella
    391; Ella Worth 391; Frank 391; Frank Leshem
    391; George W. 390, 391; George W. Jr. 390,
    391; Jesse 220; Jessie 391; Laura Craven 45;
    Margaret 391; Margaret Wey--? 391; Mary 69,
    72; Mary Christie 233; Mary E. 390, 391;
    Mr. Wilson 100, 102; Nancy 89, 90, 91; Rachel
    Byrnes 70; Samuel 391; Samuel S. 391; Samuel
    Simons 390; Sarah 229, 391; Sarah E. 384;
    Sarah Elizabeth 383; Sarah Matsinger 391;
    Thomas P. 391; Thomas Paul 390; William 90,
    91.

WINSLOW
    Benjamin C. 217, 218; Clara J. 218; Frank W.
    218; Hannah B. 218; Jerush M. 219; Jerusha
    W. 216; Rebecca 216.

WINSOR
    Alexander 234; Elise 234; Louise (Louisa)
    394, 395; Louise 393, 394, 395; Mary 394,
    395; Nicholas 393, 384, 395; Obil Anson
    394, 395; Robert 234; William 394, 395.

WINTHROP
    John 176.

WITMORE
    Jane Catherine 169.

WOLF
    George, Rev. 380.

WOLFE
    Benjamin C. 397; Charles F. 398; Clifford
    Henry 397; Effie L. 398; Ella Louise 398;
    Frank Henry 397; John 397; John White 397;
    Lizzie 397, 398; Lizzie E. 397; Louis? 398;
    Louis H. 398; Louis H. Jr. 398; Louise 398;
    Maretta 397; Mary 397; Mary Cornelia 397;
    Mary J. 397; Mary Jane 397; Reece 397;
    Reece B. 397; Samuel Cornelius 397; William
    C. 398; William Cornelius 397; William S.
    397, 398; William Smith 397.

WOLLASTON
    Elizabeth 68.

WOLVERTON
    Ann 398; Eleanor 399; Elizabeth 398, 399;
    Isabella Jane 398, 399; James 399; John 121,
    133, 399; Mary 398, 399; Rebecca Crawford
    398, 399; Sarah 399; Thomas 398, 399;
    Thomas J. 399; William 399.

WOOD
    Emaline 202; Frank W. 141; Frank Willard
    141; Frank Willard Jr. 141; Joseph Flickwii
    Wood 141; Mary 176; Sarah 15; William 196,
    198.

WOODCOCK
    Bancroft 70; Ruth 69, 72.

WOODNUT
    Hannah 69, 70.

WOODWARD
    Abner 273, 274; Abner C. 274; Blanche
    Derickson 273; Christina Kay Lilley 274;
    Eleanor 274; Eleanor Francis 273, 274;
    George 274; Margaret 194; Mary Ann 52,
    273; Susan G. 52.

WOOLEY
    Alice Stevenson 344; Benjamin T. 343, 344;
    Helen Stevinson 344; Jennie Maude 343, 344;
    Stevenson Luck 344.

WOOLLEY
    Mary 361, 362.

WOOLTEN
    Ellen Mitchell 172; George M. 172.

WOOTTEN (WOOTEN)
    Anna May 345; Orlando V. 343; Orlando
    Valentine 345.

WORLEY
    W. C. 295.

WORTHINGTON
    Francena Doone 201.

WRIGHT
    Abraham 308; Ada S. 308; Ann 308; Donald F.
    25; Hannah G. 308; Helen B. M. 308; John
    121, 122; Lizzie G. 308; Lizzie Garrett 308;
    Salem B. 308; Susan J. 246; William 246;
    308; William G. 308.

WYATT
    Francis, Sir 55.

YEARSLEY
    Nathan 146.

YOEST
    Charles 401; Christopher 183, 401; Doratha
    401; George Himes 401; Hanna 401; John 401;
    Mary 183, 401; Rachel 401; Rebekah 401.

YUCKMAN
    William, Dr. 248.

ZEBLEY
    Bessie 123; Edward 123; Jane W. 276; Mrs. 122; Mary 358, 360; Sarah E. 260, 262; Thomas 360.

ZIMMERMAN
    Martha 275; Wilhelimina 204.

Other Heritage Books by Lu Verne V. Hall:

Delaware Bible Records, Volume 6
New England Family Histories and Genealogies: State of Massachusetts

Other Heritage Books by Lu Verne V. Hall and Donald O. Virdin:

Delaware Bible Records, Volume 5
New England Family Histories and Genealogies: Miscellaneous New England States
New England Family Histories and Genealogies: States of Maine and Rhode Island
New England Family Histories and Genealogies: States of New Hampshire and Vermont
New England Family Histories: State of Connecticut
Texas Family Histories and Genealogies

www.ingramcontent.com/pod-product-compliance
Lightning Source LLC
Chambersburg PA
CBHW060908300426
44112CB00011B/1392